SAN VINCENZO AL VOLTURNO 2:

THE 1980-86 EXCAVATIONS

PART II

Published with the aid of grants from the
M. Aylwin Cotton Foundation and
the Marc Fitch Fund

SAN VINCENZO AL VOLTURNO 2:
THE 1980-86 EXCAVATIONS
PART II

Edited by Richard Hodges

with

Major contributions by
Richard Hodges and John Mitchell

Other contributions by
Samuel Barnish, Catherine M. Coutts, Sheila Gibson,
Andrew Hanasz, Ian Riddler, Chris Wickham
and David Wilkinson

ARCHAEOLOGICAL MONOGRAPHS OF THE
BRITISH SCHOOL AT ROME
No. 9

British School at Rome London
1995

Cover illustration: Excavation of the Refectory, with the present abbey in the middle ground
(Photograph: Richard Hodges)

Typeset by Alden Multimedia, Northampton, and printed by The Alden Press, Oxford
Cover design by Three's Company, 18 Henley Avenue, Oxford OX4 4DJ

TO SHEILA GIBSON

Sapiens architectus

This is the second of a number of volumes describing the 1980-86 excavations of the early medieval Benedictine abbey of San Vincenzo al Volturno. It includes accounts of the excavations in the Vestibule, the Upper Thoroughfare, the Assembly Room, the Refectory, on Terrace 2 (the late Roman Tower), on Terrace 3 (a church with an *opus sectile* floor), on the hilltop and in the hilltop cemetery. In addition there are essays on the historical context of the site: on the late Roman settlement; on Christians and countrymen; on monastic lands and monastic patrons; and on the relevance to San Vincenzo of the Plan of St Gall.

Volume 1 describes the setting of this major archaeological project and gives an overview of the remains found. It also includes detailed accounts of the excavations of the Crypt Church, the 'South Church' (the eighth-century abbey-church, which was to become the ninth-century Distinguished Guests' Refectory), the Garden Court, and the Entrance Hall. There is also a reappraisal of the cycle of paintings in the crypt in the light of the excavations.

Volume 3 will contain the reports on the finds from the 1980-86 excavations.

Volume 4 will have reports on the Samnite-Republican *vicus* discovered at San Vincenzo, the twelfth-century abbey of San Vincenzo, occupied after the early medieval site was abandoned, the survey of the upper Volturno valley, and the excavations of the early medieval sites of Colle Castellano and Colle Sant'Angelo.

Contents

List of Figures

The following abbreviations have been used to indicate the artist, draughtsperson or photographer: Nigel Baker – NB; James Barclay-Brown – JBB; Sally Cann – SC; Catherine M. Coutts – CMC; Karen Francis – KF; Sheila Gibson – SG; Andrew Hanasz – AH; Richard Hodges – RH; David Lewis – DL; John Mitchell – JM; Ian Riddler – IR; Jonathan Vickery – JV; Barry Vincent – BV; Lucy Watson – LW.

List of Colour Plates

The following abbreviations have been used to indicate the artist, draughtsperson or photographer: JBB – James Barclay-Brown; SG – Sheila Gibson; JM – John Mitchell.

The colour plates are located between pages 46 and 47.

List of Tables

PREFACE AND ACKNOWLEDGEMENTS

The second volume of San Vincenzo al Volturno comprises two parts: firstly, Chapters 1 to 8 describe the remainder of the excavations undertaken in 1980-86 (Fig. 0:1), and, secondly, Chapters 9 to 12 offer a preliminary discussion of the results described in Volume 1 as well as in the first part of this book. For the convenience of the reader, details of the archaeological phasing are repeated here (Table 0:1).

The first part focuses upon the northern buildings within the ninth-century cloister (Fig. 0:2): the Assembly Room (part of the Lower Thoroughfare), the Refectory, the Vestibule and the Upper Thoroughfare. In addition, there are descriptions of the smaller investigations made of the late Roman residential Tower which was the hub of the fifth- to sixth-century settlement, of the church on Terrace 3, of the cemetery, and of the hilltop itself. Three excavations are omitted. Trenches FF, GG and HH, excavated in 1983-84 and already described by John Moreland (1985), will be published in Volume 5 of this series, together with a full description of the ninth-century workshops and San Vincenzo Maggiore.

The discussion section draws only ephemerally upon the results of the 1990-93 excavations of San Vincenzo Maggiore and the associated workshops. The emphasis, instead, is upon settlement history – the issues which brought us to San Vincenzo al Volturno in 1980 (see Volume 1: 4-7). I wish to express my sincere thanks to Samuel Barnish and, especially, Chris Wickham for their contributions to this volume. Chris Wickham, I recall with affection, was instrumental in designing the original project.

Volume 1 contains a long list of acknowledgements to the many excavators, specialists and friends who made it possible to undertake these excavations on small budgets. Here, suffice it to repeat my great debt to Catherine M. Coutts, Karen Francis, John Mitchell and the School's Publications Manager, Gillian Clark, for their determined and skilful efforts to see this report into print. Finally, publication of this volume provides the welcome opportunity to choose a dedicatee. One of my abiding memories, as, for example, we struggled to understand the archaeological sequence in the Vestibule and the Upper Thoroughfare, is of Sheila Gibson's participation. She made sense of the seemingly incomprehensible. Hers has been an incalculable contribution to this project, for apart from her matchless drawings she, like Don Angelo Pantoni – to whom the first volume was dedicated – showed resolute support and boundless fascination for our efforts. In essence it took a *sapiens architectus* to interpret the works of Abbot Joshua's ninth-century master-architect. To Sheila we dedicate this volume.

Richard Hodges
British School at Rome
December 1993

TABLE 0:1 The archaeological phasing of San Vincenzo al Volturno following the 1980-86 excavations

0a1	Samnite sanctuary (fourth-first centuries BC). Dated by pottery.
0a2	Republican *vicus* (first century BC-first century AD). Dated by pottery, inscriptions and sculpture.
0b	Early Imperial villa (first-fourth centuries AD). Dated by pottery.
1a	Late Imperial estate centre, dominated by a Tower on Terrace 2 (early fifth century to *c.* AD 450). Dated by coins, African Red Slipwares, glass and jewellery.
1b	Late Roman additions (*c.* 450-550) to the Tower on Terrace 2; the construction of the 'South Church' and Crypt Church. Dated by coins, pottery, glass and jewellery.
1c	Late Roman addition to the 'South Church'. Stratigraphically later than phase 1b. Dated by coins to *c.* 450-550.
2	A phase of burials inserted into the ground floor of the (?)deserted phase 1 Tower and into the 'South Church'. Only approximately dated by the jewellery and beads to the later sixth or seventh century.
3a	The first monastery: 'South Church' rebuilt and a new plaster floor laid over the late Roman burials in the 'South Church'. Interpreted as the eighth-century abbey-church (termed San Vincenzo Minore), founded in *c.* 703.
3b	A primitive addition to the west end of the phase 3a 'South Church' and modifications to its apse. Possibly related to the construction of the Crypt Church and its nave, which are also attributed on architectural grounds to the later eighth century.
3c	The addition of an altar and new ambulatory to the 'South Church' and the rebuilding of the apse of the Crypt Church. Very little stratigraphic evidence was found for this phase.
4a	The massive rebuilding of the 'South Church' and comparable rebuilding of the entire area to the south. The creation of long corridors as well as terracing (between Terraces 2 and 3) suggests the replanning of the monastery, coinciding with the construction of Abbot Joshua's (791-817) new abbey-church in *c.* 808. Dating confirmed by the paintings from the 'South Church', the east portico of the Garden Court and the Assembly Room on the Lower Thoroughfare.
4b	Modifications to the undercrofts within the 'South Church'.
5a	Abbot Epyphanius's age (824-42): the blocking of the 'South Church' undercroft north doorways; construction of the painted crypt; the construction of the Crypt Church atrium; the enlargement of many other phase 4 buildings.
5b	Mid-ninth-century additions, some arising from land movement, possibly as a result of the earthquake of 848 recorded in the *Chronicon Vulturnense* (Guidoboni 1989: 614-15).
5c	A great fire clearly associated with numerous heavy arrowheads fired from composite bows of an alleged Saracen type. Attributed to the Saracen raid of 881.
6a	Makeshift additions, tombs and decay which post date 5c and pre-date the wholesale demolition. Approximately early tenth to mid-eleventh centuries.
6b	The demolition of the site which may be linked to the chronicler's description of Abbot John V's rebuilding, dated to around 1055.
7	The laying of a cream-white mortar surface, over large parts of the site, on which a pottery kiln was situated. Interpreted as a backyard area within Abbot John V's monastery.
8	Terracing overlying phase 7, which cannot be accurately dated. Construction of the present abbey complex on the edge of the plateau, dated by historical references to it as well as by the *opus sectile* pavements surviving inside the present church. Probably Abbot Gerard's monastery described in the *Chronicon Vulturnense*.

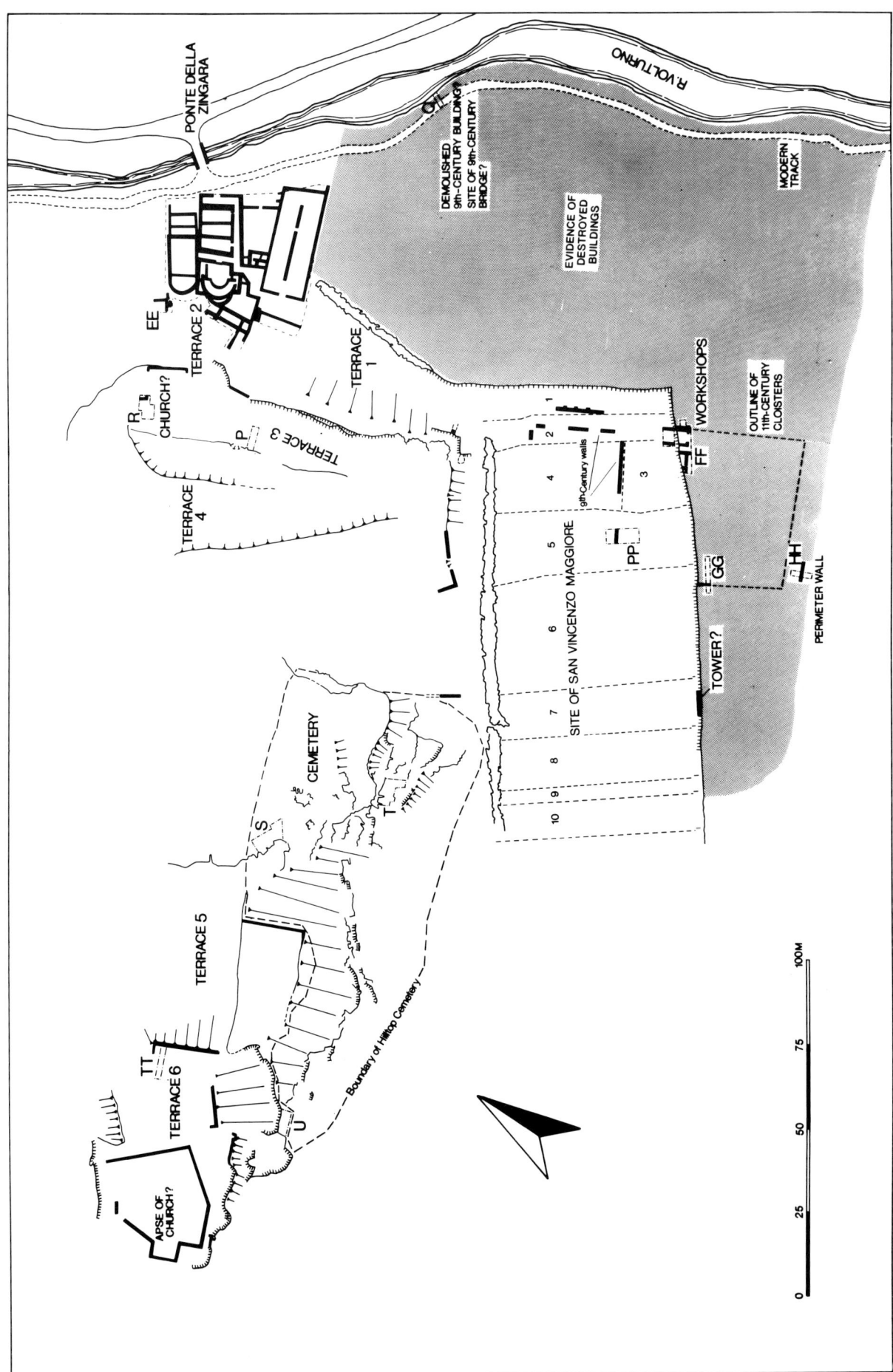

Fig. 0:1 Main site plan showing the location of the 1980-86 excavations (SC)

PONTE DELLA ZINGARA

R. VOLTURNO

DEMOLISHED
9th-CENTURY BUILDING?
SITE OF 9th-CENTURY
BRIDGE?

EVIDENCE OF
DESTROYED
BUILDINGS

MODERN
TRACK

EE?

TERRACE 2

R
CHURCH?

P

TERRACE 4

TERRACE 3

TERRACE 1

WORKSHOPS

FF

9th-Century walls

OUTLINE OF
11th-CENTURY
CLOISTERS

PP

GG

PERIMETER WALL

TOWER?

SITE OF SAN VINCENZO MAGGIORE

S

CEMETERY

T

TERRACE 5

TT

TERRACE 6

U

APSE OF
CHURCH?

Boundary of Hilltop Cemetery

0   25   50   75   100M

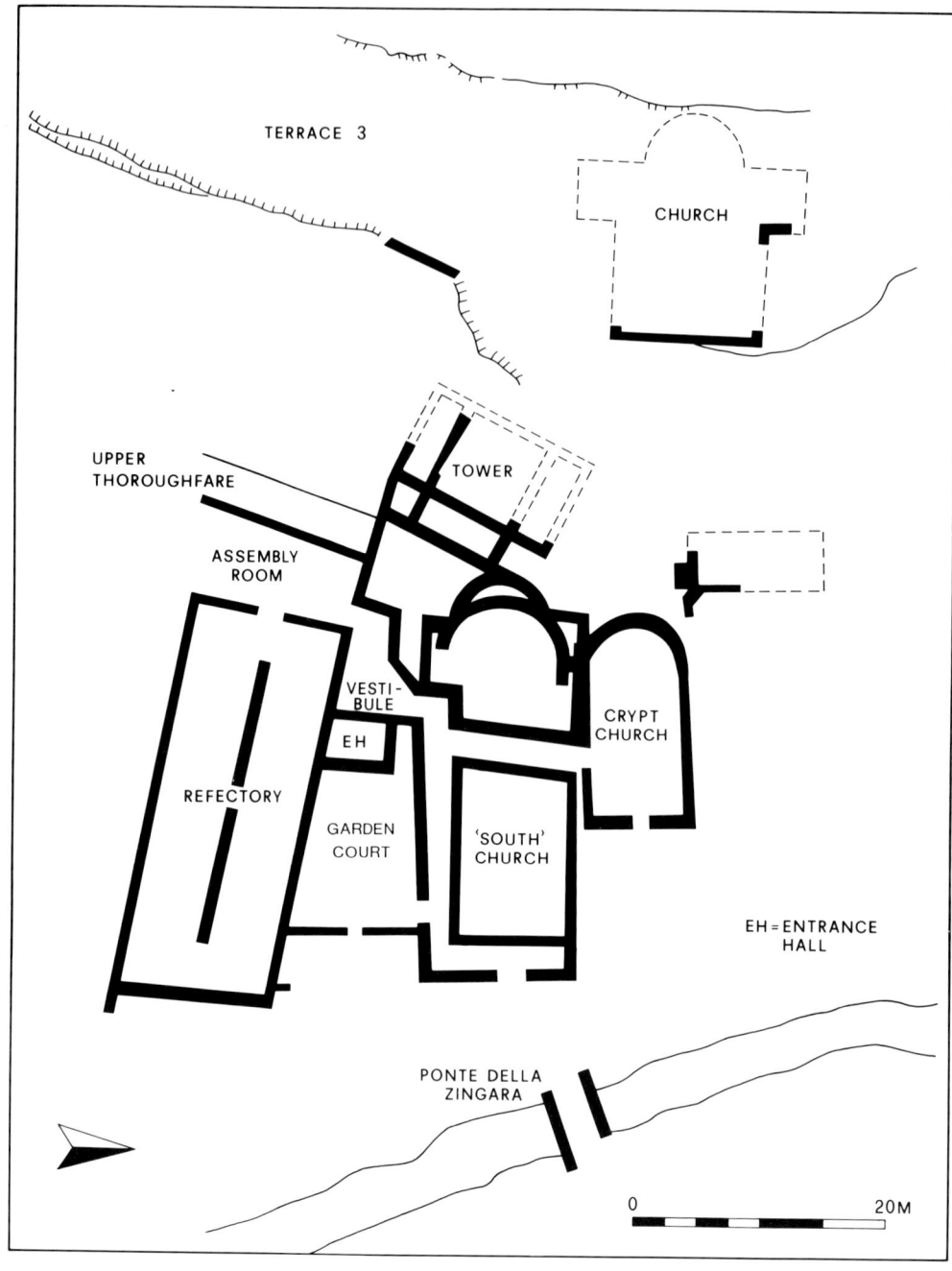

TERRACE 3

CHURCH

UPPER
THOROUGHFARE

TOWER

ASSEMBLY
ROOM

VESTI-
BULE

CRYPT
CHURCH

EH

REFECTORY

GARDEN
COURT

'SOUTH'
CHURCH

EH = ENTRANCE
HALL

PONTE DELLA
ZINGARA

0   20M

Fig. 0:2 General sketch plan of the principal buildings discussed in this volume *(SC)*

NOTE ON SPELLINGS, NAMES AND ABBREVIATIONS

A mixture of spellings for names is used in this volume. When referring to places, Italian names are used for the most part. Hence the site is called San Vincenzo rather than Saint Vincent, and the abbey-church is called San Vincenzo Maggiore. When referring to persons, however, English versions of their names have been used (for example, Abbot Joshua, Charlemagne). Names and spellings taken from the *Chronicon Vulturnense* are used sparingly and always in italics. Biblical quotations are as given in the Authorized Version. The following abbreviations have been used:

CC	*Chronica monasterii Casinensis* (see Hoffmann 1980)	*MGH D. Loth. I*	*Monumenta Germaniae Historica, Diplomata Lotharii I* (see Schieffer 1966)
CDL	*Codice Diplomatico Longobardo* (see Zielinski 1986)	*MGH Epp. III*	*Monumenta Germaniae Historica, Epistolae III* (see Gundlach *et al.* 1892/1957)
CIL	*Corpus Inscriptionum Latinarum*		
CV	*Chronicon Vulturnense* (see Federici 1925)	*MGH LL*	*Monumenta Germaniae Historica, Leges* (see Bluhme 1868)
Gelasius, *Ep.*	Gelasius, *Epistulae* (see Thiel 1868)	*MGH SRL*	*Monumenta Germaniae Historica, Scriptores Rerum Langobardicarum et Italicarum* (see Bethmann and Waite 1878)
GMD	Gregorius Magnus, *Dialogi de vita et miraculis patrum Italicorum*		
GMRE	Gregorius Magnus, *Registrum Epistularum* (see Nordberg 1982)	Paulinus, *Carm.*	Paulinus, *Carmina* (see de Hartel 1894)
HL	Paul the Deacon, *History of the Lombards* (see Foulke 1974)	*PG*	*Patrologiae cursus completus, series graeca* (see Migne 1857-76)
ILS	*Inscriptiones Latinae Selectae* (see Dessau 1892-)	*PL*	*Patrologiae cursus completus, series latina* (see Migne 1844-63)
LD	*Liber Diurnus Romanorum Pontificium* (see Sickel 1889)	*RM*	*Regula Magistri* (see de Vogüé 1964a)
LGC	*Liber in Gloria Confesorum*	*RPR*	*Regesta Pontificum Romanorum* (see Jaffé 1885)
LP	*Liber Pontificalis* (see Duchesne 1886-92)	*SM*	*Statuta Murbacensia* (see Semmler 1963)
MGH D. Kar	*Monumenta Germaniae Historica, Diplomata Karolinorum* (see Mühlbacher 1906)	*Tractatus*	*Zenonis Veronensis Tractatus* (see Löfstedt 1971)

RETRACTATIONES

The reports on the 1980-86 excavations are being published over a period of some three to four years, with work on the preparation of each also being staggered. In addition, excavation has continued apace since 1986 to the present (1994). As a result, and perhaps inevitably, in finalizing this volume we have discovered some points on which we could now revise information and/or opinions presented in Volume 1. We should like to take the opportunity here of correcting some small errors which crept into Volume 1, in particular so that there is no confusion where correct information is given in this volume.

page 3, col. 2, line 24:	for 'kingdom' read 'principality'
page 24, col. 1, lines 13-15:	should read 'Its western apsidal end was not identified, but with removal of the vegetation its eastern end could still be identified.'
page 49, col. 2, lines 25-8; fig. 6:14:	the south wall of the nave of the Crypt Church is 104 and the east wall of the nave of the Crypt Church is 100
page 51; page 56, col. 1, lines 21 and 43; page 63, col. 1, line 9:	for '148/167' read '148/267'
page 114, col. 2, line 35:	for 'Pius' read 'Pious'
page 128, col. 1, lines 21-2:	for '74/9203' read '74/9102'
page 158, col. 1, line 17:	for 'Tomb 784 (Grave 1)' read 'Tomb 746 (Grave 1)'
page 210, table 11:1, line 6:	for 'room' read 'roof'
passim:	The church with the *opus sectile* floor in Trench R is now regarded as being of phase 7 date

Chapter One

THE VESTIBULE: WHERE THE THOROUGHFARES MEET

by Richard Hodges, Sheila Gibson and John Mitchell

INTRODUCTION

The Vestibule (Fig. 1:1; cf. Fig. 0:2) was an enclosed area between the 'South Church' south corridor (Volume 1: 170-8), the Entrance Hall (Volume 1: 216-26), the Refectory and, through a wide interconnecting doorway, the Lower Thoroughfare (of which the Assembly Room formed a part). It seems to have formed an ante-room to the Assembly Room, as well as a point where the Upper and Lower Thoroughfares intersected. Significantly, this area separated the claustral area to the south from the secular, distinguished guests', sector. The Vestibule was located within Trench D and was excavated under the supervision of Amanda Claridge and Richard Hodges (1981), Nigel Baker (1982), and John Clipson (1983). The context numbers for this area run from 300 to 495, plus 507, 508, 8058, 8083, and 8348-50. The trench was initially intended to explore the zone due south of the 'South Church'. In fact, Terrace 1, beside the 'South Church', fell away to a deep and, at the time, unexpected room. The western half of the room was systematically excavated in 1981, while the rest was exposed using a machine in 1983. A summary of the main phases in the Vestibule is given in Table 1:1.

PHASES 1-3b

No definite features survived from this period. Note should be taken, however, of the drain preserved only in profile in wall 316 (Fig. 1:2). This drain evidently ran downslope beside walls 334 and 354 but was probably removed in phase 5 when the room was covered. The tile-lined drain resembled the ninth-century drain (8239) discovered running from the Distinguished Guests' Refectory across the east portico of the Garden Court. If this drain dated to the ninth century we might have expected it to have run along the north side of the Refectory and into the Garden Court. No trace of it was encountered, however, in room 1 of the Entrance Hall (Volume 1: 216-17). Therefore, it may be that it should be dated to the fifth century and that it took water away from the Tower on Terrace 2, along the south side of the phase 1b garden which then occupied the slope.

PHASE 3c (FIG. 1:3)

The eastern half of the Vestibule was probably occupied by a corridor or narrow building that in some way connected the 'South Church' to the Refectory at this date (Volume 1: 217). Wall 468 (the west wall of the Entrance Hall) formed the east side of this corridor/building, while the line of the west side was indicated by the west (terminal) end of the 'South Church' south corridor. Beyond lay the remains of the late Roman garden which was probably maintained in this phase. It occupied the slope beside the apse of the 'South Church', and was defined by walls 620 (of the Tower), 74/9102, 9208, and probably 334 (Fig. 1:3).

PHASE 4 (FIG. 1:3)

The redevelopment of the 'South Church' complex necessitated creating new access arrangements between the cloister and this area. The Vestibule, in effect, was now created as a focal point for two thoroughfares coming from the south in the

TABLE 1:1 Summary of the main phases in the Vestibule	
1-3b	This area lay at the base of the late Roman garden on the slope below the Roman Tower.
3c	The eastern half of this area was probably occupied by a corridor or narrow building, that in some way connected the South Church to the Refectory. The late Roman garden was probably maintained.
4	There was a small open courtyard, the focal point for the meeting of four passages.
5a1	There was a covered room, connected to the Lower Throughfare. Paintings occurred on at least some of the walls. A passage (part of the Upper Thoroughfare) now passed over it, at first-floor level, from the first floor of the Entrance Hall to the remodelled Upper Thoroughfare on Terrace 2.
5a2	All the walls of the Vestibule were now painted and the room was paved with tiles. A short bench was added between the new doorway into room 2 of the Entrance Hall and steps 508. A decorated tomb was placed in a prominent position in the floor.
5c	The area was badly affected by the fire of 881.
6a	A new doorway was cut through the (north) Refectory wall, close to the Entrance Hall (room 1), to replace the blocked doorway connecting the Vestibule to the Assembly Room. The Upper Thoroughfare was probably still in use.
6b	The Vestibule was systematically demolished.
7	The ruins were completely buried and abandoned.
Post 8	The site was landscaped and, more recently, used as an olive grove.

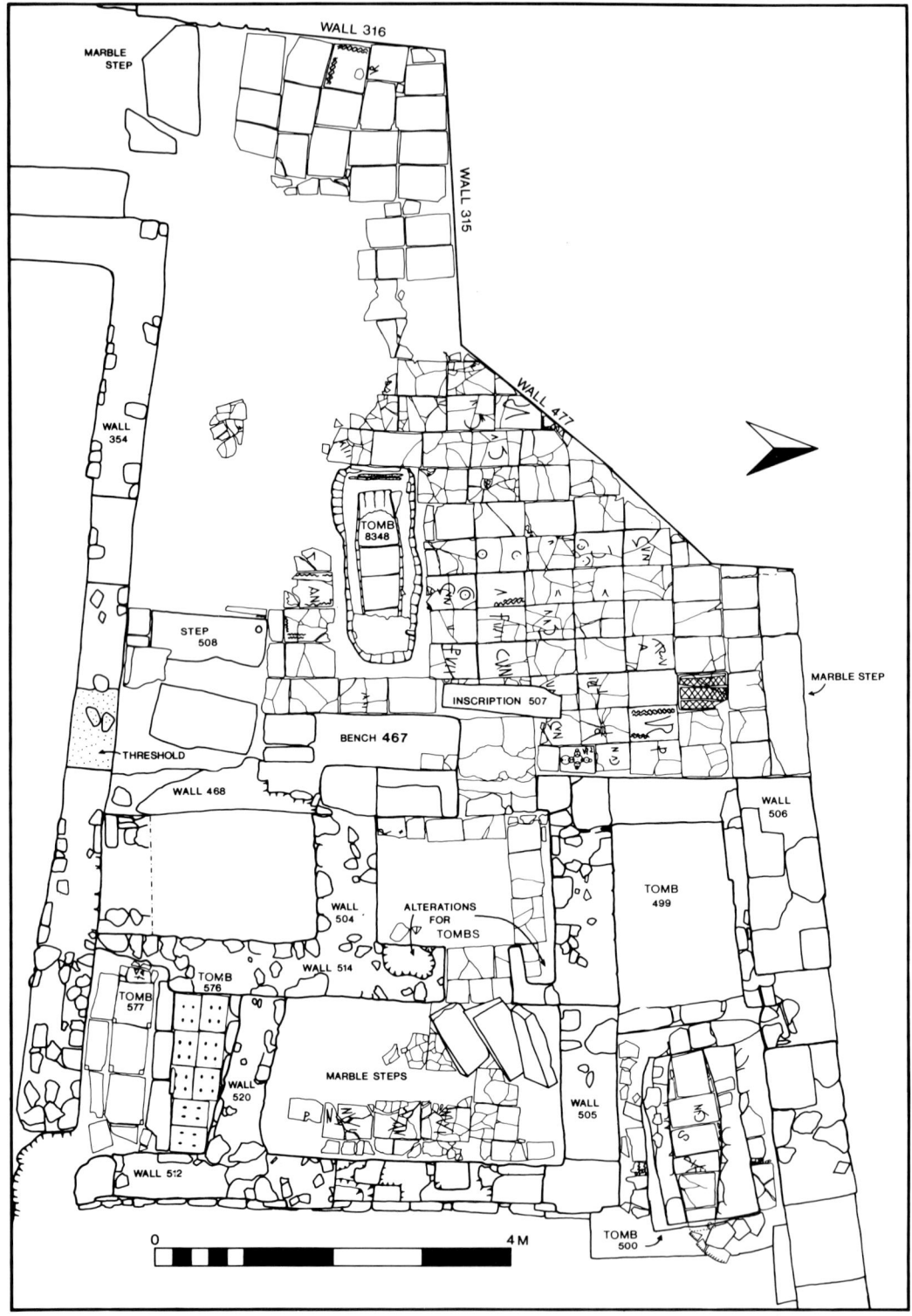

Fig. 1:1 Plan of the Vestibule and the Entrance Hall *(CMC)*

direction of the 'South Church' complex. These thoroughfares arrived at different levels: the Lower Thoroughfare came through the Assembly Room at Terrace 1 level; above it, running along the slope, lay the Upper Thoroughfare.

Very little survived of the Vestibule that could be attributed to phase 4. Some aspects of it, however, were clear. The north Refectory wall (354) formed the south side of this space; the

Entrance Hall formed the east side; and the passage which led from the 'South Church' formed the north side. The form of the west side, by contrast, could only be reconstructed with reference to the excavations of Terrace 2 (see Chapter 5). It appears that the west side of the area was defined by the Roman garden wall (9208) (see below, Chapter 9), of which one fragment was uncovered. It is proposed that this wall ran at an

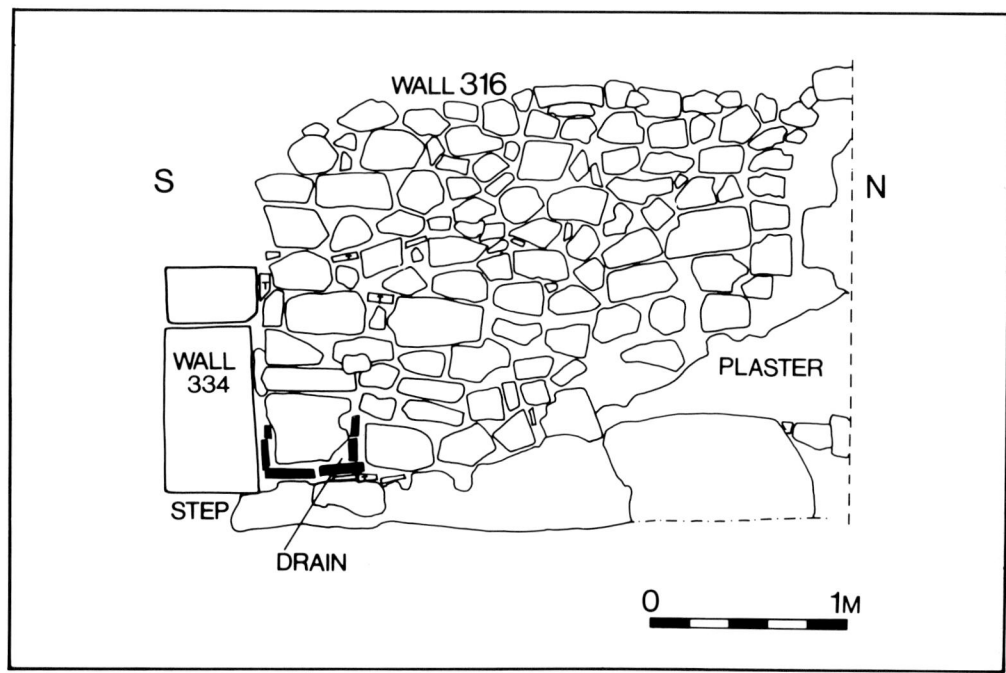

Fig. 1:2 Elevation of wall 316 showing the drain *(KF)*

angle from the point where it was exposed beside the 'South Church' towards the west side of the doorway into the Assembly Room (that is, to join with the east-west line of wall 334). Furthermore, it is proposed that the cut stone on which the phase 5 wall 316 was founded originally formed part of a stairway leading from this enclosed space up onto Terrace 2. Unfortunately no other steps survived. We might also bear in mind that the drain sealed in this wall (described above) would have lain beside the steps. The southern surface of the 'South Church' wall (the north side of this room) had been carefully plastered and lime washed. This suggests that in this phase the courtyard had whitewashed walls.

In sum, it is proposed that the essential form of the late Roman garden on the slope below the Roman Tower was preserved in phase 4. As a result, an open courtyard with whitewashed walls was created in the space between the Entrance Hall, the Refectory and the 'South Church'. The Assembly Room, and thus the Lower Thoroughfare and the heart of the monastery beyond, could be reached at the south side of the courtyard. The Upper Thoroughfare, we propose, was arrived at by a set of steps cut through the old retaining wall of the Roman garden. All trace of these steps, we conclude, was virtually removed when the phase 5 retaining walls 315 and 316 were constructed. To the north there was access to the south corridor of the 'South Church', and thus the Crypt Church and the Garden Court area. Finally, the 'South Church' could be approached via a monumental flight of marble steps (508), which led to the first floor of the Entrance Hall and, from there, to the distinguished guests' hall.

PHASE 5a1 (FIG. 1:3)

In this phase the shape of the room was altered. The late Roman garden was removed; Terrace 2 was now retained by walls 316, 315 and 303, a small courtyard being formed (Fig. 1:4). Wall 303 was constructed of rough rubble, solidly held together by a hard cement. This wall was faced on both sides. By contrast, walls 315 and 316 had faces on one side only, the inner side being rough. These walls were made of rubble held together by a poor cement. Wall 316, as was noted above, was founded on cut rock which may have originally formed part of the phase 4 steps. It also incorporated pieces of ninth-century painted plaster.

Wall 303 offered an important clue for this phase. It was a solidly constructed wall, unlike 315 and 316, yet its outer face was not painted. This indicates that it was designed to support a considerable weight, and that the enclosed area was roofed. We propose, therefore, that wall 303 was built to support the Upper Thoroughfare which crossed at first-floor level from the slope of Terrace 2 to the enlarged Entrance Hall.

The western half of the room, at least, was decorated in this phase: traces of painted decoration survived on wall 315. At its far western end, in a deposit *c.* 0.4 m above the level of the pavement, fragments of fallen plaster revealed a small passage of an original scheme of decoration below the phase 5a2 painted plaster. The fragments of phase 5a1 painting appeared to show a running plant scroll frieze on a white ground. The stems were pale blue-grey and light ochre, and the one partially preserved scroll terminated in a small round red fruit. The

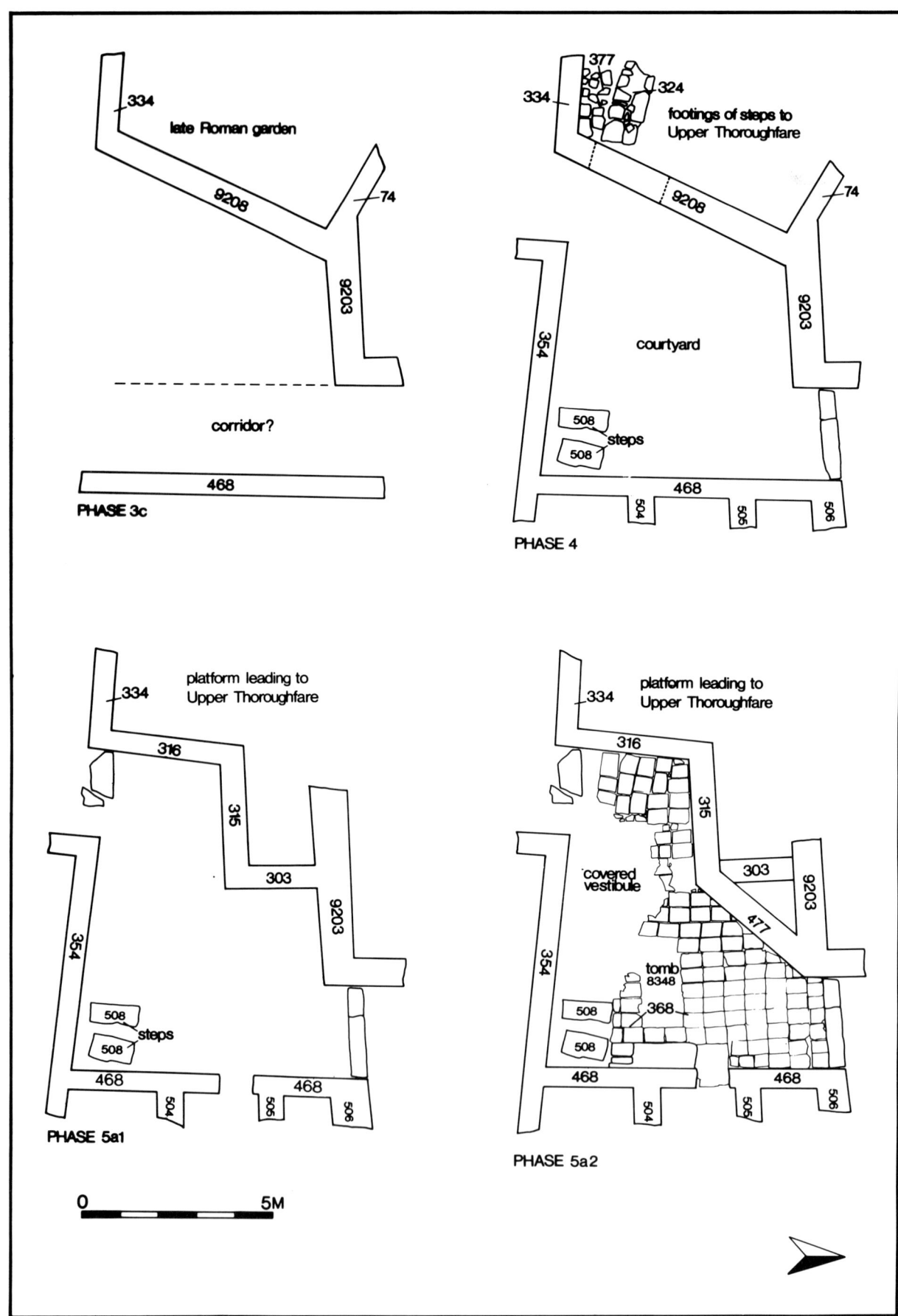

Fig. 1:3 Phase plan of the Vestibule (phases 3c-5a2) *(KF)*

Fig. 1:4 The western part of the Vestibule, showing walls 315 and 316 *(RH)*

trail was bordered at the top by a purple-black band and then by a field of strong ochre. The ochre, red and white used appeared to be very similar to the colours used in the subsequent phase 5a2 scheme. The presence of this overlying phase 5a2 plaster made a thorough examination of the lower layer impossible. However, as far as it was possible to ascertain, it seemed that the lower plaster did belong to the decoration of this wall, and was not confined to a single block of reused stone.

The monumental stairs (508) remained in use in this phase. In addition, a narrow doorway was cut through wall 468, providing access to the remodelled ground floor of the Entrance Hall (Volume 1: 218).

PHASE 5a2 (FIG. 1:3)

Wall 477 was added to the phase 5a1 configuration to close off the little corner against wall 303 (Fig. 1:5). This wall was painted at the same time as walls 315 and 316. At about the same time a pavement (368), in which a mixture of inscribed tiles was employed, was laid in the room. During the course of the ninth century, before phase 5c, the tiles between steps 508 and the doorway to the Assembly Room were removed, presumably because they had deteriorated with wear, being on the much-used route between the 'South Church' and the cloister. Another feature of this phase was the addition of a short length of bench to wall 468, between the doorway into room 2 and the marble steps (508); this too was painted.

The painted decoration of the Vestibule

Painted plaster still adhered to all of the walls of the phase 5a2 room (walls 315, 316, 354, 468 and 477). To judge from the type of plaster used and from the style of the surviving painting, it is clear that all of the walls were plastered (or replastered) and painted in one operation. At the time of excavation, considerable areas of painted surface were found in a reasonably good state of preservation on walls 315, 316 and 477. Less plaster adhered to walls 354 and 468, and what remained there had lost much of its colour. The plastered surfaces on walls 315, 316 and 477 were continuous.

A dado ran round the walls of this room, rising to a height of about 1.0 m above the tiled pavement (Figs 1:4, 1:6 and 1:7; Plate 1:1). This was painted in imitation of slabs of diagonally-veined panels of polychrome marble revetment, varying in width between 0.28 m and 0.4 m, and so cut and set that their undulating striations formed a sequence of upright and inverted chevrons. The panels had a white ground with veining which alternated in colour: on one, red and bright yellow; on the next, strong grey-blue and pale sky-blue (Plate 1:1). The veins were of two widths, broad and thin, arranged in a strictly repeating sequence. The broad veins were of two colours, with undulating bands of red and yellow or grey-blue and sky-blue running contiguously. The painted panels were bounded by vertical black lines, *c.* 5 mm wide, and they were tied one to the next, at regular intervals, by what appeared to be schematic representations of metal clamps. The black dividing lines were drawn over preparatory yellow guide-lines.

Fig. 1:5 The northern part of the Vestibule, with wall 477 and the door to the 'South Church' corridor *(JM)*

Fig. 1:6 Marbled dado on walls 315 and 316 *(JM)*

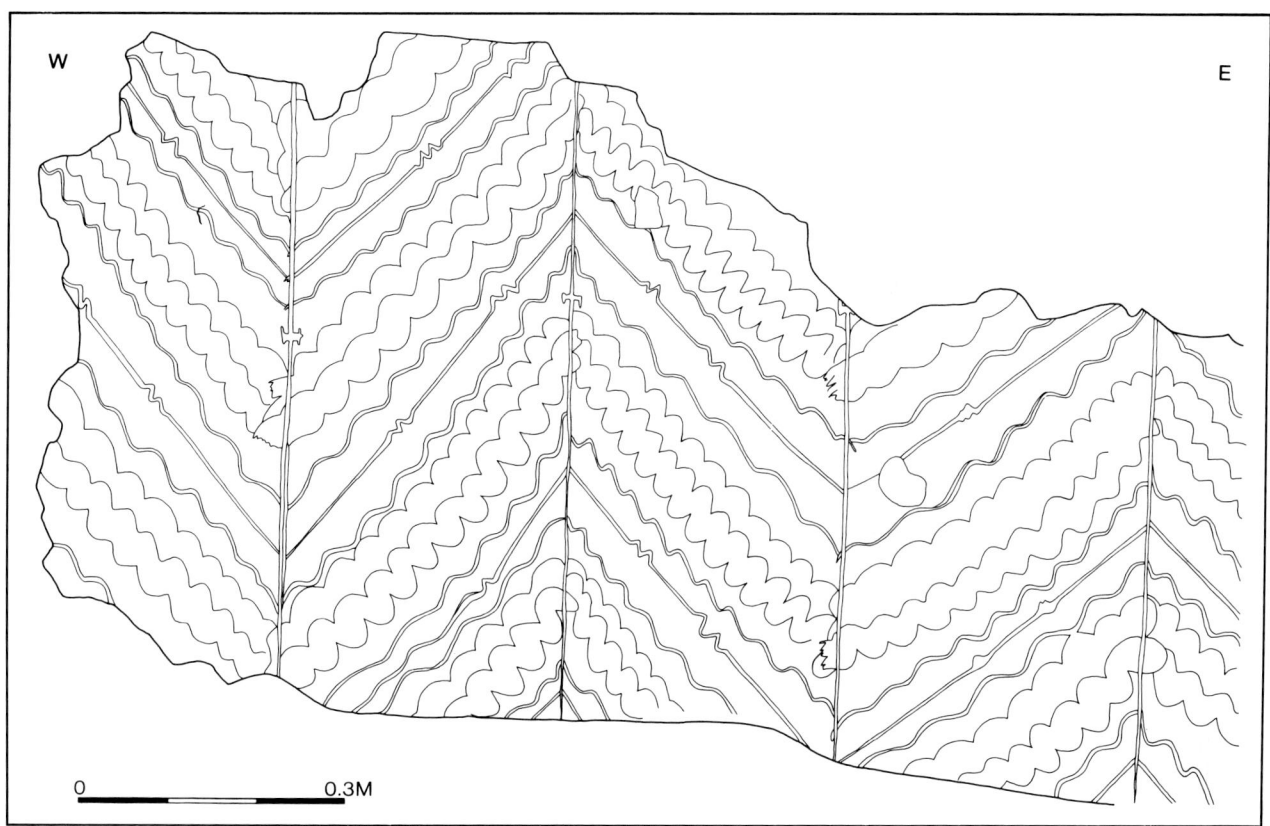

Fig. 1:7 A schematic drawing of the marbled dado on the north wall (315) of the Vestibule *(LW)*

Diagonally veined marbled dados of this kind are not uncommon in late Antique schemes of decoration, and are occasionally found in early medieval Italy: but there is one detail which distinguishes the marbling at San Vincenzo from most other surviving examples (these dados will be discussed in Volume 3; see also Mitchell 1985: 129-32; 1994). This is a thin, straight, diagonal vein, interrupted at regular intervals along its length by seismographic shakes (see Fig. 1:7). This curious twitching vein was employed in all the diagonally marbled dados so far uncovered by excavation at San Vincenzo. It is of great value for dating, approximately, the painting in this part of the monastery, since it was also found in the decoration of the crypt of the Crypt Church, painted when Abbot Epyphanius was in office (824-42) (Fig. 1:8). The style of the dado in the Vestibule differed slightly from that in the adjacent Assembly Room (see Chapter 3, Plates 3:6-7 and Fig. 3:13). In the Vestibule, yellow was used in combination with red in the broad veins of marbling, the undulations of the veins were generally tighter, and the seismographic shakes in the straight veins were sharper and more violent.

A small section of the horizontal border, which once separated the dado from the field above, survived in the northwest corner of the room, at the northern end of wall 316. Above the marbling there followed, in succession, a very thin bright yellow horizontal line, a black band *c.* 19 mm wide, a second fine yellow line, a 58 mm band of a rusty orange-red, and finally a broad band of pink. The divide between the orange-red and the pink was ornamented with large pale ochre pearls, each *c.* 22 mm in diameter, and set *c.* 10 mm apart. Projecting up from the orange-red band into the adjacent pink zone, at the far northern end of the west wall, was a small rectangular feature, in colour a deep magenta, outlined in white and enclosing a small pale blue rectangle, perhaps in imitation of a gemstone in its setting. Immediately above the upper left corner of this feature was a large white dot on a slightly larger grey-blue disc; there were traces of a similar dot just touching its upper right-hand corner. Presumably this was one of a series of such rectangles, probably alternating with black discs (see below), which ornamented the border along its length. The design would have been similar to the border above the Prophets on the west wall of the Assembly Room (see Fig. 3:18). Almost nothing of the painted plaster above the level of the dado and its upper border was found still adhering to the walls in this room (see below).

In the northwestern corner, the panels of imitation marble were bounded by a vertical black stripe *c.* 10 mm wide, followed by a band of orange-red, which continued into the angle. A similar vertical border, an orange-red band between two narrower black stripes, marked the angle between wall 315 and the slanting wall 477.

Fig. 1:8 Dado of veined marbling in the crypt of Epyphanius
(*JM*)

On the east wall, 468, on the low surface beneath the ledge which gave onto Tomb 499, some painted plaster survived immediately above the pavement. A band of black ran along the base of the wall, impinged on at one point by a descending thin red line.

On all of the plaster still adhering to the walls in this room the paint surface showed signs of flaking, and on the slanting wall 477 the flaking was severe (Fig. 1:9). This suggests that the walls were painted *al secco*, that is, after the surface of the plaster had been allowed to dry. Another detail that may also point to this conclusion is that the vertical divisions between the panels of marbling on the dado were usually not defined by lines snapped into the still-damp plaster, as was the case with most of the phase 4 painted walls which were discovered by excavation. Snapped vertical lines were found in the Vestibule only at the divisions between the first two panels of marbling at the northern end of the western wall 316.

As is the case in nearly all of the other excavated buildings of the monastery and as mentioned above,

almost nothing of the painted plaster above the level of the dado and its upper border was found still attached to the walls in this room. However, considerable quantities of fallen plaster were recovered during excavation, and from these it was possible to piece together some parts of the main painted fields of the room, and to deduce something of the nature of the others. Painted plaster was found in the following contexts in the Vestibule: 319, 321, 355, 359, 360, 367, 370, 465, 467, 469, 478, 479, 480, 481, and 489.

The principal part of the scheme so far reassembled from this material consists of one of two standing figures from the adjacent walls 315 and 316. Of the figure that probably came from the western end of the north wall (315) only a fragment of the book he once held was recognized, but more than half of his companion on the west wall (316) could be reconstructed. Most of the relevant fragments were recovered from the foot of wall 316, in the mortary layers 359 and 360.

The reassembled figure represented a young, unbearded, nimbed saint, facing half to the left

Fig. 1:9 Marbled dado on slanting wall 477 *(JM)*

(Plates 1:2-3). He held his right hand before his breast with two fingers raised in a gesture of address; and with his left hand he grasped a closed book with a jewelled cover, which rested in the crook of his arm (Fig. 1:10). His head was surrounded by a large yellow halo, which was circumscribed by an incised compass-drawn line and bounded by a narrow black band outside an even narrower ring of white. The halo was once flanked by the letters of his title and name, written in large red capitals against the surrounding white ground. Some of these letters could be attached to the reassembled parts of the saint's head and halo: the remains of an R on the left-hand side, and, on the right, part of the bowl of a rounded character, probably a C or an O, at one level, and, on the next level down, most of an A, with a flat bar at its apex and a broken median bar, followed by traces of the initial vertical stroke of the subsequent letter (Fig. 1:11). Other fragments of his title, which it was not possible to fit into the reconstruction, were SCS, VS, and the tops of two ascenders with a large contraction sign above (Fig. 1:12). The saint has not been identified.

The face was open and alive, a long oval narrowing to a rounded chin, with widely flaring eyebrows, a long nose and a small pursed mouth. Eyes, nose and mouth were precisely described with black lines and broad shading, and were accentu-

Fig. 1:10 Detail of the body of the young saint from the west wall (316) of the Vestibule *(JM)*

Fig. 1:11 Letters of the *titulus* accompanying the young saint *(JM)*

Fig. 1:12 Letters of the *titulus* accompanying the young saint *(JM)*

ated with red. The eyes were carefully painted, with striking red irises in brilliant white corneas. The shadow beneath was a muddy pinkish brown, above a swathe of pale cream. The eyelid was defined by a black and a red line, the ridge of the eyebrow was described in black, and the hollow in between was shaded with a sludgy green. The nose was formed of two parallel brush strokes, one white, the other a purplish brown, which gave it a summary relief. The nostrils and the lower part of the nose were strongly outlined with red. The philtrum was prominent, a purplish brown rectangular hollow outlined in black. The mouth was a tight black line with nail-head depressions at either end, set above a small pendulous lower lip. Two short black strokes marked the cavity below the mouth. The whole face was modelled at its edges with a soft purplish brown and a deeper brown. The lighted interior areas were worked up into a thick and brilliant white *impasto*, which was laid on last of all. The neck and hands were also strongly modelled and lighted, with vigorous strokes of white, creamy ochre, and, in the case of the neck, pink. The hair was cut to a cap with a scalloped fringe, finely striated with streaks of yellow against black.

It is difficult to make complete sense of the saint's dress. Essentially, he wore a wide-sleeved tunic with greyish blue banded folds, and an upper garment, a kind of pallium, of pale ochre with white linear highlights and long folds described with purplish brown and pale ochre, these appearing as narrow bands grouped chiefly in threes. The tunic was ornamented with at least two broad red *clavi* which fell diagonally down from his right shoulder and lay against a slanting swathe of pale pink. His right sleeve, which was in the colours of his tunic, hung down from his forearm and elbow in a steep triangle. The central break in the neck of the garment was marked by a short pointed grey-blue fork. The pallium was thrown over his left shoulder, passed round behind the neck to re-emerge along his right shoulder, and then fell down behind the left side of his body, reappearing below the elbow. Another part of it passed round the waist in the manner of a cummerbund. Strangely, the triangular sleeve on the saint's left arm was given the same colours as the pallium, although it ought to have been uniform with the tunic. On both tunic and pallium the grouped vertical folds formed a dominant banded pattern.

The long sinuous fingers of the saint's right hand were held before his breast in an attitude of speech, in the so-called Latin gesture of blessing. In his left hand he held a large closed book, angled so that the fore-edge was displayed, with densely-set parallel lines of grey-blue, pale sky-blue and white, to indicate the pages. The book had a splendidly ornate cover in yellow, presumably to represent gold, which was set with five purplish brown gems, a circular one at the centre and foliate stones in the four corners, all in black pearled settings.

Apart from a narrow passage on the left side, the saint's midriff and legs have not yet been reconstructed. However, among the fallen plaster recovered from context 359, in the northwestern corner of the room, were fragments with two butterfly-folds, from the bottom of a garment, which, to judge from their colour and design, must have come from this figure (Plate 1:4).

The dimensions of the reconstructed figure were as follows: overall height of reconstructed fragment 0.98 m, estimated overall height of figure when complete (including halo) *c.* 1.55 m, diameter of halo 0.42 m, height of head 0.2 m, width of head at temples 0.173 m.

The saint stood against a thickly painted plain white ground, but it has not yet proved possible to establish the wider context of his setting on the wall.

In style this figure is related to the painted decoration in the crypt, at the northern end of the site, which is firmly dated to the abbacy of Epyphanius (824-42) (Fig. 1:13) (see Volume 1: chapter 7). It differs markedly from the Prophets in the Assembly Room (see below, Chapter 3). The painting of the saint was more constrained than that of the Prophets, even a trifle laboured by comparison. In place of the free, irregular strokes which indicated the folds, and the play of brilliant lights and little strokes of red which illuminated and described the features of the faces of the Prophets, strictly marshalled parallel bands of colour in serried profusion ran down the saint's body, and his face was continuously modelled with a thick white *impasto* and was strongly contoured. In the crypt there was a similar, somewhat laboured, precision in the description and articulation of the figures. We also find in the crypt similar large yellow haloes ringed with white and black, similar drapery (characterized by the dark parallel lines of folds often clustered in groups of three, sharp triangular sleeves, extravagant butterfly-folds enlivening the lower hems of long tunics), and saints with scalloped fringes to their hair (Belting 1968: ills 13-60; Pantoni 1970; see also Volume 1: chapter 7). The face of the saint from the Vestibule can be seen as a simplified and abstracted version of a type which recurred a number of times in the crypt (Belting 1968: ills 52-60; Pantoni 1970: figs 39, 40, 53-5). This figure is likely to have been close in date to the paintings in the crypt. However, there is no question of it having been the work of one of the same painters. In style and execution the saint had his own idiosyncrasies: fold lines on tunic and pallium had a tendency to proliferate, to form a more general pattern of narrow parallel bands, as against the clusters of three parallel fold lines crossing surfaces of unruffled material preferred by the painters of the crypt. In addition, the two butterfly-folds from the lower hem

Fig. 1:13 St Laurence in the crypt of Abbot Epyphanius *(JM)*

of the saint's tunic had an angular rather than a rounded flowing configuration (Plate 1:4); the slanting *clavi* at the shoulder had a particular form, and the dot-trails which ornamented the garment of so many of the figures in the crypt and various passages of related drapery from the excavations were absent (although they were present in related paintings found in the northern end of the neighbouring Assembly Room). The differences between the saint and the paintings in the crypt may be the differences between two contemporaneous interpretations of the same idiom, or they may indicate a slight variance in date. If anything the saint is the earlier of the two. Its somewhat looser, more flowing, brushwork harks back to phase 4 painting at San Vincenzo, and is similar to that of the Prophets from the west wall of the Assembly Room (see Chapter 3).

Fragments of a frontal head, very like the head of this figure from 359, were found in the northern part of the adjacent room, the Assembly Room (see Chapter 3, pp. 61-2 and Plate 3:25). This may have come from a wall in the southern part of the Vestibule.

From contexts 359 and 360, in front of wall 315, came many fragments of nodding plants with red, heart-shaped flowers, field poppies, on slender bending black stalks painted on a white ground (Plate 1:5). The stems were 3-4 mm in diameter, and the red flowers themselves were about 50 mm tall. It has not proved possible to establish their original context. However, at one point a curving black band, 9 mm wide, separated the field of flowers from an area of brown-ochre densely sprinkled with small white dots. One fragment with such a plant was found in context 478, a layer of fallen plaster from wall 477. It seems likely that this scheme had its place in the decoration of the southern face of wall 315, and thus may have been associated with the two standing saints. The heart-shaped red flowers of these plants are paralleled in the fragmentary plant trail painted on the face of bench 8104 in the east portico of the Garden Court (see Volume 1: 202-3; fig. 10:14; plates 10:2 and 10:3), and in the many flowers which spring from the ground in most of the scenes in the crypt of Epyphanius (see Volume 1: figs 7:14, 7:19, 7:26; plates 7:3 and 7:5). Like these, the flowering plants from the wall in the Vestibule are to be associated with a campaign of decoration which accompanied the construction phase 5a2, in the second quarter of the ninth century.

The material from context 359 also included two adjoining fragments of border between an area of red and a pink band c. 35 mm wide, which in turn was separated from a 20 mm ochre band by a thin white line. White dots, about 15 mm in diameter, ran along the red/pink divide, punctuated by an occasional large black circular device, c. 42 mm in diameter, with a hollow centre and four white dots around it. Fragments of a similar border were found in 479, on the eastern side of the room, in the doorway leading into the northwest room (room 2) of the Entrance Hall. In design this border was similar to the one which divided the dado on wall 316 from the main painted field of the wall above (described above). These fragments were probably from either the lower or the upper main horizontal borders of the walls in the Vestibule, with the divide between red and pink bands ornamented with white dots and with periodic black discs and pale blue and magenta rectangles, both girt with white pearls. This scheme would appear to have been a variant of the pearled horizontal borders which framed the Prophets on the west wall of the Assembly Room (see Chapter 3, Fig. 3:18, Plate 3:8).

A substantial quantity of painted plaster was recovered from the neighbouring context, 360, from the foot of wall 315. Among this were fragments of the veined marbled dado and various types of drapery. One type of drapery was in blue-grey with bands of white, ochre and red, resembling drapery fragments found in context 480, concealed behind the upright Roman inscription dedicated to Afinia

Phieris (507) (see Volume 1: 223; J. Patterson in Volume 3) in the eastern side of the room; another kind of drapery was rather more roughly painted with bands of light blue-grey, deep grey-blue and cream. Two interesting but unidentifiable motifs were also found here: an extraordinary small curling configuration in blue-black and creamy white with red articulation, which in isolation rather resembled an ammonite; and a scheme with large ochre balls, c. 32 mm in diameter on a dark blue-black ground, which bordered an irregular area of white. These must have come from some quite elaborate composition. A number of fragments, apparently deriving from the decoration of the adjoining Assembly Room, also found their way into 360: these included pieces of the upper border of the western wall, and a fragment of drapery in lavender, salmon-pink and white, which in its colours and design was identical to the drapery of the Prophets.

From context 355 came fragments of a figural composition with drapery similar to that of the young saint from 359, with configurations in a creamy white on a pale ochre ground. Another passage which was also possibly drapery had rich red and pale salmon-pink bands with trails of little white dots. There was also part of a sandalled foot. It is unclear from which wall these pieces fell.

Fragments of drapery were also found in 367, at a low level in the western part of the Vestibule. Some had a red band ornamented with white pearls set against a salmon-pink ground modelled with white strokes, and others had trails of bright blue dots running down striped grey material.

In the eastern part of the room quite large quantities of painted plaster were found in 465, the uppermost layer in this area below the zone of machine clearance. These included various fragments of drapery from figurative compositions, part of a red-brown halo with a thin white rim, against a ground of pale sky-blue, and also pieces of a rough plaster floor containing inclusions of crushed red tile (cocciopesto). Some of this material showed signs of burning.

Much painting, including substantial remains of figures, was found in 467, a layer which lapped up over the bench at the foot of wall 468. It seems likely that most of this material fell from this wall after the conflagration of 881. A large percentage of these pieces was scorched, some being reduced to little more than cinders. The fire must have burnt intensely at this end of the room, or in an adjacent room, one of whose walls may have fallen into this area (see below). There were some pieces which seemed to resemble the painting of the young saint on the opposite wall of the room: these included a fragment of a yellow halo, rimmed in white and black, just like the halo of the saint. Another four pieces joined together to form a field of yellow ochre bounded by a curving incised line, with an area of red at the centre of the yellow patch. Beyond the bounding line there was a second incised circle enclosing a ring of pale blue-grey, and outside that a ground of white. This may have been the remains of another haloed saint with reddish hair. On the other hand, there were some fragments of heads and drapery from 467 which resembled the painting of the phase 4 Prophets in the Assembly Room. These included the remains of a somewhat scorched head, with part of its deep brown-red halo (Plate 1:6). The upper part of the face was preserved, with the temple worked in a very thick pink *impasto* and shaded in thick blue-grey, and the eyebrow defined by thin red lines. The head was about 90 mm wide at the level of the root of the nose, that is substantially smaller than the Prophets in the neighbouring room. Two other pieces bore thick *impasto* swathes of blue-grey, white and red, perhaps from a beard. There were six adjoining fragments of another red-brown halo, with a white line running round just inside its rim, set against a scorched sky-blue ground; and there were other fragments of a red-brown halo, associated with what may have been a pink face and a beard painted in a very thick white *impasto*. Various fragments of drapery stylistically related to that of the phase 4 Prophets from the Assembly Room were also found in this context; among them were some passages of drapery with sections of light salmon-pink lighted with white and with red linear articulation bordering on areas with white light lines on a light blue-grey. Finally there was a fragment with part of a hand, the fingers modelled in thick white *impasto* and outlined in red, again in the manner of the Prophets in the Assembly Room.

Remains of plaster still adhering to the base of wall 468 bore traces of the same scheme of marbled dado as that found on the other walls of the Vestibule (315, 316, 477, 354), with panels of blue-grey veining alternating with ones with red and yellow veining on a white ground. One would have expected the painting on the main field above the dado to have been completed in the same campaign and to have been in the same style as the saint from wall 316. It is likely that the fragments of yellow haloes from 467 belonged to this phase 5 scheme.

The fragments of figurative painting in the manner of the phase 4 Prophets in the Assembly Room which came to light in the Vestibule are likely to have fallen in from another neighbouring room. Similar painted fragments, apparently dating from phase 4, were found in the neighbouring context 479, in the doorway connecting the Vestibule with the northwestern part of the ground floor (room 2) of the Entrance Hall. This material included, apart from the usual collection of nondescript fragments bearing various colours and combinations, one piece with a scrap of a painted inscription and others which came from the head, drapery and hands of one or more figures. The inscription was in large white capitals, originally

c. 0.1 m tall, on a grey-blue ground. Only the lower extremities of two letters survived, perhaps the tip of the leg of an R, followed by the bottom of the left leg of an A. These letters had thin elegant serifs, but they showed no trace of the swelling terminals typical of much script at San Vincenzo in the ninth century. However, there is little question that this was early medieval work and a date in the early ninth century seems perfectly acceptable.

In 479 there were three fragments from the head of one individual. The face was fully frontal and about 85 mm wide at the level of the eyes – that is between a half and two-thirds of the size of the heads of the Prophets on the west wall of the Assembly Room. In design and execution, the head seemed to be quite similar to those of the Prophets, with red pupils to the eyes, the eyelids outlined with red and white lights and thick blue-grey shadows over skin which was in pink modelled both to light and to dark. The paint was laid on quite thickly. The head was surrounded by a bright brown-red halo. Two other adjoining fragments which belonged to this group were painted with thick blue-grey and white strokes on a light grey ground. On the backs of all these pieces there were marks in red-brown, which looked like offprints from fresh paint on the preliminary layer of plaster on the wall, the *arriccio*. (No sense could be made of these configurations; but it is just possible that they were the stains from underlying *sinopie*.) There was a further fragment in the same context from the head of another individual. Also from this context came two fragmentary painted hands with energetically curving contours, the fingers in a thick white *impasto* and outlined in red, after the manner of the hands of the Prophets in the Assembly Room. All this appears to be work dating to phase 4 of the construction of the monastery (*c.* AD 800). It is not clear from where these fragments came. The apparently windowless room 2 of the Entrance Hall would have been both too small and too dark to have merited an elaborate scheme of figural decoration; and they cannot have come from the west face of wall 468 in the Vestibule, since, to judge from its dado, this room was decorated in phase 5, in the second quarter of the ninth century, rather than in the years around AD 800. A possible explanation is that this plaster fell from a wall on the upper floor of the Entrance Hall, which had been painted in phase 4, a generation before the Vestibule, and that the similar material found in the adjacent context 467, against the eastern wall of the Vestibule, came from the same source.

The material from 479 also included fragments of a border between bands or fields of orange and magenta red, with pale ochre dots along the divide and periodically a round back motif modelled with pale ochre, with white highlighted grey dots at its corners. These resembled fragments of border found in 359 in the northwestern corner of the Vestibule and were probably from one of the main horizontal divisions which ran round the walls of the room (see above).

Little of any consequence was recovered from 478 at the foot of the slanting wall 477 (Fig. 1:9). There was a quantity of fallen dado, with its veined marbling, and two fragments with red flowers on black stalks against a white ground, seemingly from the decoration of wall 315. Otherwise few of the fragments were identifiable. A small number of pieces may have been from drapery, with configurations in dark blue-grey, ochre and a small white and black linear articulation on a pale sky-blue ground. One fragment had a design of tightly curling white lines on a blue-grey ground, which looked somewhat like a voluted capital. Various other configurations and colours were found on the painted plaster from this context, but it has not proved possible to identify the main subject of the scheme of decoration of the wall (477) from which much of it would appear to have fallen.

Numerous fragments of drapery from a standing figure were recovered from context 480, in the far northeastern corner of the Vestibule, at the foot of wall 468, immediately to the north of the doorway which led into room 2 of the Entrance Hall. The drapery was predominantly pale ochre and grey-blue, articulated with thick white bands and with white dot-trails running down the lines of the folds. One assembled group of fragments seemed to show a shoulder with white highlights over light blue-grey material, the contour outlined with a thin ochre line and set against a ground of warm lilac-pink. The painting was rapid and more sketchy in execution than that of the saint from 359. It is possible that this figure stood on the short stretch of wall between the doorway into the Entrance Hall and the passage leading down into the Garden Court.

A considerable number of fragments of painted plaster was found in 481, a layer which spread over Tomb 499 and overlay the tiled floor of the northeastern corner of the Vestibule, immediately to the west of the tomb. Little could be learned from this material, but there were many fragments of a corner painted a deep brick-red, bounded on one side by a field of pale blue-grey and on the other by white; and two joining pieces seemed to have come from the upper part of a head, with flesh of thickly applied pink, white hair streaked with pinkish brown strokes and a deep brown-red halo.

In addition to fragments of painted plaster of various colours, some pieces of a rough, dull red, mortar surface, probably a floor-surface, full of large flinty inclusions, were found in 489, a layer directly over the tiled floor in the northern part of the Vestibule.

Painted plaster with various combinations of colours was found in 485, 486 and 488, in the area of the doorway leading from the Vestibule down into the western end of the 'South Church' south

corridor. From 488 there was some drapery with bands of pale sky-blue and ochre-cream, resembling that of the Prophets in the Assembly Room.

In addition, some fragments found in contexts within the northern part of the Assembly Room (see below, p. 62) may in fact have been from the painted decoration of the Vestibule and have been displaced subsequently, during episodes of destruction and demolition.

Discussion

What can be reconstructed of the painted decoration of the Vestibule in phase 5a2 can be summarized as follows. A marbled dado with panels of diagonal veining, alternating in colour – red and yellow, grey-blue and pale sky-blue –, rose to a height of about 1.0 m above the pavement and circled the whole room. The border between this dado and the main field above was ornamented with a line of white pearls punctuated at intervals by black discs and magenta rectangles with pale blue centres in alternation. A similar border probably ran round the room at a higher level, above the main painted field. As regards the principle scheme on the walls above, on walls 315 and 316 there were two standing saints, a little under life-size with books in their hands, painted on a white ground. Also, it would appear that on one or both of these walls there was a concentration of red heart-shaped poppies on black waving stalks also on a white ground, perhaps associated in some way with the two saints. Fragments of other figures with similar yellow haloes were found in other parts of the Vestibule and very likely fell from other walls, probably 354 and 468, the southern and eastern walls of the room. The remains of a further standing figure were picked up in front of the northern part of wall 468. This may have stood on the wall immediately to the north of the doorway into room 2 in the Entrance Hall. The painting of this figure differed somewhat from that of the reconstructed saint from 359 at the western end of the room; it was sketchier and less precise in execution and must have been by a different hand. Large standing figures of saints seem to have predominated on the walls of this room. However, there were a few fragments from 360 which may indicate the presence of a more complex composition.

On the other hand, some fragments of figures painted in a style resembling the phase 4 Prophets in the Assembly Room were excavated in the Vestibule (360, 467, 479, 481 and 488). The pieces from 360 may have come in from the Assembly Room, which lay immediately to the south, but a group of material found in 467 and 479, at the eastern end of the room and the fragments from 481 and 488, are more likely to have come from a location closer to hand. The figures from 467 and 479 were considerably smaller than the Prophets in the Assembly Room and they had been quite severely burnt in parts. It is possible that they fell with a wall from the upper storey of the adjacent Entrance Hall, which had been decorated in phase 4, a generation earlier than the walls of the Vestibule.

The floor

The tiled pavement (368) was well laid between the northern part of wall 468 and wall 477 (Fig. 1:1), but little survived of it in the southern half of the room. The make-up layer for the floor exposed in this area (375) suggested that the fire in phase 5c was intense in this area. It must also be noted that tiles were absent along the route from the marble steps (508) to the doorway into the Assembly Room. It appears that this was a much used route within the monastery, in effect from the first floor of the Entrance Hall (where the Upper Thoroughfare joined the passage into the 'South Church') by way of the Vestibule to the cloister.

A decorated tomb

During the course of restoring the tiled pavement, the *Istituto Centrale* discovered a fine decorated tomb (8348) in an area where the tiles were missing from the Vestibule floor (see Figs 1:1 and 1:14). The tomb was lying on an east-west axis and contained a single skeleton (now lost). It was closed by five reused blocks of building stone – of roughly drafted calcareous limestone. One of these, broken into two pieces, was plain, one was lime-washed on one

face, and the remaining three bore painted plaster. Two of these three were plastered on three adjacent surfaces, the third on three surfaces. On the first of these three blocks, two opposed shorter faces were painted white, while the long face between them had the remains of a substantial rounded motif painted pale blue with red articulation set against a white ground, which was bordered by bands of pale red and purple. This block originally must have formed part of a pilaster or vertical buttress projecting from the wall of a painted room. Its dimensions more or less coincided with those of the low buttress-like projection on the west wall of the Assembly Room. The second block had on one long face a white field with a red band down one short edge, on the adjacent short face alternating broad bands of white and pink divided by gently diverging incised lines, and on the opposite long face a patch of unpainted plaster. The third of these three blocks had, on one long face, a yellow ground with the remnants of two rounded devices (one coloured pink and outlined in brown, the other red with an incised contour), and on the adjacent short face a white ground bordered on one edge by successive bands of pale red, plain plaster and dark brown, followed after an interval by curving parallel adjacent bands of yellow ochre, dark brown and red, which seemed to frame an area of white marked with orange strokes. It is not possible to reconstruct the schemes of decoration from which these fragments were torn. To judge from the range and combination of colours used and from the free and simple manner in which the various motifs were described, all of these

Fig. 1:14 The eastern part of the Vestibule, showing steps 508, the area of missing tiles above Tomb 8348 and the phase 6 blocking of the doorway into the Entrance Hall *(IR)*

Fig. 1:15 Inscribed tile from the head of Tomb 8348 *(JM)*

surfaces were painted in phase 4, and must have come from rooms which were decorated in the first decade of the ninth century.

At the head of the tomb, a tile inscribed with a cross flanked by a protective inscription was laid upright, in a setback above and immediately to the west of the cavity for the body of the deceased individual (Fig. 1:15). The tile measured 0.54 x 0.385 x 0.04 m and had been trimmed on one of its long sides. It was made of fabric B (see Volume 3). It originally bore the contracted name GVN, drawn into the leather-hard clay before firing. When the cross and inscription were cut into the tile this surface was smoothed down, partly obliterating the original letters, although much of the G was still quite visible. The cross, which was almost as tall as the tile was wide, had thin attenuated arms which swelled out into sharply cusped terminals. The inscription, which flanked the cross and was arranged in three lines above and below its horizontal bar, read: CRUX XPI CONFVSIO DIABoLI EST. The letters in all three lines were more or less uniform in size (excepting the third letter O, which was smaller (20 mm)), ranging between 37 and 45 mm in height. The man responsible for this inscription was clearly not an experienced mason, although the crudeness of execution was perhaps in part due to the fact that he was cutting tile and not stone. He first laid out the inscription by incising the contours of the letters into the surface of the tile. However, when he

initially sketched out the lines of letters, he seems to have omitted the A of DIABOLI in the final line, and subsequently had to convert the B into an A, elide the B with the A and insert a small pointed inscript O on the slant in the space between B and L. The script of the characters was a somewhat irregular and crude version of the typical epigraphic script practised at San Vincenzo in the first half of the ninth century: that is, rather square characters, with sharply cut edges; vertical shafts with more or less parallel sides which splayed out into wedge-shaped terminals; the horizontal bars of E and L in the form of triangular wedges; O drawn out on its vertical axis and pointed at top and bottom; and R open, with a leg which curved round back towards the vertical stem. The punctuation marks and the contraction sign over XPI were quite extravagant and elaborate. However, the letters were far less regular than in many of the other early ninth-century inscriptions from San Vincenzo, let alone the finest surviving examples. Their sections were rarely triangular, they were often flat in the trough, and the wedge-terminals tended to be almost grotesquely extravagant (for example, in C and L). Overall the work was not very skilled, and the forms of the letters were not well-controlled.

In general terms this has all the marks of a late product of the San Vincenzo epigraphic tradition, and must date from the second half of the ninth century (cf. Mitchell 1990).

Lighting

The lighting of the room remains an enigma. It is possible that this was a small, dark ante-room. However, the paintings suggest that some light did enter the Vestibule. Fragments of window-glass found in this room may have derived from a window which fell into the area during the conflagration in 881 (though these fragments equally may have fallen from windows situated at the west end of the Refectory, cf. Volume 1: 205; fig. 10:16).

PHASE 5c

Before this room was engulfed by fire, a fine clayey loam (370) covered the patches where tiles were absent in the southern and eastern parts of the room (that is the 'passage' between steps 508 and the doorway to the Assembly Room, discussed above). Over this was a 'trample' layer (367) in which fine charcoal had become intermixed with clay. This layer was between 0.1 and 0.3 m thick over the tiled floor (368), and clearly lipped up to the outside of the north Refectory wall (354) on the south side of the room. This is evidence that some of the tiled floor had gone before the great fire, and that localized patches of mud, at least, had formed by 881. This evidence suggests that this part of the monastery was beginning to deteriorate before the sack.

The effects of the fire in 881 varied greatly across the room. Alongside Refectory wall 354 the burning was intense. Parts of this wall actually tumbled inwards, into the Refectory, during the inferno (353, 343). Similarly, there were signs of intense burning in front of the doorway leading into room 2 of the Entrance Hall and spreading out towards the steps leading down to the 'South Church'.

The bench in front of wall 468 was likewise badly scorched, and its wooden top was turned to charcoal. By contrast, the tiled floor surviving in the room showed little sign of the burning, and the paintings on walls 316, 315 and 477 were largely unaffected by the fire or the heat it generated. It appears, therefore, that the effects of the fire were very localized.

PHASE 6a

It seems that this room was accessible, at least in part, in the tenth and eleventh centuries. At this time a doorway was chopped through the north wall of the Refectory (354) by the marble steps (508) (Fig. 1:16). This doorway indicates that there was access from the first floor of the Entrance Hall down the marble steps and into the largely destroyed western half of the Refectory. The tumble of rubble blocking the north end of the Assembly Room (see Chapter 3) presumably necessitated the creation of this makeshift doorway.

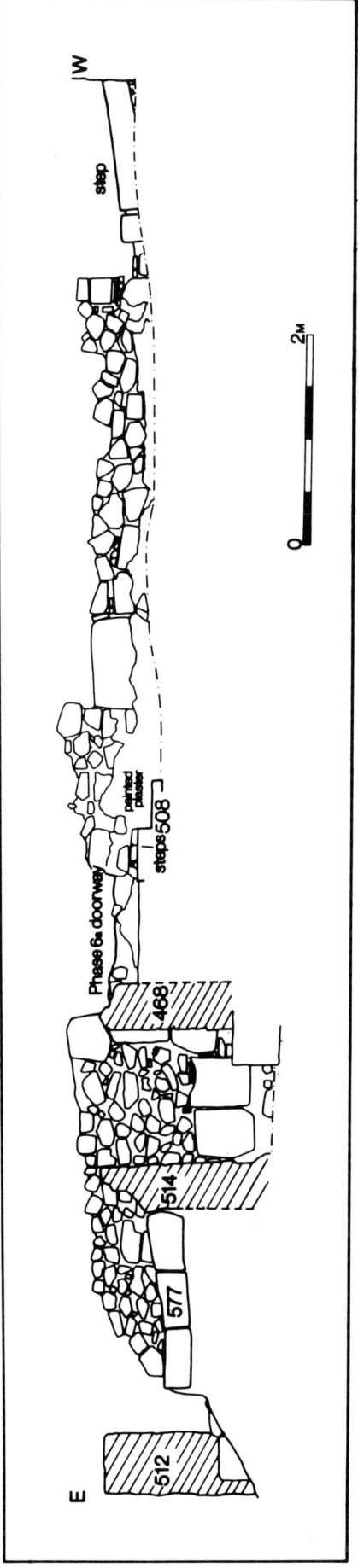

Fig. 1:16 Elevation of wall 354 showing the phase 6a doorway (KF)

In the Vestibule itself mortary layers (356-60) built up during the fire or soon afterwards: they were composed of fragmentary plaster and mortar from the partially ruined walls around about. It must have been early on in phase 6 that the large inscription (507) dedicated to the priestess Afinia Phieris was positioned in front of the doorway into room 2 of the Entrance Hall (Figs 1:1 and 1:14; cf. Volume 1: 223).

PHASE 6b

Before the demolition of the walls of the Vestibule, attempts were made to remove some of the architectural features. The threshold (369) into the Assembly Room was prised out of position. This was almost certainly done in order to release the east jamb of the doorway that hitherto had connected the Vestibule to the Assembly Room. Attempts were also made to dislodge the heavy marble steps (508) that connected the Vestibule to the first floor of the Entrance Hall.

It appears that the Vestibule was largely filled in during phase 6b with a number of tips, each *c.* 0.3 m thick, thrown from the hillslope above. Some of these tips, such as 338, contained much rubble. Thin humic tips spread across to the south wall of the 'South Church' (e.g. 466, 467, 469, 480, 485, 488), blocking off and covering the northern part of the room and covering the levelled ground floor of the Entrance Hall.

PHASE 7

The white mortar surface (contexts 335 and 346), belonging to this period and found over the area of the Assembly Room and the Refectory (see below, Chapters 3 and 4), appeared not to have extended over the old Vestibule. Wall 334 seems to have defined its northern limit. In this period it it likely that the Vestibule was completely buried and abandoned, though the upper parts of walls 316, 315, and 477 were still exposed.

POST-PHASE 8

This part of the site was landscaped after the twelfth century in two phases. Firstly, tips 310, 313, 319, 325, 327, 330, 333, were thrown into the room, bringing the soil level to the top of walls 303, 315 and 316, and covering 477. Secondly, a white mortary surface (307), possibly of post-medieval date, covered part of the old Vestibule area as well as Terrace 2. This finally sealed 334, the north wall of the Assembly Room. After this the terrace was raised once more, possibly as a result of the ploughing of the adjacent hillslope. In more recent times it became an olive grove.

DISCUSSION

The Vestibule always appears to have formed part of a thoroughfare. In late Roman times it lay beyond the eastern edge of the walled, mid-slope garden below the Tower. This arrangement was altered in phase 3c when, it is surmised, a corridor running north-south was constructed across this area, linking the 'South Church' to a large building (possibly a refectory) to the south, while leaving the walled garden intact.

The area was completely redeveloped in phase 4. The walled garden was effectively removed, and the area below it was turned into an open courtyard at the juncture between the public and the restricted, claustral areas of the complex. Lay visitors wishing to go up to the first-floor hall in the 'South Church' would have had to cross it, as would monks who had business in the areas reserved for guests at the northern end of the monastery. The Vestibule, in other words, was a critical focal point within the monastery. Four passages led into it: the passage from the first floor of the Entrance Hall and the apartments in the 'South Church', down steps 508; the passage along the south corridor of the 'South Church' (and that from the Crypt Church); the proposed passage up the steps through wall 9208, the so-called Upper Thoroughfare for lay visitors; and lastly, the passage into the Assembly Room, and thus along the Lower Thoroughfare, through the large doorway in the southwest corner of the room.

This arrangement was significantly modified in phase 5. At that time, we propose, the Upper Thoroughfare passed from the first floor of the Entrance Hall to the terrace level above the Vestibule (see Chapter 2). The open courtyard was now covered, its walls were decorated with paintings and, eventually, its floor was paved with tiles. Distinguished visitors on their way to the stairs leading up to the great chamber on the upper level of the 'South Church'/guest hall, as well as the monks, would have passed through this room. The excavated remains of expertly painted standing figures from the various walls, in particular the fresh-faced young saint from wall 315, lead us to speculate that this unprepossessing space, so close to where the monks gathered before dining, was considered, by phase 5a2, to be quite a significant focus in the monastery. It may be that this room, with solemn images of standing saints looking down from its walls, functioned not only as a place of passage, but also as a parlour, where the monks and the laity could meet formally. Bench 457 was added at about this time; and shortly afterwards Tomb 8348 was inserted into the floor. In the light of this interpretation of the room as a frequently visited public space, it is tempting to ascribe the tomb to a prominent member of the monastic community.

The room suffered considerable damage during the sack of 881. Afterwards, in phase 6, it appears to have retained its function as an intersection of passages. The routes from the Upper Thoroughfare and the first floor of the Entrance Hall seem to have remained in use, judging from the continued use of steps 508; the south corridor of the 'South Church' remained in use; and, as the doorway to the Assembly Room had collapsed, a new doorway was cut beside steps 508 into the Refectory. The continuity of the passages, albeit in this makeshift manner, was probably occasioned by the use of the Entrance Hall as a martyrium in phase 6a. Indeed, the positioning of the monumental inscription dedicated to Afinia Phieris in front of room 2 of the Entrance Hall in this phase suggests that visitors gathered here and were effectively directed towards the tombs within, arguably those of the monks who had perished at the hands of the heathen Saracens in 881.

The Vestibule, then, was a space in the public domain, at the intersection of the exterior and the interior sectors of the monastery. Not only did it function as a junction where various ways met and crossed; it may also have served as an elegant, if somewhat austerely decorated, chamber in which visitors from the outside world could converse with normally enclosed members of the community. It serves as an interesting illustration of the important role played by passageways in the organization of élite communities, both religious and secular, in the early Middle Ages. Corridor-thoroughfares were prominent features in monastic settlements, like Benedict Biscop's Wearmouth (Cramp 1976: 233-4, figs 5:9, 5:10) and Angilbert's St.-Riquier at Centula (Taylor 1975: 145-52), as they were in Charlemagne's palace at Aachen (Kreusch 1965: 511-29, fig. 1; Hugot 1965: 545, fig. 2), and in the papal palace at the Lateran (Lauer 1911). In both spheres they served both to distinguish and to unite the various sections of a dispersed complex of buildings, each of which would have had its own function and status within the overall working of the institution. They also provided a means of directing and controlling the movements of people in extended settlements in which large communities led a varied but ordered life, following an elaborately prescribed daily routine. In monasteries like St.-Riquier and San Vincenzo, passages were an essential physical expression and articulation of the daily life and liturgy of the community. They connected the different stratified sectors of the monastery, monastic areas and guest-quarters, workshop and cloister, the Abbot's apartments and the habitations of the simple monks. Similarly the passages joining the main abbey-church with the other satellite churches and chapels within the precinct would have framed the routes of the elaborate processions which played such a major role in the liturgy of daily devotion, in which the monks processed from altar to altar in their unceasing round of communal worship.

Chapter Two

THE UPPER THOROUGHFARE

by Richard Hodges

Terrace 1 ran along the side of Colle della Torre, from the old farmhouse, southward towards the site of San Vincenzo Maggiore (Volume 1: 17-19). The excavations demonstrated that the level of the terrace approximated to a level made in the ninth century. This level largely coincided with a tiled passageway, running north-south and at least 2.5 m wide, which we have called the Upper Thoroughfare. The Upper Thoroughfare was situated 1.6 to 2.0 m above the Lower Thoroughfare (of which the Assembly Room formed a part), and appeared to have followed the same line (see Chapter 3). Only two sections of the passage were found: the first, very fragmentary section, was discovered on the slope between the Vestibule, 'South Church' and Tower; the second section was found further south, directly behind the Lower Thoroughfare (Fig. 2:1).

A summary of the main phases in the Upper Thoroughfare is given in Table 2:1.

TERRACE 1 BESIDE THE 'SOUTH CHURCH'

Olive trees grew on this terrace when we arrived in 1980 (Volume 1: fig. 3:2). At that time a small clandestine probe had been made to locate the walls of the 'South Church' (cf. Pantoni 1980a: tav. V). In 1980 we tidied up this earlier excavation and recorded the uppermost layers just beyond the south edge of the 'South Church'. In 1981 we began a trench just a little to the south, avoiding the recent disturbance. Our aim at this time was to find the Roman buildings associated with (and below) the Tower on Terrace 2 (see Chapter 5). The trial trench (D), however, exposed the shallow features above tips in one half of the trench and, in the southern half, the deep deposits associated with the filling and destruction of the Vestibule (see above). The sterile nature of the archaeology of the northern half of the trench persuaded us to abandon this area; little seemed to be resolvable. However, in 1985 a small trench (9200) was cut alongside wall 303 to examine the elements of Sheila Gibson's reconstructions of the Entrance Hall pertinent to this area.

Phase 1b

The north side of the area was defined by the late Roman wall 74/9102 (the two sections being shown on Fig. 2:1 at different levels: see below). This was bonded into the (phase 1b) portico of the Tower (see Chapter 5). The wall was made of well-bonded rubble, and survived to a height of about 0.5 m close to the portico, but dipped down sharply as it proceeded eastward. The phase 5 uppermost apse of the 'South Church' was built over this wall, while it remained outside (south of) the phase 4 apse of the 'South Church'. A small trench (9200) cut in front of wall 303 picked up 74/9102 as it turned southward (9208) (Fig. 2:1). A fine-textured, clean brown soil (9110) was discovered in a cutting in front of the Tower portico. This appeared to have been the level associated with the walled enclosure of this slope. The fine, largely undisturbed quality of this level strongly suggested that it was a garden soil. It must be assumed, then, that there was a walled garden directly in front (that is, east) of the Tower, which separated the 'South Church' from the areas to the south. We can only postulate the original lines of walls 74/9102 and 9208; the latter would seem to have run as far south as either a line intersecting with the inner (south) portico bracing wall or with the south wall of the Tower, approximately the line of 334 (the north wall of the Assembly Room in the Lower Thoroughfare) and 354 (the north wall of the Refectory) (cf. Fig. 1:3).

TABLE 2:1 Summary of the main phases in the Upper Thoroughfare	
0	Traces were found of a robbed wall to the west of wall 452.
1a	A thick midden layer spilled over the northern part of the area beyond wall 452.
1b	A walled garden was created on the slope below the Tower on Terrace 2.
3	The garden remained alongside the eighth-century 'South Church' (San Vincenzo Minore).
4	Steps were cut through the garden wall, linking the Vestibule to the Upper Thoroughfare. They ran parallel to wall 452.
4-5	Remains of a tiled passageway and steps were discovered west of wall 452, running along Terrace 1.
5a1	The Roman garden wall was demolished. Walls 303, 315 and 316 were constructed to retain the hillside. Large tips were accumulated behind these walls to support a passage connecting the Entrance Hall and the Upper Thoroughfare.
5a2	Wall 477 was added to conceal wall 303 (see above).
5c	There was evidence of limited burning, associated with a shallow pit containing a hoard (320).
6b	The passage was demolished.
Post 8	Traces of a post-medieval mortar surface (307) were found.

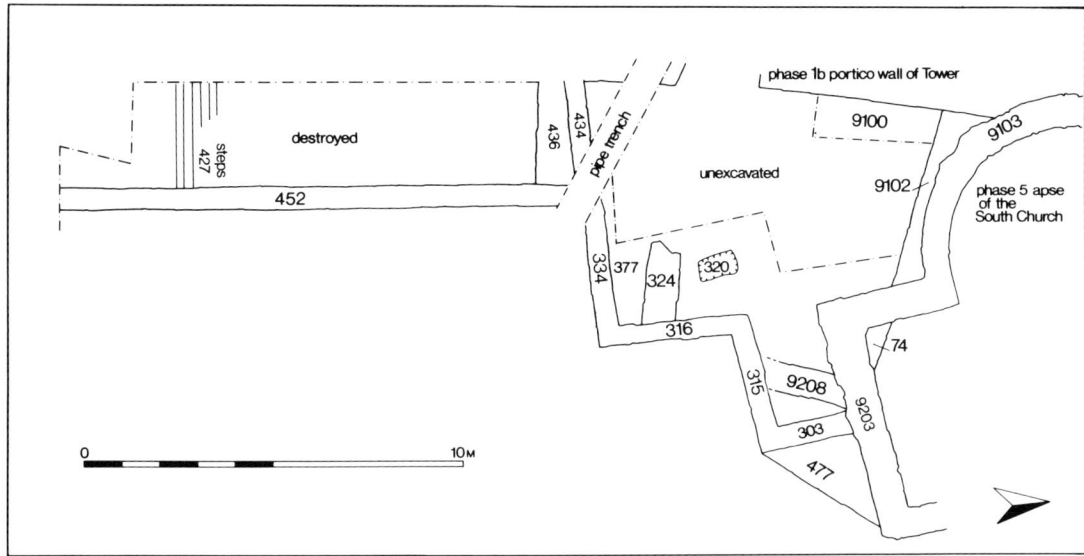

Fig. 2:1 Schematic plan showing walls and features in the Upper Thoroughfare area *(KF)*

Phase 3

The garden continued in existence, now alongside the eighth-century 'South Church' (San Vincenzo Minore).

Phase 4

The garden appeared to have been more or less intact at this time. The north garden wall, 74/9102, closed off the new (phase 3c) apse of the 'South Church'. The eastern side appeared to have connected to the north end of the Assembly Room in some way (see Fig. 1:3, phase 4). Wall 334, the north end of the Assembly Room, formed the new south side of this garden. The only feature which almost certainly belonged to this phase was a curious stump of a wall (324) which lay a little north of wall 334 (Figs 1:3 and 2:1). This stump was just over a metre wide, and poorly mortared. The narrow gap between the stump and wall 334 was filled with rubble (337) which overlaid the tile-lined drain found in section in the Vestibule area (see Chapter 1). This stump of walling, like the similar anomalous stumps beyond the junction of 334 and 452 (see Fig. 2:1), has been interpreted as the base of a set of steps. These steps would have linked the Vestibule to the Upper Thoroughfare.

Phase 5a1

In this period Terrace 1 was radically altered. Wall 74/9102 was levelled. The third, uppermost apse of the 'South Church' was either built over it or incorporated parts of it. Likewise wall 9208, the eastern side of the garden, was levelled and replaced by wall 303. Wall 303 was a solidly constructed wall to which wall 315 was linked. The latter was clearly a poorly-built retaining wall. Following the con-

struction of walls 315 and 316, the old (late Roman) ground surface was raised when a series of mortary, sandy tips (314, 322, 373, 9205-7, 9209-11, 9213-16) were thrown behind these walls. These tips contained late Roman pottery, and sealed the eastern garden wall (9208). The tips also sealed the stump of wall (324) further up the slope. In short, the old garden was replaced by a terrace to support a passage connecting the Entrance Hall to the Upper Thoroughfare. The construction work almost certainly took place as the phase 5 'South Church' was being built. Many of the tips may have come from the final demolition of the Tower on Terrace 2.

Phase 5a2

Wall 477 was constructed along the east side of the area, concealing wall 303. This wall is described in Chapter 1.

Phase 5c

Traces of a fire, possibly that of 881, were detected when the south face of the apse of the phase 5 'South Church' was cleaned in 1980. Two distinctive charcoal layers were observed, immediately beneath the topsoil on the upslope angle of the trench. Only one other feature (320), possibly belonging to this event, was noted, suggesting that the upper levels pertaining to the phase 5 passage were removed, probably in phase 6b. Feature 320 was the lower part of a pit approximately 1.0 m long, 0.6 m wide and 0.2 m deep (Fig. 2:1). The feature was filled with charcoal, burnt tiles and the fragmentary remains of many objects. In it was a collection of bronzeworking material, a *nummus* (dating to the first half of the eighth century), the twisted remains of an iron-bound box, as well as a finger-ring with a blue glass setting. The bronze-

working materials included bronze beading strips
and other pieces similar to the assemblage found in
the workshops in Trench FF (Volume 5). The
collection may have been in a chest that was burnt
in situ. Some of its contents, though, were probably
dispersed in phase 6b when bronze offcuts and
possibly the enamelled reliquary cover (see Mitchell
in Volume 3) were shovelled from this spot down the
slope to fill in the rooms (Vestibule, Entrance Hall
etc.) below. In other words, the items found in
feature 320 amounted to only a part of the original
assemblage hastily hoarded, perhaps in 881. The
discovery of an assemblage trapped in the fire in the
workshops at the south end of the monastery, in
addition to this collection near the northern limits of
the monastery, makes one wonder if a smith was
trying to flee, and dropped a pocketful of offcuts. If
so, only an odd assortment of materials was left after
the monastery was sacked. These evidently deteriorated fast and meant nothing to those in the
eleventh century who shovelled away a remaining
portion of the assemblage.

Phase 6b

The rubble layers 312 and 313 may have belonged
to phase 6 or 7. These seemed to be hillwash rather
than rubble tips. The passageway constructed over
this area appeared to have been systematically
demolished, leaving no traces. It must be assumed
that this occurred in phase 6b.

Post-medieval

The polished white mortar surface (307) which
survived in patches in this area, and extended over
wall 334 into the area above the Assembly Room,
certainly post-dated phase 8 (Fig. 2:2). The shallow
features cut into the surface may have related either
to structures or agricultural activities such as
planting olive trees. Cut 306, which ran north-
south and was filled with clean, dark brown soil,
may have been a robber trench for the wall of a
small building associated with the post-medieval
farm 293 (described in Volume 1: 14-15). The same
may be postulated for cut 311. In both cases too
little survived to specify exactly what was there.
This may have been a building of some kind
belonging to the farm which occupied the hillside
until very recently, or it could have been all that
remained of an earlier structure for which no
historical information survived.

A STEPPED SECTION OF THE UPPER
THOROUGHFARE (FIGS 2: 3 and 2:4)

A section of the Upper Thoroughfare was revealed
by accident in 1982 when a mechanical digger,
working to enlarge the Trench D area, extended the

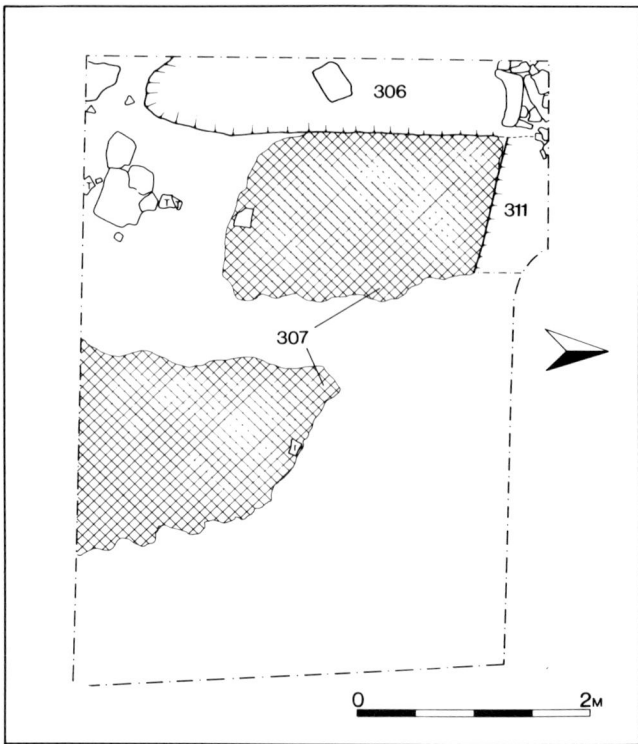

Fig. 2:2 Mortar surface 307 *(KF)*

excavation to the west and uphill. At that time it
was assumed that the west wall of the Lower
Thoroughfare in Trench D (452) was the back of
the entire complex. It was, therefore, a surprise
when the machine cut into a set of steps behind wall
452.

Phase 0

Half way along the trench the cutting revealed the
traces of a robbed wall constructed of large
boulders. The wall appeared to have run upslope,
but so vestigial were its remains that little more of
substance can be added.

Phase 1a

A thick midden layer (433/473) spilled over the
northern part of the trench. It contained much
Roman pottery and some animal bone. The midden
was similar to the spread found in Trench EE
(Volume 1, chapter 8). Wall foundations 436/7207
appeared to have cut into this material.

Phases 4-5

Remains of a tiled passageway and steps were
discovered, built on top of rubble that sealed the
earlier phases in this area. The inscriptions on the
tiles indicated that the floor (447) and the tiled steps
(427) belonged to either phase 4 or 5. These formed
part of a wide passageway which ran directly behind
wall 452 along what we have described as Terrace 1.

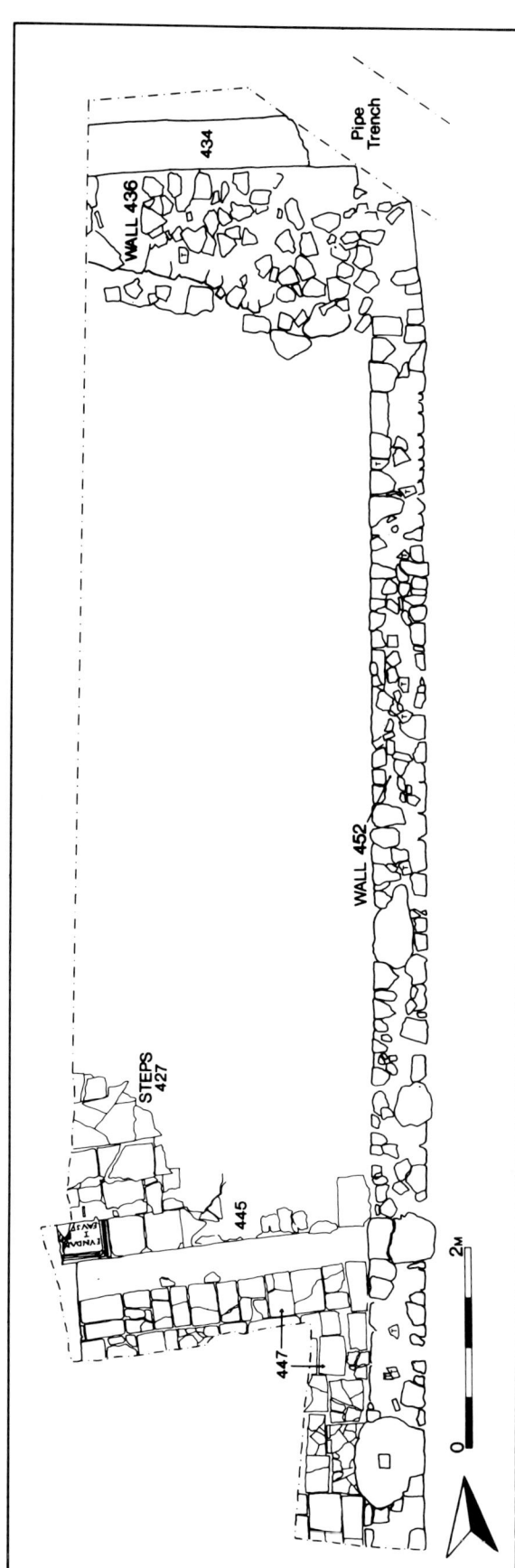

Fig. 2:3 Plan of the south sector of the Upper Thoroughfare showing steps 427 (*LW*)

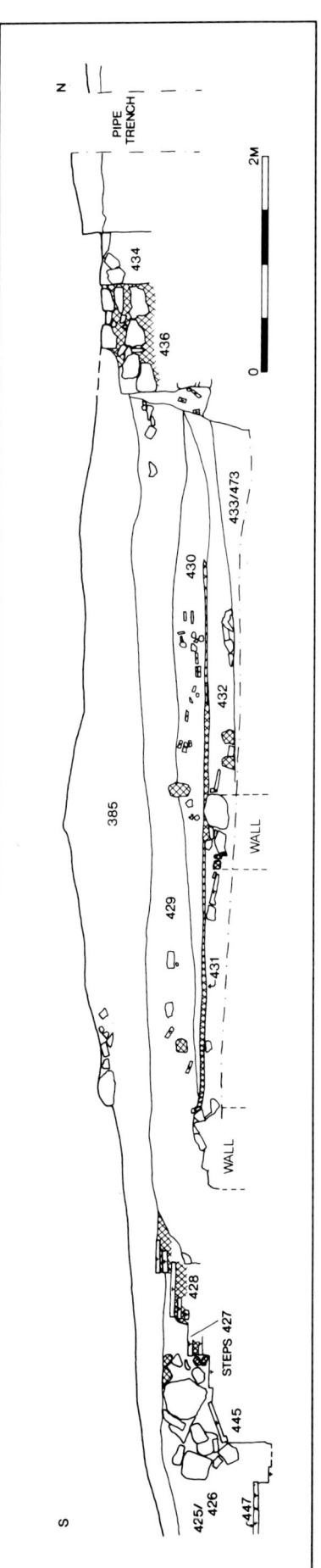

Fig. 2:4 Upper Thoroughfare, east-facing section, between steps 427 and wall 436 (*LW*)

Fig. 2:5 Inscription on Upper Thoroughfare steps *(RH)*

The tiled floor (447) was only a small section of a corridor; the tiles exposed in this area lacked makers' marks – possibly an indication that the floor itself belonged to phase 5 rather than phase 4. The steps began beside a blocked-up window in wall 452 (the wall separating the Upper and Lower Thoroughfares). The bottom step (445) had been robbed, leaving only the mortared base: this appeared to sit on top of an enigmatic wall belonging to a still earlier phase. Remains of a door jamb, or a post of some kind, on the eastern side of this robbed step proved difficult to interpret. The tiled steps were neatly revetted on the east side by a block. Four steps, constructed upon a white mortar and rubble base (428 and 429), appeared to advance towards a platform which had been thoroughly removed. The steps were each one tile's width. Set into the bottom tiled step was a fine Republican funerary inscription (Fig 2:5, and see J. Patterson in Volume 3). The full width of the steps could not be determined, but the passage looked to have been at least 2.5 m wide at this point.

The approximate line of the Upper Thoroughfare ran from the top of the steps towards 436/7207, above level 429. Below this line the machine cut through traces of mortar-mixing (431), probably for the construction of the Assembly Room, which in turn overlaid a deep clay-loam layer (432) which in other parts of the excavation has been associated with the creation of the phase 4 monastic plan. Layer 432, in turn, overlaid the late Roman midden layers 433 and 473. The bonded rubble 436/7207, which cut through the late Roman midden layers, is

in fact perhaps best interpreted as the foundations for steps. It is proposed in the section above that the passage from the Entrance Hall followed the outside of the Assembly Room to this point, at which, in addition, there was an intersection with a westward passage leading up the slope alongside the demolished Tower.

Two points are clear as a result of these excavations. Firstly, the steps belonged to a corridor resembling the Lower Thoroughfare. Secondly, the passage seems to have been cut into the later Roman configurations of the hillslope. The question remains as to why there were steps here at all. Why did the passage not simply continue at the level of the tiled surface (447), along Terrace 1? To answer these questions, we might suggest two explanations. Firstly, the steps may have risen over, rather than cut through, the construction levels associated with the making of the Assembly Room, notably layer 432, which appears to have been a terracing level, and the mortar layer 431. Secondly, the platform at the top of the tiled steps may not only have led northward, parallel to the Assembly Room, but also westward, up the slope beside Terrace 2. The section cut across the steps did not throw any real illumination on this matter, but traces of steps attached to the late Roman Tower suggested that there was a route up the hillslope from the riverside ranges in approximately this area.

Phase 5c

There was scant evidence that this area was affected

by the fire of 881. No charcoal or ashy deposits overlaid the floor or steps.

Phase 6b

It appears that the Upper Thoroughfare was blocked by rubble in the tenth century (phase 6b), after the west wall (452) of the Assembly Room had been demolished. The Upper Thoroughfare must have been used as the platform from which wall 452 was demolished, with the plaster and mortar debris (401) falling into the destroyed Assembly Room below. After the demolition of wall 452, the bottom step and the entire length of the platform running behind wall 452 were robbed. The south part of the Upper Thoroughfare area was then covered by a level of loose rubble (426), representing the destruction of upstanding walls in this area, similar to the collapse at the north end of the Assembly Room. No colluvial deposits were mixed with the rubble, suggesting that insufficient time elapsed for other deposits to form prior to the wall destruction. From this we can conjecture that the demolition of the monastery took place rapidly, and systematically, with demolition workers moving up the terraces in a methodical fashion.

DISCUSSION

This area was excavated in several trenches as the opportunity arose. The results must, therefore, be treated with caution. Until phase 4, it appears to have been a mid-slope area, above Terrace 1. Part of it was walled off as a garden serving the late Roman Tower in phase 1b. When the 'South Church' complex was transformed into a guest hall in phase 4, an access route to it from San Vincenzo Maggiore was required that did not pass through the claustral area of the monastery. Considerable landscaping was needed to create this passageway, once the Lower Thoroughfare (including the Assembly Room) and the Vestibule had been built. The Upper Thoroughfare was created by using the west wall of the Lower Thoroughfare, 452, as a retaining wall. At this point, the floor of the Upper Thoroughfare was 1.6 m above the pavement in the Lower Thoroughfare and Assembly Room. This illustrates the considerable effort invested in providing a suitable access route for lay visitors between the 'South Church'/guest hall and the abbey-church. The Upper Thoroughfare was one of a network of routes and passages which articulated the fabric of the monastery and connected its principal centres of activity (see Chapter 1, Discussion).

Chapter Three

THE ASSEMBLY ROOM: PART OF THE LOWER THOROUGHFARE

by Richard Hodges and John Mitchell

This room, which formed part of the Lower Thoroughfare, lay immediately to the west of the Refectory, and was connected by a wide doorway to the Vestibule to the north (Figs 3:1-3). It was discovered in Trench D, a deep excavation on the south side of the 'South Church', which was extended four times. In 1980-82 this area lay within the olive grove on Terrace 1, separated by a break of slope of almost 2.0 m from the low-lying ground by the riverside. As has been noted already (Chapter 1), the Assembly Room was discovered after the Vestibule had been located in 1981. The 1981 excavations had, in fact, just clipped the north side of the Assembly Room. In 1982 Nigel Baker supervised an extension trench which examined the stratigraphy in the northern half of the room in some detail. In the latter part of that season the trench was extended using a machine; the intention by this time was to expose more of the deeply buried room rather than to further the study of the stratigraphy within it. This policy was continued in 1983. In this season, too, a small exploratory trench was cut, running out from the south section of the trench, to seek the south wall of the room. As no wall was encountered at an upper level, the trench was backfilled. The excavations, therefore, were undertaken over several seasons with two explicit aims: to sample the upper stratigraphy and to record the buried ninth-century buildings in as much detail as was possible.

The account that follows is based on the work of the supervisors and archaeologists who worked in the Assembly Room in 1981-3; in particular it owes a great debt to Nigel Baker's painstaking efforts in 1982 to come to terms with the challenges posed by the exacting goals described above. The room is described in two sections: first, the excavations, and second, the painted decoration of the room.

THE EXCAVATIONS

A summary of the main phases in this area is given in Table 3:1.

Phases 1-3

No features appeared to belong to these phases, although the lowest part (434) of the north wall (334) of the room may have been late Roman in date.

Phase 4

The Assembly Room was trapezoidal in shape, being about 5.78 m wide at its northern end, and about 7.63 m wide at the southern limit of the excavation. The reason for this shape is not entirely clear, but one hypothesis is as follows. The north wall (334) seems to have followed a late Roman alignment, while the west wall (452) appears to have run parallel to a long phase 4 terrace wall dividing Terrace 2 from Terrace 3. The phase 4 Refectory (see Chapter 4) seems to have been built on top of an earlier (phase 3c) Refectory of which the wall-line 334 to 354 was the northern axis. It appears that when the Refectory was enlarged, some elements of the pre-existing plan were maintained, but changes were also necessary. In this restructuring the room was designed as a thoroughfare and a place of assembly, built into the hillside, taking a shape determined by the larger-scale programme of building undertaken under Abbot Joshua. As such the room would have served not only as a place where monks might wait before dining, but also as one of the principal routes through the claustrum to the abbey-church located to the south. In the following section the particular characteristics of this room will be considered, rather than its general function. First, it is important to emphasize that the full extent of this room was not found in the excavations. A trial trench extending out from the south section showed that the room continued southward: but its precise form south of the excavations remains a matter of speculation.

TABLE 3:1 Summary of the main phases in the Assembly Room

4	A trapezoidal hall, decorated with fine paintings, was built beside the Refectory and formed part of the Lower Thoroughfare.
5a	The opening in the west wall was blocked and the floor may have been patched.
5c	The room was gutted by fire, the roof collapsed, and the doorway leading to the Vestibule and 'South Church' was blocked by fallen debris.
6a	The room remained in a largely derelict state.
6b	The Refectory walls (and thus the east wall of the Assembly Room) were levelled, and the area was buried beneath tips.
7	A cream-coloured mortar surface was laid over the area. Several post-holes cut the surface, and a small tile-built pottery kiln was constructed on it.
8	Tips were spread across the area.

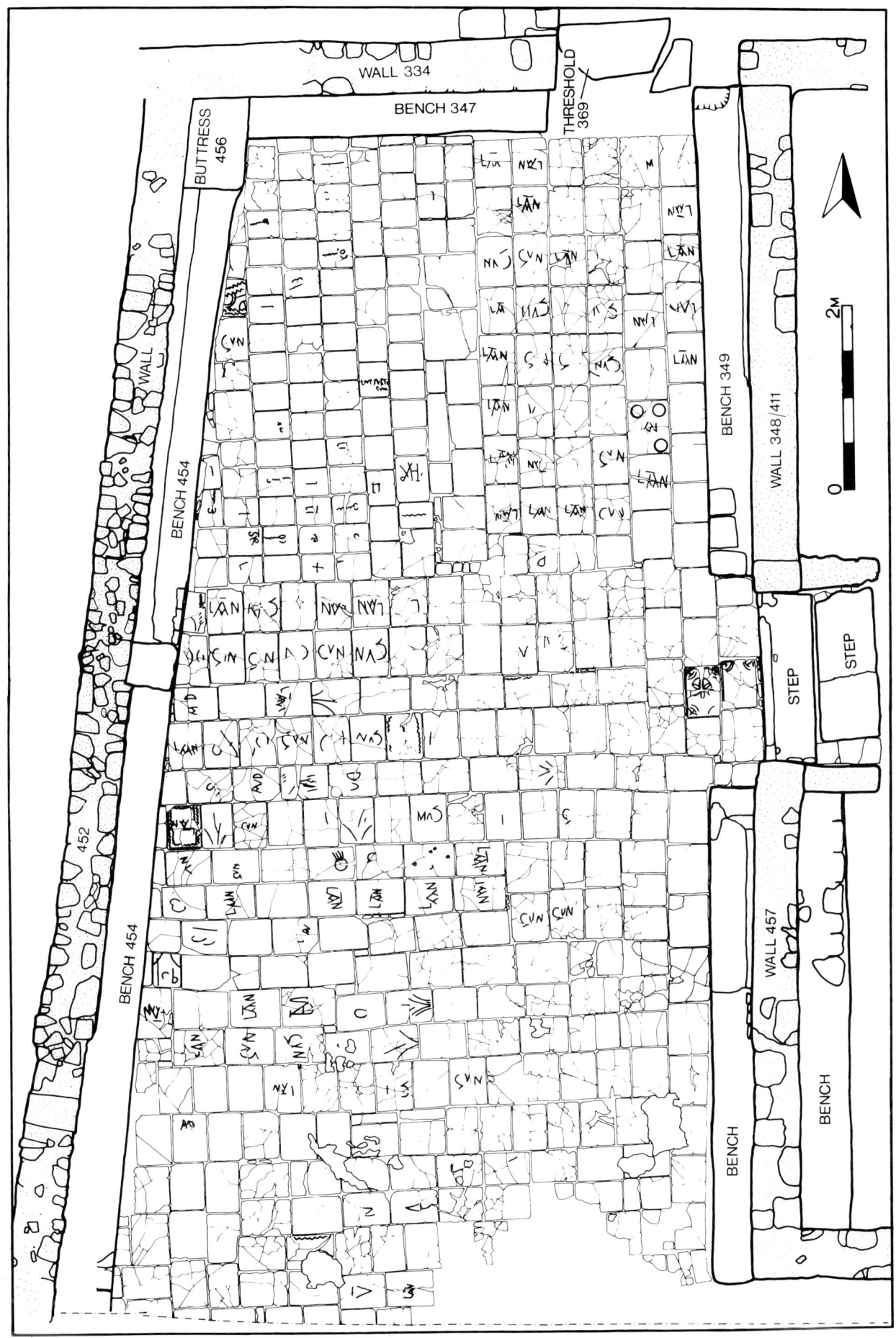

Fig. 3:1 Plan of the Assembly Room *(CMC)*

Fig. 3:2 Assembly Room, view to north (1982) *(RH)*

However, tiled floors discovered in excavations immediately south of the Refectory suggest that a passage led off from the Assembly Room alongside the south wall of the Refectory. This might have been the northern walk around a cloister garden (see below, p. 78).

Walls

The walls were of a crude rubble construction, with a pale yellow, soft mortar, and were roughly 0.5-0.6 m wide. The back (west) wall (452) of the room rose to a maximum of 2.6 m above the tiled floor; the northern wall (334) still stood (at the time it was excavated) to between 2.2 and 2.5 m above the tiled floor, while the east walls (348/411 and 457) survived to a maximum of 0.6 m. The substantial buttress (456) added to the northwest corner of the room was almost certainly designed to reinforce the junction between walls 334 and 452 at a point where the considerable combined pressure of the hillslope and the Upper Thoroughfare, which passed directly behind the room, would have been greatest. The corner buttress would have helped support the tiled roof of the Assembly Room. Painted wall plaster covered all the vertical surfaces of the room. It is estimated from the reconstruction of the decorated plaster fragments from the west wall (452) that this wall rose originally to a height of 3.85 m above the tiled floor.

Doorways

Two major doorways were found in the excavations. The northern one had a marble threshold (369), and, in all likelihood, the robbed door jamb on its east side was of similar material – in phase 6b there was an attempt to prise up the threshold, and it was probably at this time that the jamb was taken away. The east doorway, leading into the Refectory, is described in Chapter 4.

Benches

Benches constructed of rubble and mortar, in some cases with ledges above to receive wooden seats, were added in this room after the walls had been plastered and decorated. The benches rose about 0.45 m above the tiled floor, and were *c.* 0.45 m wide. The ledges varied, although they tended to rise a further 0.1 m up from the benches and were about 0.15 m wide. No ledge occurred above bench 347 on the north wall (334). All the benches were painted (see below), and on their plastered upper surface were found the carbonized remains of wooden seats (e.g. 455). Footrests, such as those which occurred in the Refectory, were absent from the bases of the benches in this room.

The floor

The tiled pavement was anything but homogeneous in its laying (Fig. 3:1). The laying of the floor and its inscribed and ornamental tiles are discussed and analysed by Mitchell in Volume 3.

Lighting

A feature towards the south end of the west wall (452) may have been a window. This was a narrow opening through which a person reaching the bottom of the steps on the terrace behind could

Fig. 3:3 Assembly Room, view to southwest (1982) *(RH)*

have looked down into the hall. The scarcity of window-glass from these excavations is in marked contrast to the Refectory, and suggests that there were few, if any, windows in this room.

The roof

It can be calculated from its reconstructed painted decoration (see below) that the west wall (452) rose to *c.* 3.85 m above the tiled floor. It appears that there was a beamed roof, the carbonized remnants of which were found where they had fallen after the fire of 881. On top of this, to judge from the thick deposit of tiles found in the area, was a covering of tiles. The presence of nails in the destruction level, as in the Refectory, indicates the rather rudimentary nature of the timber framing.

Phase 5

It is proposed that the opening in the west wall 452 was blocked in phase 5a, and the patching of the floor may also have dated to this time. The other features of this phase were associated with its destruction: that is, attributable to phase 5c. A thin veneer of clay and soil (367, 415) occurred in patches over the tiled floor and under the burning: it resembled a trample-layer, as though for some brief spell animals or large numbers of people used or passed through the room. The exact meaning of this feature eludes us, but it merits further consideration in the future. The fire-layer which sealed it is equally fascinating for its anomalies. The fire seems to have varied in its ferocity within the room. The burning layers (e.g. 413) were most conspicuous in

the western half of the room, but neither the walls, nor the benches, nor the floor seem to have been significantly scorched in the fire (with the exception of the southern end of the west wall, where the wall plaster was progressively scorched and blackened). Only the plank tops of the benches (e.g. 455) were burnt. This is in complete contrast to the Refectory where the conflagration was uniformly great. It is clear, however, that following the fire the tiled roof partially or completely collapsed, at least part of it falling into this room (context 344). At present it appears that the fire spread from the Refectory, but was rather limited in its effect. The differing composition of the roofs of the two buildings – thatch on the Refectory and tiles in the Assembly Room, and a paucity of wood in the latter room (few roof timbers, no or few window transennae and an absence of furniture in comparison to the Refectory) – may explain this anomaly.

Finally, layer 414, over the trample 415, but underneath the charcoal, merits a brief discussion. This was a buff-yellow mortar tip, in some places 0.16 m thick. It resembled the weathering of the walls which we noted following the excavations; it may also be a consequence of the heat on the plaster within the room.

Phase 6a

The building was abandoned in phase 6 and fell apart. A deep tumble of rubble in the northwest sector of the room (344 and 401) suggests that the walls either side of the buttress (456) fell inwards (Fig. 3:4). The spread of stone varied from 0.75 m to

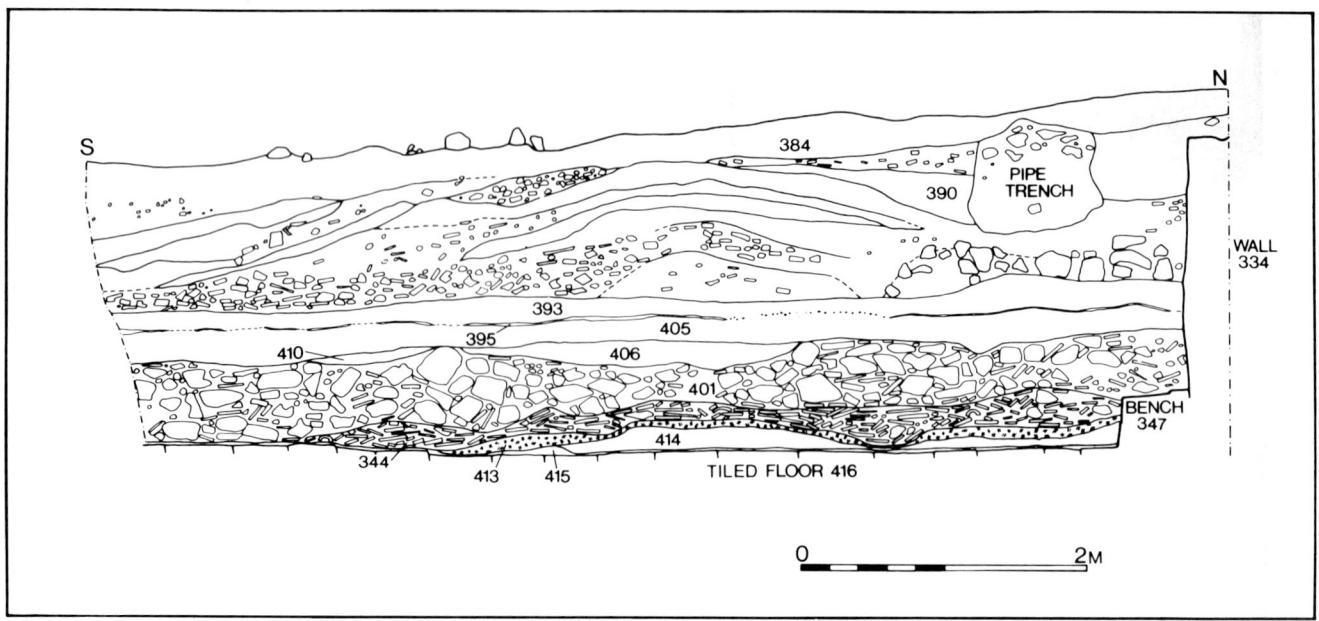

Fig. 3:4 East-facing section through the northern half of the Assembly Room, illustrating the tips and destruction levels *(SC)*

0.3 m in thickness and, in the northern part of the room, appeared clean, lacking much loam. About seven cubic metres of walling would have collapsed, and this appears to be consistent with the spread over the northern half of the room. The loamy content of the collapse in the southern half of the room suggests that the southern part of the wall decayed more gradually and became intermixed with hillwash and vegetation. The eastern walls

(348/411 and 457) seem to have tumbled into the Refectory and not into the Assembly Room. Much of the painted plaster occurred within and under the collapse in 401 and reflects the virtually instantaneous end which befell the northwestern part of the building. In this corner we may assume that the thrust from the hillslope as well as the buildings above were contributing factors in the uneven destruction of the building.

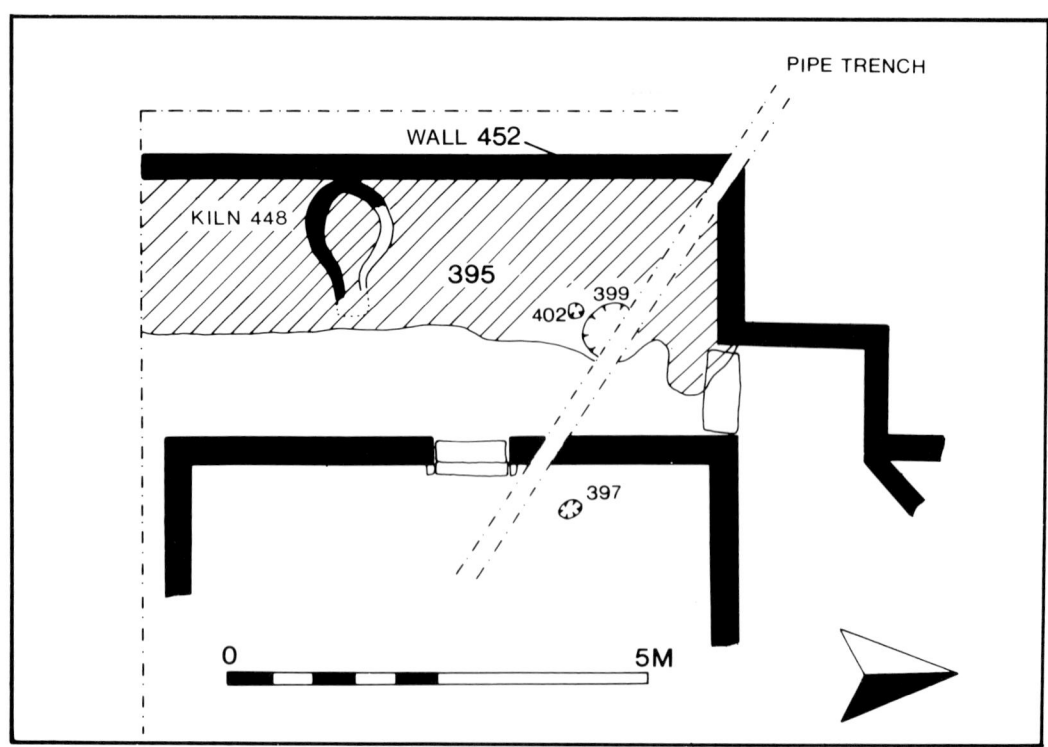

Fig. 3:5 Schematic plan showing mortar surface 395, features 397, 399, 402, and kiln 448 *(CMC)*

Fig. 3:6 Kiln 448, view to west (1982) *(RH)*

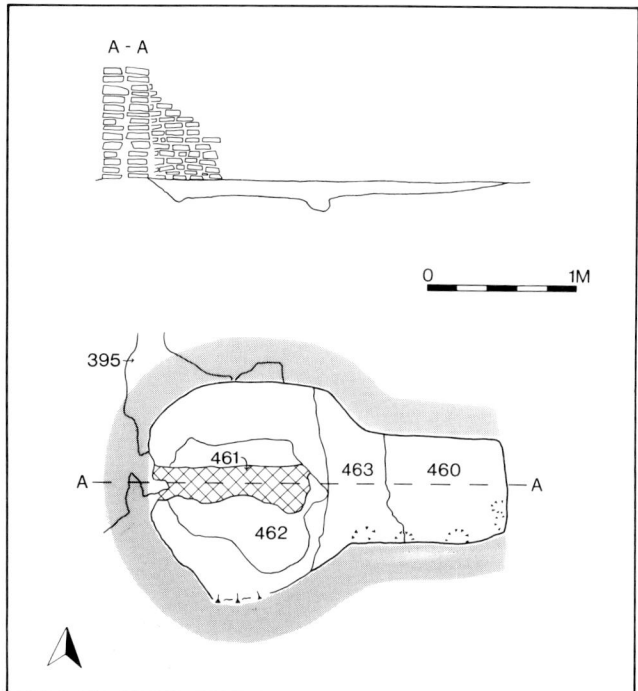

Fig. 3:7 Plan and profile of kiln 448 *(LW)*

Phase 6b

The demolition of the west wall of the Refectory (that is, the east wall of the Assembly Room) was the first of a series of changes made in this phase. Following this, a succession of deep tips (405, 406, 407, 410) were thrown across the Assembly Room, spreading over the Refectory walls (Fig. 3:4; see also below, Fig. 4:15). These tips were thrown from above wall 452, possibly from the Upper Thoroughfare. Many fragments of window-glass, pottery and animal bones were contained within these levels.

Phase 7

A cream-coloured mortar surface (395), in some places 50-100 mm thick, covered much of the area once occupied by the Assembly Room. This surface, however, was patchy, with several worn areas where the mortar was absent. Several features were cut into the surface, of which 399, a small pit, and 402, a post-hole, should be noted (Fig. 3:5). The most important feature of this phase, however, was a small single-flue tile-built kiln (448) (Figs 3:6-8). The kiln was a bottle-shaped feature, 2.6 m long and 1.25 m wide, with walls standing on its west side to a maximum height of 0.7 m above the mortar

surface. It was aligned east-west, with its stokehole at the east end. The kiln had been partly built against wall 452. Inside, the broken tiles of which it was constructed had been lined with up to three coats of baked mud. Excavation showed that all types of tile were used in its construction, and that they had been set in a baked clay matrix. The kiln was set into the mortar surface. Its stokehole was 0.35 m across, and had been constructed of wattle and daub. The removal of the structure revealed a tongue of the undisturbed mortar surface which had been retained within the kiln, presumably to act as the base of a support on which the items to be fired were stacked. A fine layer of charcoal (460) filled the stokehole. No debris was associated with the kiln. It is unlikely that it was intended for cooking or metalworking, and, therefore, it is proposed that it was a pottery kiln. The form of the kiln was certainly consistent with pottery kilns of this period known from other parts of Europe (cf. Hodges and Patterson 1986; Patterson 1989).

Phase 8

Further tips were spread across this area, on which Terrace 1 was subsequently to be constructed.

THE PAINTED DECORATION

The walls of the Assembly Room were plastered and painted soon after the completion of the building in phase 4 – that is in the first two decades of the ninth century. The underlying *arriccio* and the *intonaco* of this phase were the only layers of plaster on the walls,

Fig. 3:8 Base of kiln 448 after excavation of the walls *(RH)*

and remained essentially intact until the monastery was sacked and the room fired during the Saracen sack in 881. The room was never cleared or repaired after the return of the monks to the monastery early in the following century. At the time of excavation, plaster was found still adhering to the lower parts of each of the walls of the room and to the fronts of the benches built against these walls. In addition, large quantities of fragments of painted plaster were preserved in a relatively good state where they had fallen, together with some rubble from the upper walls. They lay above the broken tiles and charred timbers of the fallen roof, but below the phase 7 mortar surface (395) and the subsequent build-up of earth above. The following description will discuss the painted decoration of the benches, the dados, and the upper walls of the room, in turn.

There was a clear distinction between the decorative schemes on the benches and the dados on the east side of this room and those on the north and west sides (the southern end of the room still being buried) (Figs 3:9-11). On the east side the designs were more varied and were defined with more care than on the other walls. This distinction was probably also present in the principal programme of decoration on the upper surfaces of these walls.

The benches

The painted surfaces of the benches were, by and large, well-preserved. Two designs were used on those which ran along the east wall (348/411, 457) of the room. Progressing from the north end of the wall southward, the first 2.39 m were decorated with an imbricated scheme of rounded particoloured

scales (Fig. 3:12, Plate 3:1). The following section of 2.92 m, which extended as far as the doorway to the Refectory in the centre of this wall, had a design of interlocking triangles of various colours which can be read either as a sequence of large segmented squares, or as a succession of segmented lozenges laid end to end (Plate 3:2). For the first 2.8 m after the doorway there was a reversion to the scale pattern, after which the scheme of composite squares/lozenges continued almost to the southern end of this bench. In both cases the intention presumably was to imitate a revetment in *opus sectile*. The divisions between the two designs were marked by vertical lines snapped into the wet plaster with a string and subsequently heightened with white (see Plate 3:2). The changes in pattern in mid-bench were clearly planned from the outset.

The scales of the imbricated design on both sections of bench on this wall were incised into the plaster with a compass and carefully outlined with white: each had a radius of 99 mm. Scales of a particular colour were set in horizontal sequence, rather than in the diagonal rows which were invariably found in ancient Roman and late Antique examples of the motif. The colours of the scales on the northern section of bench were as follows: bottom row, light ochre/darker ochre; second row, brownish red/pink; third row, light grey-blue/dark grey-blue; top row, pink/brownish red (Plate 3:1); and on the southern section: bottom row, brownish red/pink; second row, brownish red/greyish blue or pink; third row, pale cream; top row, light ochre/darker ochre. The small concave triangles in the spandrels of the top row of scales were a light grey-blue. Above these there was a pale white

Fig. 3:9 Assembly Room looking west, showing excavation of the fresco midden and wall 452 (1983) *(RH)*

Fig. 3:10 Assembly Room, looking north at wall 334 *(RH)*

Fig. 3:11 Assembly Room (foreground) and western part of the Refectory (mid-ground), showing the west face of walls
411 and 457 (1983) *(RH)*

Fig. 3:12 Bench 349 with painted decoration of particoloured overlapping scales *(JM)*

horizontal band, 10 mm wide, followed by a strong band of white, and finally, running right along the upper margin of the front of the bench on this wall was a band of brownish red, varying in width between 35 and 45 mm. The lower edge of this upper red band followed a horizontal line snapped into the wet plaster with a string.

Essential guidelines for the scheme of composite squares/lozenges on these two sections of bench were also snapped with a string into the plaster when it was still wet. The colours of the small right-angled triangles which made up the pattern on these two sections were brownish red, pink, grey-blue and light ochre, and prominent thin white lines were drawn along the divisions. Triangles of the same colour were diametrically opposed in each composite lozenge. At the far southern end of the bench another motif was introduced. This could not be identified satisfactorily (Plate 3:3). The short northern end of the bench against wall 457, to the south of the doorway, had marbled decoration, with two adjacent panels of diagonally undulating veins, which together formed a sequence of chevrons centred on a vertical divide. The colour had decayed and was, on discovery, a reddish ochre.

On the bench against the west wall (bench 454, wall 452) the triangular shapes which made up the design were coloured yellow ochre, strong brown-red, orange-pink and dull blue-grey (Plate 3:4). Thin white lines were drawn along all the divisions in this pattern, but these were pale washy strokes, far less prominent than the sharp white outlines of the designs on the east wall opposite. On the bench (347) against the north wall (334) the colours of the triangular elements were light ochre, darker ochre, deep ox-blood and pink; white outlines were not used. As on the other benches, triangles of the same colour were set opposite one another within each composite lozenge. There were no traces of snapped guide-lines in the plaster on the western and northern benches. The eastern end of the bench against wall 334, where it stopped short of the doorway into the Vestibule, was decorated with dull

red undulating diagonal bands in imitation of veined marble revetment (Plate 3:5). This small panel of marbling was framed by a 65 mm vertical dull red band at the outside corner and a 80 mm vertical stripe of the same colour against the wall. The antecedents, parallels and cultural implications of the two designs on the benches will be discussed in Volume 3 (see also Mitchell 1994).

The dado

Above the benches a marbled dado encircled the room. Originally this was probably about a metre high, the same height as the dado in the Vestibule. On the east walls of the Assembly Room (348/411, 457) it was preserved only to a maximum height of about 0.15 m, but on the western and northern walls, which served to buttress the fore-edge of the terrace of the hill, and which still stood to over two metres in places, substantial passages of painted dado were found in place, up to a height of about 0.9 m above the level of the top of the bench. The lowest reaches of the walls, behind the benches, were not painted. The benches just covered the lower border of the dado in places. On wall 334 the mortar on the top of the bench lapped over the bottom of the marbled dado, and the painted plaster had even been scored to ensure the satisfactory adhesion of the bench to the wall. Furthermore, the plaster on the fronts of the benches was of a different consistency to that employed on the walls of this room. The former had a greyish cast and contained numerous small inclusions, while the latter was smoother and whiter. All this suggests that the walls were plastered and painted before the benches were built, but that the latter were intended for this room from the outset.

The east walls (348/411 and 457)
As was the case with the decoration on the benches, the most elaborate and differentiated scheme was deployed on the east walls (348/411 and 457). Again the arrangement will be described starting from the

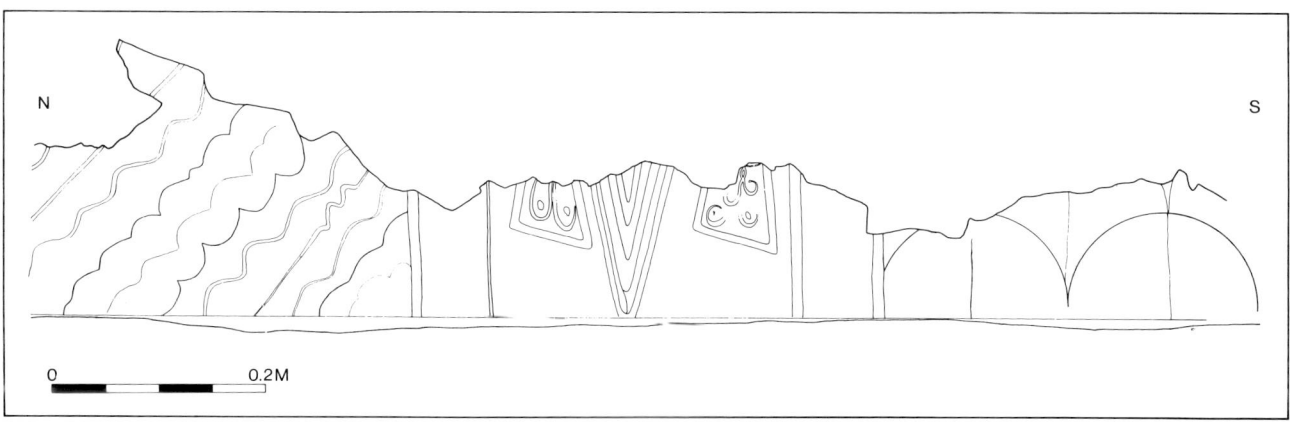

Fig. 3:13 Schematic illustration of the dado on wall 348/411 *(JV)*

north and progressing to the south. From the northern edge of wall 348/411, to a point 1.53 m to the south, the dado consisted of panels of diagonally veined marbling (Fig. 3:13; Plate 3:6). The panels were pale flamingo-pink in colour with warm pinkish red veins. The latter, like those on the other walls of this room, were of three types, broad undulating veins, narrow undulating veins, and thin straight ones with periodic seismographic twitches, in strict repeating succession. The veins of the marbling on this side of the room were executed with greater care and with less freedom and dash than those on the other two excavated walls (see below). The panels were divided by vertical black lines, 9 mm wide, drawn freehand. One painted clamp, joining two adjacent panels, was preserved (Plate 3:6). This passage of marbling was followed by a curious vertically oriented panel, which survived only to a height of 0.14 m (Fig. 3:13). This consisted of a central rectangle, 0.29 m wide, coloured a brownish red which modulated to yellow on its right edge, flanked by vertical shafts 70 mm wide, dull lilac on the left and white on the right. An acutely-angled black wedge rose from the mid-point of the base of the central rectangle, steadily expanding to the broken upper edge of the wall. A thin white line ran up the left slope of the wedge, and two nested Vs were drawn over it in lavender. On the brownish red field immediately to the left of the wedge there were angular and rounded configurations in white and black. This section was probably painted in imitation of a panel of complex marble inlay. It appears to have been a neater and more precise version of the upright panel painted in imitation of *opus sectile* and carved relief on the northern face of the pulpit in the Refectory (Figs 4:11-12).

This panel was followed by a section of imbricated particoloured scales, of the kind used on the bench below. The outlines of the scales were drawn with a compass into the wet plaster. The scales were coloured as follows: bottom row, pale yellow/strong yellow; second row, strong brown-red/pink. The upper parts of this design have been lost. The final stretch of dado, north of the doorway into the Refectory, was a further section of the diagonally veined marbling on a flamingo-pink ground with which the wall had begun.

The part of the east wall (457) to the south of the Refectory doorway was demolished down to the level of the bench at the time of the final abandonment of this part of the monastery, and nothing remained of its painted decoration (see Fig. 3:11). However, like the bench at its foot, the scheme on this wall probably corresponded in overall design to that found to the north of the doorway.

The west and north walls (452 and 334)

The dado on the west (452) and north (334) walls of the room was, in contrast to that on the east wall, unvarying in design and colour, and generally must have been lighter and less ornate in its overall effect. The design consisted of panels of diagonally veined marbling, arranged to give a repeating sequence of stacked chevrons. The ground of the design was white, and the veins, which were of the same type and which followed the same sequence as those in the similar marbling on the east wall of the room and in the adjacent Vestibule – broad and narrow undulating veins and thin straight ones with intermittent seismographic shakes along their length – alternated in colour from panel to panel, brownish-red on one, and pale greyish-blue on the next. The broad red veins were sometimes doubled with a second undulating band in a lighter shade of the same colour. The vertical divisions between the panels on the northern section of the west wall and on the north wall were snapped into the wet plaster with a string dipped in a weak solution of red paint, and were subsequently gone over in black, or sometimes in pale blue. However, on the southern part of the west wall, to the south of the low median buttress, these vertical divisions were painted onto the smooth plaster with a brush. The usual imitation clamps, joining the panels, crossed these verticals at intervals. The panels varied greatly in width, from about 0.3 to 0.54 m. In the northwest corner of the room, where the dado met the large corner buttress, which itself carried veined panels, vertical bands limited the marbling (Plate 3:7). The final panel ended about 0.11 m short of the corner itself, and was followed, in succession, by, first a strip of unpainted plaster 40-50 mm wide, then narrow vertical bands of blue-grey and black, a thin white line, and finally a border of red which turned the corner.

The overall appearance of the dado on these two walls was very similar to that in the adjacent Vestibule (see Fig. 1:7). However, in the Assembly Room, yellow was not used in combination with red in the broad veins of the marbling, and the undulations of the veins were a little looser and less angular than in the Vestibule. Furthermore, the paint on the walls of the Assembly Room did not show anything like the tendency to flake that was apparent in the Vestibule. The painting in the Assembly Room seemed to have been carried out while the plaster was still damp, and probably approached *buon fresco* in technique.

The plaster at the foot of the buttress (456) in the northwest corner had been replaced and summarily repainted with red diagonal veining (Plate 3:7). An apparently contemporary sequence of letters, in the same dull red paint, was to be found low down on the eastern face of the corner pier. The reading of this inscription was uncertain: IOTVI...; it may be a name. The buttress was probably repaired when the benches were built and plastered, immediately after the walls themselves had been completed and painted. The upper limit of the repair corresponded with the tops of the benches, and the plaster used was of the same kind as that employed on the fronts of the benches, and different to that used on the walls above.

The upper walls – the Prophets and Apostles

As is the case in all the other excavated parts of the monastery, none of the painted plaster from the upper surfaces of the walls of the Assembly Room was found in place. However, many thousands of fragments of paintings were excavated from the lower layers of fill within the room. By far the largest coherent group of painted plaster, amounting to something between 5,000 and 10,000 fragments, was deposited in context 401, a layer of soil, fallen blocks of building stone and general rubble, some 0.3 m deep, which lay along the western side of the room. The densest concentration lay immediately in front of the long west wall (452), where it had fallen subsequent to the fire of 881 which destroyed the roof of the room and scorched some of the paintings. The plaster must have fallen from the walls and have been buried soon after this fire, since the painted surfaces of the buried fragments were remarkably fresh and well-preserved, and could not have been exposed to the weather for more than a few years.

Layer 401 was excavated in rectangular metre-wide sections, assigned the letters *A* to *L*, running along the foot of the west wall and the adjoining bench, and was further subdivided into 'bench', 'middle' and 'east' zones (Fig. 3:14). The upper surface of the deposit lay just over the top of the bench, and extended down for about 0.3 m. Each metre section was excavated in spits 0.1 m deep.

The work of reassembling the broken fragments from 401 began in 1982 and continued until 1988. Substantial areas of painting were pieced together, and it proved possible to reconstruct the overall scheme of decoration of this wall for virtually its entire height and for a length of about 6.0 m. (The overall height of the painted surfaces of bench and wall, from the pavement to the roof-beams, could be estimated at about 3.85 m.)

The reconstructed scheme consists of a sequence of male figures, a little under life-size, who are identified by accompanying *tituli* as Prophets. They stand under the arches of a continuous arcade, and hold large unrolled scrolls on which lines of text are displayed.

The first phase of work on the fragments was carried out at San Vincenzo al Volturno, in the aisles of the rebuilt abbey-church, by kind permission of the Abbot of Monte Cassino (Mitchell 1985: 144-50). The principal work was done by Rosie Steele, Todd Bartel, Andrew Hanasz, Polly Hudson, Norma Jordenais, Talin Megherian, Bernadette Malizia, Laura Schmidt, Mairi Venables, Patrick Vyvyan, Nan Talbot, Catherine M. Coutts and John Mitchell. In 1986, Prof. Giuseppe Basile of the *Istituto Centrale di Restauro* assumed responsibility for reassembling the painted fragments, and the work started on the site was continued with great success in Rome by the conservators Paola Cinti, Mario Gammino, Kristine Doneux and Gianna Musatti (Basile 1988: 153-7).

Figure 3:15 records the stage the work of recomposition carried out at the site had reached by the autumn of 1985; and Plate 3:8 gives the state

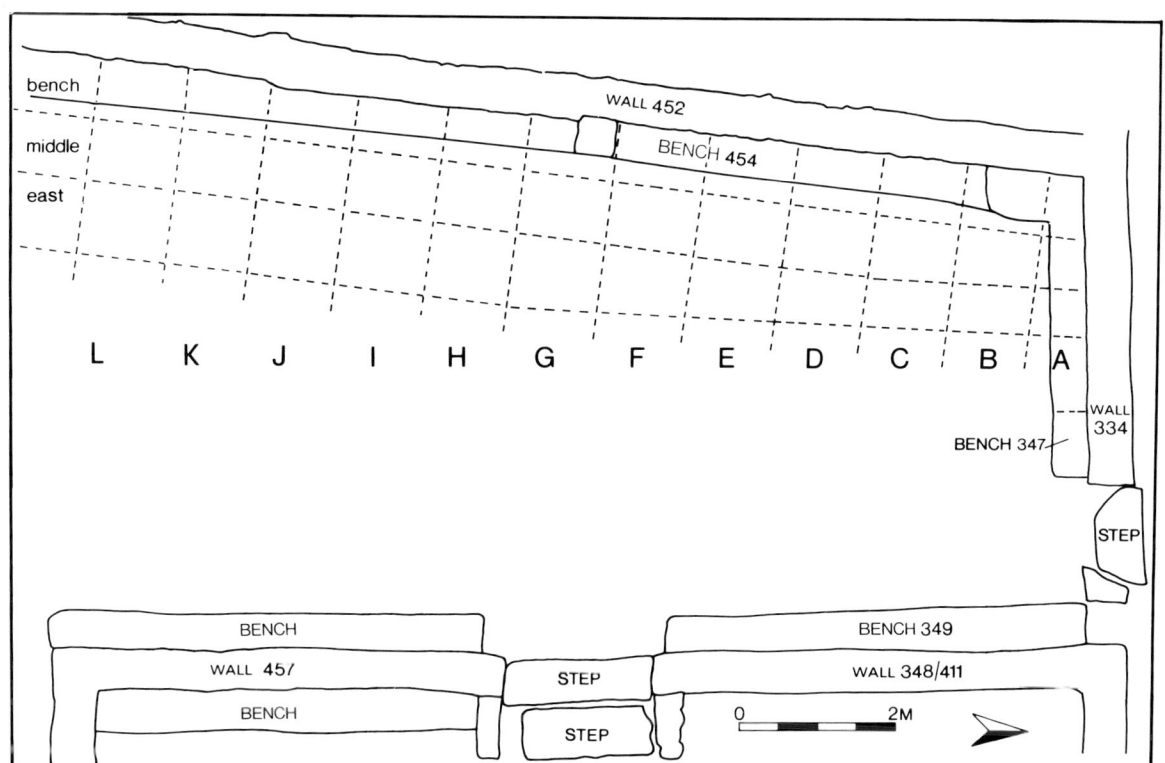

Fig. 3:14 Scheme of excavation of the zones with painted plaster in layer 401 in the Assembly Room *(CMC/JV)*

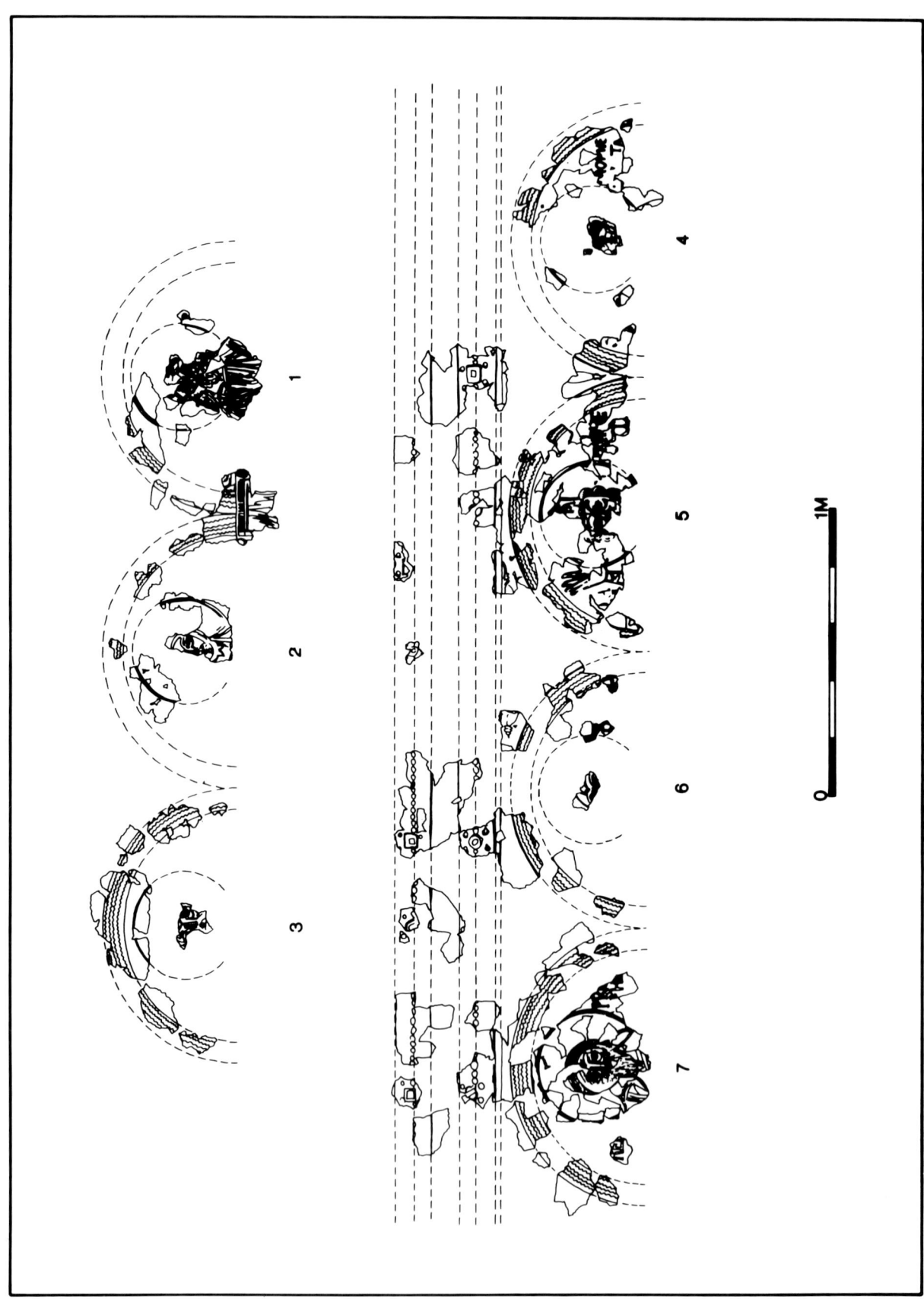

Fig. 3:15 Stage of reconstruction of the Prophets in 1985 (*AH/LW*)

HIE REM IAS PRO PHETA

ECCEDI V MVN

PROPH ETA

HECD DE DIB STRGATIO DVEAX

PA V ID

0 1M

1

Fig. 3:16 Schematic reconstruction of the painted decoration on wall 452 *(AH/JV)*

of reassembling at the time of going to press in the spring of 1994. Figure 3:16 is a schematic reconstruction of what we believe the painted decoration of wall 452 to have been.

In the case of the inscriptions, the painted letters themselves were in many cases so faded and their traces so slight that not only were they extremely difficult to identify, but sometimes it was impossible to determine if what one was looking at was the faint shadow of a character or merely an incidental and barely perceptible darkening in the colour of the scroll. The schematic partial reconstructions reproduced in Figure 3:17 incorporate observations made at various times since the excavation of the painted fragments in 1982-84, and should be regarded as tentative composite records of the surviving letters. The drawings of the individual inscriptions (below, Figs 3:21, 3:25, 3:28, 3:30, 3:36, 3:37 and 3:41), on the other hand, are records of the reassembled fragments as they appeared in January 1994.

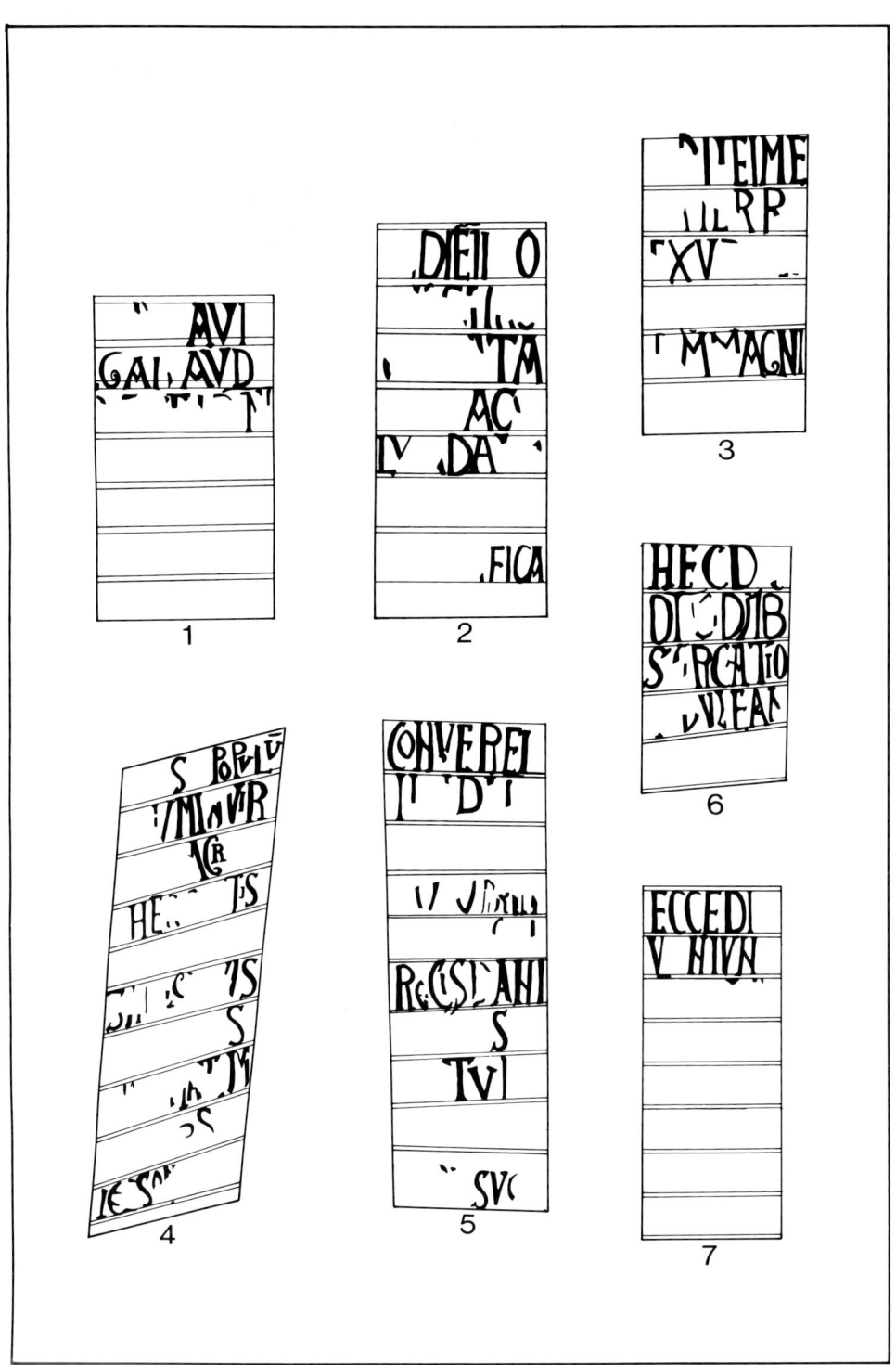

Fig. 3:17 Schematic reconstruction of the letters on the scrolls held by the Prophets *(KF/LW)*

Fig. 3:18 Detail of the painted border on wall 452 *(JM)*

Because these texts were extremely fragmentary and worn, and because the identity of many letters was uncertain, we have not attempted to transcribe the surviving letters in our description below. We have preferred to publish drawings of the scrolls, with as much of the texts as we have managed to discern, and to leave their decipherment to the reader. However, we have noted the instances in which complete words can be recognized, and have indicated when enough of a text survived to allow identification with a passage from the writings of one of the Prophets.

The ornamental setting of the Prophets

Before looking at the individual Prophets in detail, it will be as well to describe their ornamental setting. The description will start at the top and move down (Figs 3:16 and 3:18).

At the upper limit of the plastered surface a horizontal deep brown-red band, 50 mm wide, ran along the full length of the wall. The upper surfaces of the surviving fragments of plaster bearing this border carried the imprint of the horizontal roof timbers – the wall-plate – which once ran along the top of the wall. Below, contingent with the red border, was a band of pink painted over black, *c.* 60 mm wide. A line of large pink dots, each *c.* 15 mm in diameter, and set in close order, *c.* 5 mm apart, ran along the divide between the two colours. This line was broken, at more or less regular intervals, by alternate black rectangles and discs. Each of these was outlined with pink, and had four white dots set around it on its diagonal axes. The discs had white dots at their centres, and the rectangles had small

white squares. The dimensions of the small black rectangles were *c.* 42 x 48 mm. These motifs were positioned at intervals of about 0.4-0.6 m, and appear to have been more or less lined up with the standing figures and the columns of the arcade in the zone below. The lower edge of the pink band bordered on a horizontal swathe of black, *c.* 0.1 m deep, below which there was a further 60 mm strip of pink overlying black, followed by a band of rich red 75 mm wide. A white line, in places accompanied by a roughly executed brown-red line, was drawn along the divide between the black and the pink, and a chain of pink dots interspersed periodically with prominent black rectangles and discs, similar to the ones above, ran along the division between the pink and the red. In other words, apart from one thin white line, the scheme of ornamentation at the top of the wall was symmetrical about the wide horizontal band of black. The bottom edge of the lowest red band was bordered by a black stripe 10-20 mm wide, with a thin white line along the divide.

The intermittent black discs in the lower chain of dots appear to have been positioned roughly over the apices of the arches and the heads of the standing Prophets, and the black rectangles over the columns. In the upper chain, it is possible that the relative locations of the two motifs were reversed (as is in fact shown in Fig. 3:16), resulting in a chiastic relationship between rectangles and discs in the two registers. However, it is impossible to be certain about this detail since only limited passages of this upper border were reassembled, and, to judge from what was put together, the spacing of these ornaments was by no means regular. The positions of these ornaments in the upper and lower registers may well have changed more than once from one end of the wall to the other, relative to one another and relative to the positions of the arches and columns below.

Below the final horizontal black stripe was the brown-red ground which filled the triangular fields around the curving vaults of the arches. The apices of the arches lay about 30 mm below the black stripe. Some of the red-brown spandrels between the arches were embellished with configurations of painted white drapery. The original form and the full extent of these curtains cannot be determined, since all that survived were fragmentary narrowing ends of cloth in the corners of three of the spandrels. The configurations shown in the reconstruction (Fig. 3:16) are purely hypothetical.

The arches which curved over the Prophets' heads were gaily coloured affairs (Plate 3:9). Each was of the same pattern and consisted of overlapping concentric undulating bands of dark pink, light pink, white, grey and red. These were built up from the centre, with both light pink and grey overlapping the white median band, and then dark pink overlapping the light pink above, and red overlapping the grey below. The arches were struck with the help of a compass, the pivot of which was located at a point near the chin of each figure. The outer diameter of each arch was c. 0.85 m, and the inner diameter c. 0.7 m.

The arches rested on capitals, which, in turn, were supported by brightly-marbled columns (Plate 3:10). The overall dimensions of the capitals were about 0.22 x 0.22 m. They consisted of rectangles, c. 0.13 m tall and 0.17 m wide, with slender abacus-like horizontal panels above and below. Their rectangular cores were a very pale bluish white with rising flame-like configurations in salmon-pink and long white highlights. The capitals (like the columns below) were lighted from the right, and their left sides were defined with a lilac shadow. The abaci were ornamented with rectangular gem-like settings, rapidly done in pink with white highlights; they terminated at either end in little oval volutes, painted lilac with overlays of white and salmon-pink, which projected beyond the body of the capital. The columns below were 0.15-0.17 m wide and about 1.2 m tall (Plate 3:11). They were painted to imitate a rich salmon-pink marble with clusters of veins in rising arching configurations in red, grey and white, which seemed to repeat at intervals of about 0.25 m. Rising white flame-like forms, resembling those on the capitals, filled the spaces between the arching clusters. The column-bases were simple pink rectangles, c. 85 mm tall and 0.2 m wide, framed with lilac and ornamented with two rectangular pink jewel-like settings highlighted in white. All the columns were lighted from the right, and were shaded down their left-hand sides

with a c. 7 mm white band of highlight running down a broad swathe of red. The majority of the arches was more or less centred on their columns. However, in the case of the column which separated the first from the second reassembled Prophet, at the northern end of the wall (the column between Prophets 1 and 2), the base of the two springing arches was displaced to the left, leaving a space of 50 mm between the outer edge of the right arch and the right-hand end of the abacus below. Whether this displacement was due to an unintended slip on the part of the artist, or whether it was a controlled device to achieve some effect of spatial recession at this point, is not clear. Likewise, the columns were not always centred on their bases.

The lower horizontal border, which lay between this arcade and the marbled dado below, was a reduced and simplified version of the one at the top of the wall. Progressing from top to bottom, the ground on which the Prophets stood was bordered by a band of white, 15-20 mm wide. This was succeeded by a greyish pink band 60 mm wide, and then by a brown-red band, 70 mm wide, with large pale pink dots set at close but irregular intervals along the division between the two colours. The pink band appeared to have been overpainted with a murky mushroom-grey colour. Below the red-brown band, after 20 mm of pale dull pink wash, came a 15 mm stripe of red-brown. There followed a zone of white at least 50 mm deep. The panels of the marbled dado must have reached up to more or less this point. However, the precise form of the transition from the dado to the multiple border below the Prophet-arcade is still unknown.

The west wall – the Prophets

In this description, the measurements which are occasionally given for the dimensions of repeating elements in the scheme of decoration must be understood as only approximate indications of size and interval. These paintings were executed with great freedom and brio. Very little about them was regular, laboured or strictly controlled. The lines of horizontal divisions could veer radically from their anticipated rectilinear course, arches did not always hit their capitals squarely in the middle, columns were not always centred on their bases, and the schemes of marbling on the columns were anything but mechanical in their sequence.

All seven Prophets stood frontally, staring straight out ahead. It did not prove possible to reassemble any one of the figures in its entirety, but each must have stood to a height of something between 1.4 and 1.5 m, and about 0.1 m more to the top of the halo: that is, a little under (contemporary) life-size. The attitudes and gestures of the figures differed in detail, but overall, as far as can be judged from what was reassembled, they were fairly uniform in their stance and in their dress. Each had a great halo, 0.36-0.37 m in diameter, coloured a strong brown-red, with a white band, *c.* 5 mm wide, circling its circumference, just in from the edge. The outer contour of each halo was incised into the surface of the wall with a compass, whose inner pivoting point was set between the eyes at the root of the nose. Each Prophet, except for number 5, King David, wore a long loose garment which reached his ankles, with deep triangular sleeves and with red *clavi* on the breast, and, over this, a cloak worn on the right shoulder. Each held out before him a large unfurled scroll on which a substantial text was written.

Certain pictorial formulae were employed repeatedly in the construction of the faces of the figures, and these will play a critical role in any attempt to characterize the style of the paintings and to set them in an artistic context. The most obvious of these formulae are the wide arching foreheads lit with a spreading area of highlight which gathered into a prominent dipping triangular configuration just above the root of the nose; the great curling shadows below the eyes, which hung as if suspended in seas of white; the combs of brilliant white lights set either beside or below the eye; the eyes themselves with their dilated pupils in burning red or cooly smouldering lilac; the continuous red contour used to define the lower end of the nose; the little strokes of red which described the hollow between the cheek and jaw of the first Prophet; the small mouths with pursed pendulous lips, also outlined in red; the scalloped contours of the Prophets' beards and the blunt white lines which outlined two of these beards.

The painting was free and fluid, seemingly executed with rapid strokes of the brush, and stands in clear contrast to the more laboured and meticulously detailed work in Epyphanius's crypt at the northern end of the monastery (see Volume 1, chapter 7). Here, in the Assembly Room, the surfaces of the garments were articulated with clusters of folds, rendered as narrow coloured bands, in groups of three or more. However, these fold-clusters did not follow the formula of tight regular groupings of narrow bands, carefully defined and running parallel for the length of a particular passage of material, which was employed at San Vincenzo in Epyphanius's crypt, and in many other Italian centres in the ninth and tenth centuries (Matthiae 1967: pls 136, 144, 145, 176, 197; Belting 1968: figs 22, 24-6, 41, 46, 49, 147-57, 160, 179-90; Hubert, Porcher and Volbach 1969: figs 162-3). Instead, they were less regularly ordered, with individual folds often breaking off in mid-course, as if dying into the material. The overall effect was of loose, rather brightly-coloured, garments draped quite naturally about the body, but at the same time falling into a number of freely-rendered formulaic configurations which were repeated from figure to figure. One such formula, repeated on four of the figures, was a deft

little knot tied in an end of cloth which crossed the upper part of the breast, just below the neck.

Although the columns separating the figures were painted as if illuminated from the right (see Plate 3:11), the heads of the Prophets were, in schematic fashion, lighted from the left. The lighting of the columns may have been designed to correspond to the location of a window which brought light into the Assembly Room from the north, although there is no surviving archaeological evidence for the presence of a window in the north wall (334). The lighting of the faces, on the other hand, would appear to have been purely formulaic.

The faces of the Prophets were painted with particular panache, and the ones whose surfaces were well-preserved gave a vivid impression of life and energy. Their base colour was a salmon-pink, which was modelled with a darker shade of the same hue. Subsequently deeper shadows in grey or dark grey-green and areas of modulated white light were added on some of the figures. Next, features like the forehead, nose, mouth, eyebrows, ears, beard and the hollows of the cheeks were defined in red. Finally, brilliant white highlights were laid on the hair and the beard, the brow, the eyes, the nose and the cheeks. It is the manner in which these accents of white light contrasted with carefully contrived areas of shadow that gave these faces their dramatic impact.

All the Prophets displayed opened scrolls (Fig. 3:17). Six held these out by their sides with their left hands, while one grasped his in both hands and stretched it in a long diagonal across his breast. The scrolls were coloured salmon-pink, often streaked with light blue-grey. Each carried a text written in large capital letters, *c.* 40-55 mm tall. The rows of letters usually alternated between red and a darker colour of uncertain hue which in almost all cases had faded to the limits of legibility. Horizontal ruled guide-lines incised into the plaster defined the upper and lower edges of each of these rows. The texts were in a clearly legible, slightly irregular, script, characterized by the presence of variant forms of letters – for example, A with straight or broken median bar, and both square and rounded uncial forms of E – and of *litterae inscriptae*, that is half-sized letters which were tucked within or in between the full-sized characters. Both of these features were probably employed to introduce variety into the inscriptions. The texts are likely to be excerpts from the writings of the Prophets who held them (see below).

A *titulus* in white capitals flanking the haloed head within the lunette of the arch once identified each figure. Each man's name was written in the narrow space to the left of the head, with the letters arranged in three superimposed registers in the one instance in which most of the letters survived (the fifth Prophet: David) (see below, Plate 3:17). Scant remains of the names were found – the battered letters of King David's name, and a letter or two from two of the other Prophets (see below). On the right of the head was written the title PROPHETA, always divided between two registers, although the point at which the word was broken varied in the five extant examples. The script of these *tituli* was in somewhat irregularly formed white capitals which varied between 35 and 55 mm in height. Vertical members of letters ended in nail-head terminals; E had short bars with rather ill-defined dropping or rising serifs; O was a drawn-out oval and sometimes almost pointed at top and bottom; R had a straight leg; and T had dropping serifs which were set in from the ends of its cross-bar. There was little evidence here of the characteristic features of the epigraphic script used on gravestones at San Vincenzo in the ninth century (see Volume 3, chapter 2).

The fields within the arches, against which the Prophets stood, were divided into three horizontal zones, following a usage often met with in early medieval painting. The colour of the ground about the Prophets' heads, within the lunettes, changed half way along the sequence of reconstructed arches: a warm pinkish lilac towards the northern end of the wall, and a pale sky-blue towards the south. The change in colour occurred in the arch of the fourth of the reassembled Prophets from the north. The exact level of the horizontal division between the upper (lunette) and middle zone varied. In the first three arches at the northern end of the wall the divide was at the level of the abaci which surmounted the columns, while in the four remaining arches to the south it was sometimes located a little higher, at around the level of the Prophets' chins. The division was sometimes defined with a faint red-brown line. The second zone, strong lilac in colour, extended down as far as the lower legs of the figures, to a point a little above the bottom hem of their long tunics. The lower zone was not absolutely uniform in colour from arch to arch. In the first and seventh arches nothing of it survived; in the second it appears to have been an unvaried brown-red, while in the third, fourth, fifth and sixth it was a strong pink with undulating brown-red lines to indicate the terrain.

The range of colours used in this scheme was quite small. Salmon-pink, lavender, lilac, pale sky-blue, red, grey, white and various shades of brown-red predominated. But the disposition of these colours over the wall was not completely uniform. As has been described, the colours of the lunettes behind the heads of the Prophets changed from a pale warm lilac to a pale sky-blue after the third arch. In the figures of the Prophets there were similar subtle changes of emphasis. In the drapery of the first, second, third and fourth Prophets, the dominant colours were lilac, white and palest sky-blue against salmon-pink for the tunics, and brown-red or pink strongly contoured and shaded with brown-red for

the cloaks. In the case of the fifth figure, King David, the dull pink of the tunic and the brown-red of the cloak predominated. In the following figure the emphasis changed again, with striking broken configurations of red and white against strong pink.

Within the confines of a repeating sequence of figural and architectural units, and within the constraints of a very limited palette, the artists who designed and executed this wall introduced variety and incident and contrived to hold the observer's interest through the subtle manipulation of colour, through the careful deployment of bravura passages of painting, through minor variations in the attitudes of the figures, and, above all, through the freedom with which they realized the details of their scheme and through the unregimented panache of their brushwork.

A cursory glance at the heads of the first and the second Prophets (below, Plates 3:12 and 3:13) is enough to show that the figures on this wall were the work of more than one person. However, whether the seven partially reassembled figures should be assigned to two or to three different hands is difficult to say. The formal topography of the heads, the formulae employed for the various facial features and for highlighting and shading, were more or less the same in all the figures. The differences lie in the interpretation and execution of this pictorial vocabulary, and it is not easy to determine whether a particular difference should be taken as evidence of the work of two distinct hands or simply as the degree of variation likely within the production of a single artist.

Prophet 1

The surviving fragments of the first Prophet were found, for the most part, in 401 *D*. (It seems likely that two further Prophets once stood in the northernmost arches on wall 452, although we have not been able to reconstruct these – see below.) The head of this man and much of the upper part of his torso were reassembled (Fig. 3:19; Plate 3:12). His face was a striking piece of painting, with dramatically contrasting schemes of deep pink and grey shadows and brilliant white lights playing over the brow, round the eyes and on the cheeks, down the bridge of the nose, and over the hair, moustache and beard. Red accents, applied with a fine brush, were used to define many of the features, the contour of the brow, the eyebrows, the ears, the nose, the hollows of the cheeks, the mouth and the shadow under the moustache, and the broken contours of hair and beard. Most effective of all, the pupils of the eyes were red ovals which looked out from pools of brilliant white. The hair must have been particularly splendid: with an overlay of thick white lights over a pink ground, it was tightly pulled back from the brow and over the crown, and then gathered in two broadly braided bunches which fell back over his shoulders on either side.

Fig. 3:19 Upper part of the body of Prophet 1 *(JBB)*

Although this head gives the immediate impression of being the inspired invention of an artist of some power, it was in fact skilfully built up from a series of formulaic elements which recurred in the other figures on this wall and which are met with in ninth- and tenth-century painting in certain other parts of Italy. The most salient of these formulae are the broad arched brow, the scalloped beard, the striking curling crescent shadows beneath the eyes, the convention of defining the lower part of the nose with a continuous fine red contour and the hollows of the cheeks with a sequence of short red brush-strokes, and, finally, the highlighting systems (the dramatic combs of light beneath the eyes and the use of a long white brush stroke beside broad vertical strokes of grey and deep salmon-pink to describe the form of the nose). The deep brown-red of the halo must once have done much to enhance the iconic power and the immediacy of the head.

This Prophet appeared to have been wearing two principal articles of clothing, a loose tunic-like garment with sleeves which hung down from the forearm in a prominent triangular configuration, and a dark brown-red cloak which fell over his left shoulder and left breast (Fig. 3:19). (The tight sleeves of a third article of clothing, worn beneath the wide-sleeved tunic and the cloak, may perhaps be identified on the right forearm of the Prophet.) Insufficient fragments were reassembled for the overall form of either garment to be clear. However, the tunic appeared to be closed at the neck by a little knot tied in the material, and four red *clavi* ran through it on the left shoulder and breast, two of them very short and two long. The ground colour of this garment was salmon-pink, with bands and swathes of lilac and pure white, and areas of white tinged with lilac, alluding to elaborately shaded and illuminated surfaces of folded cloth. Folds tended to be clustered in groups, but these groupings were not at all regimented, and were not even immediately apparent. The Prophet's right arm was bent at the elbow, and his hand formed a gesture of address, with the middle finger bent to touch the thumb. This long, elegant hand was painted pink, with a thick overlay of white highlights, and the shaded contours of the fingers were outlined in red.

Little remained of the scroll this figure once held in his left hand. However, one of the fingers was

Fig. 3:20 Scroll held by Prophet 1 *(JBB)*

preserved, gripping the top roll which was modelled with dark pink and lit with white. The extended surface of the scroll was coloured a pale salmon-pink. It was at least 0.28 m wide. No sense can be made of the few surviving letters from the text, which was written in alternating lines of red and dull purplish red (see Figs 3:17, 3:19-21). The letters in the first line varied between 50 and 55 mm in height, and those in the second were about 48 mm tall; they repeatedly over-sailed the inscribed horizontal guide-lines. In this inscription the lower incised guide-line in each row of script was doubled, the additional line lying about 10 mm above the base-line.

Fig. 3:21 Scroll held by Prophet 1 *(LW)*

Fig. 3:22 Upper body of Prophet 2 *(JBB)*

Prophet 2

The majority of the fragments which made up the second Prophet was found in the next metre-square to the south, 401 *E.* Enough of this figure was reassembled to show that he stood with his weight on his left leg, and that, like the first, he held out a large scroll with his left hand. His face was built up of superimposed strokes of colour, dark salmon-pink, grey, greyish white, with delicate contours and accents in red, and white highlights, all over a salmon-pink ground, just as on the previous figure (Plate 3:13). But the interpretation was broader and less delicate. The face appeared to be framed by a great oval of dark pink, and the shadows above and below the eyes and on either side of the nose were bluntly applied and relatively crude in their definition. The appearance of this face had been affected by the loss of much of its scheme of white highlights. However, it was clear that the little comb of lights which ran out from the corner of the surviving eye was not as fine as the bravura passage of comb-lighting beneath the left eye of the first Prophet. In the case of the second figure, the forehead was lighted by a spherical triangle of pale greyish white with grey

shading, and the cheeks were covered with large triangles of modulated grey shadow, growing darker in the hollow above the jaw. Most telling of all, the elegant beard of the first Prophet (with its indentations precisely defined in red, its wispy little bifurcated tip and its dense tracery of highlights) was really very different from the thickly-painted pink beard of his companion, with its boldly scalloped sides and forked tip outlined with an unvarying white contour. This second Prophet must have been the work of a different hand. Although the overall design of the figure and the pictorial conventions employed for details of the head were the same in both cases, the interpretation of these conventions and the manner in which the paint was applied were markedly different.

In design and tonality, the drapery of this figure was quite similar to that of the first Prophet (Fig. 3:22). As before, the principal garment was tied at the neck with a neat little knot. Its ground colour was again pale salmon-pink, and the folds were described in pale lilac and white. The cloak on his left shoulder was coloured pink, with contour and folds in a strong brownish red, and some accents in

Plate 1:1 Marbled dado on the north wall (315) of the Vestibule *(JM)*

Plate 1:2 Young saint from the west wall (316) of the Vestibule *(JBB)*

Plate 1:3 Head of the young saint *(JM)*

Plate 1:4 Butterfly-folds from the lower hem of the tunic of the young saint *(JM)*

Plate 1:5 Poppies on white ground from the north wall of the Vestibule *(JM)*

Plate 1:6 Fragment of a phase 4 head *(JM)*

Plate 3:1 Painted decoration of overlapping particoloured scales on the bench against the east wall of the Assembly Room *(JM)*

Plate 3:2 Painted decoration with segmented lozenges on the bench against the east wall of the Assembly Room *(JM)*

Plate 3:3 Painted decoration at the southern end of the west face of bench 349 *(JM)*

Plate 3:4 Painted decoration with segmented lozenges on bench 454 against the west wall (452) of the Assembly Room *(JM)*

Plate 3:5 Painted decoration on bench 347 against wall 334 *(JM)*

Plate 3:8 Reassembled painted decoration of wall 452, with Prophets within a running arcade *(JBB)*

Plate 3:6 Dado on northern section of wall 348/411, with bench 349 *(JM)*

Plate 3:9 Detail of one of the arches from the Prophet arcade *(JM)*

Plate 3:7 Painted decoration on the east face of buttress 456 *(JM)*

Plate 3:10 Detail of one of the capitals from the columns on the Prophet arcade *(JBB)*

Plate 3:11 Column from the Prophet arcade *(JBB)*

Plate 3:12 Head of Prophet 1 *(JM)*

Plate 3:13 Head of Prophet 2 *(JBB)*

Plate 3:14 Head of Prophet 3 *(JBB)*

Plate 3:15 Head of Prophet 4 *(JBB)*

Plate 3:16 Detail of the scroll held by Prophet 4 *(JBB)*

Plate 3:17 Head of Prophet 5 *(JBB)*

Plate 3:18 Head of Prophet 6 *(JBB)*

Plate 3:19 Detail of the body and scroll of Prophet 6 *(JBB)*

Plate 3:21 Fragmentary head of a Prophet from the north end of wall 452 *(JM)*

Plate 3:20 Head of Prophet 7 *(JBB)*

Plate 3:22 Scroll held by a Prophet from the northwest corner of the Assembly Room *(JBB)*

Plate 3:23 Upper body of a standing figure from the northern end of the Assembly Room *(JM)*

Plate 3:25 Head of a figure from the northern end of the Assembly Room *(JM)*

Plate 3:24 Fragment of a standing figure from the northern end of the Assembly Room *(JM)*

Plate 3:26 Head of a figure from the northern end of the Assembly Room *(JM)*

Plate 3:27 Body of a turning figure, found in the Assembly Room *(JM)*

Plate 3:28 Head of a young man turning to the right, found in the Assembly Room *(JM)*

Plate 3:29 Fragment of a spirally fluted column from the northern end of the Assembly Room *(JM)*

Plate 12:1 Reconstruction of San Vincenzo al Volturno (*SG, 1985*)

Fig. 3:23 Detail of the legs and feet of Prophet 2 *(JBB)*

white. Much of the man's body was missing, but it was clear that he held his right hand before his breast in a gesture of speech. Lower down, the bottom of his tunic and both feet were partially reconstructed (Fig. 3:23; and see Basile 1988: fig. 4). The lower reaches of this garment were salmon-pink, contoured in pale lilac, and with folds indicated in pale lilac and white. The rear hem was visible below the front hem, and the long triangular area which resulted was filled with curving strokes in white and red over the pink of the ground, presumably to represent the lining of the garment. This pictorial device presented the viewer with a crude semblance of foreshortening and so some kind of allusion of pictorial depth at this point. The Prophet's legs were bare, painted pink with thin white channels of light running down the ankles and feet and over the toes, which were defined in red.

Enough of this Prophet's scroll was reassembled to show that it was originally about 0.54 m long and 0.22 m wide (Figs 3:17, 3:22, 3:24 and 3:25). The text was written in letters varying in height between *c.* 50 and 63 mm, in alternating lines of strong red and a dull pinkish purple against a pale pink ground. At the bottom the scroll was modelled in darker pink and white to indicate the lower cylinder of still rolled paper. Parts of various words and individual letters could be recognized, but the surviving passages were too fragmentary, and their surfaces too abraded, for the text to be identified.

Fig. 3:24 Scroll held by Prophet 2 *(JBB)*

Fig. 3:25 Scroll held by Prophet 2 *(LW)*

Prophet 3

The fragments of the third Prophet on this wall were found principally in 401 *F*. Little of this figure survived – vestiges of his halo, the central section of his face, a substantial proportion of his scroll, some passages of drapery from his clothed body, and much of his feet. However, to judge from what little remained, his head must have been one of the most impressive of the whole sequence (Plate 3:14). The ground colour of the face was again salmon-pink. This was modelled with an orange shade of the same hue round the edges of the face, above and below the eyes and down the right side of the nose. A deep blue-grey was used to model the forehead, the left side of the nose and the nostrils, the mouth and upper lip, the hollows of the cheeks, the hollows beneath the

eyebrows, the areas around the ears, and the shaded parts of the neck. As usual, red, applied with a fine brush, defined the features, the bottom of the nose, the eyebrows and the mouth, and the hollows of the cheeks. Then, powerful white lights, which fell off into grey shadow, accentuated the base of the brow and the nose, enframed the curling areas of shadow beneath the eyes, and articulated the moustache and the hair. In addition, the artist had also used a pale lilac to great effect. This colour was used for the hair, moustache and beard, which were all liberally lighted with white, and also for the pupil of the eye. On the lower half of the face, with the colour of the skin showing through the beard in places, the artist managed to achieve the same combination of pink, lilac and white that was found on the drapery

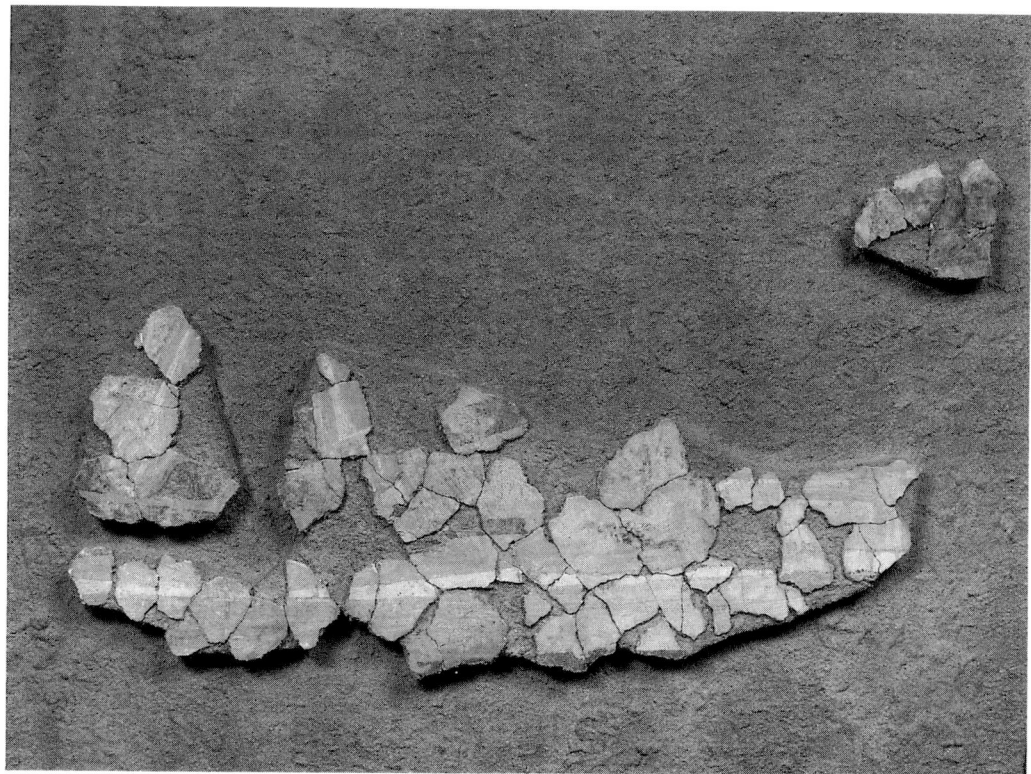

Fig. 3:26 Detail of the feet of the Prophet 3 *(JBB)*

of the Prophets. The result was a wonderfully striking and delicate colour scheme, which was both warm and cool at the same time.

This man's tunic was the same colour as before, that is salmon-pink with prominent shaded folds in lilac and lighted in white. Immediately below the neck the material of the garment was secured in a little knot, and one long and two short red *clavi* were positioned on a small curling grey patch high upon the Prophet's right breast. Lower down, a cluster of three red folds, probably also *clavi*, which fell diagonally away to the right of the scroll, formed a prominent accent in the scheme of the drapery. On his left shoulder he wore the usual cloak, again pink, deeply shaded with grey and with contours and folds in brown-red. The hand with which he grasped his scroll was shown outlined in red in deep grey shadow. He stood on a strong pink ground unevenly banded with brownish red; and his feet were again pink with a rather abstract scheme of highlights which ran down over his toes (Fig. 3:26).

The scroll, which the Prophet held by his side with his left hand, was 0.2 m wide and must originally have been more that 0.45 m long (Figs 3:17, 3:27 and 3:28). To judge from what was reassembled, there were once letters on at least six lines, varying in height between 55 mm and 60 mm, in alternating rows of red and a colour which had faded to a faint dark salmon-pink. These were set against a salmon-pink ground streaked in places with grey and white. Although a number of groups of sequential letters and perhaps one whole word,

Fig. 3:27 Scroll held by Prophet 3 *(JBB)*

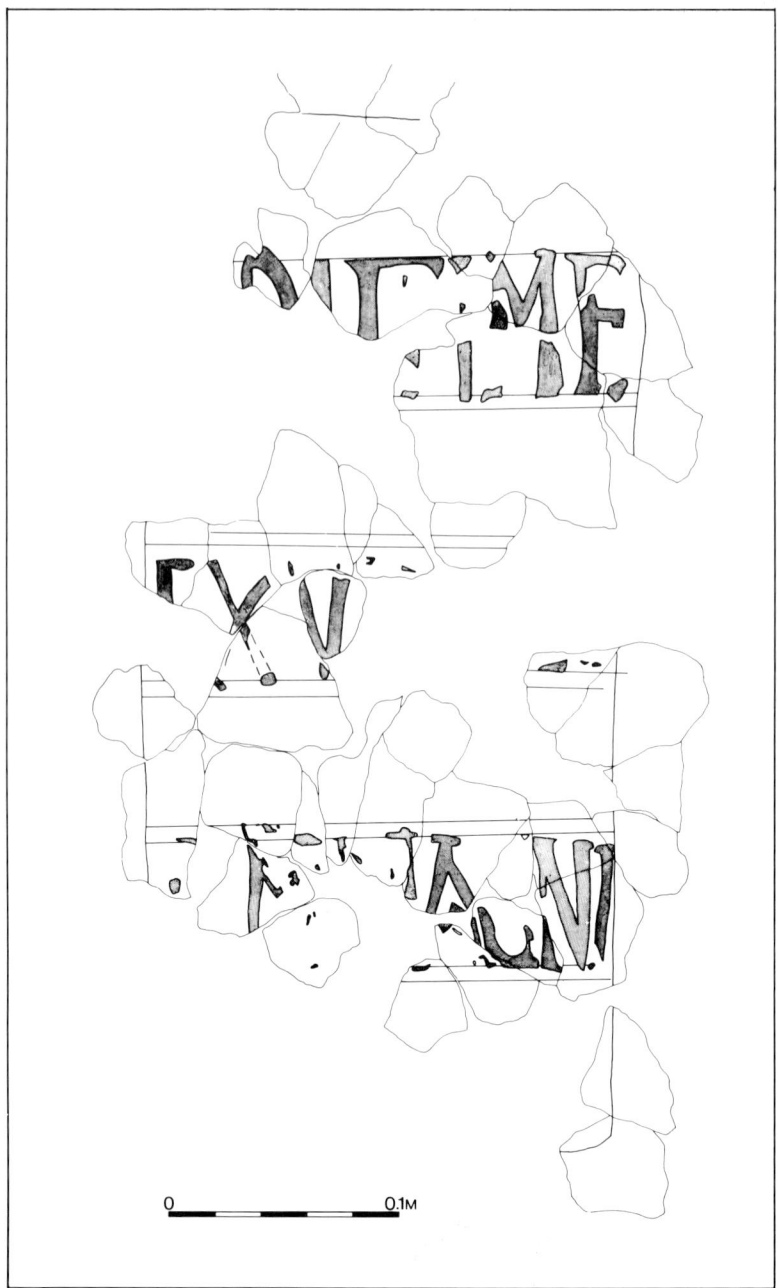

Fig. 3:28 Scroll held by Prophet 3 *(LW)*

MAGNI, were preserved, it did not prove possible to identify the text of this inscription.

Prophet 4 – Micah
The fragments of the fourth Prophet were found in 401 *G*, around the foot of the truncated 'buttress' which rose out of the bench against the north wall of this room. He had a youthful face of which the central part was preserved. To judge from what little remained, he had a scalloped beard, rather like the one worn by the second Prophet on the wall, that was thickly painted in strong pink and summarily contoured in white (Plate 3:15). His face was coloured, modelled and lighted in the usual fashion, with strong shading in deep pink and grey,

with greyish white lighted surfaces and lines of brilliant white illuminating prominent ridges. He had the usual small and rather pendulous lower lip, coloured a dull lilac and defined in red, burning red eyes enfurled in brilliant white, and a short comb of white rays beside the surviving eye, very like those lying beside the eyes of the second and the seventh figures on the wall. What little remained of his hair suggested that this was in two tones of red-brown, encompassing his head and falling down onto his shoulders in a broadly scalloped contour.

His tunic was generally similar in colour and design to those of his companions, with lilac folds lighted with white on a salmon-pink material which was modulated with patches of very pale sky-blue

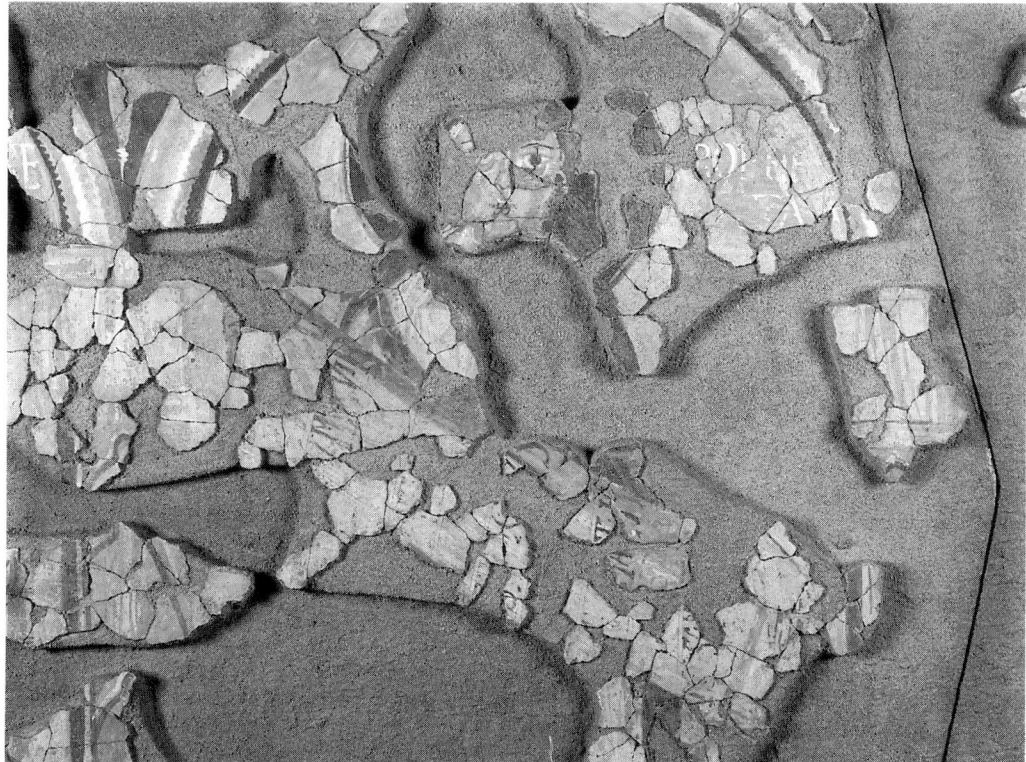

Fig. 3:29 Upper body of Prophet 4 *(JBB)*

(Fig. 3:29). As with the three preceding figures, the garment was tied at the neck in a little knot. Under his right shoulder was again a curling patch of grey bearing four vestigial red *clavi*, all executed with great freedom and élan; just beside this was another bravura passage of painting, an overlay of lilac and white bands and areas of the palest sky-blue with the pale salmon-pink of the material showing through in between. Like the others, this Prophet wore a cloak on his left shoulder, this time coloured a deep pink, and broadly contoured and articulated in brown-red. Below, one of his feet was reconstructed, and shown to have been well modelled all over in dull lilac with white highlights, and with the contours and the toes defined in red. As with the preceding Prophet, the ground on which he stood was a strong pink, irregularly banded with brownish red.

The one striking anomaly about this figure was his scroll (Figs 3:17 and 3:30; Plate 3:16). Instead of holding it out so that it hung vertically at his left side, he grasped it with both hands and stretched it in a long diagonal across his body, providing a welcome variant accent in this somewhat uniform rank of figures. The scroll extended from a point close to the left-hand capital of the arch to within 40 mm of the right-hand column. It was about 0.78 m in length and 0.19 m wide, with eleven lines of script, varying in height between 41 mm and 52 mm, and alternating in colour between dull violet-grey and red, against a pink ground streaked with a pale duck-egg blue. The words of the inscription were written on the slant within their lines, to complement the diagonal slope of the scroll. The text was fragmentary, and many of the surviving letters were faded to the limits of decipherability. However, what could be made out of the first four lines seems to accord with the wording of a verse in the book of Micah (7.14): '*Pasce populum tuum in virga tua, gregem haereditatis tuae, habitantes solos in saltu in medio Carmeli; pascentur Basan et Galaad iuxta dies antiquos*' (Feed thy people with thy rod, the flock of thine heritage, which dwell solitarily in the wood, in the midst of Carmel: let them feed in Bashan and Gilead, as in the days of old).

In the lunette of the arch, much of the right-hand side of the title accompanying this figure was reassembled, with the white letters of 'PROPHETA' (Fig. 3:31). The illegible remains of what may have been the first letter of the man's name were preserved on pale sky-blue ground just inside the arch on the left-hand side of his head.

Prophet 5 – David
The fifth Prophet came principally from the next square to the south, 401 *H*. He wore a crown, raised his right hand in a gesture of address, and was identified by the *titulus* by his head as the Prophet-king David (Fig. 3:32; Plate 3:17). Parts of all but one of the letters of his name, DAV[I]D, and almost all of his title, PROPHETA, were preserved (Fig. 3:33). He appeared to be clean shaven, and his face

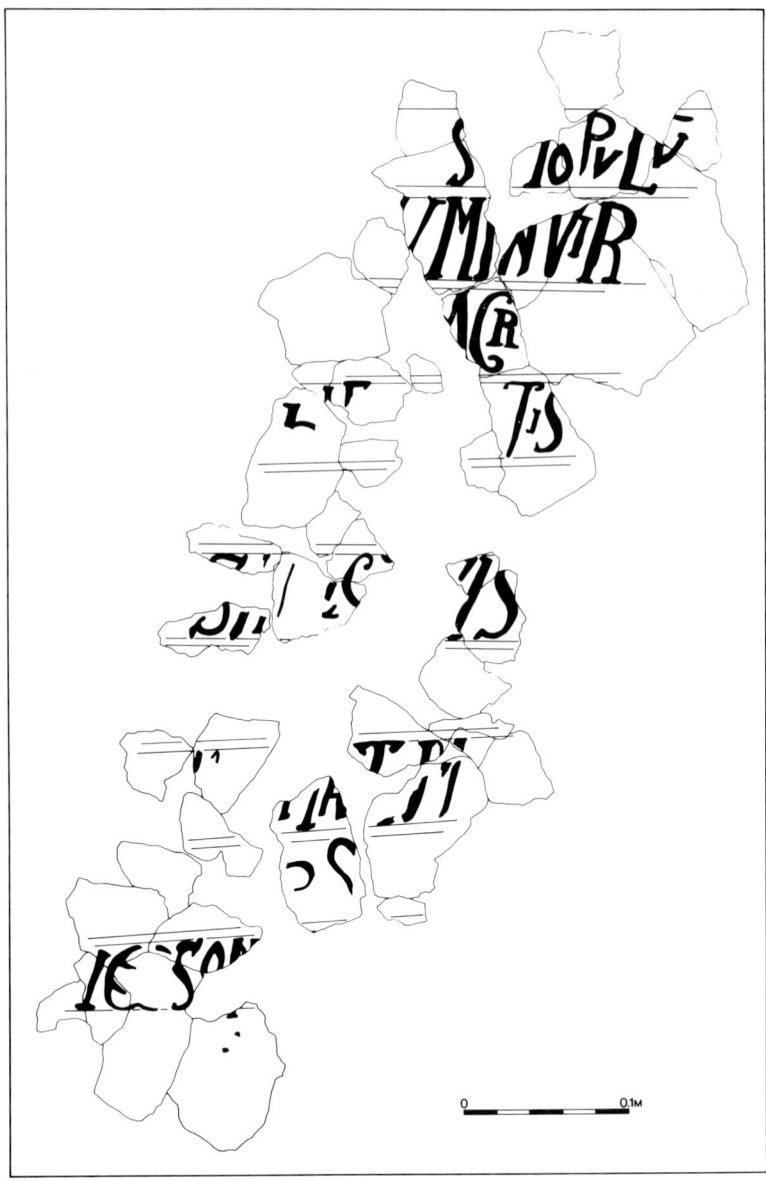

Fig. 3:30 Scroll held by Prophet 4 *(KF)*

was the usual salmon-pink, shaded with a deeper mix of the same colour which turned in some areas to a deep mushroom hue, and was illuminated by broad areas of pinkish white on his forehead and cheeks and by brilliant white lights along his eyebrows and on the inner side of his left eye. As usual his eyebrows, nose and mouth were defined in red. His hair crossed his brow in a ragged fringe and fell around the sides of his face in thick and deeply scalloped curls, like that of the previous figure. In colour it was a light brownish red, with darker strands within, and with dark contours. His crown resembled a mitre, with straight sides which turned in and curved up to a peak. It was coloured a dull salmon-pink, articulated with red-brown and outlined in white, and bore on its front a bilaterally symmetrical plant motif with scrolling branches in white. The division between the pale sky-blue ground of the lunette and the zone of lilac below

was extremely irregular in this case and was not marked by a red-brown line.

David's right hand, which he held up beside his head, was strongly modelled with lilac-white over a pink base, and was outlined in brown-red. He wore a tight-sleeved tunic, dull pink in colour, its contours and folds defined in brown-red (Fig. 3:32). This was embellished with three long and close-set red clavi which ran diagonally down from his right shoulder across his breast. Lower down, immediately to the left of his scroll, two red lines, perhaps the lower ends of *clavi*, ran down over a small patch of dull mauve overlying pink. Over the tunic he wore a brown-red cloak highlighted with white, which may have been secured at the shoulder by a brooch. From the reassembled fragments it is hard to discern the original form of this cloak and to reconstruct how it fell about his body. However, it should be observed that the tight sleeve of David's tunic changed colour

Fig. 3:31 *Titulus* PROPHETA accompanying Prophet 4 *(JM)*

from dull pink to the brown-red of the cloak at a point 50 mm below the wrist. The lower hem of his cloak was preserved, and a detached band of the same colour followed its contour below at a distance of 10 to 20 mm (Fig. 3:34). His feet were coloured white, with the palest pinkish wash, and shaded in lilac. There was no indication of toes. He, alone of the surviving figures from this wall, seemed to have been shown wearing shoes, as is appropriate for a king, and it is possible that these were originally painted over the white, *al secco*, in some bright colour which had flaked off the wall leaving no traces. The ground behind the feet was a strong pink.

Various fragments of this Prophet's scroll were

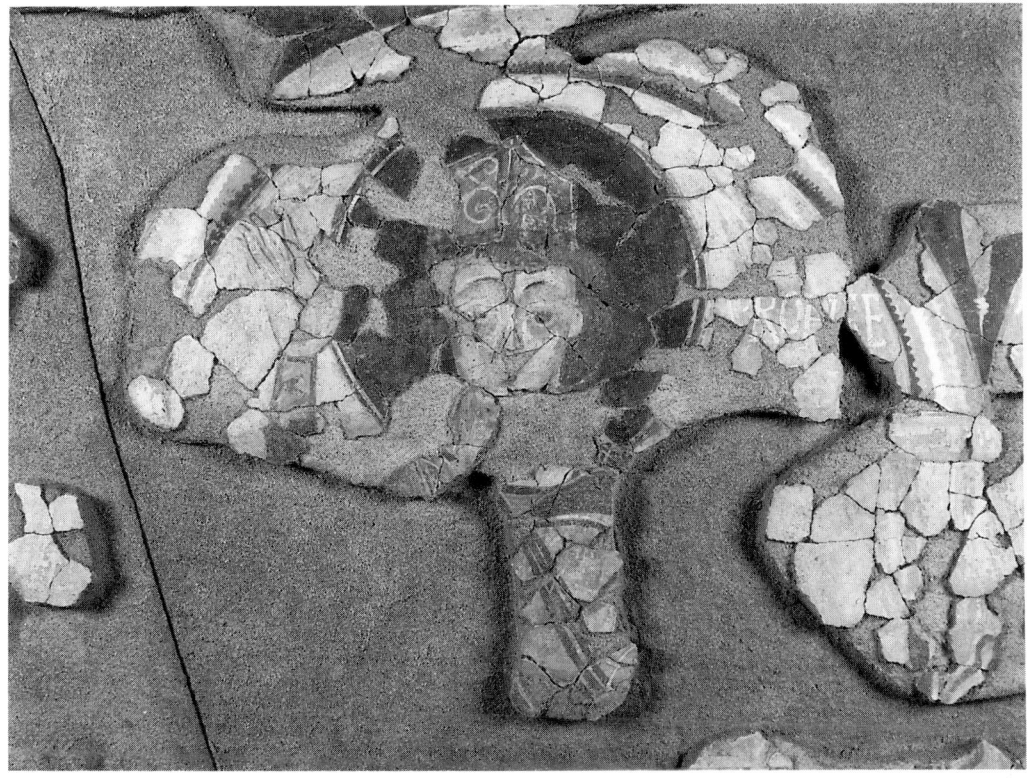

Fig. 3:32 Upper body of Prophet 5 *(JBB)*

Fig. 3:33 Detail of the *titulus* DAVID accompanying Prophet 5 *(JBB)*

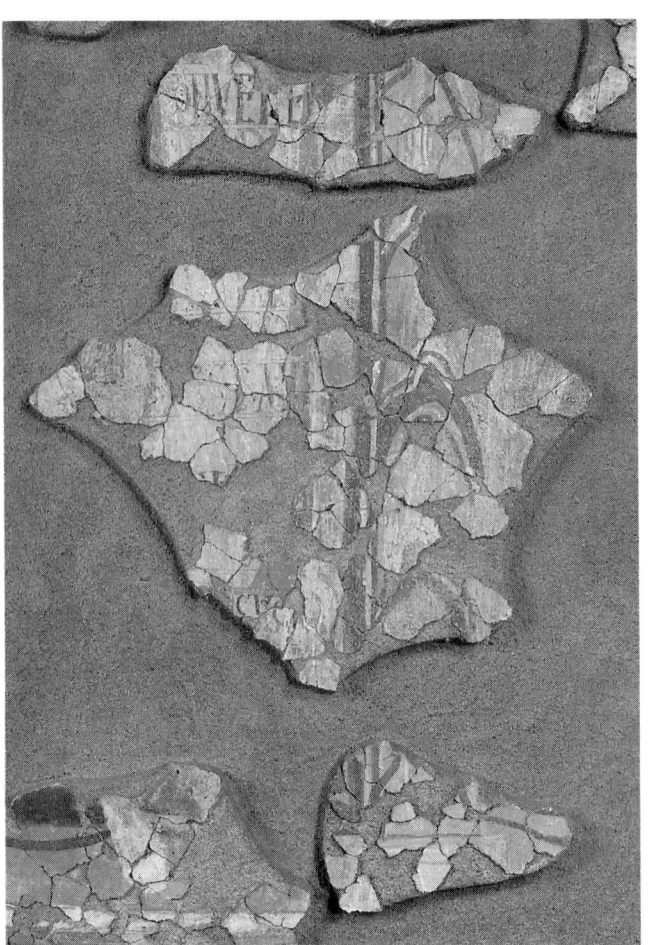

Fig. 3:35 Scroll held by Prophet 5 *(JBB)*

Fig. 3:34 Detail of the feet of Prophet 5 *(JBB)*

Fig. 3:36 Scroll held by Prophet 5 *(LW)*

reassembled (Figs 3:17, 3:35 and 3:36). It was quite long and was ruled for probably ten lines of script. It was about 0.71 m long and 0.19 m wide, and its characters varied in height between *c.* 53 mm and 62.5 mm. The scroll was pink with repeated swathes of very pale lilac running down its length, and a vertical band of dark pink, 28 mm wide, defined its right-hand contour. The lines of letters alternated between red and a colour which had faded drastically to a dark salmon-pink. Although various sequences of letters could be recognized, it did not prove possible to identify the text. It seems that a number of the lines ruled for script may have been left blank.

Prophet 6

The painted plaster from the sixth Prophet was found principally in areas 401 *I* and *J*. The plaster from this figure had, for the most part, been scorched by fire, and its surfaces tended to be darkened and discoloured. It is clear that the fire which burnt and carbonized the timbers of the roof of this room, presumably the conflagration of October 881, swept up to the painted wall at this point. Consequently it is hard to be sure of the original values of the colours used. The remains of this man's head were vestigial. Only three fragments were recovered (retrieved from disparate contexts, 401 *I*, *J* and *K*), and these showed his right eye, the

Fig. 3:37 Scroll held by Prophet 6 *(KF)*

root of his nose, and part of his forehead (Plate 3:18). The scheme of modelling of the face was the normal one and was as powerful as ever, with emphatic use of blue-grey shadows on the forehead and the nose, and a dipping greyish white light above the root of the nose. The hair too appeared to have been coloured the same blue-grey, perhaps with touches of lilac here and there. Red was much in evidence, in the eye, strongly outlining the brow, and defining the eyelid and the eyebrow.

Enough of the right-hand side of this figure was reassembled to show that he was clothed in a loose garment with passages of drapery wound about his waist and falling across his legs in the region of the knees (Plate 3:19). The colour of this material was basically a bright salmon-pink, with folds represented in striking configurations of red and brilliant white. Immediately to the left of the Prophet's scroll, there was a passage of densely folded drapery, with four narrow red bands and four white bands falling

vertically in a cluster, one of the white bands being delicately ornamented with a sequence of tiny white *impasto* dots along its length. The narrow red bands here should probably be read as *clavi*. Below this there was a further sequence of thin red bands against pink dropping down below the Prophet's knees, probably the continuation of these same *clavi*. A bent finger from the gesturing right hand of the Prophet was preserved at the upper left-hand corner of this reassembled area. The passage of ruffled, broken, drapery on the Prophet's upper arm, just above the scroll which he held in his left hand, provided another virtuoso display, this time of brilliantly-lit broken flame-like configurations in red and white against the pink of the material. The ground behind the man's feet was the usual pink, irregularly banded with brown-red.

His scroll (Figs 3:17 and 3:37; Plate 3:19) hung by his side, with somewhat more of a swing than usual. It was 0.21 m wide, and was originally over 0.5 m long. There seemed to have been at least eight lines of text. Various complete and fragmentary letters were preserved in the first four of these, but only one word, the initial H(a)EC, was readily recognizable, and the text could not be identified. The script of the first and fourth lines was in red, and that of the second and third was in a colour which had faded to a dull mauve. The letters varied in height between 48 mm and 58 mm. The upper roll of the scroll was modelled with bands of pink and white, to indicate its cylindrical form, and the inscriptional field below was salmon-pink, lighted on the left with streaks of white, and with a wide band of deeper salmon-pink defining its right-hand edge.

Prophet 7 – Jeremiah

The remains of the seventh Prophet came, in large part, from 401 *J*. Most of the head, parts of the shoulders, and a fragment of the scroll held by this figure were reassembled. Much of the plaster from this figure had been scorched by fire, and its surfaces tended to be darkened and discoloured. This implies that the fire of October 881 came into contact with this section of the painted wall.

The face was powerfully designed with broad areas of highlighting and deep contrasting shadows (Plate 3:20). Pale greyish white swathes of light were laid on his brow, around his eyes, and over his cheeks, on his nose and all over his moustache and beard. Brilliant lines of white light were then added to give form to the hair and beard, to put life into the white of the eyes, to define and to accentuate the great curling crescents of deep salmon-pink shadow below, and to articulate nose, mouth, brow and ears. As always, red had been used to contour the brow and the beard, and to describe the eyebrows and eyelids, the ears, the nose, the mouth and the hollows of the cheeks; and red had also been chosen for the eyes, which glared out from this ecstatic countenance. In type, this head was related to that of the first Prophet. There was the same long pointed beard, and the hair seems similarly to have been tied back over the shoulders in two braided bunches. However, a glance at the ways in which red was used to articulate the cheeks and the beards of the two men, and white to describe their illumination, is sufficient to show that these heads were the work of two different artists.

The line of this last Prophet's shoulders was firmly outlined in red. However, below this too little of the body was retrieved for it to be possible to say anything about the design of his clothing.

A few of the letters of the identifying *titulus* in white letters, which once flanked this man's head, were recovered: part of the title PROPHETA, from the right-hand side, and, from the left-hand side, the letters RE followed by the initial vertical stroke of a subsequent character (Fig. 3:38). Unfortunately the letters from the name were omitted from the definitive reassembly of the plaster from this wall.

Fig. 3:38 Fragment of *titulus* [ie]RE[mias] accompanying Prophet 7 (*JM*)

Among the names of the Prophets, this combination fits only Jeremiah (IEREMIAS). The third letter must, therefore, have been an M.

This identification is supported by the few surviving words from the text on the scroll (Figs 3:17, 3:39 and 3:40). All that was found of this were sequences of letters from two successive lines which appear to have read: ECCE DI[ES] V[E]NIVN[T...]. ('Behold, the days come ...'). This is a favourite phrase of Jeremiah, being used eight times as the opening phrase of a verse (9.25; 16.14; 19.6; 23.5; 31.27; 31.38; 33.14; 48.12). Elsewhere in the Old Testament it appears only three times (1 Samuel 2.31; Amos 8.11, 9.13). There can be little doubt that this figure did indeed represent the Prophet Jeremiah, and that the two surviving lines of script were the opening words on his scroll. The scroll seemed to have been coloured salmon-pink and streaked with a pale sky-blue. The first line of letters was red and the second was a colour which had faded to a pale pinkish purple.

Fig. 3:39 Scroll held by Prophet 7 (*JBB*)

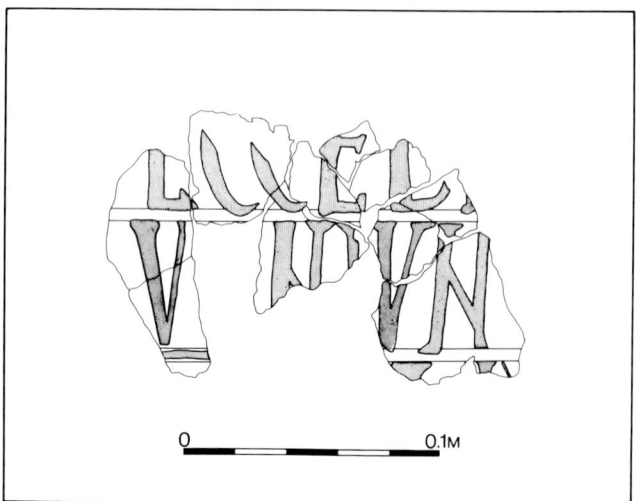

Fig. 3:40 Scroll held by Prophet 7 *(LW)*

Other elements from the west wall

Although so far it has not proved possible to reassemble the first two figures from the northern end of wall 452, numerous fragments of painted plaster excavated in this area testify to their existence. These included numerous fragments of a pearled upper border and of drapery, four adjoining pieces of a head (Plate 3:21) and many scraps of white *tituli* on bluish-lavender ground, all in the idiom of the Prophets. At least one of the figures at this end of wall 452 seems to have worn garments in which red, white and lavender predominated. In this it must have contrasted with its immediate neighbours to the south and have been in accord with the more distant Prophet 6 (Plate 3:18). To judge from the material excavated from these contexts, it would appear that there was a subtle but definite change in the way paint was applied between fragments recovered in areas 401 *C* and *B*. The application appears to have become stronger and more decisive at the northern end of the wall. On the plaster recovered from *B*, the area of red above the painted arch was distinctly richer in tonality than on plaster found in *C* and in the contexts further to the south, and the black lines defining this area were *c.* 4 mm wide and were very strong and black. More of this type of painting was retrieved from 358, in the area just in front of the doorway into the Vestibule.

Of the reassembled figures, only David, Jeremiah and Micah could be identified from their titles or from their scrolls. However, the presence of Isaiah seems to be indicated by a fragment of painted plaster with the letters AI in white against a bluish lavender ground, found in the middle of the room in 392. The A had a broken bar and the script was typical of that used for the titles of the Prophets. The combination of letters would fit none of the Prophets except for ISAIAS.

The most complete of all the reassembled scrolls also came from the northwest corner of the room (401 *A*), and must have been held by a Prophet who stood either at the northern end of the west wall (452), or possibly on the short northern wall (334) (Fig. 3:41; Plate 3:22). This was *c.* 0.465 m long and 0.235 m wide. It was clearly held up by a figure in colourful vestments, generally uniform with those worn by the Prophets on the west wall. Its left side lay against the curving edge of a brown cloak, strongly contoured in black and lighted with thin streaks of white. Below this was part of a lower white tunic, densely banded with vertical folds in lilac. Four long red parallel *clavi* ran down through this material, following the margin of the scroll. On the right, the scroll stood against an area of lilac faintly tinged with blue, which must have been the ground which encompassed the figure of the Prophet within his arch. The scroll carried eight lines of script, coloured alternately red and black, set against a salmon-pink ground; the whole was outlined in black, and shaded down the left side and at the bottom. The letters of the inscription varied in height between *c.* 38 and 52 mm, except for the final line in which they were only *c.* 29 mm tall. As usual, the characters stood between incised horizontal guide-lines. The text was a variant of the usual reading of a passage from Micah: *IN D[I]E ILLA DICIT D(omi)N(u)S CONGREGABO C[LA]V-DICANTEM ET EAM QVAM EIECERAM CON-GREGAB[O]* (Micah 4.6). The Vulgate reading is '*In die illa, dicit Dominus, congregabo claudicantem, et eam quam eieceram, colligam, et quam afflixeram*' ('In that day, saith the Lord, will I assemble her that halteth, and I will gather her that is driven out, and her that I have afflicted'). One might presume that the Prophet to whom this scroll belonged was Micah.

The only other scroll from this wall for which it has been possible to propose an identification, that held by the fourth figure, would appear to have carried a text from the same Prophet (Fig. 3:30; Plate 3:16). It is unusual for a prophet to be represented twice in a single scheme in the Middle Ages. However, it is not unknown, and a parallel case would seem to be the great twelfth-century ivory cross in the Cloisters Collection of the Metropolitan Museum in New York. On this Jeremiah is represented twice on the rear face and again on the front face, in each case holding a scroll bearing a text from his writings (Parker and Little 1994: fig. 12 and ill. 96). (St John, the author of the Apocalypse, similarly is shown twice on the rear face of the cross (Parker and Little 1994: fig. 10 and ill. 30).) In this case the repetition of the prophet was demanded by the programme of imagery, which required three texts from the one author. The rationale behind the repetition of Micah at San Vincenzo may have been a similar one.

The two texts which can be identified suggest that

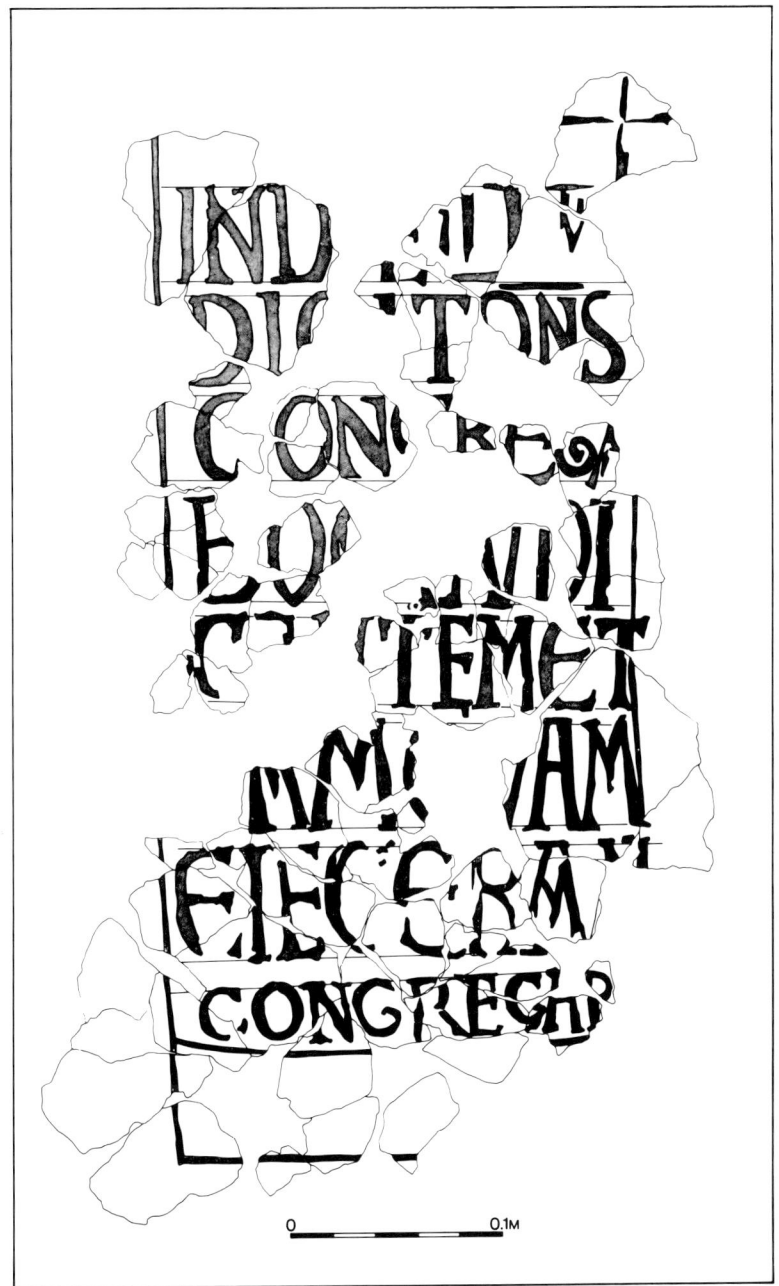

Fig. 3:41 Scroll held by a Prophet from the northwest corner of the Assembly Room *(KF)*

the passages displayed on the scrolls held out by the Prophets in the Assembly Room may have been selected with the function of the room in mind. To judge from its location, from the benches round its walls and from its size, this was a place where the monks could come together before processing into the Refectory to eat. The theme of the text on the scroll from the northern end of the room is the assembly and gathering together of the weak and persecuted, while that of the text displayed by the fourth Prophet ('Feed thy people with thy rod, the flock of thine heritage, which dwell solitarily in the wood, in the midst of Carmel: let them feed in Bashan and Gilead, as in the days of old' (Micah 7.14)) is God's feeding of his chosen people, dwellers in a harsh silvan wilderness. Both would appear to have been appropriate to the ante-room to the Refectory of a monastery whose foundation legend had it that, when its first monks came to the area, the Upper Volturno valley was a desolate and dangerous region of thick forests, the haunts of wild beasts and of thieves (*CV* i: 111. See also Chapter 12).

The east walls – the Apostles

The scheme of painting on the east walls of the Assembly Room is likely to have been even finer than the scheme described above. However, the almost complete demolition of these walls (to a level of 0.6 m) means that very little painted plaster survived to help us reconstruct the design.

Layer 401 contained much lower concentrations of painted plaster in the central and eastern parts of the room. Too little was preserved for it to be possible to reassemble any coherent passages from the northern or eastern walls. However, the decoration of the benches and the dados showed that these walls were once painted in a similar fashion to the reconstructed western wall, and the more careful and more varied scheme of decoration deployed on the benches and dado on the eastern side of the room (see above) indicated that the eastern walls (348/411 and 457) were singled out for particular emphasis. The reason for this is almost certainly the fact that the main doorway into the Refectory passed through this wall. Given that one of the principal functions of the Assembly Room must have been to serve as an ante-room to the Refectory, where the monks could assemble before going in to dine, the main focus in the Assembly Room would have been this doorway into the Refectory. The wall surfaces flanking the opening were given a particularly elaborate scheme of decoration in accordance with the almost universal practice of signifying passage from a space of lesser importance to one of greater significance by ornamenting the outer face of the opening which leads from the one to the other (Fernie 1983: 141-3, 148). It follows that the Prophets were probably subordinate to the principal scheme on the east wall of the room.

The subject of this principal scheme can be identified from a fragmentary painted inscription found near the northern end of the wall in layer 401 (Fig. 3:42). The letters of this inscription were white capitals, *c.* 55 mm tall, set against a lilac ground. This ground was bordered on the right by a convex curving line. In design, in the *ductus* of the script and in colour, this fragment was uniform with the identifying *tituli* which flanked the heads of the Prophets on the opposite wall. The only difference is that in this case the painter had scored guide-lines at the heads and feet of the letters to define the lines of script. The surviving letters were: ...HILIP/P... The word is broken after the first P, and continued at a lower level, with the second P set beneath the first I. The full word can only have been PHILIPPVS. This name, together with the accompanying title APOS-TOLVS, like the names of the Prophets opposite, must have flanked the head of a standing figure.

Fragments of figures with large brown-red haloes and dressed in garments in the same range of colours used for the Prophets were recovered from contexts close to the foot of the northern section of the eastern wall of the room (wall 348/411, in contexts 343, 350 and 409). Other related fragments were found at the western end of the north aisle of the adjoining Refectory, into which the Apostle wall had collapsed (in context 409; see Chapter 4, p. 74). Many of these bits of drapery were coloured a pale salmon-pink articulated with bands of deep brown-red, and

Fig. 3:42 Fragment of the *titulus* of the Apostle Philip from wall 348/411 *(JM)*

with prominent red *clavi* and other marks in white and red. An assemblage of three adjoining fragments from 343 showed the shoulder of a figure, with three red *clavi* running down over a lilac tunic articulated with black and the occasional streak of white. The head of the figure was set against a lavender ground, while the body was surrounded by a somewhat more purplish variant of the same colour, the two zones being divided by a faint horizontal red line. A *titulus* in white characters flanked the head. The scheme was clearly very similar in design and colour to that of the Prophet-arcade opposite; yet the painting was rather flatter than that of the Prophets. This was most obvious in the heavy black contour of the shoulder and in the hard flat *clavi* which ran down over the breast. Fragments of backgrounds from this area were mostly in various tones of lavender and there were some other very abraded fragments of white letters from *tituli* of the type which flanked the heads of the Prophets.

It is fairly certain, therefore, that the Apostles, painted in the same idiom as the Prophets, were presented on the east wall of the room, beneath an arcade similar to the one on the facing wall. Presumably the twelve figures were arranged symmetrically on either side of the doorway into the Refectory.

Other elements of painted decoration

Although it did not prove possible to reconstruct more of the decorative scheme of the room, various other elements were reassembled from fragments recovered from 401 and other related contexts.

A large number of fragments of drapery, with folds indicated in deep grey-blue, light grey-blue, cream, yellow and white, with strokes of red indicating *clavi*, was found at the northern end of the room in 401 and in other related contexts (for example, 396). From this material it was possible to reassemble an area measuring *c*. 0.33 x 0.355 m which showed the torso of a figure with his right arm bent across his chest (Plate 3:23). Sharply defined bands and daggers of dark and pale grey-blue defined a scheme of folds against the yellow material of his tunic. The deep grey-blue folds tended to be contoured with white and the prominent clavate bands on the shoulder and on the sleeve were ornamented with trails of white dots. The flesh of the man's bent arm was painted yellow and was highlighted with white. Its upper contour was defined in red, while the lower edge was shaded in greyish green. To judge from the area in which the majority of this plaster was found, it seems likely that it originally formed part of a standing figure on the short north wall of the room. However, in style, in the relatively fussy precision with which the fold lines were arrayed and delineated and in the colours employed, this work has certain affinities with the phase 5 paintings in the crypt of Epyphanius at the northern end of the site, which date from the 830s (see Volume 1, chapters 6 and 7). If this plaster really did come from the northern wall of the Assembly Room, it must have been the work of an artist whose work anticipated the developed version of the idiom employed on the Prophet wall, which was to be practised at San Vincenzo in the following generation.

A well-preserved lower leg and foot in profile was found in the same area (401 *A*) and must also have come from a large standing figure from this end of the room (Fig. 3:43). The leg protruded some 0.17 m from the lower hem of the individual's garment and the foot was *c*. 0.18 m long. In colour, leg and foot were a pale salmon-pink, with a prominent white light running down both of them. Black sandal-straps crossed the foot. The garment above was also a salmon-pink, with vertical folds in brownish red. The ground around the leg was a rich red-brown, the same colour as that used for the haloes of the Prophets on the west wall.

Other sections of draped figures were assembled from fragments found at the foot of the north wall of the room (wall 334, in contexts 343 and 344, with one stray fragment found in 401 *F*). The principle piece was of an area *c*. 0.36 m by 0.13 m, with dark brown bands, apparently representing folds on a dark grey-blue ground, flanked by areas of yellow which were articulated with brownish yellow and pale ochre folds, one of which was doubled with black (Plate 3:24). The yellow areas were set with rectangular jewel-settings with red and yellow

Fig. 3:43 Foot of a large standing figure, from the northern end of the Assembly Room *(JM)*

stones framed in brown. At one point a thin red line defined the contour of an unidentifiable feature. The background to this configuration was a deep blue-grey. This may have been the remains of a man splendidly dressed in a jewelled yellow cloak falling over a dark undergarment. The design and the combination of colours used recall the paintings in the crypt of Abbot Epyphanius, of the 830s, although the brush strokes which defined the various elements were not so tight and fussy as they were there (Pantoni 1970: ills 59 and 62; Volume 1, pls 7:2 and 7:4). Another section of drapery from this context which looked forward to the work in the crypt was a light sandy brown with an overlay of cream and light ochre lines, some of which followed a zigzagging course. This was articulated by black lines and small areas of dull red.

Another assemblage from 344 showed the shoulder of a figure together with a section of his head. This was framed by a square halo, usually the mark of a portrait of a living individual. The garment worn by the figure was brown, contoured with black and with an ornamental overlay of ochre lozenges. The face was a pale ochre and the hair brown with dull yellow striations. The square halo was a dark slate-grey-blue, just like the ones in Epyphanius's crypt, and the background against which the figure stood was a dull salmon-pink.

Much of the head of a frontally-facing man was assembled from six joining fragments retrieved from 401 at the northern end of the room (Plate 3:25).

Although of similar size to the heads of the Prophets and related in style, in colouring and in execution it was different. The base colour of the face was yellow, with prominent curling shaded areas beneath the eyes and a straight band of shadow down the nose in a pale olive-green. White was employed to highlight the brow, nose and the pupil of the eye. The pupil itself was a yellowish brown. Thin red contours defined the surviving upper eyelid and the lower part of the nose, and a touch of red brightened the eye. The hair was light brown with dull ochre striations and a scalloped fringe was thickly contoured in black. The surviving area measured 0.125 m x 85 mm. It is possible that this was the head of a figure from the short north wall of the room; but in its colours and in its form, it was strikingly reminiscent of various heads by one of the hands responsible for the painting in the crypt of Abbot Epyphanius (Pantoni 1970: ills 53-6).

Another fragmentary head found in 401 was very like the head of the beardless saint from the short north wall of the Vestibule, which was put together from fragments recovered from 359 (Plate 3:26 and Plate 1:3). The face was a yellowish cream. White strokes modelled the cheeks and lit the mouth, and small white rays issued from the corner of the remaining eye. The eyelids were delineated in red, the eyebrows in black and a prominent yoke of white ran over the brow. The scalloped cap of hair was a dull ochre with striations in light brown. The head was strongly contoured in black and stood against a deep grey-blue background. It may have been accompanied by an inscription in white characters on the same deep grey-blue ground. As has just been said, this head and the one of the saint from the north wall of the Vestibule were very similar in type. Both were oviform and both were clean-shaven, with the hair cut to a scalloped fringe over the brow. The same conventions were used for the eyebrows, the eyelids and the mouth. However, although typologically alike, the two differed in execution. The head from 401 was far flatter and more linear in appearance than the one from the Vestibule. This was most apparent in the continuous black line which outlined the face and in the peculiar rectangular configuration used for the mouth. As far as one can tell, the two heads must have had roughly the same dimensions and it seems possible that they formed part of the same scheme of decoration. These fragments, found in the northern end of the Assembly Room, may have been translocated to the south after they had fallen from their original position on one of the walls of the Vestibule.

Two joining fragments from 401, at the northern end of the room, showed part of the body of a man. He appeared to turn half to the right and wore what may have been a short tunic in pale sky-blue which was contoured and articulated in various shades of blue-grey (Plate 3:27). This was a small figure compared to the Prophets. The head of a young man, also turning to the right, resulted from the joining of two fragments, one from 401 and the other from 396 (Plate 3:28). This also belonged to a figure of moderate size: the measurement from crown to chin must have been originally something in the order of 0.12-0.13 m. The ground colour of the face was a pale ochre, with soft greyish green shading around the eyes and on the nose. The eyes were delineated in black, with a touch of red, and the pupils were a deep ochre. The hair was a light yellowish brown and was strongly outlined in black. The head was set against a strong ochre ground. The fragment measured 0.12 x 0.105 m. In style this had various mannerisms in common with the work of one of the artists who painted the walls of the crypt of Abbot Epyphanius in the 830s (Belting 1968: pl. XXX, ill. 59; Pantoni 1970: ills 53-6).

Fragments of a fluted column, outlined in red and set against a salmon-pink ground, were found in 344 (Plate 3:29). The fluting was in dull-green and brown. From the top of the column the flutes spiralled across the column, before changing to a vertical alignment. This column may have supported a blue capital. Other fragments of a spirally fluted column of exactly the same design and colours were recovered from 344. A fragment of a projecting corner with what may have been the remains of a red and white fluted column painted on one face was found at the northern end of the Assembly Room in 401 *A*. There is a possibility that these spirally fluted columns formed major visual accents at the corners of the room.

Further fragments which may possibly have derived from the painted decoration of this room were discovered in the Refectory and are discussed below (pp. 73-4).

Discussion

The original scheme of decoration in the room thus consisted of sequences of standing figures beneath running arcades. The principal focus of the pro- gramme was on the west wall, where the Apostles, possibly grouped about the figure of Christ, flanked the main entrance into the Refectory. The eye of an observer must have been drawn immediately to this wall by the more brightly coloured and varied nature of the decorative elements, still discernible in the decoration of the benches and dados. The Apostles were faced by the Prophets. The Prophets, and presumably the Apostles also, held large scrolls displaying texts, which, to judge from the two identifiable examples, appear to have commented on the function of the room in the life of the community. There may have been other categories of figures on the two end walls of the room. The enclosing arches were brightly coloured and were set within framing horizontal bands ornamented with fictive white pearls and gemstones. Below, a dado painted in imitation of a revetment of panels of diagonally-veined marble ran round the room, broken and enriched on the east Refectory wall by sections imitating marble *opus sectile* and an imbricated scheme of particoloured overlapping semi-circular tiles. The benches, under the dado, were ornamented with a design of interrelating coloured triangles, which similarly was interrupted in the central section of the east wall by the more striking pattern of particoloured tiles.

The stylistic affiliations of these paintings, their formal iconography and their place and role in the visual articulation of the monastery will be discussed in Volume 3. The implications of the large scrolls held up by the Prophets have been addressed in two preliminary studies (Mitchell 1990; 1994) and will again be the subject of discussion in Volume 3.

The date and artistic context of the painted decoration of the Assembly Room

Two categories of evidence can be drawn on for dating the scheme of decoration on the walls of the Assembly Room. The first of these concerns their architectural context; the second concerns the painted surfaces themselves and involves their style and composition.

The walls of the Assembly Room, which constitute the setting and the support for the paintings, are associated with phase 4 at San Vincenzo. This phase corresponds to a period of construction during which the small early eighth-century monastery was completely transformed, in which some of its principal structures, including the abbey-church of San Vincenzo itself, were re-sited, and in which the area covered by the monastic buildings was expanded by something approaching a factor of ten (see Table 0:1; and Volume 1: 32).

A number of converging indices help to establish an absolute date for this phase. These indices include:

(1) the fire of 881;
(2) the phasing as indicated by the archaeological stratigraphy;
(3) the painting of the crypt of Epyphanius;
(4) the tiles;
(5) the style of the paintings.

The fire of 881

There was plentiful material evidence of a great fire which brought down the roof of the Assembly Room and scorched its painted walls at some points. This fire was part of an extensive conflagration which left unmistakable traces in most parts of the monastery and which must have effectively destroyed the majority of its buildings. The stratigraphy of the associated burning level and the presence of many heavy arrowheads suggest that this fire should be identified with the conflagration which consumed the greater part of the monastic complex during its

sack by the Emir of Bari, Sawdan, and his Saracen war-band, in October 881. If the identification of this fire is correct, it follows that the Assembly Room and its paintings must date from before the Saracen attack of 881.

Phasing

The stratigraphic relationship of phase 4 to the preceding phases of the eighth-century monastery makes a dating much before 800 out of the question. The sequence of building-phases which have been identified as lying between the foundation of San Vincenzo and its comprehensive replanning and expansion cannot all be crowded into a few decades. Phase 4 must be assigned, at the earliest, to the last years of the eighth century, and more probably to the first two decades of the ninth. We have associated this phase with the abbacy of Joshua (792-817) (cf. Volume 1: 32), and the dedication of Joshua's new church is recorded as having taken place in 808 (*CV* i: 221). Consequently, it would seem likely that the construction and decoration of the Assembly Room and the rest of the phase 4 ranges at the monastery occurred in the first or second decade of the ninth century.

The painting in the crypt of Epyphanius

A third index is provided by the relationship between the phase 4 buildings associated with the Assembly Room, on the one hand, and, on the other, the construction and decoration of the crypt of the Crypt Church. It has already been argued that the Crypt Church post-dates the building phase associated with the Assembly Room (phase 4), and the former has been assigned to the subsequent phase – phase 5a (see Volume 1, chapter 6). Consequently the construction and the painted decoration of the Assembly Room must be earlier than the phase 5a painted crypt. The earliest possible date for the crypt is the mid-820s, and it may well not have been constructed until a decade later.

The tiles

A fourth index is the inscribed tiles with which the phase 4 floors were paved and the phase 4 roofs were clad. As is observed in Volume 3, the only real parallels for these are some very similar inscribed tiles from Monte Cassino which are firmly associated with the abbacy of Theodemar (778-97) and possibly also with his successor Gisulf (797-817) (Mitchell 1990: 201-3; 1994: 901-3). To judge from this comparison, the most likely date for this quite exceptional production of tiles at San Vincenzo would be the last quarter of the eighth century or the first quarter of the ninth, the period of the construction phase 4. The decorative patterns scratched onto some of the tiles, those involving undulating and zigzag squiggles which are clearly derived from the diagonally-veined panels of marbling first introduced at San Vincenzo on the phase 4 painted walls, not only confirm that tiles and painted dados belong to one and the same coherent scheme of decoration, but also suggest that when the tilers made these tiles they were already acquainted with the decorative scheme devised by the painters for the dados of the newly-constructed ranges of rooms and halls.

The style of the paintings

The style of the paintings in the Assembly Room and the pictorial formulae employed also fit most happily into the context of painting of the late eighth and the early ninth centuries in the Lombard areas in northern and southern Italy. The artistic context of the paintings is discussed in Volume 3.

DISCUSSION

The function of the Assembly Room in phases 4 and 5 remains a matter of speculation. It appears to have formed the northern part of the Lower Thoroughfare. The room was provided with painted benches and was elaborately decorated, yet it had a utilitarian as opposed to an elegant, ornamental pavement (Fig. 3:1). It is likely that the wall with the finest paintings was that on the eastern side of the room, flanking the doorway into the proposed Refectory. The assembled monks would have focused in this direction as they prepared to enter the dining hall. The west wall, by contrast, would have been at their backs as they entered the Refectory, though facing them as they took their leave after dining. The west wall shows that the room was decorated with a major programme of paintings (see Fig. 3:16; Plate 3:8). The striking line of Prophets, each holding a scroll, suggests that this room served as more than a passageway. The programme of fine painting on the north wall in the phase 5 refurbishment of the Vestibule further emphasizes this point.

It is tempting to think that this long hall, its walls ringed with benches, may have been designed as a chapter house. However, various considerations make this most unlikely. Firstly, the location of the room makes this improbable. It would be most unusual for a chapter house to lead directly into the main Refectory of a monastery. Secondly, the dimensions and design of the room suggest it was meant to accommodate only a portion of the full monastic community. A chapter house has to accommodate all of the regular members of a monastic community in assembly at chapter. To judge both from the size of the Refectory and from the account of the Saracen sack of 881, given in the *Chronicon Vulturnense*, it seems that the community at San Vincenzo consisted of several hundred monks in the ninth century. Nothing approaching this number could have been seated in the Assembly Room. Thirdly, it is by no means certain that purpose-built chapter houses were regular features of monasteries in the early ninth century (cf. Horn and Born 1979: vol. 2, 336; Zettler 1990: 678-9). The walks of the cloister (see below, p. 78) or the warming-room were spaces which could be used for this purpose. It seems most likely that this room served as an informal meeting place where some of the monks could gather before and after dining, benches being provided for the many aged and infirm members of the community. The two decipherable inscriptions held by the Prophets allude to assembly and feeding, themes which would be most appropriate for the area in which the brothers met before going in to eat. Thus we may suppose that this room was one of the most familiar to the community of monks, and for this reason its programme of paintings would have had considerable significance.

Chapter Four

THE REFECTORY

by Richard Hodges, Catherine M. Coutts, Sheila Gibson and John Mitchell,
with a contribution by Andrew Hanasz and Ian Riddler

INTRODUCTION

In 1980-82 a terrace wall running north-south crossed the centre of the site of the Refectory, creating a difference in height of about 2.0 m between Terrace 1 and the fields beside the river (Volume 1: 15-17; fig. 3:5). In 1982 the stratigraphy of this terrace was first examined in Trench D. In this excavation the stratigraphy was deep and well-preserved. By contrast, the exploratory trenches (X, Y, Z) (Fig. 4:1) within the low-lying riverside field to the east of Terrace 1 – designed to examine the character of the tile scatter covering these fields – revealed a shallow stratigraphy in which the upper-most early medieval levels had been destroyed by ploughing. In 1982 Trench D was first excavated by hand under the supervision of Nigel Baker, and then extended with a mechanical excavator. Trenches X, Y and Z were excavated by hand. The trenches were then merged (as Trench X) and enlarged with a bulldozer: excavations of Trenches X, Y and Z were supervised by Cameron Moffett. In 1982, because of the pronounced difference of level between the western and eastern trenches, it was difficult to relate the two, separated excavations. In 1983 the excavation of the western area of the room was enlarged. During this season the base of a decorated pulpit (509) was discovered in the southwest corner of the room: this indicated that this building might have been the ninth-century Refectory, forming one side of a rectangular- (or square-) shaped cloister. These excavations were supervised by John Clipson. In 1984 the *Soprintendenza Archeologica* excavated six test-pits (X1-X6) of which three (X1-X3) lay in the Refectory area (X4-X6 being within the Distinguished Guests' Refectory and Garden Court). (The test-pits are not discussed further in this report, but the documentation can be found in the archive.) The *Soprintendenza* then invited us to uncover the entire Refectory (Fig. 4:2). This led to the two excavation areas (D and X) being merged. The enlargement of the trench to encompass the entire building was undertaken by Italian workers and by archaeologists, supervised by Catherine M. Coutts and Ian Riddler. At this stage a small cutting was made to the south of the Refectory to investigate what lay alongside this building. The detail of the results consequently differs as the strategy developed year by year. The

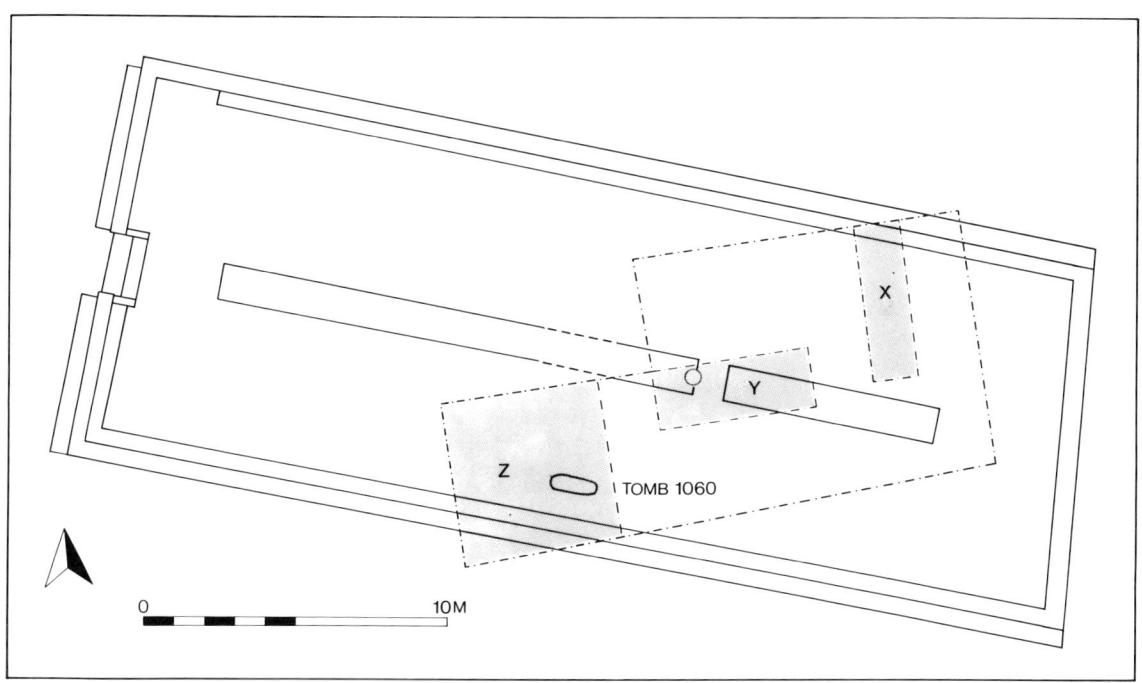

Fig. 4:1 Plan showing the positions of trial trenches X, Y and Z, and Tomb 1060 *(LW)*

65

TABLE 4:1 Summary of the main phases in the Refectory	
3c	The outline of a building 11.6 m wide and 21 m long was suggested by the profile of the phase 4 floor, as well as by walls observed in the pipe-trench cutting this area.
4	The Refectory consisted of a building 12.5 m wide and 31.7 m long. The floor was tiled. The remains of a small pulpit were discovered in the southwestern corner.
5a-b	An annexe was added to the east (riverside) end of the building.
5c	The building was destroyed in a fierce conflagration.
6a	Traces were found of some kind of occupation in the northwestern corner of the building. Tomb 543 was cut into the north bench of the ruinous Refectory.
6b	This building was systematically demolished.
7	A mortar surface covered parts of the western end of the building.
Modern	The area was made into two fields, separated by a terrace wall. A shallow tomb, containing the skeleton of a woman, was found in the topsoil of the lower (riverside) field.

tips in the Refectory in Trench X, like the deep tips in the Assembly Room, only merited detailed attention in the first stage of the operations. To have continued a detailed, stratigraphic excavation would have meant sacrificing work elsewhere. The second stage, therefore, involved clearance excavation in order to reveal the whole building. Much of this proceeded at speed and in far from satisfactory conditions (cf. Volume 1: 30). A summary of the main phases in this area is given in Table 4:1.

PHASE 3c(?)

The pipe-trench (386) running across the southwest sector of the building provided us with a glimpse of the stratigraphy pre-dating the phase 4 building (Fig. 4:3). The trench appeared to have sliced through the southwest corner of a building, revealing the levelled remains of one wall on a north-south alignment, and of one on an east-west alignment (Fig. 4:4). These remains probably belonged to a phase 3c building, but might be all that remained of an even earlier, late Roman range in this area. The wall on the north-south alignment would appear to have been an extension of wall 468, the phase 3c wall which later formed the west side of the Entrance Hall. This wall was termed 468 south extension. The east-west wall appears to have been the south wall of the building which could be traced in the uneven pavement of the phase 4 Refectory. This wall (368a) ran along a line 2.0 m north of the phase 4 south wall (502/561/1072) of the Refectory, to a point 5.0 m from the east wall of the phase 4 Refectory. At this point it turned to the north. In Figure 4:4 this eastern wall is shown as continuing to join a putative north wall which, it is proposed, was on exactly the same alignment as the phase 4 north wall of the Refectory, thus accounting for the 0.4 m difference in level between the Garden Court (to the north) and the floor of the phase 4 Refectory. This difference indicates that a deep deposit existed within this area, arising from repeated rebuilding on the same spot (as in the 'South Church'). It is proposed, therefore, that the phase 3c precursor of the Refectory was a substantial building approximately 11.6 m wide and 21 m long.

The pipe-trench sections (Fig. 4:3) showed that the west and south walls of this building were levelled when the phase 4 Refectory was built, and

Fig. 4:2 The Refectory after excavation, looking westward *(RH)*

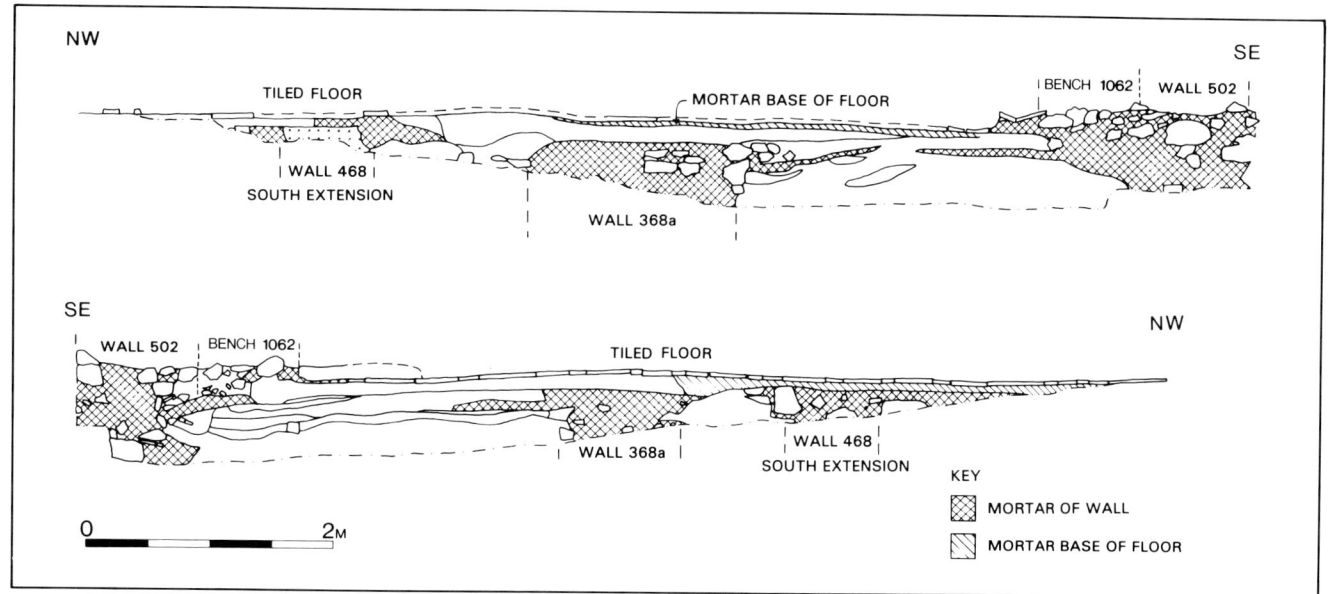

Fig. 4:3 Pipe-trench sections *(LW)*

the areas beside were filled with a series of tips. They also revealed the shallow footings of wall 502/561/1072, the south wall of the phase 4 Refectory, which was constructed directly on top of these tips.

PHASE 4 (FIG. 4:5)

A new building was constructed in phase 4, which appears to have been typical of the workmanship of this period. The pulpit (509) discovered in the southwest corner of the room indicates, for reasons which will be described in more detail below, that

this was the monks' Refectory and, therefore, in all likelihood, the north side of the monastic cloister.

General features

The building was built on a slope, with a difference of 0.8 m between the west and east ends. It was not quite a rectangle, being 30.4 m long on its north side and 31.7 m on the south; it was 12.5 m wide (all internal measurements). It seems that there was only one major doorway into the Refectory, situated at the west end. The spine began about 4.0 m in

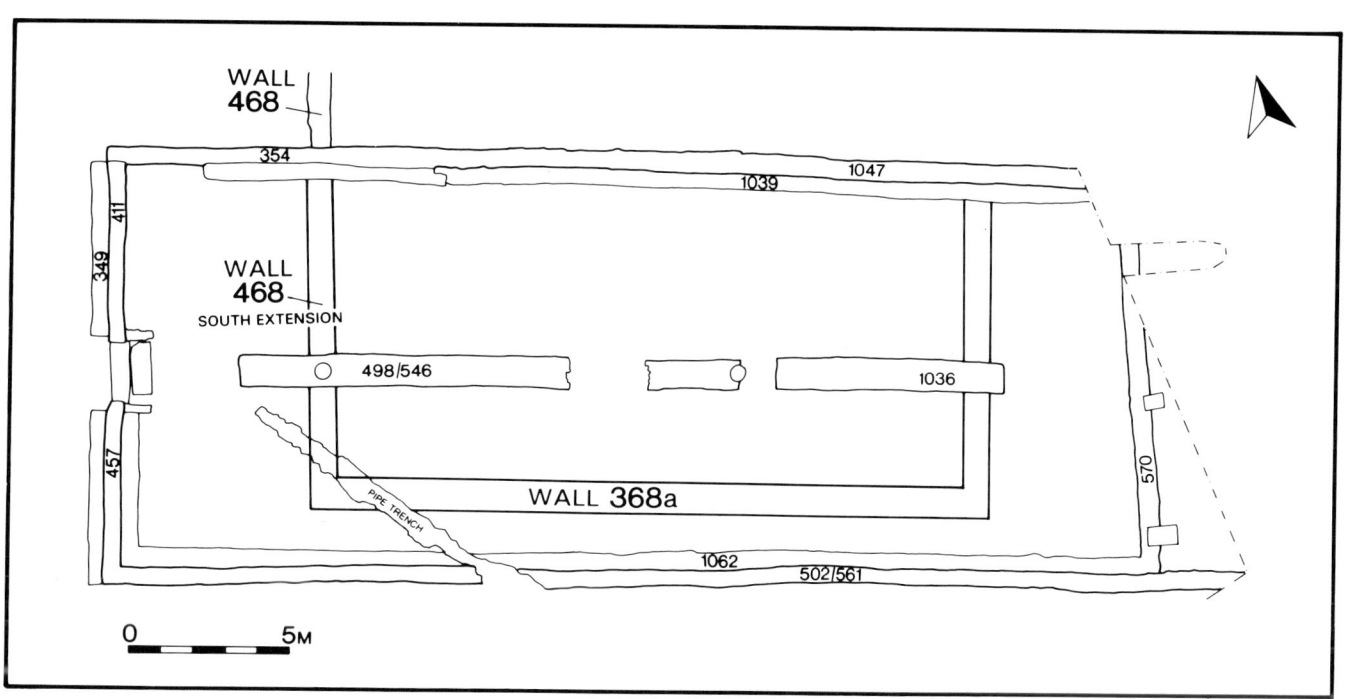

Fig. 4:4 Plan showing the proposed phase 3 Refectory in relation to the phase 4 Refectory *(KF)*

from the west and east ends; a 'doorway' was apparently cut through it about two-thirds along its length (towards the eastern end). Columns placed on a central spine provided additional support for the roof. Benches, in some cases with footrests, were sited along the south and north walls and along the southern part of the west wall, but not the east wall. The central spine provided further benching. The pulpit lay immediately to the south of the doorway, tucked in the southwest corner. In the opposite corner was a blank space that may have been the location of a cupboard for items such as eating utensils. The floor was paved with tiles. Of the many tiles found in the excavations, 429 (c. 36 per cent) had some form of inscription or decoration. The room was painted, but in the fire which destroyed the building all the plaster was badly scorched. From the excavations of the Garden Court, we estimated that there were between thirteen and fifteen glazed windows along the north of the building, and probably the same number on the south side. The thick deposit of ash indicates that the roof was made of timber, supporting thatch. The roof timbers, to judge from the nails found in the destruction level, were about 0.12-0.15 m in thickness. The structure as a whole, however, was not entirely sound: buttresses to provide additional support were bonded into the north and east walls.

Walls

The walls of the Refectory were about 0.6 m wide, roughly constructed of small stones, as well as a little broken tile, and bonded by hard, yellow mortar. The height of the walls at excavation varied. The north wall (354) survived to a height of about 0.6-0.7 m, and may in part have contained two or more phases of construction. The evidence for this is as follows.

(1) The north wall (354) appeared to have very deep footings while the south wall (502/561/1072), robbed to a point level with the tile floor (418) and consisting only of footings, did not.

(2) Buttress 8066, added to the north side of wall 354 and incorporated into a bench in the east portico of the Garden Court, was bonded at a point roughly level with the floor of the Refectory. The bottom courses of the north wall may have belonged to the preceding (phase 1-3) building, while the south wall was constructed in this period to replace an earlier wall (see above) a little to the north of it.

The west walls (348/411 and 457) survived to about 0.6 m above the tiled floor, and on each some badly scorched painted plaster survived. By contrast, the east wall (570) existed as little more than footings. This wall was also buttressed on the outside. Wall 570, in fact, is a little perplexing. It was bonded into bench 1062 (running alongside the south wall of the building), and so it is tempting to

interpret 570 as a continuation of the bench, in which case the east wall of the building was removed in phase 5 and lies beneath the phase 5 tiles of the extension. Traces of such a wall (571) were located in the 1984 excavations, immediately east of wall 570. This would mean that the two 'buttresses' inserted into 570 were in fact supports for the roof, similar to those found in the central spine. Only excavation below the floor-tiles of the extension would resolve this issue.

The doorway

There was only one major doorway into the room, that is on the west side, though there were traces of a narrow squint which pierced the east wall (570), opposite the remains of a possible stair (8048) discovered in the annexe to the east of 570. The remaining blocks of 8048 suggest that it was approximately on the same axis as the fine west doorway and the Refectory spine. Dating the squint doorway and possible stairway was not possible as 570 had been comprehensively robbed: however *if* the annexe was a phase 5 addition then it follows that these features must have belonged to phase 5. The main doorway in the west wall was monumental in its proportions. The doorway was 2.0 m wide and had a reused Roman threshold. Two side-arms to the bench, taken from an ornamented Roman structure (probably a tomb of 40-30 BC), flanked the steps from the doorway to the pavement of the Refectory (Fig. 4:6). It should be noted that the threshold was very similar, if rather larger than, the threshold into the Distinguished Guests' Refectory (8226) (Volume 1: 210-11).

The central spine

The central spine of the Refectory was in two parts; the west part (498/546) was a little over twice as long as the east part (1036) – 15.5 m as opposed to 7.1 m. On this stood a row of pillars which helped to support the timber roof. The exact number of supports can only be estimated (see Fig. 4:5) although the distance between the two most westerly extant pillars suggests that the long section of spine (498/546) supported seven pillars, and the shorter section (1036) three pillars. Some of the roof supports were of grey Egyptian granite and of cipollino, while others may have been of wood or brick. A large fragment of a granite column was found at the west terminal of the spine (in 482), as was a capital. A similar granite column, in poor condition, was found actually on the spine. At least one of the cipollino columns had split and shattered when the building was destroyed in the great fire of 881: fragmentary remains were found either side of the spine in 1982 in contexts 1048 and 1049. All of the granite-cipollino columns appear to have been removed from a classical building. Two holes cut

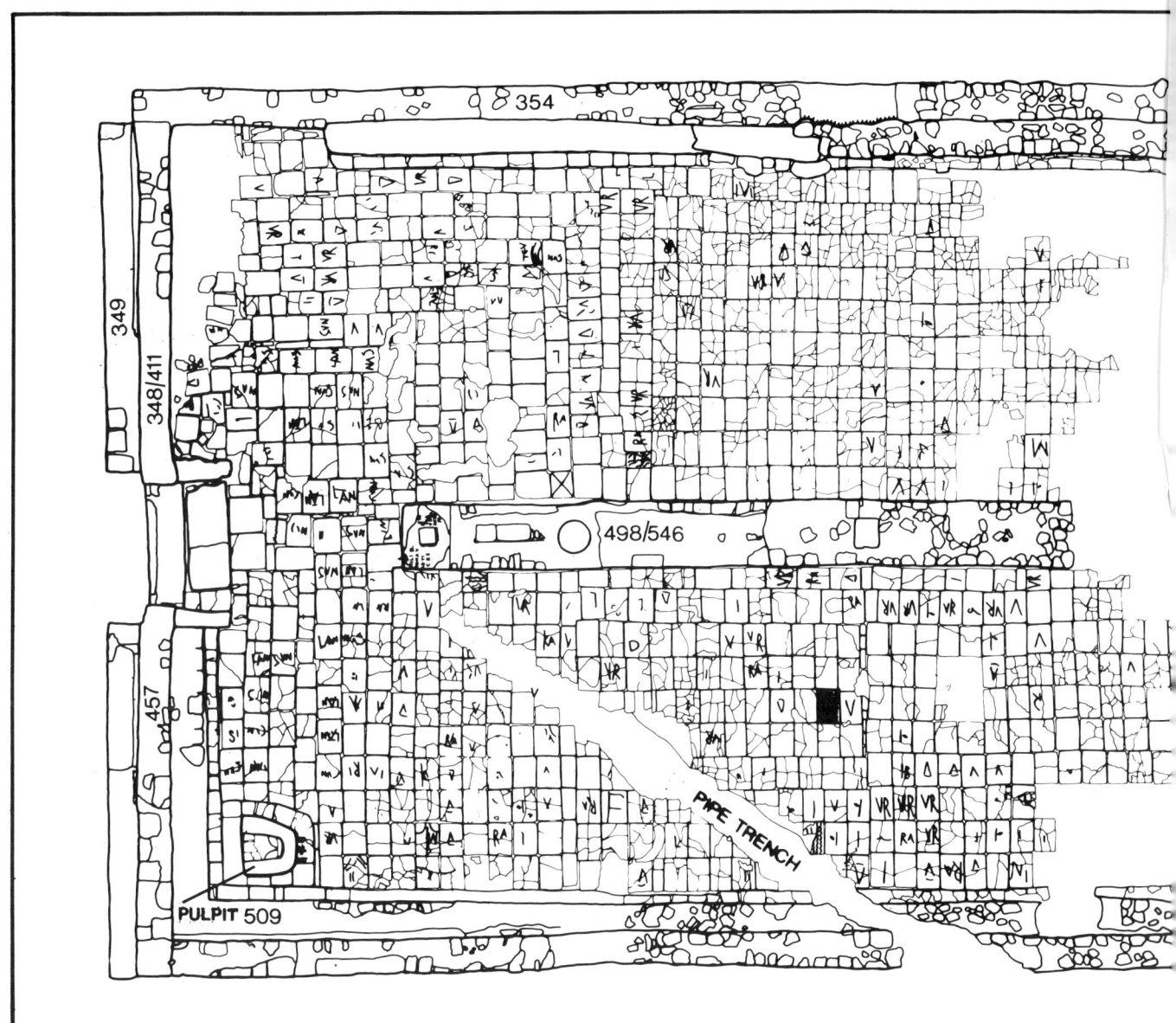

354

349

348/411

457

498/546

PULPIT 509

PIPE TRENCH

Fig. 4:5 Pla

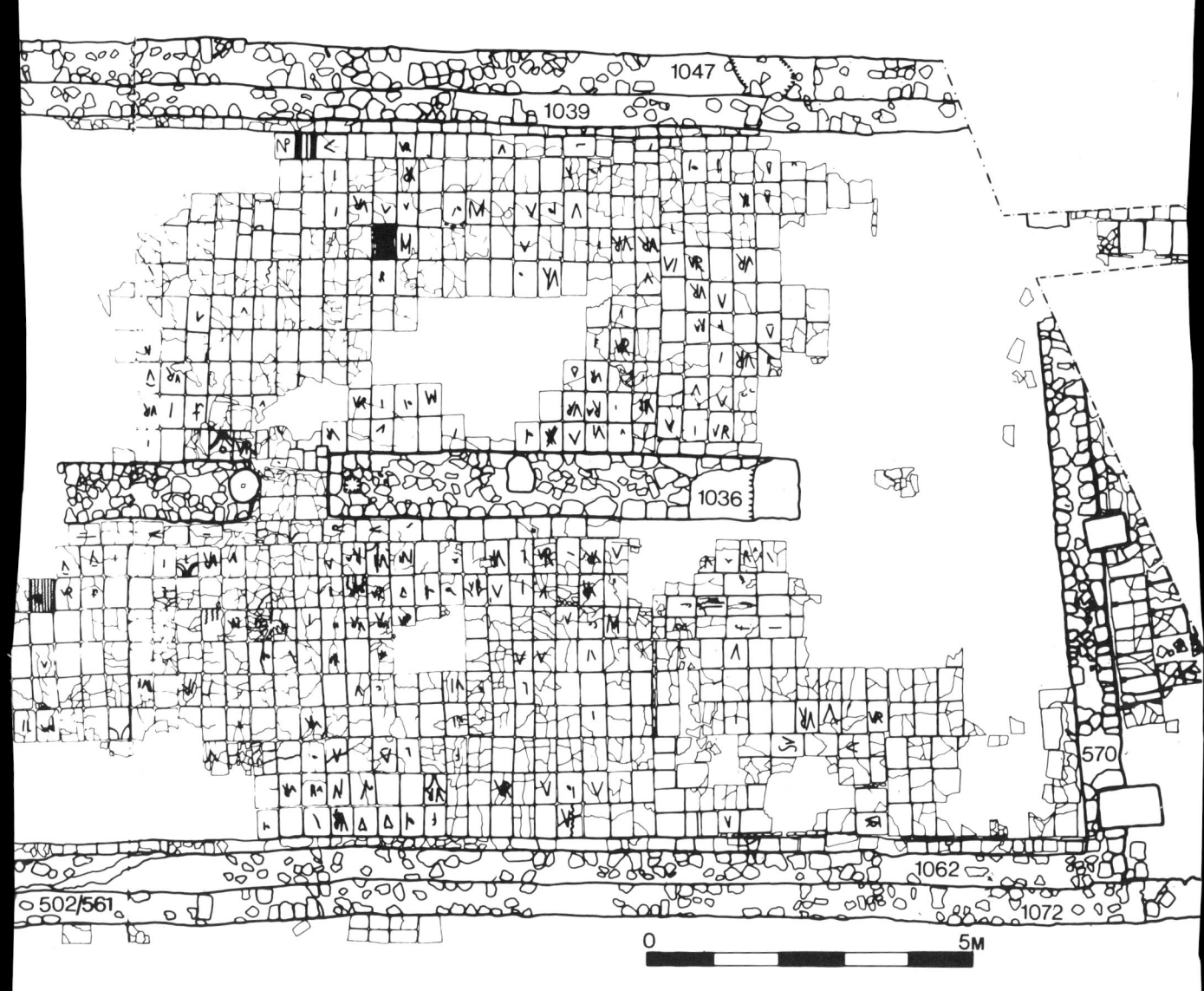

n of the Refectory showing the tiled floor *(CMC)*

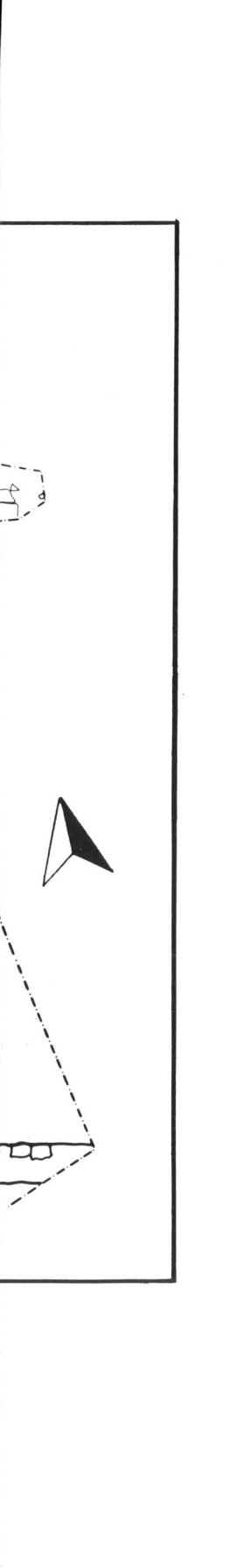

into the spine (8053 and 1055/8070), each roughly 0.2 m square, may have been cut to provide a base for roof supports, as must the square socket cut into the reused Roman inscription (see J. Patterson in Volume 3) employed as a terminal at the west end of the spine. A similar inscription may have once existed at the east end, given the hollow at the east terminus of the spine. Finally, the spine itself was used as a bench, the north and south sides being separated by a low central divide. Unlike the benches alongside the walls, these lacked footrests.

The benches

The benches formed an integral part of the north and south walls and of the southern half of the west wall. It is also possible that 'wall' 570 was in fact the remains of a bench that, before the addition of the phase 5 extension, ran alongside the eastern wall of the building. The room was designed, in other words, to have plenty of seating. The spine, which provided further benching, was also built at the same time. Most of the benches suffered badly in the fire. They rose to about 0.4 m above the floor level, slightly lower than those in the Assembly Room, and were about 0.45 m wide. They were roughly constructed of rubble, loosely bonded with mortar. Each bench top was plastered for wooden surfaces (of which fragments survived on bench 1039). In addition, a footrest ran along the front of the benches situated around the walls (Fig. 4:6). This was tidily made of tiles, cleanly chopped to fit. The footrest rose about 0.1-0.13 m above the tiled floor, and was about 0.2 m wide.

The benches were painted in a manner similar to those in the Assembly Room, but in all cases they had been scorched severely. Where the painted surface was preserved on the benches against both the northern and southern walls, the design was that of composite coloured triangles which was employed on the benches in the Assembly Room (Plate 3:4; cf. below, Fig. 4:8). The scorched colours of the triangles were orange-red, black, and an uncertain lighter colour, perhaps white. The forms were outlined with prominent white contours. A 30 mm band, burnt to a white colour, ran along the top of the south bench over the triangular configurations. In addition, on the south bench the vertical axes in the design had been faintly snapped into the wet plaster.

One well-preserved fragment from a scheme of particoloured tiles, like that used on the eastern benches in the Assembly Room, was found in 407, in the western part of the Refectory. This may have derived from the Assembly Room, but it is also possible that it could have come from a bench in the Refectory intended for prominent members of the community or for distinguished guests.

The pulpit or lectern (Figs 4:6-13)

The pulpit (509) was discovered in the southwest corner of the room. It had been constructed upon a small podium, about 0.1 m high, which raised it above the level of the tiled floor. This was built after the benches and their footrests had been added to walls 457 and 502/561/1072 in this corner. The podium neatly joined the footrests and was level

Fig. 4:6 The doorway from the Assembly Room to the Refectory, showing also the pulpit and the bench and footrest against wall 457 *(RH)*

Fig. 4:7 The pulpit, from the west *(RH)*

with them. It had a tiled surface, and the tile set in front, on the central axis, was particularly elaborate, with a large five-pointed star, which had been drawn into the leather hard fabric with a compass, framed by undulating lines (Fig. 4:9). The pulpit was constructed of tiles and mortar, and its exterior surfaces were plastered and painted. In form it followed the pattern of late Antique pulpits known from the eastern Mediterranean: a rounded front, gently bowed sides, and a straight back; and in its original state, it must have risen to a peak at the fore edge, and sloped down to the rear. Its width was

somewhat greater than its length, *c.* 1.0 x 0.94 m, and the interior space for the reader measured 0.4 m from side to side and 0.61 m from front to back (Fig. 4:10). It was entered from the rear, and the reader's platform was paved with a phase 4 inscribed tile, measuring 0.55 x 0.4 m, of fabric A (see Volume 3). When excavated, the sides of the pulpit had been cut down to the height of the demolished Refectory walls either side of it, so that little remained above the level of the platform.

The exterior surfaces of the pulpit were decorated with a striking scheme of painted marble revetment,

Fig. 4:8 The pulpit, from the east *(RH)*

Fig. 4:9 Tile set in front of the pulpit *(JM)*

consisting of broad and narrow undulating red veins framing prominent hollow ring-discs (Figs 4:11-13). The curving front face carried a large disc with an outer radius of 0.102 m and an inner radius of 71 mm, set within veins of marbling which sloped down from either side to meet and form chevrons on the central vertical axis of the pulpit. The action of the intense fire which consumed the Refectory had reduced the original colour of the ring of the hollow disc to white, and the veins of marbling had been burnt to a deep red. A very similar configuration of hollow ring-disc set within chevrons of veined marbling was found on the south side of the pulpit which faced the adjacent south wall of the building. The ring-disc on this side had an outer radius of 0.111 m and an inner radius of 81 mm. The northern face seems to have carried a similar scheme. However, on this side, which would have been the side most visible to the company seated in the two parts of the Refectory, the design had been curtailed somewhat (in comparison to the southern side) and shifted to the west, to make room for a prominent vertical panel on the northeast corner of the pulpit, in effect the most prominent surface of all (Fig. 4:11). This was a tall rectangle enclosing a drawn-out lozenge, which, in turn, contained a

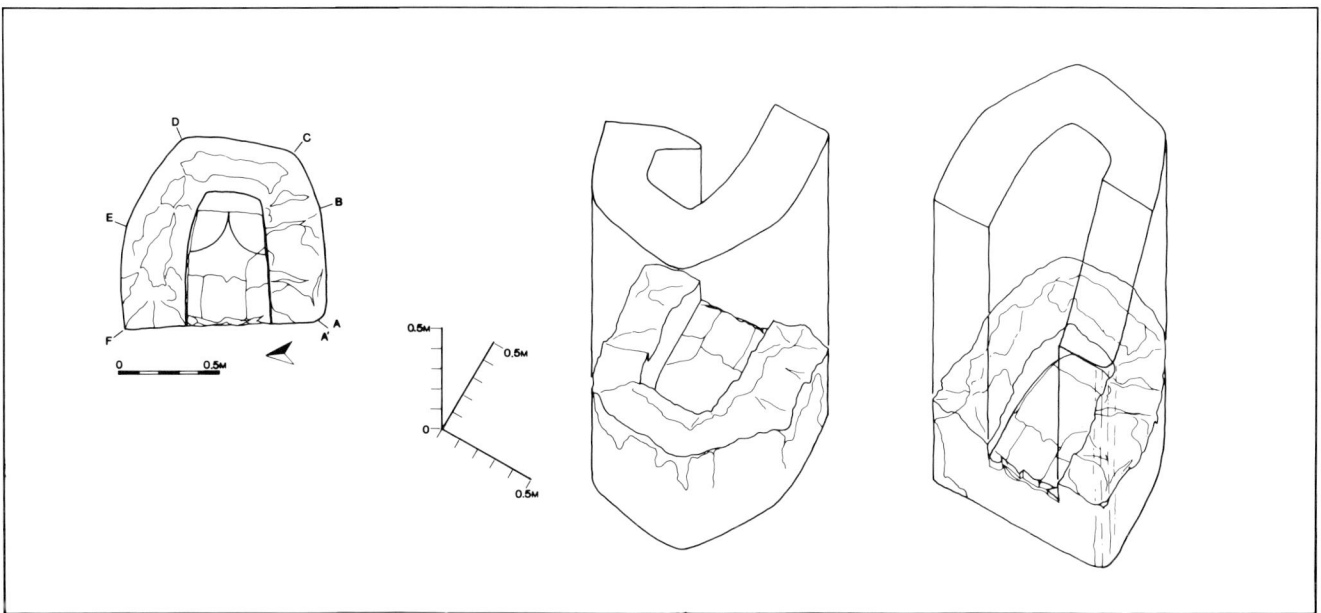

Fig. 4:10 The pulpit, plan and axonometric reconstructions *(DL)*

Fig. 4:11 Detail of the decoration of the northern face of the pulpit *(JM)*

small ring-disc, with outer radius of 63.5 mm and inner radius of 42 mm; all in imitation of *opus sectile* panelled stone revetment. The ring-disc was burnt black, but the slender vertical lozenge was outlined with a line which, after the fire, was reddish orange. The surviving lower point of the lozenge was flanked by narrow spandrels, filled with a striking scrolling ornament (Fig. 4:13) in reddish brown, which had been burnt to a red-orange, and dull blue. These spandrels appear to have been painted in imitation of stone panels carved in relief with plant *rinceaux*. The differentiated and relatively dense patterns of this panel must have helped to attract the wandering eye and the attention of the monk to the pulpit and to the words of the reader. The rear face was decorated with a variant of the pattern found on the other sides, with, it seems, a small ring-disc at the bottom of each of the narrow surfaces flanking the entrance, surrounded by veined marbling in undulating chevrons. In its complete form, the pulpit would have risen to a height of *c*. 1.3-1.5 m above its low base. The ring-discs, which were the most prominent elements in the painted decoration, may have been grouped in pairs, one above the other, on each of its principal faces.

The little triangular panels on the northeastern face, which seem to have been painted to mimic carved relief, show that the people who designed and executed the pulpit were aware of the tradition of church furniture, involving elaborately carved stone panels, which was widespread in Italy in this period. It is unclear why they resorted to this painted imitation of the real thing; it may have been to ensure overall uniformity and harmony in the embellishment of this hall, or it may have been

part of a time- and effort-saving strategy to enable the Refectory to be completed and equipped speedily using readily available expertise and resources. However, to judge from what has been found so far, it would appear that in fact the monastery did not have at its disposal masons who could undertake major items of church furniture in carved stone.

The cupboard

Immediately north of the doorway was an anomalous space where the tiled floor was patchy and benches were absent. In fact, no bench was found on the east face of wall 348/411, or for the first 2.5 m of the south-facing side of wall 354. The tile-less patch occupied an area about 1.0 m deep (from wall 348/411) and roughly 2.0 m long (i.e. north-south). Was this where the Refectory cupboard containing the tableware was positioned? It is worth noting that a solid charcoal tip (417) was encountered in this area, suggesting that something wooden had occupied this position or a point close by. A lock mechanism (from 482; small find no. 2161), similar to one used in the workshops (Trench FF), was also found in this area (see Volume 3, chapter 15).

The floor

The tiled floor suffered during its lifetime from being poorly laid on top of the preceding building and was evidently patched in parts. The tiles themselves were laid on fine sand (e.g. 1051), usually white but sometimes yellow in colour. Of the tiles which survived, 429 had some form of decoration (*c*. 36 per cent) (Fig. 4:5). There was an uneven survival of tiles within the Refectory, with a large number missing from the eastern end. There was also an uneven distribution of tile sizes, although the majority was of the standard (*c.* 0.4 x 0.52 m) size, oriented north-south. It is interesting to note that by estimating the number of tiles per square metre, it appears that there would have been around 1,740 tiles in the building (not including the tiled footrests). When the tile fragments in the footrests and the roof tiles are also taken into account it is apparent that the monastic tilers had a mighty challenge to face. The tiled floors will be discussed at length in Volume 3, chapter 6.

Decoration

At the time of excavation, traces of a painted dado were still just discernible on the northern and southern sections of the west wall (348/411 and 457), and on the extreme western end of the south wall (502/561/1072), in the corner behind the pulpit. This seems to have been generally uniform with the dado in the Assembly Room: painted panels imitating marble revetment, with undulating

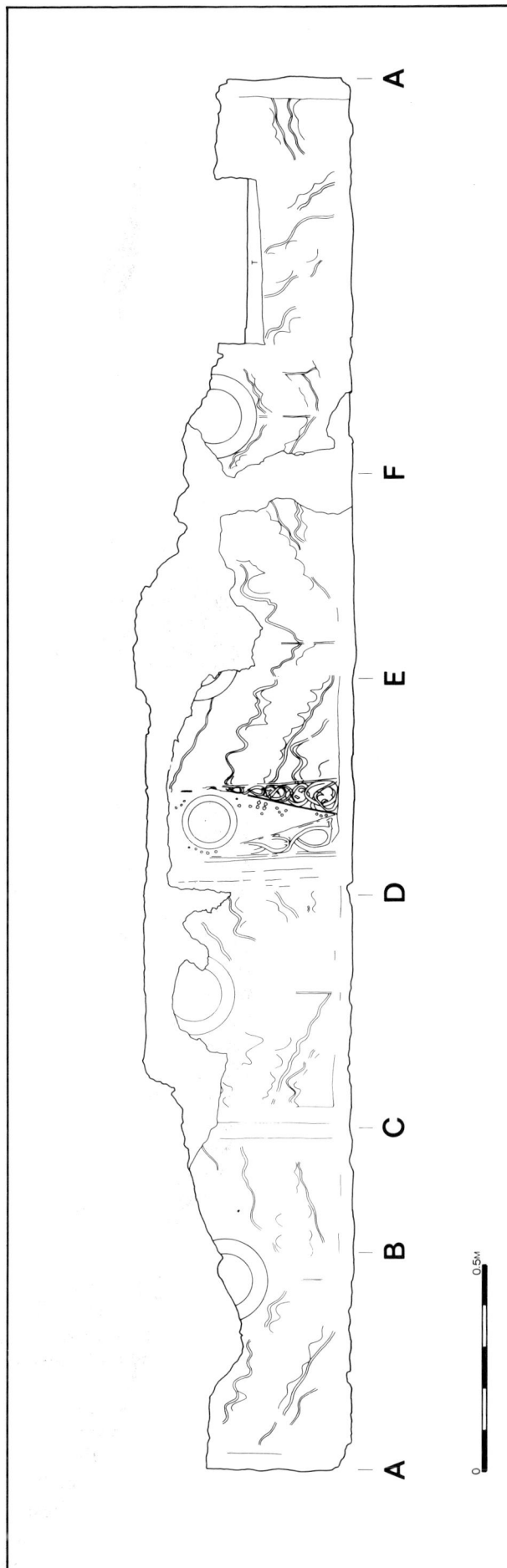

Fig. 4:12 The painted decoration on the pulpit *(JV)*

Fig. 4:13 Detail of the painted decoration of the pulpit *(JV)*

diagonal veining disposed so as to form a sequence of upright and inverted chevrons. However, in the Refectory the veining on all of the panels seems to have been in red, whereas in the Assembly Room red alternated with grey. There were also traces of yellow in the veining on the northern section of the west wall. Although most of the painted surface had been scorched off, the design of wavy veining was still just discernible in places and the vertical edges of the panels were plainly visible where they had been snapped into the still-wet plaster. These panels varied in width between 0.306 m and 0.392 m. Fragments of red veined dado were excavated in three contexts in the western part of the Refectory (482, 491 and 494).

The presence of an imitation marble dado in the Refectory suggests that the upper walls once carried an elaborate, in all likelihood figurative, scheme of decoration. Fugitive evidence of this was found in the badly burnt plaster recovered during excavation. Scorched fragments of painted drapery were excavated in the southwestern part of the room (in 491). Some had bands of yellow, beige, rose red, dull apricot and grey-blue; others had bands of grey-blue and salmon pink highlighted with white, which bordered on an area of red. Another fragment of drapery from this context resembled, in execution, that of the Prophets in the Assembly Room, with bands of strong grey-blue on a pale sky-blue ground, and articulations in light ochre and *impasto* highlights in white. Pieces of a pearled border, very similar to those which ran above and below the Prophets, were also found in this layer. From the same area (494), there was a fragment of what looked like another kind of border, coloured ochre and carrying a configuration of running white festoons. Other rather vestigial fragments which probably derived from vested figures were retrieved from the northern half of the building (from 482). Two adjoining pieces from this context formed part of a head, with a pale creamy yellow face, finely delineated red eyebrows, and brown striated hair. This head was set against a ground of brownish yellow.

A considerable amount of painted plaster was retrieved from 409, a layer which ran up against wall 348/411. This included many pieces painted in the idiom of the Prophets and others with bands of pale blue and cream highlighted with white, from drapery like that found in the northern end of the Assembly Room in 401 (see Plate 3:23), and fragments of pearled borders similar to those from the Prophet wall (452). Parts of the head of a figure were also recovered from this layer, with a face coloured a pale ochre and lighted with white, with light brown and ochre hair, and set against a blue-grey ground. It seems quite likely that much of this material derived from the eastern wall of the Assembly Room, and fell into the Refectory when the dividing wall 348/411 collapsed eastward, following the fire in 881.

Lighting

No windows, of course, survived, but piles of window-glass were found within the building, as well as to the north of wall 354, in the Garden Court (contexts 8022-31 – see Volume 1: fig. 10:16). The piles in the Garden Court suggest windows at approximately every 2.0 m. In all we might postulate thirteen to fifteen windows, high up in each of the long north and south walls. The piles of glass indicate large, multicoloured windows, possibly set in wooden transennae (see D. Hodges in Volume 3). A blue roundel found in 491, however, suggests that a small circular window may have been set high up in the west end of the building.

Heating

No trace of any fireplace was found in the excavations. It is possible that the Refectory was heated by braziers. However, the illustration of the Plan of St Gall similarly makes no allowance for integral heating facilities for the refectory, and Horn and Born suggest that this was deliberate (see Horn and Born 1979: vol. 1, 271-2). The Rule of Saint Benedict was unequivocal on the sin of gluttony; an unheated Refectory would lessen the desire to linger over food.

The roof

The thick layer of ash, charcoal and rubble over much of the Refectory (417, 545, 1037, 1048, 1049, 1050, 1063, 1064) was one of the most distinctive features of the excavation. The evidence indicates that the conflagration was spectacular and of enormous power. Very few fragments of tile were found in the destruction level. The lightness of the ash points to thatching, possibly of reeds or locally grown straw. A thatched roof, with timber bracing (as well as wooden benches and tables), might have generated a fire sufficient to account for the archaeological evidence of intense burning. A number of large nails, on average about 0.12-0.15 m long, was found in the excavations; almost certainly these were used in the roof (Fig. 4:14). The pointed ends of most of these nails were still bent over, as though they had been hammered flat to the timbers and had been burnt *in situ*. Accordingly, we might postulate that timbers, of about 0.12 m thick, were used to construct the frame that supported the roof.

The annexe

A possible annexe existed at the east end of the building; this is attributed to phase 5a and discussed in the following section. However, it is likely that some ante-room to the Refectory, connected to the kitchen, existed in phase 4, as arranging to serve

Fig. 4:14 Roof nails from the Refectory *(RH)*

food to several hundred people would have been an awkward affair either in the Refectory itself or in the kitchen.

PHASES 5a-b

The eastern annexe of the Refectory is difficult to date. Whether there was a building here in phase 4 remains a subject of speculation. In phase 5 it *appears* that an earlier ante-room was transformed into an integral part of the Refectory, possibly to act as a servery. Wall 570, quite possibly conceived of as a phase 4 bench, was retained as seating or made into a serving bench. The roof of this annexe was supported

by uprights positioned on blocks which served as post-pads. At this time a new tiled pavement (573) was laid in the annexe at a level about 0.4 m lower than the pavement in the Refectory. This pavement was not meant for display, being made of inverted roofing tiles rather than purpose-built floor tiles. Wall 502/561/1072 was extended eastward (579), though little of it survived. During the course of phase 5 the floor level was then raised with a clean yellow sand (572), as well as other thin layers of loam, being laid over the old pavement (573). Little, however, remained of the pavement associated with this period, although the blocks (8048) against the east side of 570 indicates that there were steps leading between the extension and the main dining-hall, steps which had since been robbed.

PHASE 5c

The ferocity of the fire appears to have destroyed all but the most durable features of this building.

PHASE 6a

The best preserved archaeological contexts were encountered in the northwestern sector of the building. It appears that the fire was at its fiercest where the cupboard had been situated. The fire deposit (417) had a 0.4 m destruction deposit (409) over the top of it (Fig. 4:15). For some reason a heap of material began to build up here. The top of 409 butted up against wall 348/411, and appeared to have been trampled into a beaten earth surface. A doorway was smashed through wall 354, providing access to the Vestibule and thus to the foot of the marble steps (508) (which led to the Entrance Hall) (cf. Chapter 1). Passing from the Vestibule, and through the doorway, one would have arrived on a surface now level with the top of the bench. In sum, it seems that there was some modest use made of this corner of the building, though its function is not now apparent. This is probably the context for Tomb

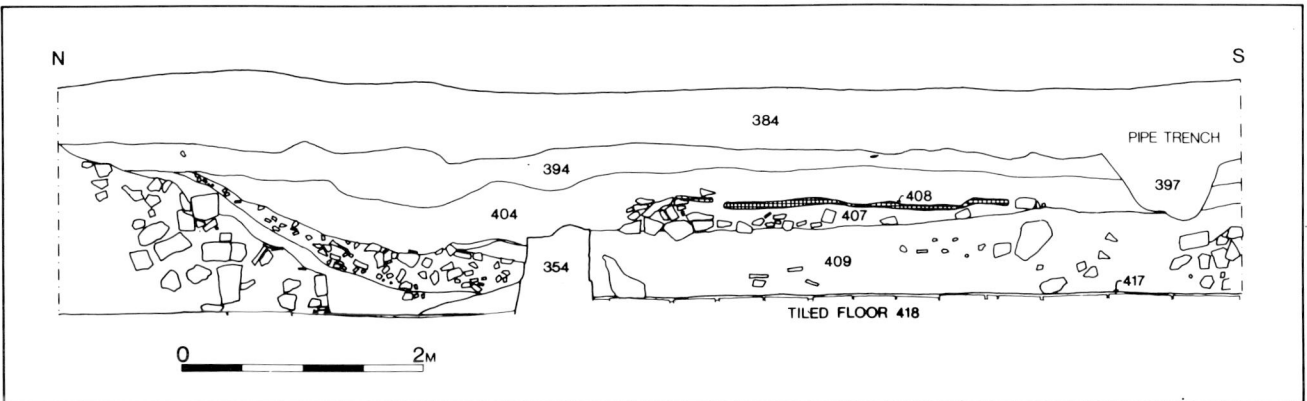

Fig. 4:15 West-facing sections showing the phase 6b tips in the Vestibule and the Refectory *(LW)*

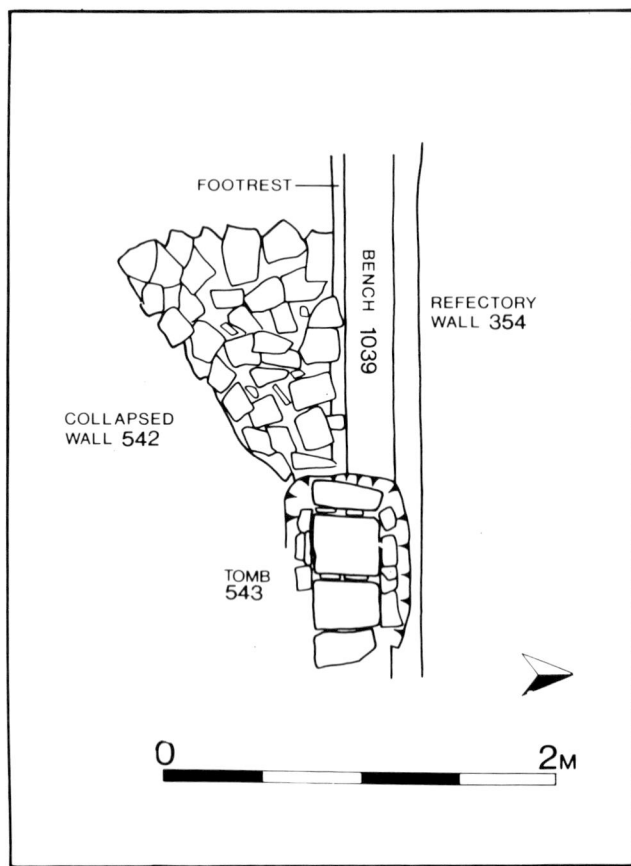

Fig. 4:16 Phase 6a Tomb 543 cut into the Refectory bench and collapsed wall 542 *(SC)*

seemingly systematic destruction proceeded, leaving the walls levelled to the point where they met the then ground surface. Hence, the trampled surface 409 protected the bottom 0.6 m of wall 348/411, while the absence of such a context led to the obliteration of the Refectory walls in the eastern half of the building. With the destruction went the concurrent levelling-up of the site, and the creation of a new raised surface in this area. (The tips are discussed more fully in Chapter 3.)

PHASE 7

One fragment of the white mortar surface encountered in the Lower Thoroughfare was found in the Refectory area (408). This occurred above 409 in the northwest corner of the area (Fig. 4:15), having been preserved from ploughing by the medieval/modern terracing. The layer, nonetheless, had been badly damaged, possibly in medieval times. We can only postulate that it once extended all over the abandoned Refectory.

MODERN

The tips (391, 394, 404) over the white mortar surface (408) probably relate to recent agricultural activities on the site. However, the shallow tomb (1060) within the ploughsoil, toward the eastern end of the Refectory, belonged to very recent times indeed (Fig. 4:17). The tomb contained the articu-

543 (Fig. 4:16). This tomb belonged to the cemetery found primarily in the Entrance Hall to the north (Volume 1, chapter 12). The tomb had been cut in part out of the bench, the cut removing the incinerated wooden top and part of the rubble fill of the seat. Four large blocks – one square and three rectangular – were tightly bonded together to form the cover. The bench was trimmed and part of wall 354 was removed, so that the blocks would sit comfortably. The southern side was also constructed of blocks, some of which reached down to the tiled floor (418), though most were bedded on the footrest (but projecting 0.1 m or so in some cases). Inside was a grey loam with stones and some plaster fragments, and below this there was an articulated skeleton of an elderly woman with her head at the western end (8057). The deep cut into wall 354 (features 8039, 8040, 8041) may have been a second tomb placed a little east of 543; however, no skeletal material survived, so for the moment this feature must remain an anomaly.

PHASE 6b

The destruction of the building occurred at some date after the tomb had been cut inside the Refectory. A fall of stone (542), presumably from a collapsed wall, actually covered 543. Elsewhere a

Fig. 4:17 Tomb 1060 *(CMC)*

lated skeleton of a female, oriented with her head to the east. The body appeared to have been buried in the low-lying field that we encountered when we began the excavations (cf. Volume 1: 15). The workmen employed by the project expressed the strong belief that she was a victim of the hostilities concentrated hereabouts between November 1943 and May 1944, when the Allies were held by the Germans at the Gustav Line which ran along the Mainarde (cf. Linklater 1951: 147; Artese 1993: 300).

EXCAVATIONS ON THE SOUTH SIDE OF THE REFECTORY (AH, IR)

During 1984 workmen cut several holes to the south of the Refectory as footings for the posts which were to support a cover over the archaeological remains (cf. Fig. 4:2). One of these holes revealed a fine Roman funerary relief (see J. Patterson in Volume 3), set into a mortared surface (Fig. 4:18). The excavation was too small to determine whether this was part of a passageway, perhaps a cloister walk, along the south side of the Refectory. Hence, a cutting, 2.0 m square, was made from the edge of the Refectory trench.

Phase 4

Fragments of a tiled pavement were discovered immediately below the topsoil (8284). Two tiles showed obvious signs of burning and most were cracked and shattered; only one revealed a complete form. The tiles were bedded on a hard clay matrix with flecks of tile and mortar (8281), as seen elsewhere. The tiles extended approximately 1.7 m from the Refectory wall (502), although they were not present up to and directly against the substantial wall (8282) discovered running east-west at the south end of the trench. This wall was formed of substantial stone blocks bonded by a loose flaky yellow mortar (8283). The wall could not be traced over the entire trench, having been robbed in one part when a pit for an olive tree was dug. A section at the south end of the trench revealed that neither the clay bedding nor the tiles above extended to wall 8282. Indeed, it was only the underlying layer (8287), a relatively thin sand and clay mix, which extended to the wall. In the intervening space, between the tiles and wall, lay a row of small, irregular stones (8290).

These stones appear to be all that remained of a kerb similar to the one which ran along the north

Fig. 4:18 Roman funerary relief and inscription from the north cloister walk *(RH)*

side of Refectory wall 354, in the Garden Court. With this parallel in mind, it is tempting to speculate that two phases of a covered portico were revealed in this small trench. Wall 8282 was built first, to support the outer wall of the covered way; its foundation trench was covered by an earthen surface (8287). The kerb was created at this phase, being set into this surface. Following this, a new surface made of tiles was laid down, butting up to the edge of the kerb.

In conclusion, this small excavation suggests that the passageway or northern portico of the cloister was about 1.7 m wide and was probably covered. Further excavations are necessary to test these observations.

DISCUSSION (FIG. 4:19)

The pulpit base discovered in the southwest corner of the room is the principal reason for interpreting this large room as the Refectory. If the interpretation is correct, the building formed the north side of a rectangular- or square-shaped cloister. It would seem most likely that the kitchen and stores formed

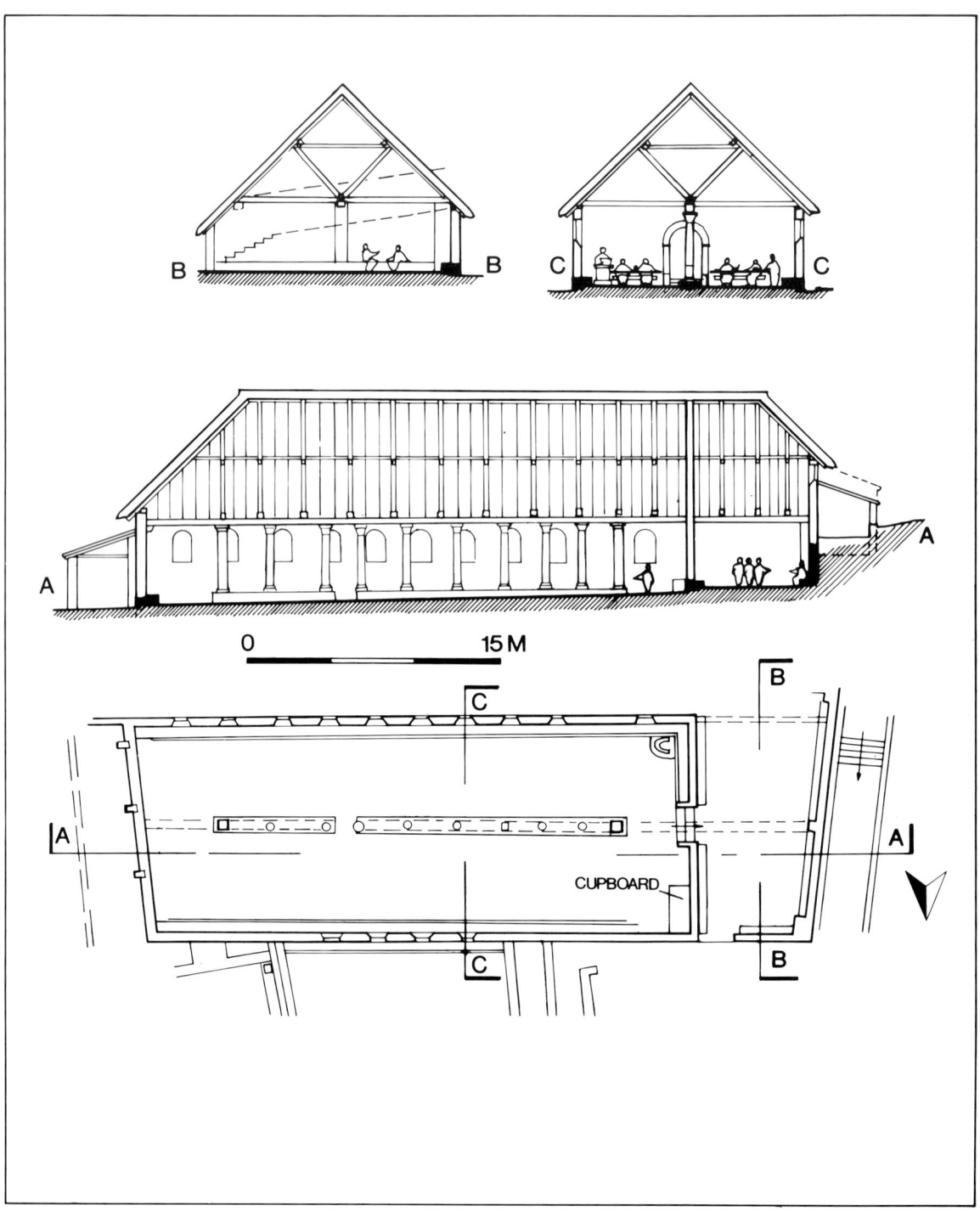

Fig. 4:19 Reconstruction of the Refectory *(SG)*

the eastern side of the cloister, and that the dormitory was located on the south side. The western side was formed, as we know, by the Assembly Room and Lower Thoroughfare. Until it is excavated, the exact shape and dimensions of the cloister can only be matter of speculation.

This formation has been the subject of much discussion. Walter Horn ascribes the origins of the cloister square to the eighth century; he proposes that the form of the cloister owes much to the Roman sites on which many of these monasteries were built (Horn and Born 1979: vol. 1, 243; cf. James 1981: 47). The cloister seems to have been absent at early eighth-century Anglo-Saxon monasteries, such as that at Monkwearmouth (Cramp 1976: figs 5.9-10), Jarrow (Cramp 1976: fig. 5.12), Whithorn (cf. Higham 1993: 151), Irish monasteries (cf. Horn and Born 1979: vol. 1, 243) and even later Merovingian- to early Carolingian-period monasteries such as Echternach (Krier and Wagner 1985) and Fulda (Jacobsen 1992: 145-6). The earliest examples of the medieval cloister square appear to be at the German monasteries of Lorsch and Reichenau. The monastery of Saint Peter's at Altenmünster, Lorsch, was built by Bishop Chrodegang, its first abbot, between 760 and 774 (Behn 1934; Rhein 1986). The monastic plan, according to its excavator Friedrich Behn, was determined by the pre-existing *villa rustica* (Behn 1934; Horn and Born 1979: vol. 1, 245) (Fig. 4:20). Recent excavations at Mittelzell, Reichenau, have identified part of the eighth-century cloister attached to the church (Zettler 1988: 156-262). Excavations at Rouen, beside the early cathedral, have identified a similar relationship. The early medieval cloister plan was determined in this case by a preceding Gallo-Roman *domus* (Le Maho 1993). At San Salvatore at Brescia, the eighth-century cloister built in the age of King Desiderius took advantage of the remains of a ruinous, but extant Roman town house (Brogiolo 1992: 204-5). At Farfa the circumstances are similar. The abbey occupied a large, pre-existing Roman villa, and it is quite probable that the high medieval cloister followed the layout of the eighth- to ninth-century one, which in turn made use of pre-existing Roman ranges (cf. McClendon

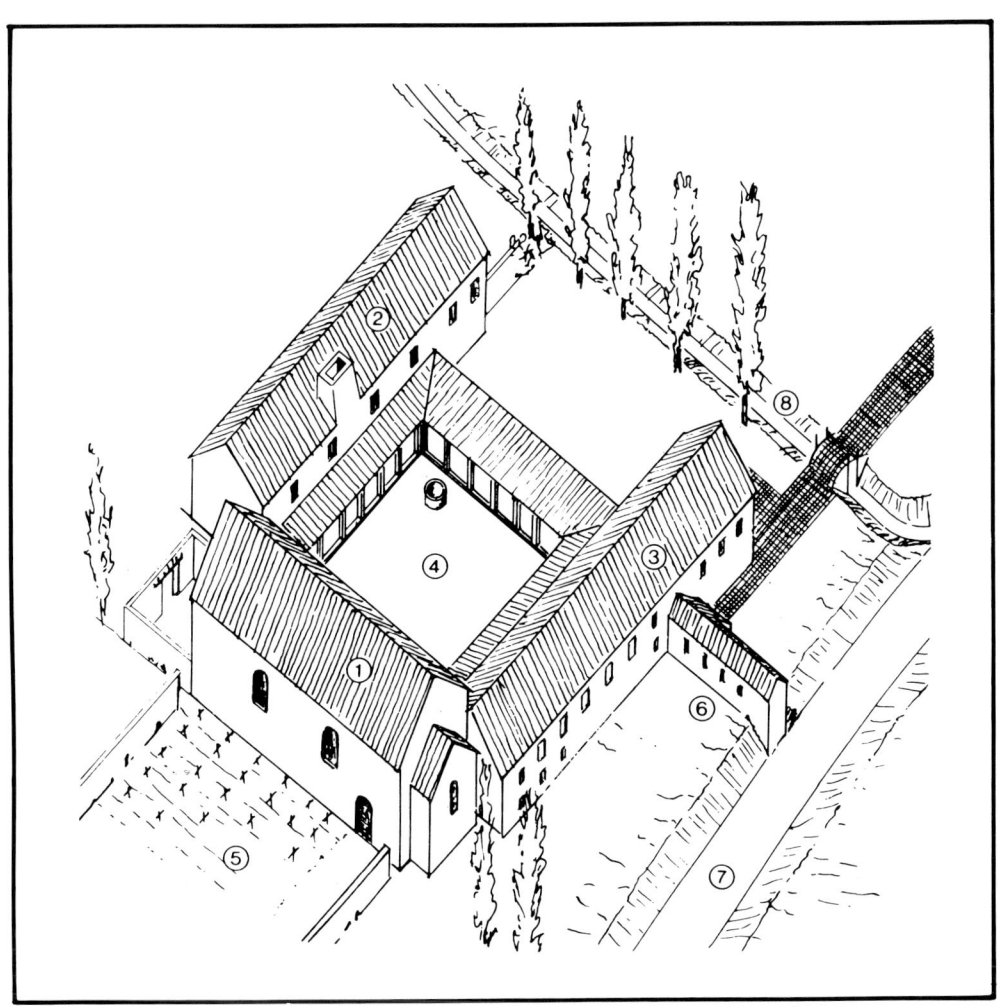

Fig. 4:20 Altenmünster monastery at Lorsch *c.* 750: 1. Church; 2. West range; 3. East range; 4. Cloister garden; 5. Cemetery; 6. Latrines; 7. Boundary ditch; 8. Infilled drainage ditch
(After Rhein 1986, back cover)

1987). The cloister at San Vincenzo al Volturno, therefore, was no exception. In the original nucleus of the monastery, layout had been determined to some extent by the plan of the late Roman settlement in which the Garden Court appears to have been an open space surrounded by buildings on three sides. Unfortunately, too little survived to indicate. whether a square cloister existed here in phase 3 (that is, during the eighth century).

The ninth-century Refectory was probably built over a smaller late eighth-century (phase 3c) Refectory, which may in turn have been located within a late Roman building. This phase 3c building was approximately 11.6 m wide by 21 m long, and clearly quite spacious. Using the permutations described below, this eighth-century building might have contained two long tables, each about 1.0 m wide and about 15.0 m long. Some 60 m of benching might have been provided, able to seat about a hundred monks. By phase 3c, in short, the community was already quite large.

The ninth-century Refectory was presumably part of the new, enlarged cloister-complex which was associated with the new abbey-church constructed by Abbot Joshua. Its size offers some impression of the new scale of building in the monastery. Amongst other things it makes it possible to calculate the size of the monastic community at its zenith. Before considering this aspect, though, let us first examine the appearance and architectural form of the building.

The paintings in the Assembly Room in the Lower Thoroughfare, where the monks gathered before entering the Refectory, were designed to lay emphasis on the entry to the Refectory. The decoration of the east wall of the Assembly Room, as was noted in Chapter 3, was particularly rich. This sense of grandeur may have been reinforced by an elaborately decorated feature – such as a carved lintel or an arch set above the doorway into the Refectory – to complement the reused Roman threshold. The Refectory itself must have resembled a barn. As far as we can judge, it had severe high walls pierced by about thirteen to fifteen windows in the long sides and possibly a small blue roundel in each of the gable ends. It is proposed in Volume 3 that the multicoloured window glass, comprising a variety of shapes such as rectangular and triangular panels, were fixed together by lead cames set in wooden (?oak) transennae.

The Refectory at San Vincenzo was graced with a 'robe of colour' (cf. Riché 1978: 152), but unfortunately the surviving plaster on the interior surfaces of the walls of this building had suffered terribly from fire. Snapped vertical lines defining the panels of marbled dado were preserved where the original plaster surface still existed. The paint of these surfaces was, for the most part, burnt away, but red and perhaps yellow veining could still be traced in some places on the west wall, to the north of the

central doorway. A scheme of coloured triangles, similar to that found on the benches of the Assembly Room, was preserved on the front faces of the benches built against both the north and south walls of the Refectory at their western ends, and this design may have continued over all of the other benches in the building. The individual triangles were outlined by thin white lines and they were bordered at the top of the face by a band of indistinguishable colour about 30 mm wide. Evidence of figurative painting, similar in idiom to the phase 4 Prophets next door, was found among the fragments of painted plaster excavated in this area. These must have derived from the elaborate scheme which once covered the upper walls. To judge from what remained, it seems that the decoration of the Refectory may have formed part of a larger programme which included the adjacent Assembly Room.

The ashy fire deposits (and absence of fallen roofing tiles) indicate that the roof of the Refectory was thatched in 881. A steep-pitched roof is proposed in Figure 4:19, braced with regularly-spaced timber trusses supported at intervals by pillars and columns mounted on the central spine. The exact number of supports is unknown, but an upright post every two metres or so along the spine might account for the otherwise enigmatic features left in this largely destroyed central feature. The roof timbers seem to have been held together, as everywhere, by a multitude of nails, mostly 0.12-0.15 m long. The points of the nails were bent over, suggesting that these poked through the timbers by 30 mm. In other words, much of the timber was of about 0.12-0.15 m in diameter, as used in the modern barn at Colli a Volturno illustrated here (Figs 4:21-22). The prolific quantity of nails is a telling comment on the poor carpentry skills of the builders. Likewise, the buttresses incorporated into the outer walls of the building confirm an impression gained from examining the foundations of the walls that the construction was far from proficient. The conspicuous drop of some 0.8 m in the level of the floor from west to east, like the unevenly laid tiled pavement over the previous building, reinforces the notion that the Refectory was built in haste.

The existence of thatched roofs within the ensemble of tile-roofed buildings is at first a little puzzling. (It is proposed that the Distinguished Guests' Refectory also had a thatched roof (Volume 1: chapter 11), though the 'South Church', Entrance Hall, Vestibule and Assembly Room had tile roofs.) How is the thatch to be explained? In Ardo's biography of Saint Benedict of Aniane, emphasis is given in the description of his monastery to its 'simple walls and the use of straw to cover the roofs' as an illustration of Benedict's humility in an era of grandiose building (Davis-Weyer 1986: 97). At San Vincenzo the use of thatch as an expression of

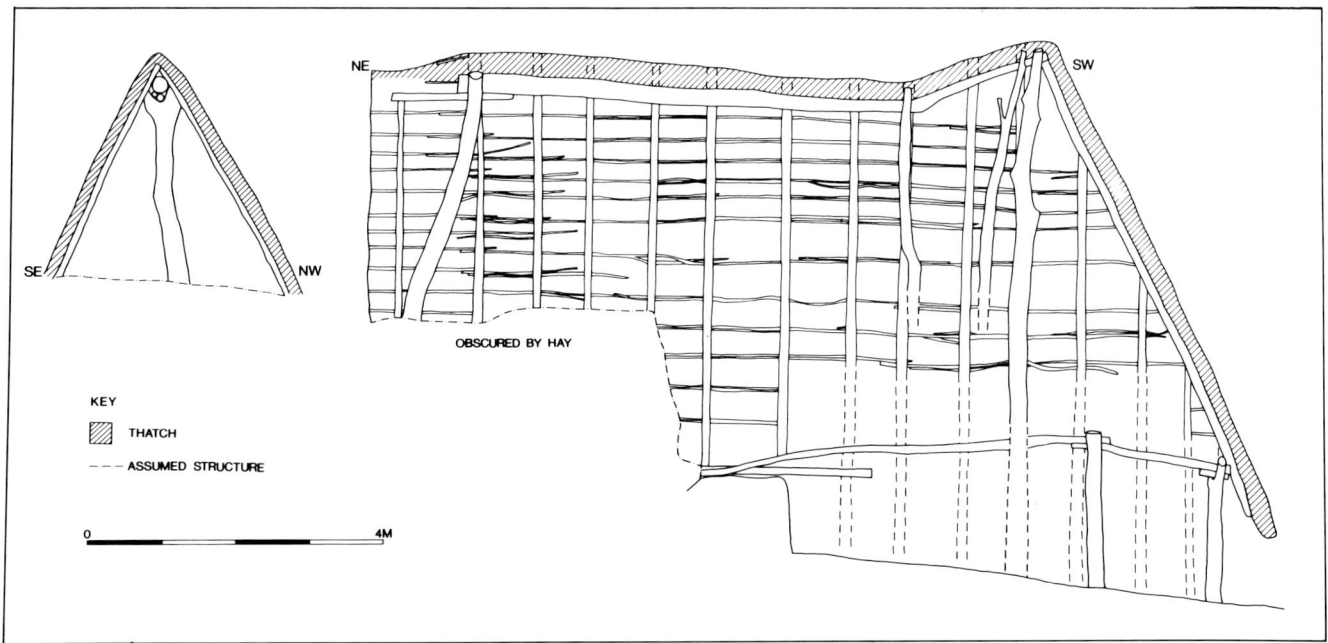

KEY

THATCH

--- ASSUMED STRUCTURE

0   4M

Fig. 4:21 Elevations of the east end and interior of a thatched barn *(pagliaio)* at Colli a Volturno *(LW)*

humility is hardly tenable. The monastery was clearly an opulent environment by contemporary secular standards, and, judging from its decoration, the Refectory was no exception. More practical explanations need to be sought. It is tempting to speculate that the roof-span was too great to cover with the heavy tiles made in the monastery. Nevertheless, this would not account for the thatched roof of the narrower Distinguished Guests' Refectory. A simpler explanation which has become apparent after recording a thatched barn with a hipped roof at Colli a Volturno (Figs 4:21-22) is that this kind of roofing retains the heat inside the building in winter. A thatched building was also easy to construct, as all the materials were readily available locally. This would have been a significant factor if the number of monks at San Vincenzo grew rapidly to several hundreds in a short space of time.

The most significant remaining feature of this building is the pulpit base. The pulpit was mounted on a low tile podium, and made of tile and brick, plastered, then brightly painted. In this respect it is strikingly different from the eighth- to ninth-century ornamented prefabricated stone pulpits from Lazio and Rome in this period (Rossi 1993). On the Plan of St Gall the reader's pulpit *(analogium)* is marked by a square with a circle inside (Horn and Born 1979: vol. 1, 268). It too appears to have been raised on a podium. The St Gall pulpit faces the entrance to the Refectory, whereas the San Vincenzo pulpit is situated in a corner close to the main doorway. In form, of course, it is very different from the grand Romanesque and high medieval balconied pulpits surviving in many west European monasteries. The simplicity in form of this example seems to have

been counterbalanced by elegant painting on the face exposed to the nearest tables.

To the left (north) of the doorway was a patch of floor without tiles and benches around the walls. This seems a likely position for the tableware cupboard. A prominent layer of charcoal and a large lock mechanism were discovered in this area and support this hypothesis. A large cupboard *(toregma)* existed in the Refectory on the Plan of St Gall (Horn and Born 1979: vol. 1, 269). The exact form of the cupboard at San Vincenzo remains unknown. Indeed, the absence of pottery in this corner lends some support to the idea that much of the tableware was made of wood.

The monastic Refectory was intended to accommodate the entire ecclesiastical community. As is stated on the Plan of St Gall: '*Haec domus adsistit cunctis qua porgitur aesca*' (This hall, where the food is laid out, has a place for everyone (Horn and Born 1979: vol. 1, 267).) The Plan of St Gall shows the Refectory as being amply fitted with furnishings to cope with such numbers. The hall had a table for the abbot *(mensa abbatis)*, tables sufficient for 120 monks to dine simultaneously, and tables set for visiting monks *(ad sedendum cum hospitibus)*. At San Vincenzo monks might have been seated on the benches alongside the walls. In total there was about 55 m of usable benching along the north and south walls; roughly 2.0 m by the pulpit; and approximately 40 m of benching along the sides of the central spine. In all there was about 97 m of integral benching which, using an estimated seating space of 0.6 m per monk indicates a seating capacity of about 160 persons. In addition, a further 160 monks might have been seated on the other side of the long tables. Another

Fig. 4:22 A thatched barn *(pagliaio)* at Colli a Volturno *(RH)*

fifteen to twenty monks could have been seated around a table at the east end of the Refectory without any difficulty. (The calculation for San Vincenzo uses Hope-Taylor's figure of 0.6 m per person for the estimated seating capacity at the seventh-century royal *cuneus* at Yeavering, Northumberland (Hope-Taylor 1977). However, Horn and Born (1979: vol. 1, 268) estimated individual

seating needs at the slightly more generous 2.5 feet (0.75 m): this would result in seating being available on the benches for 130 monks.) In all, 335-40 monks could have been seated (Fig. 4:23). This is more than twice the size of the monastic community estimated for St Gall. It should be noted that the refectory at St Gall was estimated at about 30 m by 12 m, if we accept Horn and Born's interpretation of scale

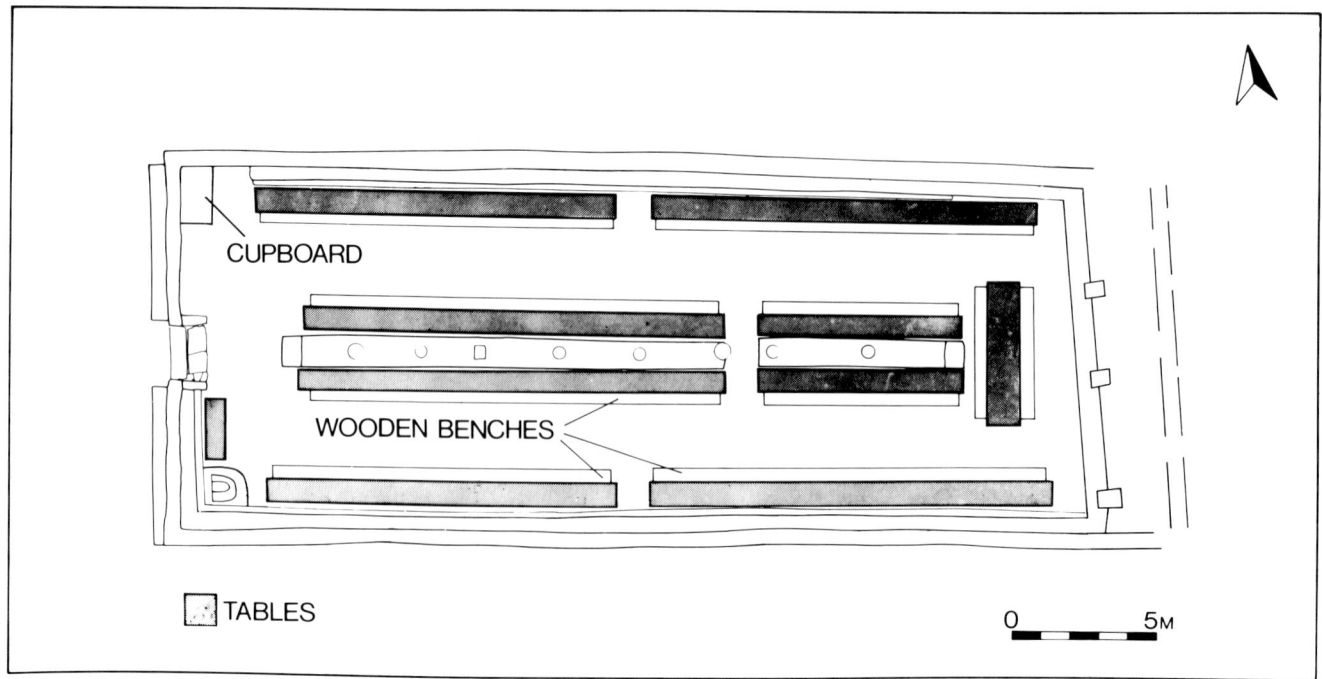

Fig. 4:23 Plan of the proposed Refectory seating arrangement in phase 4 *(KF)*

(Horn and Born 1979: vol 1, 77-97), a size comparable with the San Vincenzo Refectory: however, the central spine of the San Vincenzo Refectory, by dividing the room, necessitated a different arrangement of tables to that illustrated in the St Gall plan. These calculations further emphasize the extraordinary size of San Vincenzo early in the ninth century. A gathering of some three hundred monks might have provided the heat necessary to warm this barn of a building! However, any coldness would have been perfectly consistent with reformist Benedictine rules. Similarly, the silence imposed on the congregation at table, and the solitary voice of the Reader, constituted a further means of discouraging any improper preoccupation with the physical pleasures of eating.

The Refectory focuses attention upon the capacity of the kitchens, the storage facilities, the agrarian resource base and the size of the monastic dormitory. Each can and has to be calculated in terms of the capacity of the Refectory, given the intention of being able to accommodate the entire ecclesiastical community at one time. It also focuses attention upon a range of hitherto poorly developed crafts (if indeed these had existed at all in the preceding period), such as carpentry, tile-making, nail-production. Similar quantities of materials and similar amounts of labour would have been needed to construct the stores and dormitory forming the other sides of the cloister.

The full capacity of the Refectory was probably required only for the first half of the ninth century. All the signs indicate that the size of the community had diminished substantially by the time of the building's destruction in 881. If this was so, the spacious barn-like character of the Refectory (and indeed the dormitory?) must have made the monastery's decline all the more apparent to its community, and at the same time, without the warmth generated by so many bodies, it must have been noticeably colder in the winter months.

After the Refectory was burnt down in 881, only the northwest corner was used for some makeshift purpose. The eleventh-century (phase 7) Refectory was probably positioned on the south side of the cloister, on the edge of the Rocchetta plain (Hodges 1985: 24-5). The phase 7 cloister was considerably smaller than that of the ninth century. Moreover, its site was readily warmed by the sun at all times of the year. Similarly, it is likely that the twelfth-century (phase 8) monastery, on its new site, included a Refectory situated on the south side of the cloister, again a position that might be warmed at all times of the year (Volume 4). Judging by Pantoni's brief description (1980a: 75-80; fig. 1), this Refectory, like the eleventh-century (phase 7) version, was longer but narrower than Abbot Joshua's building (cf. Volume 4). In each case the number of monks was probably less than half that attributed to the early ninth-century community.

Chapter Five

EXCAVATIONS ON TERRACE 2: THE LATE ROMAN TOWER

by David Wilkinson,
with Sheila Gibson, Richard Hodges and John Mitchell

INTRODUCTION

The terrace on the slope behind the 'South Church' is prominent for little more than 20 m. Beyond this, to the south, the hillslope runs directly up from Terrace 1 to Terrace 3 (Fig. 0:1). In 1980 we discovered that sometime previously a small, clandestine excavation had been done at the north end of Terrace 2. This cutting was cleaned and a small area excavated. A substantial late Roman building was identified, associated with midden layers which spilled down the hillside in front of it. In 1981 and 1983 attempts were made to identify ninth-century levels on the terrace, but to no avail. Accordingly, rather more substantial excavations were undertaken in 1984 and 1985 to clarify the stratigraphy on the terrace. In all about 120 square metres were examined, though it was not possible to remove all the contexts (Fig. 5:1). Erosion on the hillside and extensive disturbance caused by burials and later robbing meant that clear stratigraphy relating to the structures was present only in a small area to the south of the large Roman building. This means that not all the developments described below can be placed in a definite sequence: some can be identified as distinct activities, but others float within the sequence to a greater or lesser extent (see phases 4-6). Moreover, only a portion of the building and sequence on this terrace has been investigated. A summary of the main phases on Terrace 2 is given in Table 5:1.

PHASE 0

Three features were noted as being earlier than the late Roman Tower (Fig. 5:1). Each probably amounted to a wall running north-south along the face of the slope. Firstly, 7234 and 7237 appear to have been foundations which were partly destroyed when the Tower was built. Footings 7234 lie beneath the late Roman (phase 1b) cistern attached to the steep slope on the south side of the Tower. 7237 was rather enigmatic, being a base about 0.7 m wide under, and at right angles to, the south wall of the Tower (683). Part of the feature may have been the underlying travertine bedrock; the rest was made of a hard, off-white mortar in which unshaped limestone fragments were set. The third and most substantial feature was a wall

fragment (7212) running along the face of the hillslope from the south side of the portico (see below). In fact, this wall ran beneath the portico walls 620 and 643 and may have extended along the full length of the terrace, as far as the back of the 'South Church'. Its large, rough-hewn limestone blocks were similar to the largely-destroyed walls of phase 0 date in the Crypt Church and 'South Church' areas. Wall 7212 strongly suggests that a late Samnite or Republican structure occupied this slope, overlooking the riverside area.

PHASE 1a

A substantial building, only partially exposed by the excavations, was built over the phase 0 structures (Fig. 5:2). The building, hereafter referred to as the Tower (see the discussion below), which we shall consider as being oriented north-south, measured about 10.0 m on its east-west axis and approximately 14.7 m on its north-south axis. The east-west axis was measured from a point at the back of the terrace at which a short length of wall, probably the remains of the west wall of the building, could be observed on the surface (not illustrated on Figs 5:1 and 5:2).

The outer walls of the Tower were of limestone rubble, with rough faces both inside and out, set in hard creamy-white mortar. The east wall (602/641/ 642), towards the front of the terrace, was just over 1.0 m wide and survived to a height of 0.8 m in

TABLE 5:1 Summary of the main phases on Terrace 2	
0	Traces were found of a substantial, stone-built structure, which had been largely destroyed by later activity.
1a	A large building, 14.7 m wide and about 10.0 m long, with deep foundations was constructed. It was a two- or three-storey residential Tower. There were remains of an extensive and deep midden below the building on the downslope side.
1b	A portico was added to the east front of the building, overlying the midden. Traces of a walled garden enclosing the slope below the portico were found. A cistern was added to the south side.
2-3	Remains were found of at least two burials which had been placed within the building. The cistern may have been disused by or become disused in these phases.
4	Major alterations were made, linked to the construction of the Upper Thoroughfare.
5	The building was demolished.
6a	Block-built tombs were inserted into the Tower.
7-8	The site was levelled with a series of fills.

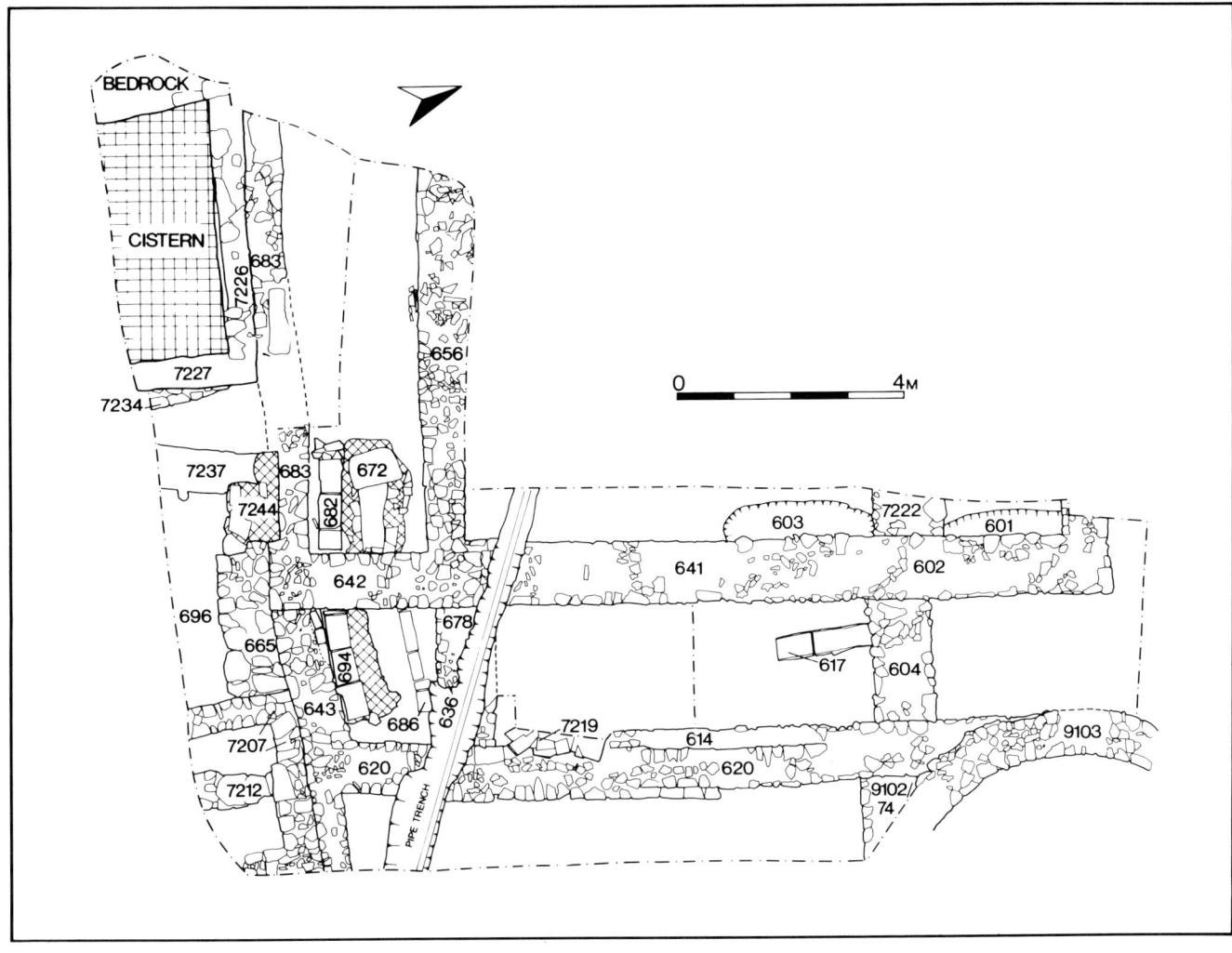

Fig. 5:1 Plan of Trench F showing the Tower walls and other major features *(KF)*

places. Below this were footings of similar stone and mortar, approximately 0.1 m wider than the wall itself and at least 0.4 m deep. The outer walls on the north and south sides were 0.7 m wide. The south outer wall (683) survived to a height of 1.2 m where it was abutted by the later cistern. The Tower had two internal walls (656 and 7222) running east-west and situated parallel to and 2.0 m from the north and south walls of the Tower. These had a similar construction to the outer wall; both were 1.2 m wide and abutted the east (front) wall of the Tower. Where it was possible to observe wall 656 in section it had shallower foundations than the outer walls. The Tower walls were later levelled, probably to create a ninth-century ground surface, and consequently almost nothing survived of the internal decoration and fittings. However, the south-flanking room formed by walls 642, 683 and 656 had white plaster on the inside of the walls. In addition, the external (south) face of wall 683, which was sealed by the construction of the phase 1b cistern against it, had white plaster.

During the first phase of the Tower a midden was

created on the slopes immediately below it. This sticky black deposit (696) was at least 0.5 m deep in some places, and was observed both in the area defined by the phase 1b portico (that is, immediately in front of the east face of the Tower) and along the south side (7209). In places this midden extended down to the back (west) side of the Lower Thoroughfare (where it was cut by the construction of the Assembly Room), as well as to the south side of the phase 1a funerary church. More of the midden was also discovered behind the Crypt Church. The deposit is manifestly full of archaeological material and warrants detailed examination at some future date.

PHASE 1b

The principal features of this phase were (Fig. 5:3):
  (1) the addition to the Tower of an eastward extension, resembling a portico;
  (2) the making of a garden below the portico;
  (3) the addition of a cistern to the south side of the Tower.

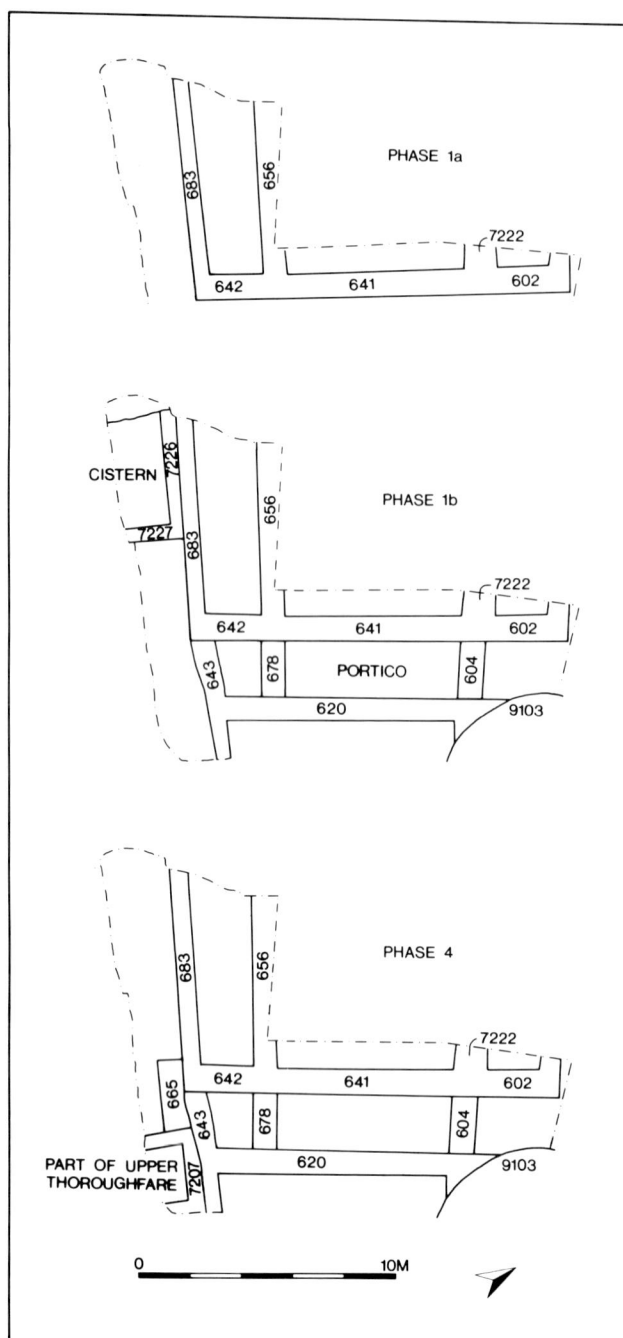

Fig. 5:2 Phase plan of the Tower *(LW)*

same width as the internal walls of the Tower. The portico walls clearly cut through the phase 1a midden (Fig. 5:3). The construction of the portico walls varied from that of the earlier walls of the Tower only in that the wall footings were slightly cruder, using less stone and more mortar. The front (east-facing) wall (620) was 0.9-1.0 m wide. A narrower section of walling (Fig. 5:1), of identical build, ran along its front edge, surviving one course high for a length of 3.6 m. This could have been either a narrower section of the upstanding wall, founded upon a wider plinth, or a narrow balustrade of some kind. The construction of the portico probably occurred as the hillslope below it was walled off. A wall (643) abutted the southeast corner of the Tower and ran down the hillslope at a slight angle to the Tower, to merge into wall 434 at the north end of the Assembly Room in the Lower Thoroughfare. This is roughly the same alignment as that of the Refectory north wall (354) (see Figs 0:1 and 0:2). Wall 643 was of similar construction to the other Tower walls, but was only 0.8 m wide. A similar wall ran from the portico on the north side, where the bracing wall met 620. This wall (74/9102) ran eastward downhill at a slight angle for about 8.0 m and would have returned southward along the face of the slope (see also Volume 1, chapter 9: 128). The light-brown loamy fill within these walls suggests that this was a garden made on the existing hillside (see Chapter 9).

A cistern, located high on the south side of the Tower, probably belonged to this phase as well (Fig. 5:4). The construction work began with the digging of a deep hole against the Tower. This hole cut through the phase 1a midden layer (7209) as well as the phase 0 footings (7237 and 7234). The cistern was then built up against the Tower. In the excavated section (Fig. 5:5) of the cistern it appears that the west side was natural rock while to the north and east there were well-built walls (7226 and 7227 respectively). (The excavation did not extend to the southern edge of the cistern.) The walls were each 0.5 m wide. The part of the structure exposed measured 5.1 m (north-south) externally, and 4.5 m internally; it had a depth of 1.4 m at its deepest point. Inside, the structure was lined with plaster, of which two layers could be seen. Plaster layer 7230 was *c.* 10 mm thick and overlay an earlier plaster layer (7231). At present, it seems that the cistern was rectangular on a north-south axis; but it is just possible that it was square.

A little downslope from the cistern, also attached to the south wall of the Tower, was what appeared to be the base of a small external staircase (7244). It was constructed of stone, large tile fragments and plenty of yellow mortar. This could have been the point of entry to the Tower when the closed garden below the portico was constructed. However, the feature was crudely built and could even post-date the destruction of the Tower. In such a case it would have provided access to the later tombs.

These features probably belonged to the later fifth or the first quarter or half of the sixth century. The only coin found associated with this phase, a bronze *nummus* from the construction fill (632) of the portico, proved to be illegible (see Grierson and Barrett in Volume 3).

The main wall (620) of the eastward extension or portico ran north-south, parallel to the phase 1a east wall (602/641/642), 2.2 m to the west. Two internal bracing walls running east-west (604 and 678), butting Tower wall 620, connected the new façade to the old one. These internal walls were aligned with the internal walls of the Tower. They survived to a height of 1.3 m and were 1.0 m thick, almost the

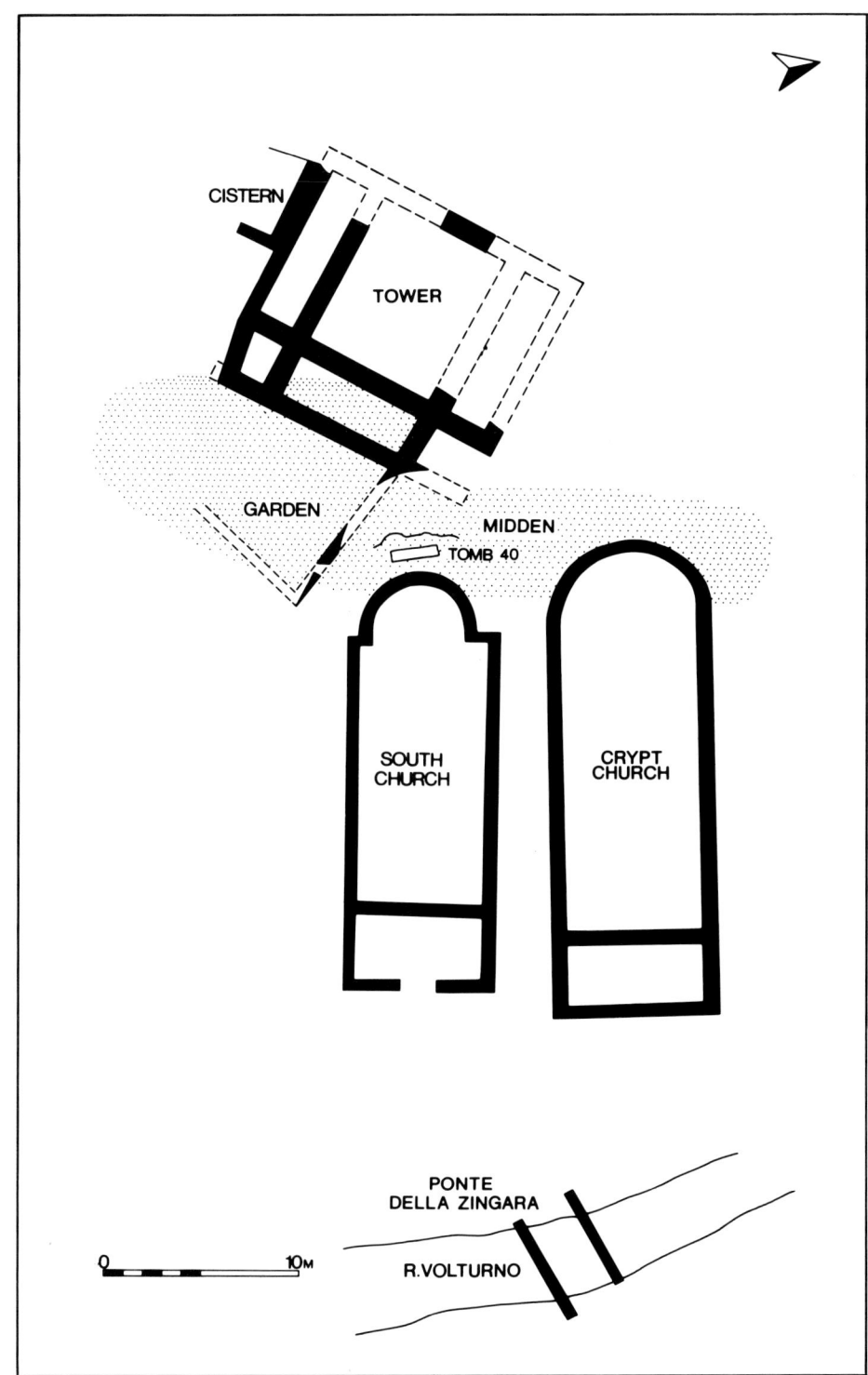

Fig. 5:3 The Tower as in phase 1b, showing also the extent of the phase 1a midden *(SC)*

The only closely-datable find belonging to this phase was a sherd of ARS, Hayes form 99b, assigned to *c*. AD 530-80, which was found in the fill (689) of feature 688 (a post-hole cut) (see H. Patterson in Volume 3).

PHASES 2-3

Several tombs found in this area probably belonged to the period between the late-sixth and late-eighth centuries. The most accurately dated of this group was Tomb 617. It was positioned within the portico, just south of the northern bracing wall (604). The skeleton within the tomb was articulated and lay with its head to the south. The body was adorned with a bronze bracelet and a string of simple pear-shaped paste beads of a type readily paralleled to sixth- and seventh-century Apulian/Basilicatan finds (see Filippucci in Volume 3). Part of the body had already been removed; the remaining part lay on

Fig. 5:4 View of the cistern, looking west *(RH)*

(7229) may have belonged to phase 2, given that it contained an assemblage of late Roman pottery and no later material. At face value this would indicate that the cistern was disused and filled in by the sixth or seventh century: however, it must be borne in mind that elsewhere on the site groups of late Roman material occurred commonly in eighth and ninth century deposits. The cistern fills (7224, 7225, 7228, 7229) contained much limestone rubble, mortar and tile, but no human bone.

PHASE 4

There were considerable changes to the area after phase 2, probably when the monastery was at its apogee in the ninth century. Wall 7207 (see Fig. 5:1), attached to the south side of the portico-blocking, probably formed some part of the construction of the Upper Thoroughfare described in Chapter 2. Its construction was certainly similar to 354, the north Refectory wall, which followed the same alignment. Wall 7207 followed the portico/ south garden wall to the back of the Assembly Room of the Lower Thoroughfare; it turned on the slope and then ran southward. The wall was 0.5 m wide and of very rough limestone. Its wide footings clearly cut the phase 1a midden (7209). It seems feasible that this wall formed the western side of a corridor approximately 4.5-5.0 m wide (the Upper Thoroughfare), running towards the steps found 12.0 m to the south (Chapter 2).

After the foundation trench for wall 7207 was filled in, a layer of dense clay (7208) was laid down, decreasing the angle of the slope. This was covered in two ways. Firstly, a stone feature (665), one course high, measuring 1.0 m wide, was laid over the clay against wall 7207. Secondly, a series of small tips (7203) containing much mortar and burnt material was deposited to the south. On the surface of 7203 was a patch of fine, white mortar similar to that used for tile bedding in the Refectory. This strengthens the argument for both of these features

three basal tiles. A similar tomb (7219) was encountered in 1983, cut into wall 620 to the south of 617, but only photographed and backfilled. This again was a single inhumation with its head to the south. The fragmentary remains of two further skeletons (623, 625) may also have belonged to this phase.

In the cistern, beside the Tower, the lowest fill

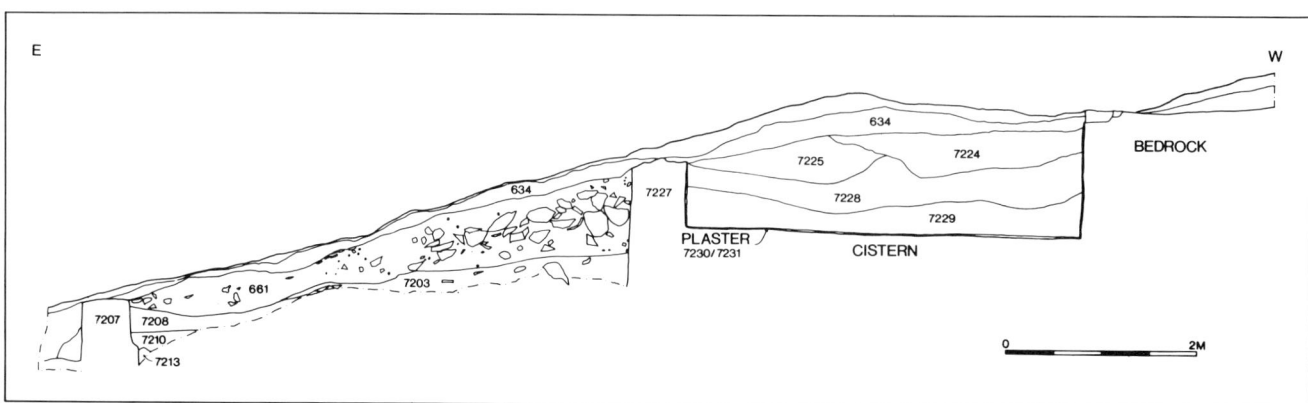

Fig. 5:5 North-facing section through the cistern and Trench F layers *(LW)*

(665 and 7203) belonging to the ninth century, suggesting an up-slope path might have followed the south face of the Tower.

PHASE 5

In phase 5a the high western apse of the 'South Church' was constructed over the north end of the Tower portico. At the same time the north wall (74/9102) of the phase 1b garden was partly dismantled and incorporated into the new apse of the 'South Church' (see Volume 1, chapter 9: 142-4). It seems likely that the construction of the 'South Church' involved at least the partial demolition of the late Roman Tower. It is possible that a thick mortary rubble layer (609, 637, 658), spread between the surviving walls and covering the phase 2-3 tombs, may have been related to this phase. This mortary level preceded several block-built tombs which had bases made of ninth-century tiles. These tombs are tentatively attributed to phase 6 (see below).

The painted plaster from contexts 639, 648 and 661 offers a small clue to enable us to interpret the sequence. These fragments probably belonged to this phase of demolition. None showed signs of marked scorching, and so all probably pre-dated the fire of 881 (phase 5c). From context 639 there was a number of pieces painted plain white. Other fragments had a thin grey line on a white ground, white bordering a field of pale blue-grey, and blue-black-grey bordering pale grey-blue. One piece was painted with white bordering light brown-red, with brick-red bands on the white ground. This material was light and airy in hue. From 648 there were fragments with white bordering black and black bordering pink. From 661, the rubble destruction layer just to the south of the south wall of the Tower, and immediately east of the cistern, there was a small group which included fragments with a dark brown swathe crossing a ground of ox-blood red, and others with a brown swathe and other marks on a ground of ochre which bordered a deep red field. Other fragments showed light blue bordering deep brown-red, with an incised line along the divide; and there were two fragments with red splodges on an ochre ground, in one case with the ochre bordering an area of pale olive-green. The most interesting fragment from this context (661) had two concentric circles incised in its surface about a compass point, one circle 34.5 mm and the other 20.2 mm in diameter. A sickle-shaped area of red-brown changing to yellow developed from the inner circle. Another fragment with the same configuration was found unstratified in Trench F. These may have been fragments of an elaborate imbricated design of little overlapping tiles, analogous to the pattern employed on the benches in the Assembly Room (see Chapter 3, Plate 3:1). The manner in which the design was laid out and the colours employed suggest an early ninth-century date.

PHASE 6a

Two sets of block-built tombs were inserted into the Tower complex; one set was within the south room of the initial Tower and one set was within the blocked portico. There were no means of independently dating these tombs, so it is possible that they belonged to phase 5. The belief that they belonged to the tenth to eleventh centuries rests upon their similarity to the phase 6 tombs in the Entrance Hall, notably in their block-built construction and tile bases, and the suggestion that the Tower complex would have been an unusual place for a graveyard in the ninth century. The tombs within the original Tower had been cut into the series of mortary layers (669) belonging to phase 0 or 1. One of the internal walls of the Tower (656) was also cut, confirming that the building was definitely a ruin by this time, if not already demolished. The original position of burials within the cut is unknown as the central tomb (672; Fig. 5:1) was inserted later, causing some disturbance. Nevertheless, the tomb to the south (682) largely survived. The skeleton lay on three large roofing tiles, with its head positioned on a fourth, broken, tile. The tiles appeared to be Roman, but were almost certainly reused. The central tomb (672) had rough walls, of tile, mortar and stone, standing 0.3-0.4 m high, and varying in width. Originally the tomb was covered by large stone slabs of which only one survived, at the west end, where it had been pushed out of position by later robbing. The same robbing presumably removed any flooring of the tomb along with the skeleton. Excavation of the disturbed layers here produced one notable find: a pair of bronze bangles in context 670 (fill c), a context with much disturbed human bone and therefore possibly the remains of a tomb, just north of the central tomb. These bangles were of late Roman date (see Filippucci in Volume 3), but in this context they are of little help in establishing an absolute date for the structures in this area.

Within the blocked portico, east of the tombs described above, lay a second set of tombs which were inserted into the ruin. Wall 643 (blocking the portico on its southern side) had clearly been repaired with two stone blocks when the tombs were built. Two definite tombs were uncovered (677 and 694), one above the other in the space defined by wall 643 and a rough 'wall', 686 (see below). The lower tomb (694) contained two skeletons, neither complete, laid on three phase 4 floor tiles. An upright tile fragment of the same type defined the head of the tomb. It was filled with loose rubble, containing much broken human bone. Over this was the second burial (677), which had been partially destroyed by later robbing. The tiles were again medieval: two were inscribed but none were complete. Of the skeleton in this tomb, only the lower jaw and part of the torso were preserved.

Undoubtedly, there were once more tombs in this area. A narrow 'wall' (686), just to the north, was built of four stone blocks 0.2-0.25 m wide. This presumably defined the edge of another tomb but no further trace of it was found.

PHASES 7-8

After the area was no longer used as a cemetery a series of fills accumulated, many containing powdery rubble and fragmented human bones. These are difficult to date because the terrace was evidently cultivated regularly until recent times, causing much disturbance. A certain amount of the ninth-century painted plaster, described above, came from these levels.

DISCUSSION

The late Roman Tower at San Vincenzo, especially in its monastic context, conjures up images of the *aedificium* in Umberto Eco's fictional monastery in *The Name of the Rose*. Unfortunately, it appears that the Tower at San Vincenzo was probably in a ruinous state when Paldo, Tato and Taso arrived here in the early eighth century. Nevertheless, it may have been the tall Tower which drew the monks to the uninhabited late Roman settlement. Moreover, with such firm foundations, like the *gsar* towers of the Libyan desert or the tower mausolea of Imperial times, it is possible that the Tower was still a prominent feature within the monastic complex when Joshua took charge of San Vincenzo at the end of the eighth century.

The Tower appears to have had two phases of occupation before it became the intermittent focus of a cemetery. In its first phase it comprised a solid central part with narrower rooms along its north and south sides. Two different building forms can be proposed. First, the central and side rooms may have risen in unison to at least three storeys. The early Imperial tower at Anguillara, Lazio, recently excavated by the British School at Rome (Van der Noort and Whitehouse 1992), provides an illustration of this model. A second hypothesis would be to postulate a three- or four-storey central structure with one- or two-storey flanking buildings on the north and south sides. This temple-like form is difficult to parallel, but it goes some way towards explaining the great strength of the inner walls in contrast to the slightly less-stout outer walls.

In the reconstruction (Fig. 5:6) we have opted for the first hypothesis since it is a more straightforward design. The precise features of this building, of course, remain unknown. We do not know whether the floors were supported by vaulting or a central pillar at ground-floor level. The windows, doorways, floors and decoration remain a mystery. Clearly, the rooms were plastered but it is not possible to tell whether these were painted as well.

The roof is assumed to have been made of tile, but no trace of a destruction level was discovered to provide any supporting evidence.

Tower houses occur in the earlier Roman centuries, but they are a particular feature of the late Empire. Small versions are known in fourth-century Britain (Neal 1982; Potter and Whitehouse 1982); from Germany (Neal 1982); from Italy at Capena (Pallottino 1937) and Anguillara in Lazio (Whitehouse 1980; Van der Noort and Whitehouse 1992), and at San Giovanni di Ruoti in Basilicata (Small 1983). The Romano-Libyan *gsars* are more modest versions of the same phenomenon (cf. Pringle 1981). In size and possible form the closest parallel is at Vaga Theodoriana near Béja in Tunisia. This later fifth- or sixth-century three-storey tower measured 18.0 x 16.0 m externally; it was entered at ground-floor level through an arched doorway with a relieving arch resting on two engaged pillars just inside it. The ground-floor chamber was 10.0 m high and lit by two windows. A cistern existed beside the tower (Pringle 1981: 251, fig. 4, pl. LVIIb). A vivid contemporary illustration of the form is depicted on mosaics from Tabarka, Tunisia (Dunbabin 1978: 122-3, XLIV, fig. 111; see below, Fig. 9:2). This villa apparently possessed several turrets. Like many North African villas, Tabarka's seems to represent the final phase of the classic courtyard arrangement of the earlier Roman period, now fortified, which was to be a harbinger of Carolingian and high medieval private élite settlements (cf. Février 1978; Leveau 1983).

In Italy, nevertheless, some care should be taken to avoid creating a group from buildings which vary considerably in detail. For example, the tower at Anguillara is much larger than the one at San Vincenzo, while the example excavated at San Giovanni di Ruoti is much smaller. Even so, some interesting observations about this building at San Vincenzo can be made, despite the ephemeral nature of the remains. Firstly, it was undeniably the principal building in the late Roman ensemble, dominating the churches below, to the northeast, and any ranges which existed on the site of the ninth-century Refectory. Yet this was almost certainly a residential complex from which a great deal of refuse was thrown. Indeed, refuse was thrown out of the front as well as the sides, leaving the building half-surrounded by rubbish. The range of pottery and glassware implies that the residents were neither extravagantly rich nor, for that matter, poor (cf. Stevenson 1988, for a preliminary description of the glassware). The quantity of rubbish, in some places 0.5 m deep, implies a considerable population or lengthy occupation. The building must have had either about 380 or 500 square metres of floor-area, calculated on the basis of three and four storeys respectively – sufficient space for a population of between about 38 and 50 people (using Narroll's constant of one person = 10 square metres (Narroll 1962)). This seems a high figure by medieval standards for feudal castles, and represents the greater proportion of the population of approximately 50 to 60 persons estimated from an analysis of the phase 1b cemetery in the funerary church which served this community during this later period (Volume 1, chapter 9: 181).

The addition of the portico and the creation of a garden on the slope below the Tower marks an interesting alteration to the plan of the late Roman settlement. In phase 1a, midden material was tumbling down to the place where the funerary church was to be built (Volume 1, chapter 9: 128).

The portico must have been designed as a new, more imposing façade for the Tower. The hillslope garden brought an end to the dumping of rubbish in an untidy and doubtless smelly way beside the new cemetery. Instead, this hillslope was separated off as if to protect the apsidal end of the churches both from rubbish and the prying eyes of those who now had to approach the Tower from its south side. A small staircase may have been attached to the south side of the Tower at this time. The construction of a large cistern may have been part of the general change in the management of the building. The earlier Roman cisterns investigated at the Posto villa

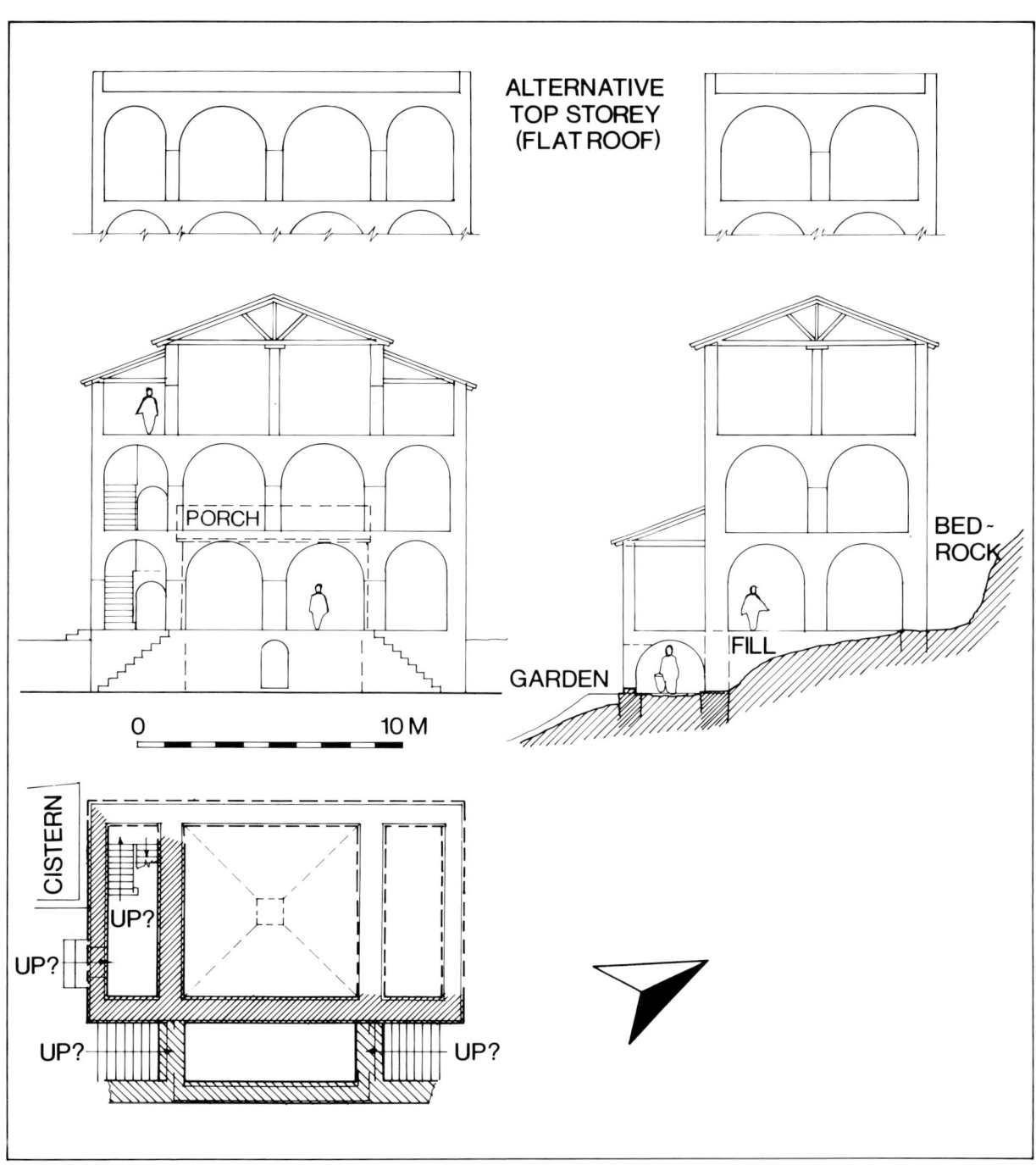

Fig. 5:6 Reconstruction of the Tower *(SG)*

in Campania were long, narrow structures (roughly 11.0 x 3.0 m) (Cotton 1979: 27). A cistern, say, 10.0 m long would have stopped at a point where a ninth-century up-slope path appears to have run between the stepped Upper Thoroughfare behind the Assembly Room and Terrace 3. A cistern 10.0 x 5.0 m and, in all likelihood, at least 2.0-3.0 m deep, would have held a good supply of water even for so large a community. But what became of their refuse in phase 1b? Some of it may have been used to fill up the narthex area of the Crypt Church (Volume 1, chapter 6: 55-6); but clearly another midden has yet to be located, as rubbish of this date, thrown out as manure, was not detected in any of the surrounding fields during the survey.

The exact date of the desertion of the building cannot be pinpointed. A sherd of ARS, Hayes form 99b (c. AD 530-80), was found in context 689 and may have belonged to the latest phase of occupation. Equally, this sherd may have been associated with some much later activity on the site. It would be unwise to place too great an emphasis on this solitary piece of evidence to suggest that the building was inhabited, for example, until the end of the sixth century. Instead, the assemblage of sixth-century pottery from the filling of the cistern offers some limited support for the hypothesis that it was deserted along with the rest of the settlement during the central decades of the sixth century.

Like many Roman villas, after being abandoned the Tower at San Vincenzo was used as a burial-ground. Post-abandonment burials are a feature of villas as far apart as those in southern England and southern Italy. In central and southern Italy burials were cut into the deserted villa at Posto, Campania (Cotton 1979), at Buccino, Basilicata (Dyson 1983) and at Casignana Palazzi, Calabria (Barello and Cardosa 1991). Late burials were also found in the largely ruinous villa at Matrice near Campobasso, Molise (J. Lloyd, pers. comm.). The unusual feature in the case of San Vincenzo is that phase 2 burials were placed not only in the ground floor of the Tower, but within the funerary church as well (Volume 1,

chapter 9). The cemetery, in other words, was still perceived to be in use. So why bury the dead inside the Tower? The answer must be sought in the volatile liturgical history of these generations, caught between classical and medieval traditions (cf. Brown 1982). The Tower certainly constituted a link with the past: by the eighth century a grand mausoleum for a population inhabiting timber rather than stone structures, for whom imperial society and its economy was but a faint memory.

The eighth-, and possibly the tenth-, century cemetery on the terrace in part continued this rather confused tradition. But the cemetery in the first place is most readily explained in terms of the 'South Church' which, it is proposed, was the first abbey-church (Volume 1, chapter 9). If the phase 3 'South Church' was the abbey-church, its burial-ground must have been located nearby. Traditionally Benedictine cemeteries are close to the principal church, often beyond or beside the apse (cf. at Mittelzell, Reichenau: Zettler 1988: TA 12). The ground either side of the eighth-century abbey-church was occupied by buildings. Only Terrace 2 could be employed as a cemetery. This might explain why the ground was left unused in the great ninth-century monastery. It might also explain why this zone was used as a burial-ground once again in phase 6, during the tenth to eleventh centuries.

These late tombs, however, must be considered in terms of the first-floor passage (the Upper Thoroughfare) which started at the Entrance Hall. The Entrance Hall may have constituted a mausoleum of sorts in phase 6, possibly housing, amongst others, the remains of the martyrs of 881 (Volume 1, chapter 12: 226). The burials in the 'South Church' south corridor (Volume 1, chapter 9: 175-6), as well as those on Terrace 2, were a short step from these venerated tombs. The passage, too, may have been one surviving connection between the church constructed in front of the gate at this date, according to the *Chronicon Vulturnense*, and the church on Terrace 3. By this time, though, the Tower had long gone.

Chapter Six

EXCAVATIONS ON TERRACE 3: THE CHURCH WITH AN *OPUS SECTILE* FLOOR

by Richard Hodges and John Mitchell

Terrace 3 (Fig. 0:1) is a well-defined shelf, unlike Terrace 2 (Volume 1: 21-4). A natural ledge appears to have been cut back to accommodate buildings. The terrace is about 120 m long and would once have been between 10.0 and 20 m wide. The northern end is the widest part. At one point, after clearance of the vegetation, the back wall of the terrace was particularly clear. At some stage the travertine had been chopped back to a vertical face; a stub projecting from it had been neatly trimmed as though it constituted the springing for a small wall running out across the width of the terrace. Two small trenches, P and R, were excavated on the terrace, to establish the nature of the remains here. First, an earlier, unpublished excavation (made when the trench for a water-pipe leading from Castel San Vincenzo to the present abbey cut through the site) was enlarged at the north end of the terrace. The pipe-layers on this occasion expanded their trench to examine what they were destroying. This excavation was called Trench R. We were informed by several local people that a pavement of some kind had been discovered in this area. The second excavation, Trench P, was designed to examine the sequence of deposits on the terrace at the point where the cut rock-face and the projecting stub occurred. Were these features part of a building, or part of the cemetery discovered further up the hill? Trench P was supervised by Jim Symonds and Trench R by Amanda Claridge.

We shall describe them in the order they were excavated, as this appears to make their interpretation most clear. A summary of the main phases is given in Table 6:1.

TRENCH R (FIG. 6:1)

Clearance of the area in 1981 led to the discovery of the old pipe-trench excavation, and demonstrated that there was a distinctive wide platform forming the northern terminal of the terrace. The platform projected out beyond the edge of the terrace, where traces of a wall could be identified. This might have been the eastern part of a building or have related to early medieval terracing.

A trench 4.2 m (north-south) by 6.5 m (east-west) was excavated in August 1981.

Beneath the humus was a mixture of loam and rubble (much of the rubble still having plaster adhering to it) (2004, 2008, 2009, 2010). Beneath the rubble was a thin but uniform ash and charcoal layer (2007), which in turn overlaid a cream-coloured plaster surface (2005). The surface was badly disturbed in several places, but the impressions of an *opus sectile* pavement could be clearly recognized, with a marble border (2006) defining its north side. The floor seems to have been contemporary with two walls (2002 and 2003) which were found in the northeast corner of the trench. These were sturdy, well-built walls, made with cut blocks, different in construction to the phase 4-5 walls. A small trial trench through the plaster surface showed that it was once about 0.1-0.2 m thick, and overlaid rubble that was on top of natural limestone bedrock. The bedding (2015) for the plaster surface varied from 50 to 100 mm deep and contained tile fragments, some marble and other building debris.

The pavement appears to be all that remained of an *opus sectile* floor in the chancel of the church. This was a small investigation so the form and date of the building cannot be deduced with any certainty. However, a few features warrant further discussion.

The church must have been at least 15.0 m long (east-west), to stretch from the (eastern) edge of Terrace 3 to the western edge of the excavation (without the addition of an apse, which could have added a further four metres). However, no return wall was found, so the precise dimensions are unknown. The exposed east wall, if it formed the eastern front of the church as opposed to the revetment of the terrace supporting the church, indicates that the building was about 12.0 m wide (see Fig. 6:2 for a reconstruction plan).

Only a relatively small quantity of painted plaster was recovered from this trench. Plaster fragments occurred in contexts 2001, 2008, 2011, 2013, 2015

TABLE 6:1 Summary of the main phases of the excavations on Terrace 3	
4-5	A rock-cut passage was made (Trench P).
7	The church found in Trench R was constructed. It had an *opus sectile* floor in its chancel.
7 or 8	There was systematic demolition of the church and covered passage.

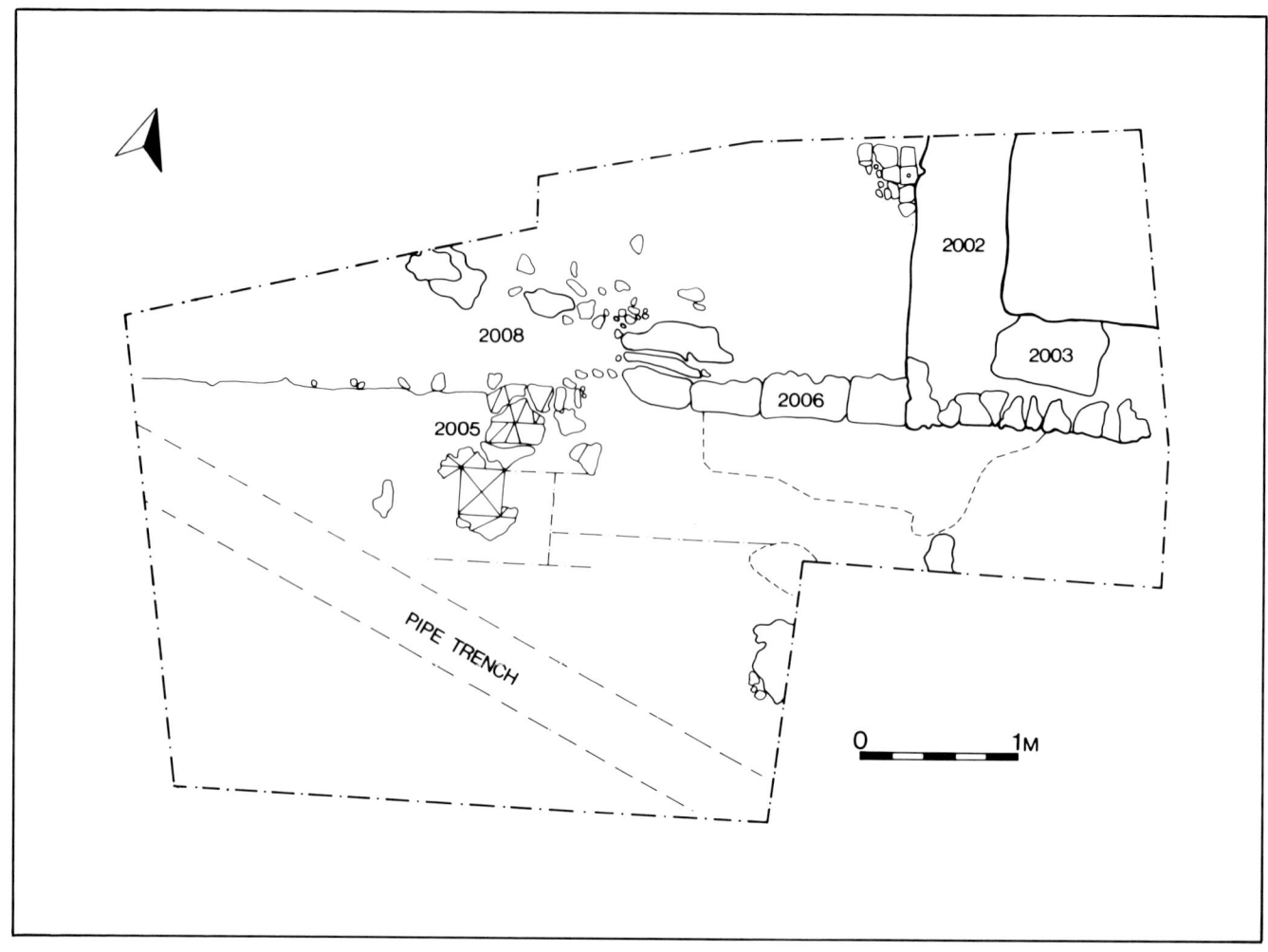

Fig. 6:1 Plan of Trench R *(KF)*

and 2025. Generally the painted surfaces of these fragments were in a moderate condition. However, in some they were much worn and faded; and in others they survived in a remarkably good state of preservation (particularly in 2008). Much of the plaster was white in colour and contained dense inclusions of tiny stones. A small group of fragments from 2013 was greyish in colour, with prominent inclusions of small stones, and rather hard and brittle in consistency. The surfaces of these were painted dark red, in one case straight-bordering white, and were rather worn. From 2008 there were remains of elaborate painting, combinations of brush strokes and colours which suggested drapery and figurative imagery. The paint was laid on with free, fast strokes of the brush which were sometimes quite controlled, but in other instances relatively unregimented and almost awkward in configuration. One large passage of plaster still attached to a block of stone was painted with an arching configuration, with an interior field consisting of branching 3-4 mm red lines against a pink ground, followed by a curving 6 mm white band, outside which was an arching 21 mm green band with prominent rounded dentations. These impinged on

an outer band of white, which, in turn, after 40 mm, was bounded by an arching field of yellow. This must have derived from a large painted arcade or some similar configuration. Another fragment had two gently diverging curving 8 mm bands of red-brown on a field of yellow – perhaps from a passage of rather schematically articulated drapery. The predominant colours in the plaster from this church were yellow, black, red, blue-black, white, and an eye-catching medium green. This latter colour was usually associated with white, black, greenish black, dull red or orange. It was not found in the paintings associated with the ninth-century phases 4 and 5 at San Vincenzo. The prominent role played by this colour in the decoration of this church, particularly in combination with black, and the manner in which the paint was applied, suggest that this was not ninth-century work.

In two contexts, 2001 and 2008, there were fragments of inscriptions, with large white letters set against a black ground. It was not possible to identify or to estimate the full, original height of any of the broken scraps of letters that survived. On one fragment, from 2008, a prominent serif, with rounded end, projected at right angles from the shaft of a character. This is untypical of the painted inscriptions from ninth-century phases at San Vincenzo. From 2008 there was also a fragment from a second inscription, painted onto a different quality plaster – part of a white letter set against a black ground.

Discussion

The building, to judge from its wall construction and from the fragments of painted plaster, dates from phase 7, and is likely to have been one of the churches refurbished by Abbot Ilarius (1011-45).

Little can be deduced about the architecture of the building. It seems possible, though, that the square east end was a façade, constructed over the edge of Terrace 3, so that the building might impress those looking up from below. If so, we might expect the apse to have lain at the west end. In the reconstruction (Fig. 6:2) it is proposed that the building was axially-aligned and approximately 19.0 m long. The flanking chapels or transepts are somewhat unusual features, and must be regarded with caution. If the church was 12.0 m wide, as is tentatively proposed in Figure 6:2, it seems likely that it was aisled, the aisles perhaps being each approximately 2.0 m wide. If so, the nave would have been about 7.0 m wide. Much of this remains to be demonstrated by further excavations. Nevertheless, it is clear that this was a major building, similar in its width to the 'South Church' in phases

4-5, and must have been of some importance. Access to this church, from the level of the Upper Thoroughfare, was along the terrace to the cemetery. Local sources suggest that a set of steps led down from this church to the building found in Trench EE, and thence to the Crypt Church (cf. Volume 1, chapter 8: 122).

Evidently there was plenty of building rubble available on which the *opus sectile* floor could be bedded; possibly it was derived from the refurbishment of an earlier building on this spot. The *opus sectile* floor is of special interest. No fragments of marble remained in place, but many pieces were discovered in the rubble of the demolition. These included red and green porphyry, and white marble; some pieces had been carefully cut comparatively small, but most had been rudely chopped from larger marble blocks or slabs. This is the only example we encountered of a fine pavement which was more-or-less *in situ*. (Remains of the floor of the phase 4-5 'South Church', however, are discussed in Volume 1, chapter 9.)

The *opus sectile* floor itself is difficult to reconstruct in detail as so little of it remained. However, it appears that a wide border of plain marble divided the chancel from the north transept. As can be seen in Figure 6:1 the fragments of floor within the chancel showed that a line of sawtooth-shaped tesserae formed an edge immediately south of the marble border, and that the main field was composed of a chequer-board design. The tesserae in the main field were cut into triangles, roughly 0.15-0.25 m on each side, and probably formed geometric patterns. Similar designs of a rather more ambitious cosmatesque variety were found by Pantoni when the present abbey-church at San Vincenzo was being restored (1980a: 59-64; figs 30-34, tav. I). But these pavements, laid by Abbot Benedict, early in the twelfth century, contain much smaller tesserae which were neatly trimmed. Those from Trench R, in contrast were poorly cut, and may represent either an earlier phase of making floors of this kind or a provincial realization of a metropolitan fashion.

The ash and charcoal mixed in with the debris lying over the pavement of the building must belong to its demolition at the end of phase 7. The faded condition of some of the plaster implies that the paintings may have been exposed to the elements before the building was demolished.

TRENCH P (FIG. 6:3)

Trench P was excavated in 1983 to examine the archaeology towards the centre of the terrace, where the cut rock-face and a stub of neatly finished rock projecting out towards the terrace occurred (see Fig. 0:1). The right-hand side of this stub carried the remnants of a plastered surface painted a deep rich

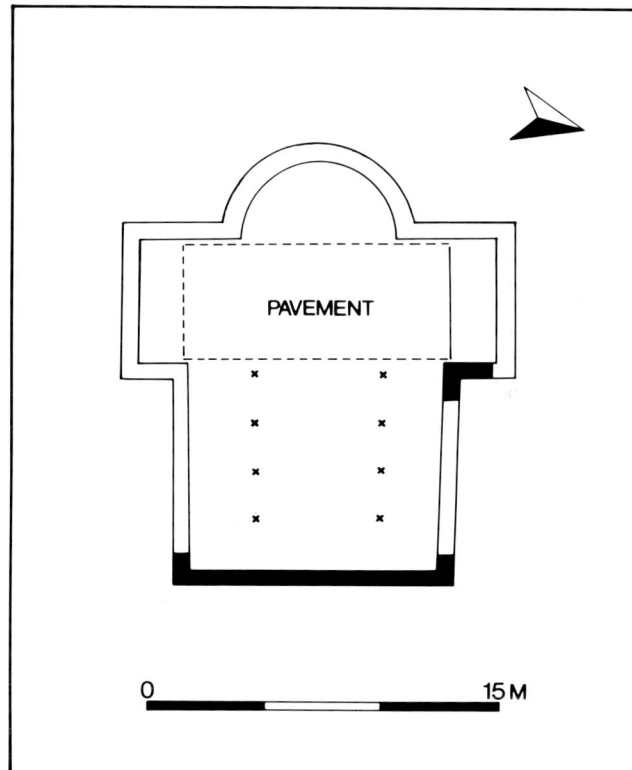

Fig. 6:2 A hypothetical reconstruction of the church found in Trench R, showing the approximate location of the *opus sectile* pavement *(KF)*

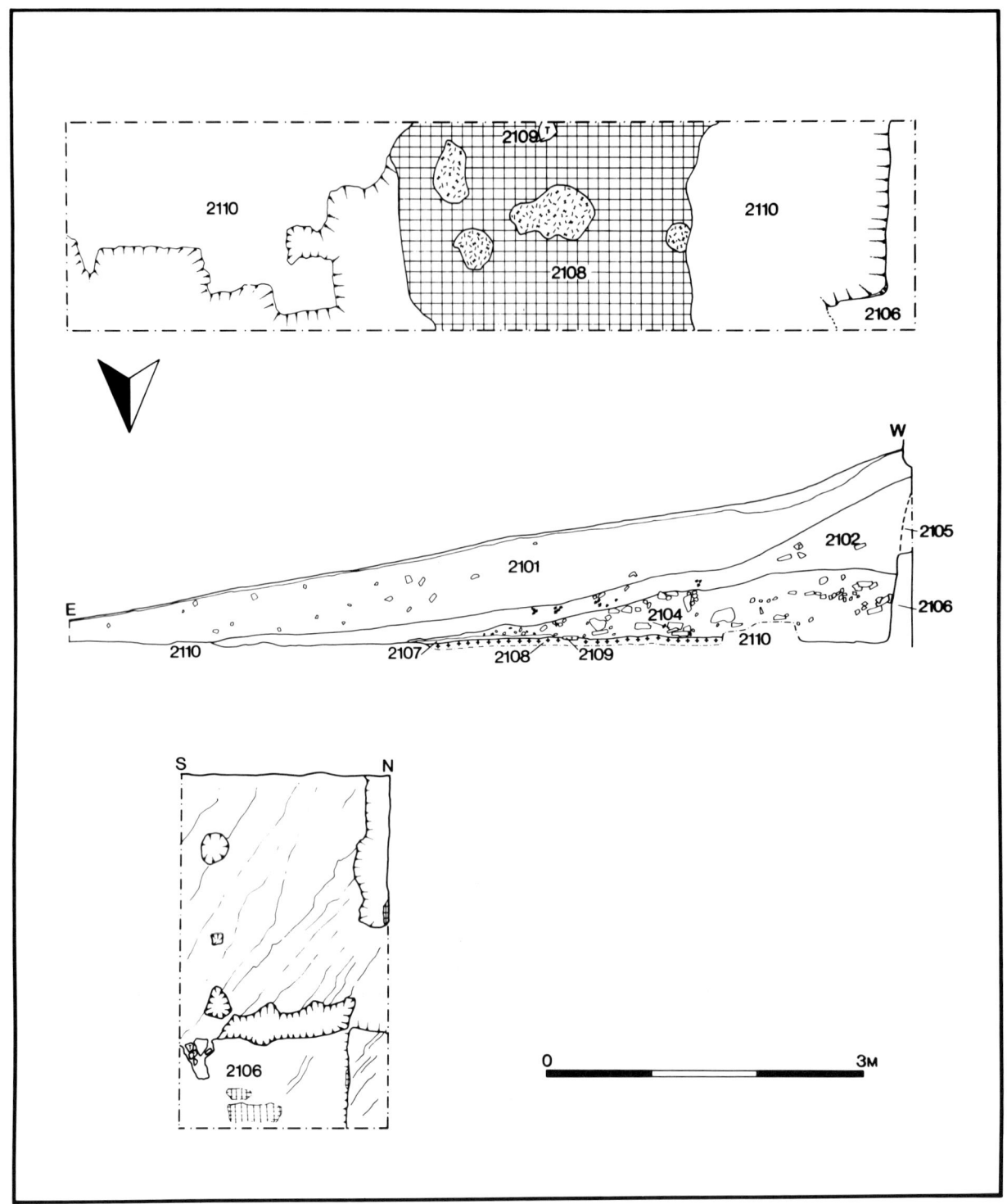

Fig. 6:3 Plan (top), north-facing section (centre) and east-facing elevation (bottom) of the rock-face *(KF)*

salmon-pink. The trial trench was 8.0 m long, extending at right angles out from the cut rock-face, and 2.0 m wide.

Beneath the topsoil there was a patchy spread of ash (2103) which overlaid a deep deposit of rubble (2104) (including a few tile fragments). Sealed beneath the rubble was a thin layer of dark earth (2107), flecked with charcoal: this also contained crushed limestone fragments and many smashed tile fragments. Removal of 2107 revealed a ledge (2106) cut into the rock-face (2110), with traces of plaster on it, and also a roughly plastered surface (2108) which covered about half the trench, set into which at a few places were tiles for a floor (2109). Further out from the rock-face, however, there was no plaster surface, only the levelled natural rock into which the surface merged. The plaster lay directly on top of the natural rock.

Again, the trench was too small to reveal the nature of the structures at this point on the terrace.

None the less, some salient features do emerge from this trial excavation.

The demolition was similar to that in Trench R, and probably belonged to the end of phase 7. The rubble overlaid some burning. In this case, however, the rubble contained ninth- or tenth-century pottery fragments and a few fragments of scorched plaster. The structure was evidently close to, or was associated with, domestic activities in which pottery was employed. It was not a particularly fine building to judge from the rubble masonry, the few fragments of plaster, and the absence of marble tesserae. Indeed, it looks as if it was a passage or hall of some kind with a crudely-cut bench set into the natural rock-face, and a tiled floor that was laid directly upon the natural limestone. The nature of layer 2107 remains uncertain, as it appears to have been a mixture of charcoal and smashed rubble, as though it represented a trampled destruction layer or a phase of temporary occupation whilst the structure was falling into ruin. The absence of a front wall strongly suggests it was either an open passage or, more probably, a simple open-colonnaded affair of some kind.

The preliminary evidence points to this area having been occupied by either a building or passage leading from the church discovered in Trench R to the substantial buildings discovered on the same level, but running at right angles (that is east-west), at the south end of Terrace 3 (Volume 1: 24). It is striking, nevertheless, that there were no traces of any late Roman features on this terrace (though sherds of pottery belonging to this phase were found), and so we must provisionally assign the rock-cutting to the phase 4-5 expansion of the monastery, that is to the ninth century.

OTHER FEATURES ON TERRACE 3

Signore Ernesto Staffieri and other workmen pointed out the existence of a well-made, stone-lined culvert which crosses the terrace about 10.0 m south of Trench P. This culvert seems to be on a similar alignment to the water-pipe encountered in Trench R, though running 30 m to the south. All our informants believe that it is an old water-course taking a supply from the hill to the main settlement (that is the ninth-century monastery). Only excavations will resolve this matter, but if it is an early medieval culvert, it may shed light on the function of buildings not only on this terrace, but on those below as well.

DISCUSSION

The excavations on Terrace 3 were designed as evaluation trenches (see Volume 1: 24). Trench R was essentially an enlargement of an earlier investigation, while Trench P was intended to examine the stratigraphy towards the centre of the terrace. The limited archaeological discoveries must be interpreted with caution. The fragments of wall plaster from Trench R suggest that the building was an eleventh-century church, while in Trench P traces of ninth-century levels were found. Trench R is especially interesting because the limited excavation suggested a single-period church, although its plan seems curious for a structure of eleventh-century (or, for that matter, ninth-century) date. One possibility is that the remains in Trench R belong to an earlier church that was radically refurbished, in the eleventh century, with wall paintings and an *opus sectile* floor. If so, this might be one of the three churches which the chronicler records, which were rebuilt in the eleventh century: either Santa Maria Maggiore, founded by Abbot Taso (729-39) but rebuilt by Abbot Ilarius (1011-45) (*CV* iii: 77), or San Pietro, built by Abbot Ato (739-60) and rebuilt by Abbot Ilarius (*CV* iii: 77), or San Michele, built by Abbot Talaricus (817-23) and also rebuilt by Abbot Ilarius (*CV* iii: 77). Only further excavations will shed light on these intriguing discoveries.

Chapter Seven

THE HILLTOP CEMETERY

by Catherine M. Coutts

INTRODUCTION

This chapter presents a description and analysis of one of the major cemetery areas at San Vincenzo al Volturno, and attempts to set the cemetery and its occupants in their social context. The study of the dead has always played a major part in archaeology; for mortuary practices are a component of social expression and interaction and can be seen to represent 'the direct and purposeful culmination of conscious behaviour, rather than its incidental residue' (O'Shea 1981: 39). Even within a single society the range of expression surrounding death can be enormous. Individuals of different sex, age, economic or political power, religious affiliation, personal charisma, occupation and status, may all be treated differently in death, as perhaps they were in life. This apparent association between differences in life and in death led archaeologists in the 1970s to believe that the social identity or 'persona' of an individual would be crystallized at death, and would be expressed in archaeologically detectable mortuary ritual. This was seen to be particularly so in relation to status. For example, the correlation between energy expenditure on mortuary edifices and the status of the individual buried therein has been asserted repeatedly (see Saxe 1970; Binford 1971; Tainter 1975; Huntington and Metcalf 1979; Goldstein 1981). The presence and nature of grave-goods have also received much attention (for examples, see Shennan 1975; Peebles and Kus 1977; Bradley 1990; Garwood *et al.* 1991).

The rituals undertaken at the time of an individual's death are primarily for the benefit of the living, whether to comfort them, allow expression of their feelings about the dead person, or to establish, legitimate or consolidate their own social position. Mortuary ritual is about interaction amongst the living and between the living and the dead; 'It is through death that the social relationships of the living are defined and expressed' (Douglass 1969: 12; cf. Parker Pearson 1993).

The dead can be transformed into an eternal and transcendent force, to be utilized by those in positions of religious authority, and feared by those without power. All Christian dead are part of the Church, and therefore the collective dead can be seen as an indomitable force, particularly dead saints, martyrs and priests. As Maximus of Turin wrote in the fifth century, 'The martyrs will keep guard over us, who live with our bodies, and they will take us into their own care when we have forsaken our bodies. Here they prevent us from the horrors of hell. That is why our ancestors were careful to unite our bodies with the bones of martyrs' (quoted in Gutmann 1977: 337). The dead may have enormous power at their disposal, far beyond anything available to them in their earthly existence. They may be feared, manipulated or worshipped; they are rarely, if ever, overlooked or denied.

The power of the dead over the lives of the living makes the investigation of archaeological manifestations of death of particular interest. The analysis of the organization and structure of a cemetery, how it changes over space and time, and the treatment of the population within it, will illuminate our picture of a society's construction of reality. It is generally accepted that in pagan and early Christian funerary systems, the presence of grave-goods was a device for displaying individual prestige. However, in some circumstances, the non-deposition of grave-goods may well have been an attempt to show allegiance to a Christian ideology of poverty and equality, a superficial rejection of pagan displays of individual wealth. Grave architecture is another medium that may be used to proclaim status, and was certainly used in this way in both the Roman and early Christian worlds (cf. Colvin 1991).

At San Vincenzo we are dealing with a society in which organized religion played a major part, where the role and power of the Church in relation to power struggles within the secular élite can be seen in activities such as giving gifts and endowments to the Church (cf. Chapter 11), as well as in mortuary ritual. The arena in which status at the time of death could be proclaimed and legitimated in fact had shifted by the ninth century, from the grave to the Church. Gifts, whether of buildings (cf. the Crypt, Volume 1, chapter 7), luxury items, endowments of land and property, for example, were given to the Church without expectation of an earthly reward. Thus the status of the gift-giver (and his/her descendants) was publicly and permanently enhanced. William the Good of Aquitaine, when founding Cluny in AD 909, made this relationship quite explicit; 'desiring to provide for my own salvation while I am still able, I have considered it advisable, indeed most necessary, that from the temporal goods which have been conferred upon me I should give some little portion for the gain of my soul' (see Breul 1876: 124-63, at p. 132).

HISTORY OF THE HILLTOP CEMETERY EXCAVATIONS

Investigations of the hilltop cemetery began in 1981. A survey of Colle della Torre was undertaken by Denis Dennehy: this suggested that a number of rock-hewn structures lay buried beneath the dense vegetation and olive groves on the south- and east-facing terraces of the hill. As a result of the survey, two of these structures were investigated as part of an overall sampling programme of the area around the monastery (see Volume 1: chapter 3). The removal of the scrub and thorns that covered the cliff-face revealed two apse-like niches. These initially seemed to confirm the local tradition that there had once been a church on this site. Both this area and what was thought to be a good example of an eremitic cell on the south-facing terrace were chosen for excavation. The two areas were respectively called S and T. Trench S was supervised by Nigel Baker and Cameron Moffett, and Trench T by Jacqueline Nowakowski.

It soon became apparent that neither of these structures was quite what it had appeared to be at first. Clearance of the dense vegetation and removal of the topsoil revealed that the rock-hewn features on the hillside were the remnants of a substantial cemetery, probably covering about 2,000 square metres. Above ground, most of these features consisted of cut rock-faces with low rock-hewn walls projecting out from them. The tombs themselves lay between these walls, and were of two types. The majority was cut into the bedrock in a coffin- or elliptical-shape. Others were built from tufa or limestone blocks embedded in the ground, their capping stones flush with the ground surface.

The excavation of these areas revealed that the cemetery had suffered considerable damage in the centuries between its construction and excavation, both from deliberate disturbance and from agricultural activities. Indeed, much of the hilltop cemetery has been cultivated as an olive grove in modern times. Most of the tombs excavated in 1981 were badly disturbed; some had been largely emptied of their skeletal remains, leaving only a few fragments of loose bones. As a result, no conclusive dating evidence was produced. The fact that cemeteries with rock-cut tombs and arcosolia feature in the Roman as well as the early medieval periods, posed a serious chronological problem.

Investigations of the cemetery continued in 1983 (under the author's supervison), with two aims:
(1) to define the extent of the cemetery;
(2) to locate and excavate undisturbed tombs with intact stratigraphy in order to date the cemetery.

Before we began the excavations, the vegetation had to be cut back over a large area of the hill, the brambles having returned to a tangled and overgrown mass since the clearance of 1981. Clearance was followed by a systematic search for undisturbed tombs. When the hill had been thoroughly examined for indications of interference with the natural rock-faces and outcrops (which might indicate the position of a tomb), a sampling strategy was devised.

The sampling strategy for the hilltop cemetery was devised by Valerie Higgins, who was working on the palaeopathological analysis of the skeletal remains, Eric Hansen, an anthropologist, and the present author. The skeletal remains were subsequently analysed by Dr Higgins, and it is her analysis that was used to form the basis of the descriptions which relate to the ageing and sexing of the cemetery population (see Higgins in Volume 3). (This sample was also included in Higgins's more general study of health patterns in rural agricultural communities of the late Roman and early medieval periods (Higgins 1990).)

The sampling design was based on an apparent distinction between isolated tombs and 'cells' which included a number of tombs. It was hypothesized that the cells were prepared for family groups, while single tombs were prepared for some other element of the population, such as people who died without kin. The hypothesis was based on the presumption that all of the tombs, irrespective of whether they were isolated or in cells, contained single burials. Excavation in fact showed that this expectation was misconceived, and that half of the tombs contained the remains of multiple inhumations, irrespective of whether they were isolated or in cells.

The isolated tombs and multiple tomb cells which were provisionally identified in the survey were numbered consecutively (with each cell constituting a single unit from which one tomb would be sampled), and ten per cent of these were selected randomly for excavation.

TRENCH S: THE EXCAVATION

The area to be excavated was first cleared of the undergrowth, heaps of rubble (3037, possibly a clearance cairn relating to previous use of this area as an olive grove), and topsoil (3036, 3038) that had covered it in recent years. The northern arcosolium (B) had been reused in the post-medieval period as part of a lean-to structure associated with a dry-stone building at the northern edge of the trench. This was probably a *baracca* associated with the management of the olive grove of farm 293 (see Volume 1: chapter 3, fig. 3:2). The walls of this structure (3039 and 3089), which ran eastward from the arcosolia, measured 0.8 m wide and consisted of a rubble core faced with cut blocks; only a single course survived. Wall 3039 projected directly out from the division between the two arcosolia. The wall to the north of niche B reached almost 1.0 m high in places, and formed the northern wall of the structure. The *baracca* measured 2.5 m across internally.

Below the rubble piles and the post-medieval walls, but above the level of the graves, were two layers of soil (3060 and 3111) which contained smashed bones. These layers must represent a post-abandonment phase, and are perhaps indicative of a period of tomb-robbing in this part of the cemetery.

The excavated sequence shows four general phases of activity:

(1) the cemetery was in use as a burial ground;

(2) the cemetery was abandoned, with tomb-robbing and/or disturbance;

(3) the cemetery area was used for olive cultivation;

(4) the cemetery area was used for olive cultivation, but was encroached upon by natural woodland (this being the current situation).

The arcosolia

As was mentioned earlier, the two rock-hewn niches located on the terrace provided the original reason for excavating in this area. These niches were originally thought to belong to some ecclesiastical

building, perhaps one of the churches referred to in the *Chronicon Vulturnense*. When the arch-shaped niches were cleared and excavated each was shown to contain a single tomb (Fig. 7:1). Both of the niches contained shallow recesses in their back walls, measuring *c.* 0.3 x 0.4 m, perhaps cut to hold painted portrait-panels or other offerings.

The more northerly niche (B) had been partly cut through a fault in the rock which had been packed with loose rock and soil. It measured 2.2 x 1.8 m, and was *c.* 0.5 m deep (containing Tomb 3076 (Grave S5)). It was cut in the form of a rough arch, flanked by two shallow vertical rebates and capped by a gable shaped slot, 0.2 m deep (see Fig. 7:1). These cuts may once have provided the mortice for a pair of rafters supporting the roof of a simple wooden porch-like structure projecting out from the arcosolium. The rebates and slots would have been unable to support a prominent structure, indicating that this edifice would not have been particularly substantial, probably extending outwards for less than a metre. Such façades are paralleled in the classicizing treatment of arcosolia in the catacombs (Stevenson 1978: 66, 125, 156). An attached façade would have protected the tomb within the arcosolium from rain running down the face of the cliff. No traces of a structure were found on the ground in front of the arcosolia: but this area

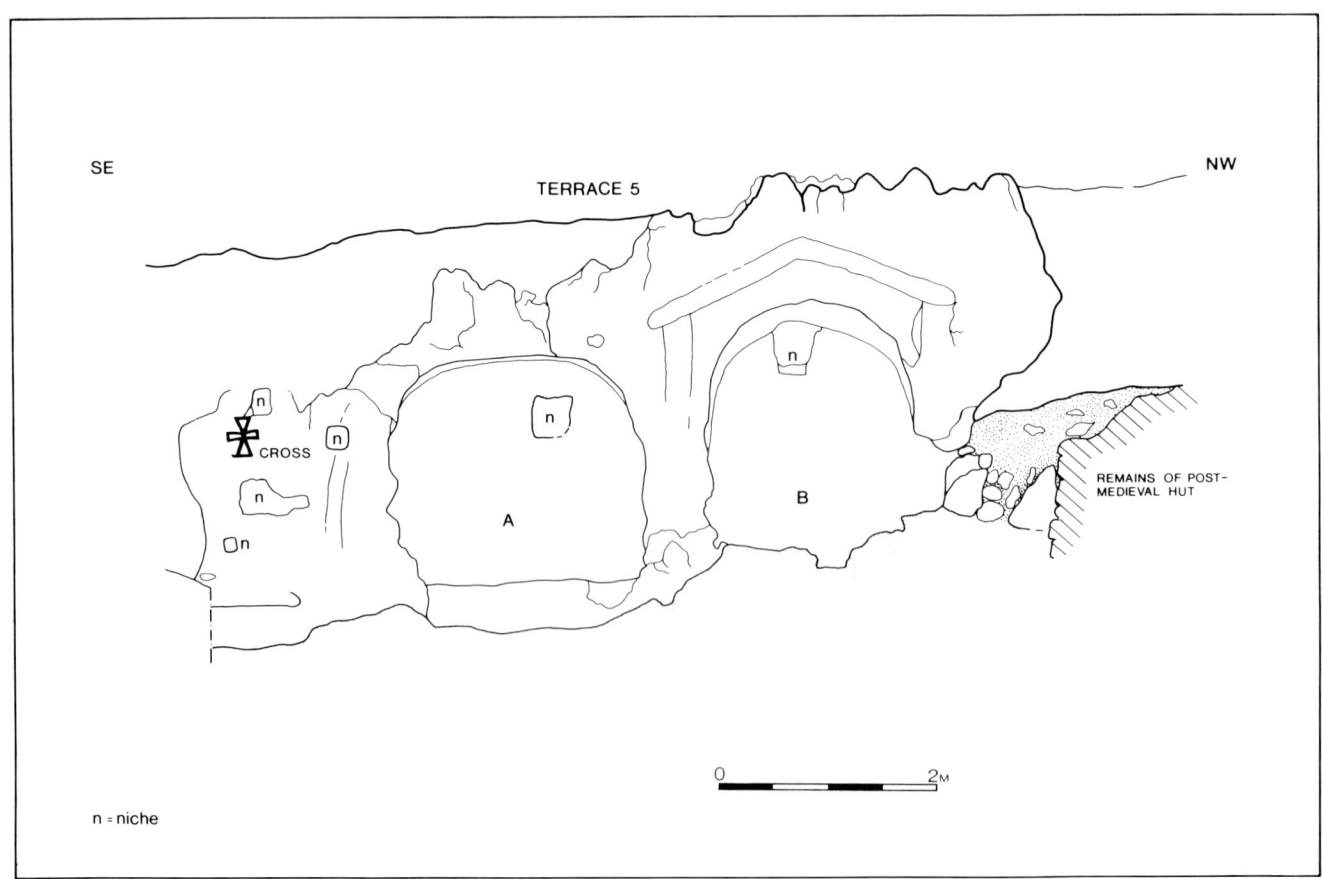

Fig. 7:1 East-facing elevation of the rock-face containing arcosolia A and B *(BV/JV)*

Fig. 7:2 The cross carved in the rock-face near arcosolium A *(JM)*

1955: 6; La Rosa 1971: 575; Tamponi 1897: 84-5). Lastly, a cross with splayed head and foot was carved onto the rock-face overlooking Tomb 3103 (Grave S6): it measured 0.36 m high and 0.27 m across (see Figs 7:1 and 7:2).

The southern niche (A) is likely to have been the earlier of the two. Unlike the northern one, it was cut into solid, almost unfissured limestone. Tomb 3074 (Grave S4) lay within this arcosolium. The southern niche was slightly squatter than its neighbour, and rather less regularly cut. The rock-face below arcosolium A was cut in such a way as to indicate that the tomb was approached from the lower level of a slabbed surface covering the tombs that lay immediately in front (Tombs 3103 (Grave S6), 3113 (Grave S10), 3124 (Grave S9) and 3126 (Grave 11); see Fig. 7:3).

The arcosolia appear to have been the focus of the terrace on which much of the cemetery lay. The possibility that they were created as martyria cannot be dismissed.

had been cut by two tombs and disturbed by later robbing, so this is not necessarily surprising. If these burials (Tomb 3108 (Grave S7) and Tomb 3119 (Grave S8)) were later than the arcosolia they would have destroyed any foundations for a façade. The south end of the rock-face was cut by several small niches, measuring on average 0.2 x 0.2 m, and about 0.1 m deep. These may have been used for lamps, flowers and votive offerings (see Cassels

Trench S: the tombs (Fig. 7:4)

The tombs in Trench S differ from the others in the hilltop cemetery in a number of respects. Firstly, they were grouped around a rock-face that had been laboriously worked in such a way as to attract immediately the attention of visitors. Secondly, the tombs grouped around here were of both the rock-cut and slab-built types, with some tombs being of a composite form. Their orientation varied more than in Trench T, probably because of variations within the rock itself. Most of the tombs appeared to be

Fig. 7:3 The arcosolia *(NB)*

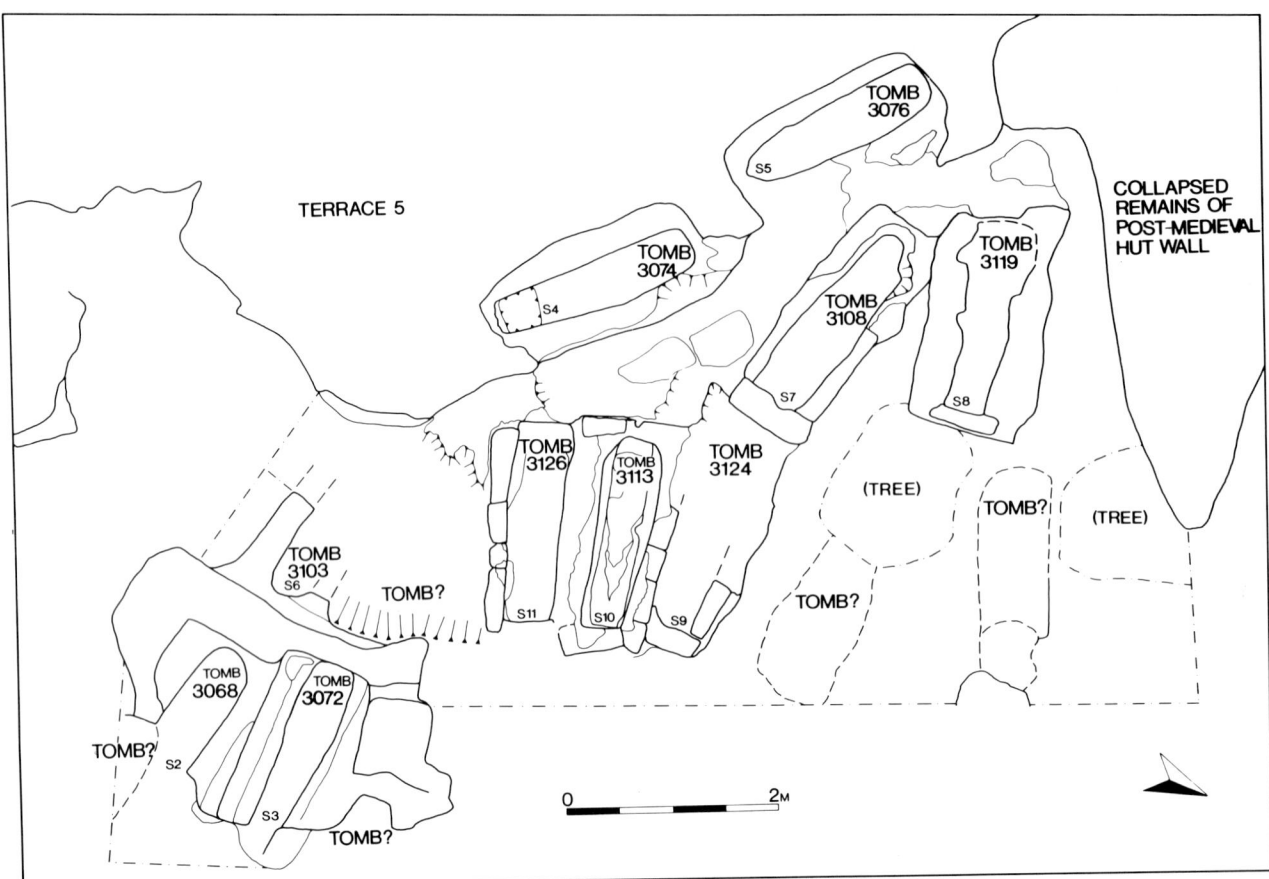

Fig. 7:4 Plan of Trench S *(CMC/LW)*

oriented towards the arcosolia, that is, towards the west, an orientation traditionally associated with Christian burial.

Tomb 3008 (Grave S1; contexts 3009-10, 3042) (Fig. 7:5)

This tomb actually lay outside the Trench S area, but was excavated in 1981 with the specific intention of looking at one of the tombs away from the arcosolia. As such, it more properly belongs to the group of tombs excavated in 1983, in area V (see below, pp. 110-14). The tomb, which was rock-cut and unplastered, was readily visible on the ground surface prior to excavation. It was oriented west-east. One of the fills (3009) contained a fragment of ninth-century blue window-glass. There was no apparent evidence of covering in the form of capping stones, or traces of mortar, but the tomb was surrounded by a narrow ledge which suggested that it had originally been covered. The tomb contained one complete articulated burial, with three additional crania arranged at the head of the tomb, and large quantities of disarticulated bones along the north side and at the east end, all within the primary fill (3042). A total of eight individuals was identified from the skeletal remains: two adult females, two adult males, two unsexed adults, and two juveniles.

Tomb 3068 (Grave S2; context 3071) (Fig. 7:6)

Rock-cut tomb 3068 was situated within an outcrop of limestone to the southeast of the arcosolia. The bedrock had been cut into a flat shelf prior to the removal of the stone for the tomb. The tomb was oriented west-east. It had been badly disturbed and contained only a few fragments of loose bones (of an unsexed adult) within a crumbly clay-loam soil (3071).

Tomb 3072 (Grave S3; context 3073) (Fig. 7:7)

This tomb, oriented west-east, was to the north of Tomb 3068 (Grave S2); it resembled the latter tomb in that a shelf had been cut before the tomb itself was dug. However, in addition, a 40 mm deep ledge had been cut immediately around the tomb to hold capping stones – traces of the mortar which would have held the capping stones in place were visible on this ledge. The tomb contained many fragments of disarticulated bones, and the still articulated ribs and lower arm of an individual within a crumbly clay-loam soil. Although a comparatively large number of bones was recovered from this tomb, the skeletal remains of only one adult could be identified positively.

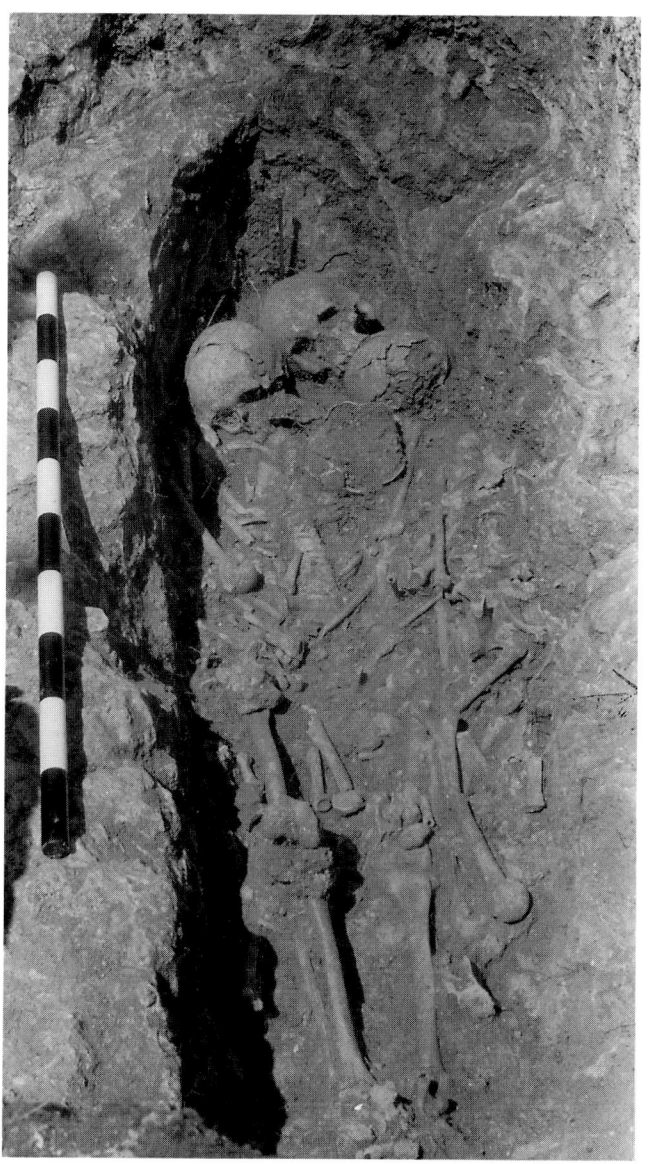

Fig. 7:5 Tomb 3008 (Grave S1) showing inhumations *(NB)*

Fig. 7:6 Tomb 3068 (Grave S2) showing the grave cut *(NB)*

Fig. 7:7 Tomb 3072 (Grave S3) showing the grave cut *(NB)*

Tomb 3074 (Grave S4; contexts 3075, 3088, 3099, 3101) (Fig. 7:8)

This was the rock-cut tomb in the south arcosolium (A), cut into the rock-face so that the top of the tomb was at knee height, rather than underfoot. It was oriented northwest-southeast. The floor of the tomb showed some traces of plaster-lining. It contained the disarticulated remains of three individuals (two adults, one juvenile) within a clayey fill that had lenses of loose grey ash incorporated within it (3088, 3099). A square hole (over 0.3 m deep) had been cut into the foot of the tomb through the bedrock: it contained remains of the primary fill (3101). It has been suggested that such recesses were for grave-goods (Davies 1977: 14), although no such finds were unearthed here.

Tomb 3076 (Grave S5; contexts 3077-8) (Fig. 7:8)

This tomb was cut into the rock of the northern arcosolium (B). Part of a lip survived at the front of the tomb, suggesting that it may have been covered originally by slabs. The tomb was oriented north-west-southeast. It contained only disarticulated fragments of human bones (from one adult), within a hard clay fill (3078). The upper fill of the tomb (3077) was loose and powdery, containing extensive wood-ash, which suggests post-abandonment burning. The sides of this tomb were plastered smooth.

Tomb 3093 (Grave S12)

This rock-cut tomb lay outside the Trench S area. It had been roughly cut into the surface bedrock at the western end of Tomb 3008 (Grave S1). It is unique in the hilltop cemetery, being the only excavated tomb that had been specifically cut for an infant burial.

Tomb 3103 (Grave S6; context 3104)

Tomb 3103 cut into the natural limestone on its eastern side and for part of the south side: it is assumed that the remaining parts were built of slabs. There was no limestone capping *in situ*. The tomb was probably oriented west-east. In common with Tombs 3074 (Grave S4) and 3076 (Grave S5), it

Fig. 7:8 The arcosolia and tombs to their east *(NB)*

contained only loose bones within a hard, crumbly, light-brown soil, indistinguishable from the general layer 3102. One individual (an adult) was identified from the skeletal remains.

Tomb 3108 (Grave S7; contexts 3109, 3112, 3118)

A rock-cut and slab-built tomb was discovered lying in front of the northern arcosolium, but was cut by a robbing pit (3105). The sides of this tomb were smoothly plastered, and two fragments of red-painted plaster were found in the fill. The tomb had been disturbed and some of the slabs forming the sides had been removed, leaving only traces of mortar. Additional mortar impressions around the tomb showed that it had once been capped. The tomb, which was oriented west-east, contained small fragments of loose bones (one adult) within two distinct layers: 3112 and 3118.

Tomb 3113 (Grave S10; contexts 3114-6) (Fig. 7:8)

Slab-built tomb 3113 originally had a base of perforated tiles similar to that found in Tomb 576 in room 4 of the Entrance Hall (see Volume 1: 224, fig. 12:12). These tiles are of phase 4 date (that is, ninth-century) (see Volume 3: chapter 6). The sides of the tomb were lined with plaster. This tomb had suffered considerable disturbance as a result of root action and robbing, but appeared to have been oriented westsouthwest-eastnortheast. Within layer 3115 some human bones remained, from which one individual (an adult) was identified.

Tomb 3119 (Grave S8; contexts 3120-3)

This tomb was cut into mixed bedrock and weathered limestone, and lay next to Tomb 3108 (Grave S7) in front of the northern arcosolium (B). It was completely sealed by two capping stones (3121) and therefore was undisturbed. The tomb was oriented west-east. A single early Roman coin (probably a late first-century bronze *as* (see Grierson and Barrett in Volume 3)) was found in the coarse gravel fill (3122). Below this fill, a fully articulated skeleton (adult female) was present, with two additional (earlier) skeletons (of an adult female and another adult) arranged at the head and foot of the tomb, within a grey-brown sandy soil (3123). Tomb 3119 (Grave S8) cut Tomb 3108 (Grave S7), and both tombs were probably later than the others in Trench S.

Tomb 3124 (Grave S9; contexts 3125, 3128) (Fig. 7:8)

Tomb 3124 was slab-built, with the side slabs partially robbed and the gaps filled with a reddish brown clay-loam, especially on the south side. The sides were plastered smooth. This grave, oriented west-east, was very disturbed and contained minimal skeletal material, although it was possible to identify some of it as being from an adult. An early Roman bronze coin was recovered from the upper fill (3125), as was a large amount of plaster. Twenty-two of the 37 fragments of plaster bore traces of red paint.

Tomb 3126 (Grave S11; context 3127) (Fig. 7:8)

Slab-built tomb 3126 lay in front of the southern arcosolium (A), cut into rock at the western end. It was oriented westsouthwest-eastnortheast. The tomb was lined with plaster on its sides. The fill (3127) was very disturbed and contained large quantities of disarticulated bones. The tops of Tombs 3124 (Grave S9), 3113 (Grave S10) and 3126 (Grave S11) were level, and all were probably sealed by limestone slabs which formed a flat pavement in front of the southern arcosolium. It is likely that there was once another slab-built tomb in the space between Tombs 3103 (Grave S6) and 3126 (Grave S11) (Fig. 7:4), but this had been completely robbed. Large quantities of smashed human bones were found in 3127. When the skeletal remains were analysed, two adult males, two adult females, and an unsexed adult were identified.

Trench T: the excavation

In 1981 two cell-like structures cut into the travertine limestone of the south-facing hillside were selected for examination. Prior to excavation these were believed to have been monastic dwellings. After the vegetation was cleared back and the topsoil (3012) removed, it became apparent that these two cells housed discrete groups of tombs, divided by a low rock-cut wall (Fig. 7:9). Two rock-cut tombs lay perpendicular to the rock-face in the west cell, and a further six were included in the east cell. The full extent of the east cell was not ascertained, but it is thought that it contained at least another two tombs of this type. These eight to ten tombs appear to have been the primary constituents of the cells, with two more, Tomb 3048 (Grave T4) and Tomb 3027 (Grave T5), being added later.

The tombs are described in full below, but to put them in their context, let us begin with the other structural features of these cells.

A feature (3018), possibly a post-hole, to the south of Tomb 3047 (Grave T7), filled with a mixture of limestone blocks and soil (3017 and 3020), suggests that the east cell might have been covered by some sort of wooden superstructure, as we proposed also for the front of the arcosolium. Two other possible post-slots (3091, 3092) were

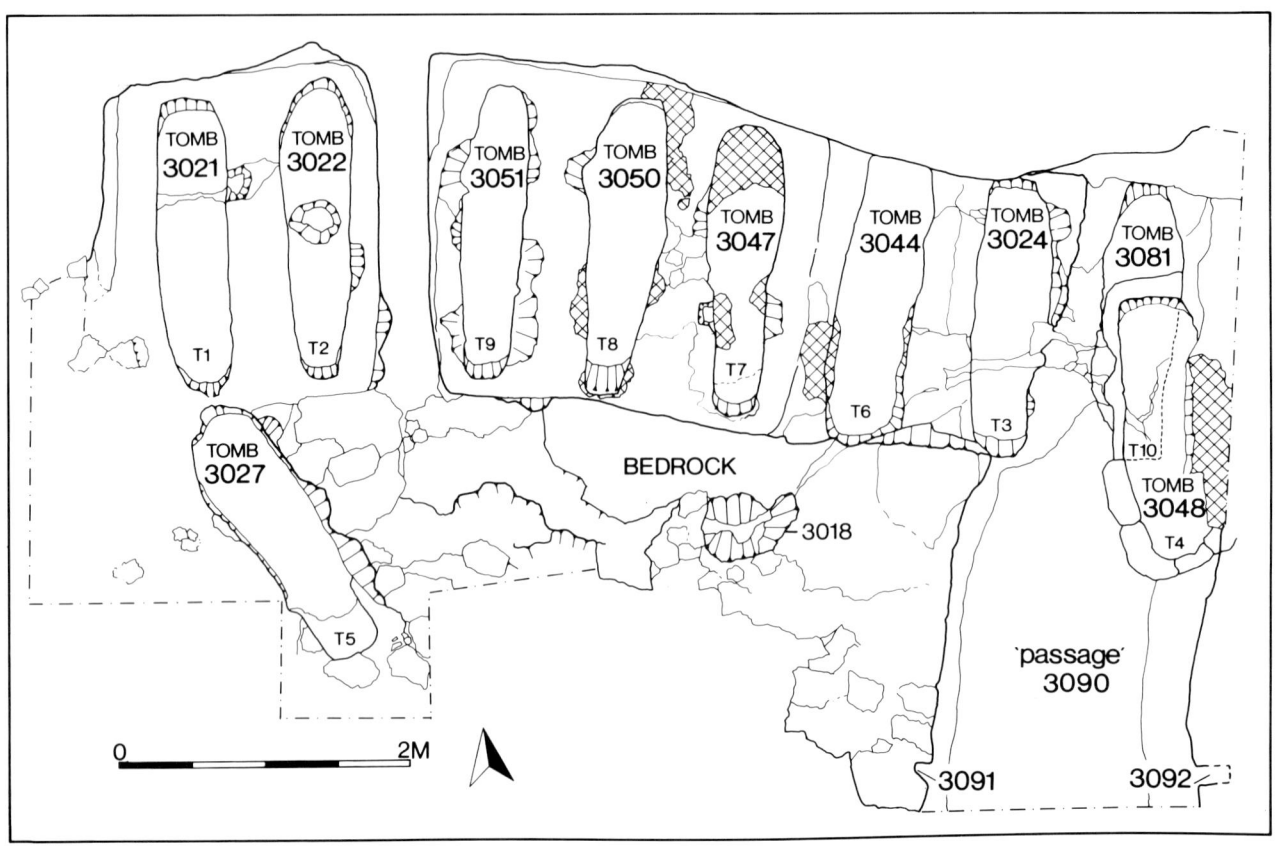

Fig. 7:9 Plan of Trench T *(CMC/LW)*

found in the east and west walls of a 'passage' (3090), which was cut into the limestone and ran north-south upslope towards Tombs 3024 (Grave T3), 3081 (Grave T10) and 3048 (Grave T4).

The tomb fills were generally composed of loose humic topsoil mixed with human bones: sometimes these overlay the remains of an articulated skeleton. A small amount of pottery was found in this disturbed infill and also in the soil that overlay the tombs. The pottery from these layers ranged in date from early Roman to post-medieval, with later material dominating the assemblages, demonstrating the amount of disturbance which had taken place. More significantly, two midden deposits were excavated, producing larger quantities of material. These were (a) a localized deposit of bones, pottery, and ninth-century window-glass (layer 3015) lying under the topsoil, and (b) a midden of pottery and bones (3085) below the subsoil layer (3030) – located in the southern part of the passage described above – which produced a large sample of early medieval red-painted and domestic wares. These two deposits are of importance for they represent later phases of activity on the site, and date to a period (the ninth to eleventh centuries) when this part of the site was possibly not in use as a mortuary area. Thus we have three phases represented in this area; firstly, the phase during which the cemetery was in use; secondly, a phase in which

the area was used as a midden; and finally, an abandonment phase which seals the earlier deposits.

Trench T: the tombs (Figs 7:9 and 7:10)

The tombs that are described in the following section share a number of features in common. All of them except one were rock-cut, and most of them were lined with plaster. It is likely that most, if not all, of the tombs were originally sealed by capping stones, but despite this they had usually been disturbed. With the exception of Tomb 3027, they were oriented more-or-less north-south.

Tomb 3021 (Grave T1; contexts 3029, 3033-4)

This tomb was one of the two primary tombs in the west cell, and was cut neatly into the bedrock. A natural fissure on the floor of the tomb had been sealed with mortar. A cut shelf around the tomb suggested that it had once been sealed by capping stones. It had been badly disturbed by robbing activity, and contained many loose bones in the main fill (3034). On the floor of the tomb a number of articulated vertebrae was recovered from the skeleton of an adult female. Some animal bones were found in the upper fill (3033), in this instance probably the result of disturbance rather than deliberate deposition.

Fig. 7:10 Trench T tombs, looking southeast *(RH)*

Tomb 3022 (Grave T2; contexts 3023, 3031-2) (Fig. 7:11)

Tomb 3022 (Grave T2), which was also in the west structure, was rock-cut and probably was originally covered by capping stones, from which traces of mortar remained. This tomb had undoubtedly been disturbed in relatively recent times; a five *lire* coin, minted in 1936, was found in the upper, disturbed fill (3031) in the centre of the tomb. This disturbance left the upper half of an articulated skeleton intact, while the rest of the tomb contained disarticulated material within a light, sandy brown lower fill (3032). Two individuals, an adult female and an unsexed adult, could be identified from the articulated and disarticulated bones.

Tomb 3024 (Grave T3; contexts 3025, 3063-4, 3079)

This was a rock-cut tomb in the east structure. One of its limestone capping stones (3063) remained mortared into place, at the south end of the tomb, but the remainder had been removed. The tomb had been badly disturbed, with only a few bones still being articulated – those from the legs and ankles – and lying undisturbed on the floor of the tomb. The soil fills (3064, 3079) contained large quantities of disarticulated material. Fill 3064 also contained a fragment of blue ninth-century window-glass. As with Tomb 3022 (Grave T2), two individuals could be identified, in this case, an unaged female and an adult male.

Tomb 3027 (Grave T5; context 3028)

This was the third tomb located in the west

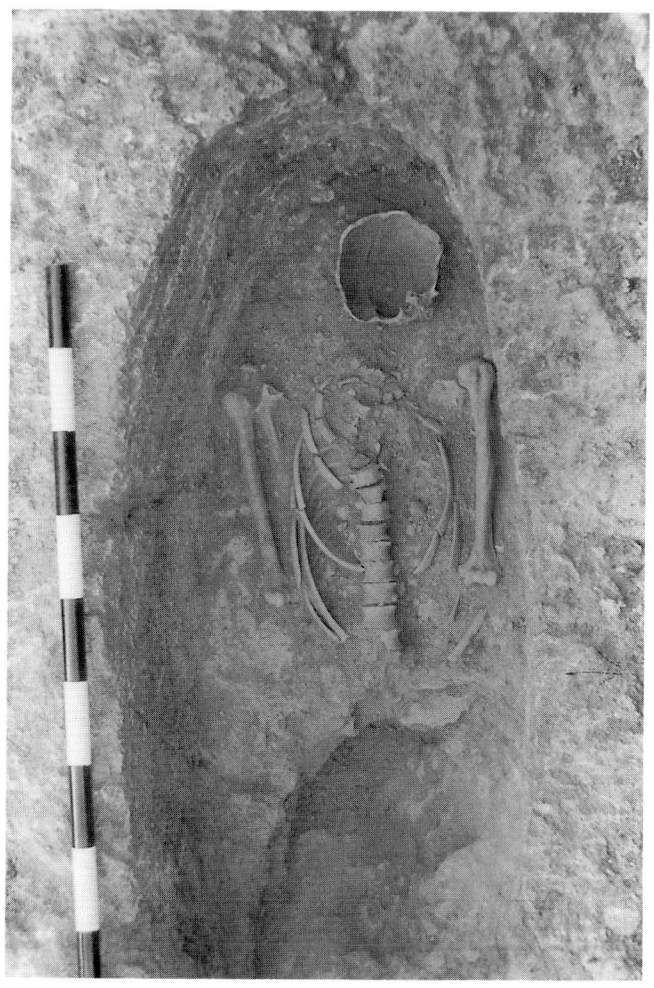

Fig. 7:11 Tomb 3022 (Grave T2) showing the upper part of the inhumation *(RH)*

structure, but it differed from the other two in both its orientation (northnorthwest-southsoutheast) and the finesse of its construction. It was cut into the bedrock unevenly, running upslope towards Tomb 3021 (Grave T1). It contained an articulated skeleton in a mid-brown fill (3028). However, the skull and the lower parts of the legs (from the distal ends of the femurs) were missing: in fact it appeared that the lower parts of the legs had been sawn off prior to the unsexed adult individual's burial. There were also fragmentary remains of another individual. The tomb lay just below the topsoil (3013) and was probably later than Tombs 3021 (Grave T1) and 3022 (Grave T2).

Tomb 3044 (Grave T6; context 3045) (Fig. 7:12)

This was a somewhat irregularly cut tomb with smoothly plastered sides and floor. A ledge around the tomb suggested that it had once been capped. The remains of part of an articulated adult male skeleton (head and shoulders) lay in place at the northern end of the tomb. The skull of a second burial (an adult female) also lay at the head of the tomb, and the fill (3045) contained loose human

Fig. 7:12 Tomb 3044 (Grave T6) showing a fragmentary inhumation *(RH)*

bones, and a little animal bone. Tomb 3044 cut into the edge of a trampled layer (3046), which covered Tombs 3047 (Grave T7), 3050 (Grave T8) and 3051 (Grave T9), to the west, and therefore may be assumed to have been constructed after the tombs to the west of it.

Tomb 3047 (Grave T7; contexts 3066-7, 3070)

This was a well-cut tomb, the floor and sides of which had been smoothly plastered. At the head of the tomb a 'pillow' of stone, probably covered with plaster, had been constructed. A ledge around the tomb suggested that it had once been covered by slabs. The fills (3066-3067, 3070) were severely disturbed, and contained only scattered fragments of bones, from which one juvenile was identified.

Tomb 3048 (Grave T4; contexts 3049, 3052, 3062, 3080) (Figs 7:13-14)

This tomb differed from the others in Trench T in that it was constructed from hewn blocks, set into a compacted layer (3065) of limestone and sand. The blocks were mortared together to form a rectangular coffin-shape (3080), which cut into Tomb 3081 (Grave T10) – one of the original graves of the east structure – and the tomb was completely sealed by capping stones (3049) mortared together by a mixture of cement and tile fragments. One of these blocks had traces of plaster on it, and a fragment of yellow and red painted plaster was found in the fill. The tomb contained the remains of a fully articulated adult male skeleton lying on a decayed mortar floor which partly sealed the natural bedrock. The partial remains of two unsexed adult skeletons were piled up at the northern end of the tomb, around the skull of the articulated individual. The skeletons were found within a mid-brown sandy soil (3052), as were two fragments of ninth-century window-glass.

Tomb 3050 (Grave T8; contexts 3053-4, 3056-7, 3059) (Fig. 7:15)

This was a rock-cut tomb with plastered sides and floor. It was partially covered by sealing slabs (3053) at its north end. The tomb contained a mixture of disturbed soil (fills 3054 and 3056), bones, and mortar from its former sealing. At its base lay a compacted layer of gritty brown soil (3059) containing large amounts of disarticulated skeletal material. Four individuals were identified from the bones in this tomb, one adult female and three unsexed adults.

Tomb 3051 (Grave T9; contexts 3055, 3058)

This rock-cut tomb had been disturbed. No indications of capping were found. It contained a large amount of disarticulated bones within the loose rubble and soil fills (3055, 3058). Three individuals, all adults, were identified from this tomb.

Fig. 7:13 Tomb 3048 (Grave T4) showing the capping stones *(RH)*

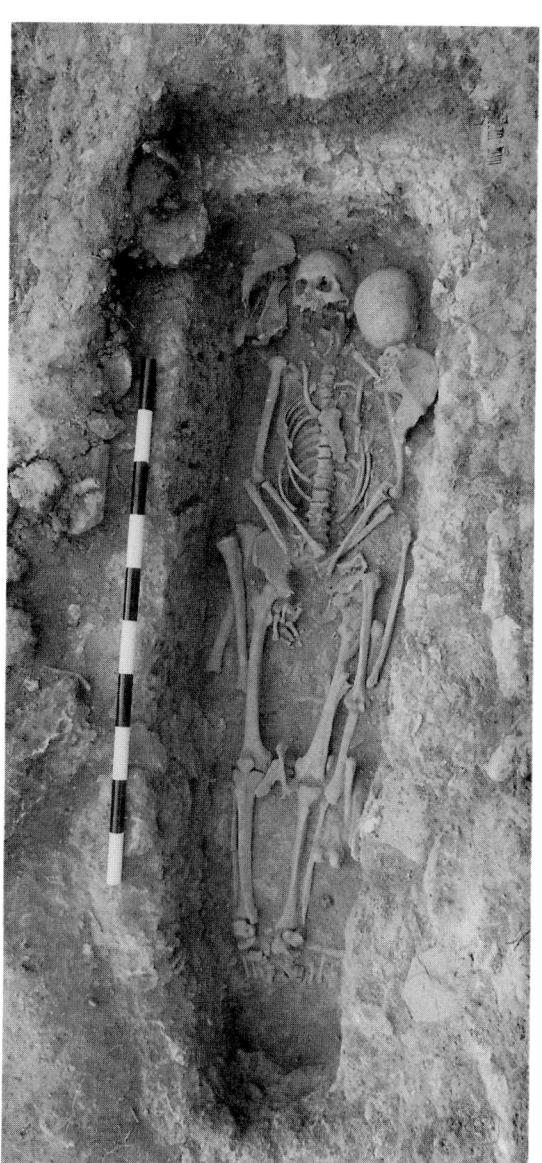

Fig. 7:14 Tomb 3048 (Grave T4) showing the inhumations *(RH)*

Fig. 7:15 Tomb 3050 (Grave T8) showing the inhumations *(RH)*

Tomb 3081 (Grave T10; contexts 3082-4)

No traces of sealing (slabs or mortar) were found, but this rock-cut tomb had been severely disturbed by Tomb 3048 (Grave T4) which lay directly above it. A layer of limestone blocks (3082) filled the west end of the tomb. A minimum of one individual was found within the two fills (3083, 3084): the skeletal remains were too fragmented to analyse.

Trench U: the excavation

In 1983 an area measuring 7.0 x 3.0 m on the western part of the south-facing terrace was selected for excavation (Trench U, see Fig. 0:1). It was hoped that this excavation would allow us to ascertain how far west the cemetery extended, and perhaps recover some datable material from an undisturbed area. Prior to excavation Trench U looked very similar to Trench T, and we assumed that we had located another large cell group, lying in a right angle between two high rock-faces.

The rock-faces themselves had been worked (Fig. 7:16):

(1) a bench or shelf (3206), measuring 1.25 x 0.2 m, had been cut into the north face (at the eastern end of the trench), c. 0.8 m above the bedrock;

(2) the southwestern extent of the rock-face had been cut into a corner (3205), leaving a remnant of rock projecting outwards, which suggested preparation for a tomb or some other structure;

(3) a 1.0 m diagonal line (3207) had been cut into the north face at its western end.

Fragments of pottery, possibly all from the same vessel, were recovered from the topsoil. These appeared to be from a jar of early Roman date. The sherds were concentrated in a defined area and their position might suggest that the pot had fallen from the terrace above (the most southerly stretch of Terrace 5). This gives credence to the suggestion that the hilltop was at least frequented during the early Roman period (see Chapter 8).

The removal of 0.1-0.15 m of loose humic topsoil (layers 3201 and 3202) and weathered bedrock (3203) revealed that the bedrock in this area had never been cut for burials. Rather, the limestone had been levelled deliberately, suggesting that the area had been prepared for the cutting of tombs, but had never been used for this purpose. Moreover, the position of this semi-prepared mortuary area suggests that the edge of the cemetery lay somewhere on the 150 m stretch between Trenches T and U.

Area V: the tombs

In 1983 a further eight tombs were excavated in the hilltop cemetery. Four were located on Terrace 4, east of Trench S, and four were on the south-facing terrace where Trench T lay.

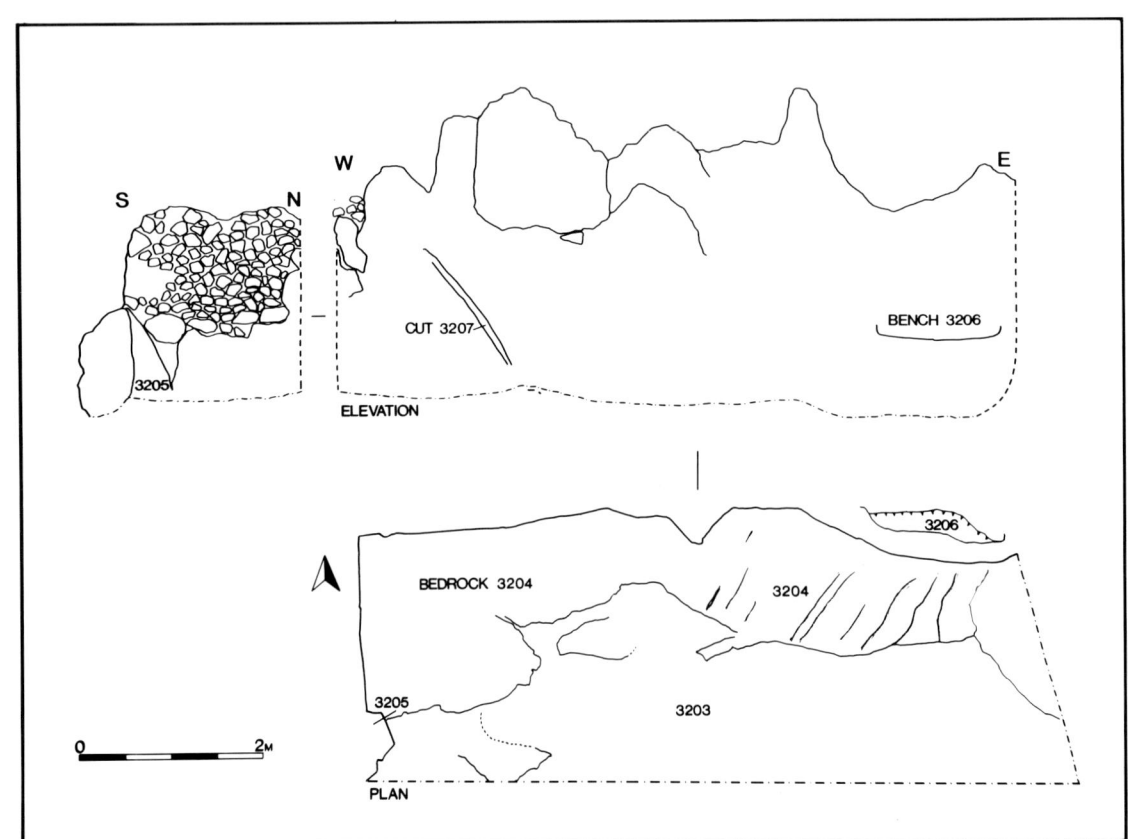

Fig. 7:16 Elevation and plan of Trench U *(KF)*

Tomb 3222 (Grave V7; contexts 3215-21, 3223) (Figs 7:17-18)

This was a block-built tomb, inserted into the decaying bedrock on the main terrace. It was firmly constructed and sealed with large capping stones (3219), heavily mortared into place. The tomb itself lay under an unusually deep (0.6 m) layer of topsoil (3216-18), and had been undisturbed. It contained the remains of an articulated adult male skeleton (3221), plus the disarticulated remains of another two adult males, and two juveniles (within grave fill 3220).

Tomb 3228 (Grave V8; contexts 3225-7) (Fig. 7:19)

Tomb 3228 was inserted into an outcrop of bedrock. The limestone of this tomb was badly weathered at the eastern (foot) end, and the tomb had been cut quite roughly. The western (head) end was cut considerably deeper (0.4 m) and better than the eastern end. The remains of eight skeletons were found, within the brown humic fill (3226), with one of them (3227) lying articulated in its original position. The skulls of two of the disarticulated skeletons had been placed at the foot and north side of the articulated skeleton. The skeletons were as follows: three adult females, three adult males, an unsexed adult and a juvenile.

Tomb 3234 (Grave V22; contexts 3230-3) (Fig. 7:20)

This tomb was well-constructed, with smooth and even side walls. It was uncapped and displayed none of the features (ledges or mortar for example) usually associated with capping stones. It contained an articulated adult female skeleton (3233), and there were also disarticulated remains of at least three other individuals (two adults and one juvenile) within a compacted brown sandy fill (3232). The crania present were arranged at the eastern (foot) end of the grave.

Fig. 7:17 Tomb 3222 (Grave V7) showing multiple inhumations *(CMC)*

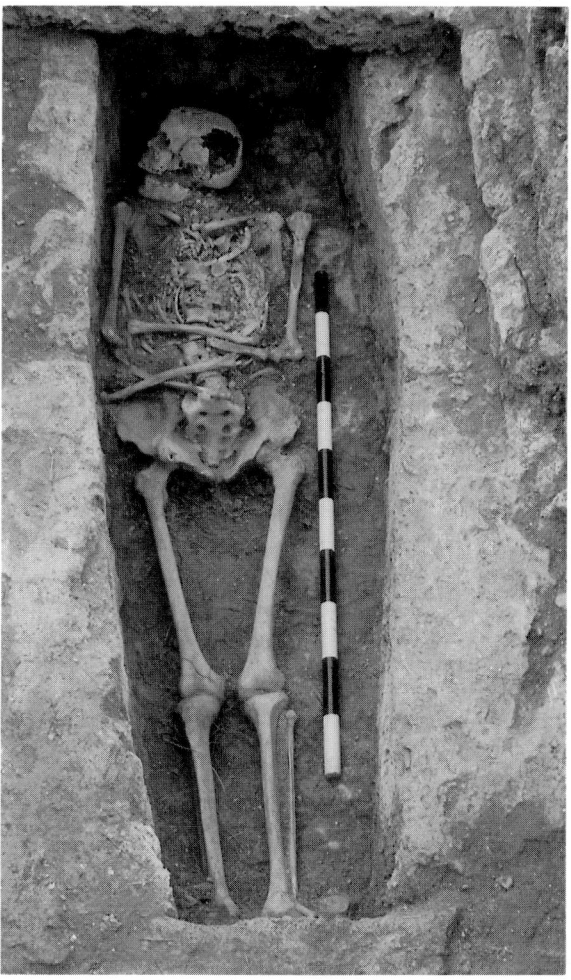

Fig. 7:18 Tomb 3222 (Grave V7) showing the primary inhumation *(CMC)*

Fig. 7:19 Tomb 3228 (Grave V8) showing an inhumation
(CMC)

Fig. 7:20 Tomb 3234 (Grave V22) showing an inhumation
(CMC)

Tomb 3238 (Grave V39; contexts 3235-7) (Fig. 7:21)

This deep, rock-cut tomb was well-constructed. It had a cut ledge running around it, but there was no other evidence of capping. The tomb had been badly disturbed by root action. An articulated skeleton (3237), without a skull, lay beneath a jumble of disarticulated bones (five individuals) in a brown sandy loam (3236). Three of the skeletons were of adult females, one of an adult male, and two were of juveniles.

Tomb 3244 (Grave V12a (cell 12); contexts 3240-3) (Fig. 7:22)

This tomb lay to the east of Trench T and displayed similar features to the tombs in that trench. It was rock-cut and well-constructed, but completely empty in terms of skeletal remains. It was oriented west-east, running parallel to the rock-face, unlike those in Trench T, which ran perpendicular to the rock-face. Layers 3240 (topsoil) and 3242 (subsoil) contained small amounts of medieval and post-medieval pottery.

Tomb 3247 (Grave V12b (cell 12); contexts 3240-2, 3245-6, 3248-9) (Fig. 7:22)

This tomb lay immediately north of, and parallel to,

Tomb 3244. It was covered with four large capping stones (3245) which were heavily mortared into place. The tomb was lined with smooth plaster and contained the remains of a single articulated skeleton (3248). Although the cement between the capping stones was intact when the tomb was discovered, the skeleton itself was in an unusually fragmentary and desiccated condition. This may have been due to the micro-climate within the tomb, or perhaps was the result of disease (see Higgins in Volume 3).

Tomb 3253 (Grave V6 (cell 6); contexts 3250-2) (Fig. 7:23)

This well-constructed rock-cut tomb was lined with plaster. There was no evidence for it ever having been capped. It contained some articulated material (3252) – the lower legs – below a jumble of disarticulated bones (three additional individuals) in a mid-brown sandy loam (3251). Two adult females and two unsexed adults were identified from the skeletal remains. The tomb was somewhat disturbed by tree roots.

Fig. 7:21 Tomb 3238 (Grave V39) showing an inhumation *(CMC)*

Tomb 3265 (Grave V4 (cell 4); contexts 3260-4, 3266) (Fig. 7:24)

This tomb was cut into poor quality weathered rock, the weathering being especially marked at the south (foot) end. It was partially covered by thin, irregular slabs (3262) of schist, very different to the usual solid limestone or tufa blocks covering other tombs. This tomb was in the most westerly cell found on this terrace. The soil fill (3263-4) within the tomb was clayey and compacted, and stained blue in places (in contrast to the sandy loam found in most of the other tombs within the hilltop cemetery). This blue staining may be the result of environmental factors such as mineral leaching, but has not been investigated fully. The tomb contained an undisturbed, fully articulated adult male skeleton.

Four further areas were opened up, all of which had been designated as tombs on the basis of cut rock-faces above the ground. Three of these proved to be illusory. The fourth (V1, contexts 3273-7) proved more problematic. This was similar in some senses to Trench U: that is, an area which appears to have been prepared for the cutting of tombs, but not used as such. However, the soil that was excavated from the front of the rock-face did contain skeletal material (of an infant and an adult). Two possible explanations may be put forward: firstly, that the area was used for burial, but that tombs were not actually cut into the rock itself; secondly, that the skeletal material, disturbed and fragmentary as it was, had fallen from the terrace above.

Fig. 7:22 Tombs 3244 and 3247 (Graves V12a and V12b) showing an empty tomb and a poorly preserved inhumation *(CMC)*

Fig. 7:23 Tomb 3253 (Grave V6) showing the articulated
legs of a skeleton *(CMC)*

Fig. 7:24 Tomb 3265 (Grave V4) showing an inhumation
(CMC)

DISCUSSION

The following questions were considered when
investigating the archaeology of the hilltop cemetery.
   (1) How big was the cemetery?
   (2) When and for how long was the cemetery in
        use?
   (3) Who was buried in the cemetery?
   (4) Were there any spatial or chronological
        variations?
   (5) Did the treatment of the dead vary – can we
        observe differences according to the sex, age
        or number of individuals in each tomb?
Each of these questions will now be addressed as
fully as possible, given the limitations imposed by
the small area excavated and the nature of the finds,
and the social context of the individuals buried (cf.
above) assessed.

(1) How big was the cemetery?

Number of tombs
The excavation of Trenches S and T, and of
individual tombs located across the terrace between
them, gave us some indication as to the size of the
cemetery. As was suggested earlier, it appears to
have covered some 2,000 square metres. However,
the density of tombs was not uniform. Trench T
represented a highly efficient use of space. Eight of
these tombs were cut parallel to each other into a
defined area of bedrock, with only 0.25-0.5 m
between them. However, we cannot assume that the
total area of the hilltop cemetery was utilized so
effectively. In Trench S the tombs appear, for
unclear reasons, but perhaps related to the nature of
the bedrock, to have been cut with less regard for
maximizing burial space.

Our investigations into the hilltop cemetery in
1983 showed clearly that there was not a simple
relationship between the presence of cuts on a rock-
face or outcrop, and the presence of a tomb in the
bedrock below. Some rock-faces had been cut in
preparation for a burial, but had not ultimately been
utilized; whereas evidence for other tombs may be
hidden below ground, in rock-pits, or behind heavy
vegetation. It is possible that the number of tombs in
the cemetery was a low as *c.* 120, although obviously
it could have been, and probably was, much higher.

Number of individuals buried

Any attempt to determine how many individuals were originally buried within any single tomb is hindered by the apparent *modus operandi* of burial within the hilltop cemetery. It should also be noted that any calculation has, perforce, to be based upon the number of tombs present, a calculation which, as has been shown, has its own uncertainties. The use of a tomb appears to have been as follows. The tomb was cut for an individual, who was subsequently buried there. The tomb was later opened and reused for the burial of a second individual; at this time the tomb was temporarily emptied of its primary occupant for the burial of the second, and the primary occupant (disarticulated or partly disarticulated) was then replaced in the tomb (usually alongside the second occupant). This process could be repeated a number of times, with the result that the articulated skeleton at the bottom of the tomb was the latest burial. However, it appears that in some cases tombs were not disturbed or that the remains of the earlier burial(s) were not replaced, resulting in a single, articulated occupant. Such practices would also account for the quantity of disarticulated bones within the layers above the tombs, and the fragmentary nature of much of the skeletal material in the upper fills of the tombs.

A minimum of 76 skeletons was identified from the 30 tombs excavated in the hilltop cemetery. This means, on average, a minimum of 2.53 individuals per tomb and, by extrapolation from the estimate of *c.* 120 tombs in the cemetery (see previous section), would mean a minimum total of *c.* 304 individuals buried in the cemetery (and we would anticipate that it was probably much higher).

(2) When and for how long was the cemetery in use?

Dating the cemetery has been a major problem. The absence of grave-goods, indicating either robbing or non-deposition, combined with a series of inconclusive grave typologies (given that both rock-cut and block-built tombs can be paralleled in Italy from the pre-Roman to the earlier medieval periods (Raspi Serra 1976; Davies 1977: 14)), merely served to increase our confusion regarding the chronology. This was compounded further by the fact that tombs were reused through the history of the cemetery, resulting in the mixing of fills. Therefore our tentative conclusion regarding the date of the cemetery rests upon slight artefactual and artistic evidence, and, in particular, upon the wider historical and archaeological context.

Painted plaster was found in a small number of tombs. Unfortunately its colour and design did not suggest any clear patterns and no traces of inscriptions were found. However, parallels might be sought with the ninth-century tombs in the Crypt Church. A ninth-century date would be supported by the window-glass found in a number of the tombs. The tiles in the base of Tomb 3113 are, on the basis of the fabric, of phase 4 date (that is the ninth century): therefore this tomb cannot have been constructed earlier than phase 4, although it could, of course, have been later. However, it must be acknowledged that medieval and post-medieval pottery was found in many of the tombs, as a result, in all probability, of disturbance and post-abandonment activity: this emphasizes the need for caution. The cross carved on the rock-face just to the south of the arcosolia, whilst of a fairly distinctive type, could date from any point between the fifth and the twelfth centuries.

The quantity of finds from the hilltop cemetery contrasts sharply with that from the late Roman funerary church (the 'South Church'). In the latter, the fills and associated deposits were rich in glass, pottery and animal bones, as well as grave-goods. How should we interpret this? Firstly, it may be that grave-goods were placed with the deceased but were subsequently 'lost' (during later clearances) or stolen by grave-robbers (cf. James 1977: 163). Some support for this hypothesis would be given by the pit at the foot of Tomb 3074, as such recesses are thought to have been cut for the placing of grave-goods. Secondly, it may be that these burials never had any associated grave-goods. This theory would be supported by the fact that not a single bead or bronze pin (which might easily have been overlooked by a grave-robber or in the clearance of the primary burial) was found and that grave-goods were absent in the few undisturbed tombs which were found. This also has some historical/ideological support in that the disposal of wealth via the grave was not a characteristic of the eighth and ninth centuries. (The status of the population buried here is, of course, also pertinent.)

Evidence for the late Roman funerary church has already been presented and discussed in some detail (Volume 1: chapter 9). A number of late sixth- or seventh-century burials was found in the Tower (Chapter 5) and in the 'South Church' (Volume 1: 161, 182; cf. 128). It has been proposed also that some of the burials in the Tower are of eighth-century date, this area forming the cemetery for that period. In sum, whilst some tombs may be earlier, it seems most likely that the cemetery's main period of use coincided with the efflorescence of the early medieval monastery (that is, the ninth century), at a time when the population would have been at its greatest. Use might have continued, however, until the focus of the monastery (and the settlement) shifted to the eastern side of the Volturno.

(3) Who was buried in the cemetery?

As has been seen, the skeletons buried in the tombs in the hilltop cemetery belong to males and females, adults and juveniles (and, in one instance only, an infant). Such a mixed sex and age distribution precludes this from being the resting place purely of the monastic population (given that San Vincenzo was not a double house). However, it was normal for the monastic community to have associated with it a lay community of broadly similar size (Horn and Born 1979: vol. 1, 268; below, Chapter 12, p. 160). It seems probable that this is the cemetery for the lay workers and lay population of the eighth- to ninth-century (and possibly also later) monastery. It would have been close enough to the monastery to be considered sanctified, but not in direct association with a church.

There was a relative dearth of infant and child burials, though it is extremely unlikely that such deaths did not occur. Although such bones would be more susceptible to destruction in the ground, it is probable that this is not the reason for this phenomenon, but that it is due to burial practices for such young individuals being different (cf. Higgins 1990: vol. 2, 120).

The observation of mixed sex and age groups within the tombs led to the suggestion that each of the multiple tombs housed a family unit. From her analysis of the skeletal material, Higgins has suggested (1985: 117) that consanguinity is in fact observable within the hilltop cemetery population.

It had been hoped that analysis of the skeletal material would yield information on the health and lifestyle of the community. However, this proved impossible, given the poor level of preservation (Higgins 1990: vol. 2, 159; see also Volume 3).

(4) Were there any spatial or chronological variations?

As was noted earlier, the hilltop cemetery did not cover the hill with a uniform density. The regular, parallel spacing of the tombs in Trench T is most likely to have been contingent upon an even and easily worked stretch of bedrock, whereas the uneven quality of bedrock on the terrace above promoted a more irregular placement and cutting of tombs.

Tomb form varied across the hill. Most of the tombs on the south-facing terrace(on which Trench T was situated) were simple, rock-cut structures, whereas those on the terrace above combined rock-cut and block-built features. It appears most likely that this was the direct result of the differential quality of the bedrock, but chronological or social patterning cannot be discounted as the cause of variation.

One aspect of the cemetery which is important to consider is its visual impact, for this may have had spatial and chronological repercussions. The carved rock-face of the arcosolia can be seen from across the terrace, and is an impressive monument. It was doubtless even more striking when it was in use; the arcosolia may well have been painted and decorated

with flowers and offerings, as can still be seen around shrines and tombs in this area of Europe. The arcosolia may have been the earliest features of the cemetery, with the rock-face acting as a focus for development. Such a phenomenon has been discerned in sixth-century Frankish cemeteries, where tombs clustered around earlier Roman tombs and mausolea (James 1978: 83). As such, the arcosolia may have formed the focal point of the cemetery, and therefore should be comparatively early in date, with the other tombs in Trench S and those fanning out across the terrace (in area V) being of a slightly later date. However, nothing in the form of the tombs independently suggests any chronological patterning.

(5) Did the treatment of the dead vary – can we observe differences according to the sex and/or age of an individual or to the number of individuals in each tomb?

At first glance there appears to have been very little variation in the treatment of the dead interred in the hilltop cemetery. The conclusion is determined in great part, however, by the small sample size, the lack of grave-goods, and a fairly uniform pattern of entombment. The evidence merits a slighty more detailed examination.

The arcosolia stand out as obvious exceptions to this uniformity. The two tombs were conspicuous because of the elaborate treatment of the rock-face above them. It could be postulated that the arcosolia were public monuments, constructed with their visibility as a primary feature. They may have been a statement of public memory, set up to remind observers of the power of the dead interred there, or of the living who buried them (see above, p. 98; cf. Fentress and Wickham (1992) for a general discussion of memory). The painted arcosolium tomb in the corridor of the 'South Church' would have fulfilled a similar public function (Volume 1: 147-50; cf. Osborne 1983). It should also be noted that the amount of energy expended on their construction was substantial in comparison to the other tombs. Tainter has proposed (1977) that the amount of energy expended in mortuary ritual varies in direct relation to the position of the deceased in the society of the living. Whilst this may be true in some instances, the fact that mortuary ritual may in fact be expressing, primarily or in addition, the aspirations and status of the living people involved in the burial of the deceased (cf. above, p. 98) should not be overlooked.

The construction of the tombs varied, some being cut into the bedrock, whilst others were built of slabs (and some combined the two methods). This seems to have been related to the quality and features of the bedrock. Whilst most of the tombs showed evidence of originally having had capping stones, there were a few which did not. However, it is impossible to determine from so few examples whether the few uncapped examples shared a common chronological and/or social factor.

The dimensions of the tombs varied little across the cemetery. It appears that the maximum depth and width of the tombs were standardized: 80 per cent were between 0.35 m and 0.45 m deep; 86 per cent were between 0.45 m and 0.55 m wide. The length of the tombs varied much more, increasing steadily from 1.68 m to 2.12 m. This suggests that the tombs may have been 'made to measure' for their primary occupants. We would propose that the tombs were cut approximately 0.15-0.2 m longer than the height of the person to be buried (as is the practice of contemporary undertakers). This proposition gains broad support from the skeletal data which give, for this cemetery population, a mean height for women of 1.6 m (standard deviation 0.0277) and for men of 1.7 m (standard deviation 0.0682) (Higgins 1990: vol. 2, 108-9).

Whilst it was clear from the evidence excavated that some tombs were plastered, in some cases the plaster had weathered, leaving only vestigial remains: the apparent prevalence of unplastered tombs therefore may be misleading. However, two-thirds of the tombs *appear* not to have been plastered. A greater proportion of the block-built tombs were plastered than the rock-cut ones (seven out of 23 rock-cut; cf. three out of five block-built; cf. one out of two rock-cut/block-built).

The painting of the plaster in some of the tombs should be noted. However, this treatment is a much less conspicuous expression of 'status' (whether of the deceased or the living involved in the burial) than above ground modification (such as the arcosolia). Whereas the arcosolia would be visible from across the terrace, the painting within a tomb would only be noticed when the tomb was open, and then only to those in the immediate vicinity. Thus, the painted tombs may be regarded as essentially private monuments, fabricated for a limited group of viewers (and, perhaps, for the 'benefit' of the deceased).

There are three tombs which displayed unique features. Tomb 3047 had a 'pillow', probably of plastered stone, at the head of the tomb. In Tomb 3074, in the southern arcosolium, a 0.3 m-deep square hole had been cut into the foot of the tomb. Such features have been interpreted often as the repositories for grave-goods, but in this case conclusive evidence was lacking (although such items would not have been surprising in such a prestigiously placed tomb). Tomb 3113 was unique in the part of the hilltop cemetery excavated so far in that it had been lined with perforated tiles. Tile-based tombs were common in the phase 1b tombs in the funerary church (Volume 1: chapter 9). However, the tiles of this tomb were of phase 4 date (comparable to those reused in the base of the phase 6a Tomb 576 in the Entrance Hall (Volume 1: fig. 12:12)).

The number of individuals interred in each tomb varied across the cemetery, with no noticeable spatial differentiation or correlation with tomb structure. The range appears have been between one and eight in a single tomb. However, it is difficult to assess this matter properly, as the skeletal material in many of the tombs had been disturbed so badly that the pattern as revealed by excavation may bear little relation to the original depositional arrangement. In addition, the analysis of the skeletal material concentrated upon that material which could be sexed and/or aged, so that the figures given must be regarded as an absolute minimum number of individuals represented in each tomb. As mentioned previously, the number of individuals in each of the multiple burials and their mixed sex and age range support the hypothesis that individual tombs were being used by consaguineous groups (Higgins 1985: 117; pers. comm.).

The occupants of the hilltop cemetery do not appear to have been buried with lavish ceremony at their funerals, or at least not the sort of ceremony that leaves archaeological remains. The tomb fills and deposits here lacked the animal bones and scatters of charcoal which characterized the fifth- to sixth-century funerary church burials which we have suggested elsewhere are the result of funerary feasts and, possibly, charcoal purification (Coutts and Mithen 1985: 65; cf. Young 1975: 118-31). However, the apparent lack of ceremony may be illusory: it may be the result of poor preservation and continued disturbance in this part of the site. It may, of course, be that practices had changed by this period. Moreover, it should be recalled that we cannot assume that the visibility of ceremony in an archaeological context has a direct correlation with past activity (cf. above, p. 98).

Within archaeology in general much emphasis has been placed upon the presence and nature of grave-goods for drawing inferences on social factors and ideological practices. However, in the case of the hilltop cemetery, such analysis and interpretation is prevented by the lack, for whatever reasons, of such items.

CONCLUSION

The hilltop cemetery at San Vincenzo has been described here in some detail. The excavations have been, by necessity, small and problem-oriented. The small size of the sample and its disturbed nature limit analysis and perforce throw an element of uncertainty on discussions. A fuller appreciation would only be possible once the funerary evidence (including the skeletal remains) from the whole site has been examined. However, some general inferences may be made and some preliminary conclusions drawn.

Many of the tombs excavated contained the remains of more than one individual. The mixing of the remains of individuals is an important factor in relation to the social process of burial. It does not reflect a lack of concern with the welfare of the dead: 'as yet unborn was the modern idea that the dead person should be installed in a sort of house unto himself, a house of which he was the perpetual owner or at least the long-term tenant, a house in which he would be at home and from which he could not be evicted' (Ariès 1976: 22). This intermingling may or may not be seen as significant by those attending the burial. However, if tombs are used to construct an idealized material map of the permanent social order, as Bloch and Parry (1982: 35) maintain, then the reuse of tombs and the mixing of skeletal remains is a salient phenomenon.

The evidence from the hilltop cemetery expresses the importance of familial unity. The family was the dominant social and economic unit, and even in the monastery, directly under divine auspices, the family maintained its structure within the lay population. Historical descriptions of the eighth and ninth centuries affirm the importance of the family unit to the people of this time. The biography of the fourth-century saint, Severus of Ravenna, which was compiled in the middle of the ninth-century, illustrates the ninth-century ideology of the family. Severus was considered to be a 'family man' and built a family sepulchre for his wife and daughter. He was buried there himself at a later date: 'We who lived a common life in this world, should also have a common burial' (*Acta sanctorum*

quotquot toto orbe coluntur, quoted in Herlihy 1985: 58). Thus Severus's family was perceived as a moral unit, in life and in death.

The social context of the population and of the individuals associated with and buried in this cemetery remains, as a result of the problems and factors outlined above, enigmatic. There is some evidence for some tombs being a 'cut above' (that is, more superior than, whether in public or private terms) the others, but it has not, so far, proved possible to interpret this convincingly and correlate it with other factors. Detailed study of the documentary sources on the status of the lay populations associated with monastic houses and on the perseverance of or changes in ideology relating to burial and the dead may provide invaluable guidance.

In brief, the hilltop cemetery at San Vincenzo is interpreted tentatively as being the burial ground for the lay population associated with the monastery, in particular during its zenith in the ninth century. Differences in the nature of the burial monument provide some indication of 'persona' and social position, whether of the deceased or those organizing the burial. It seems clear that the fundamental social unit was the family, so the burial ritual may well be seen to be a reflection upon the living as well as the dead. When these tantalizing glimpses are fully integrated with the evidence from other burial areas discovered in these and more recent excavations, and placed within their precise historical and ideological contexts, our picture of the world of the dead and the society of the living may gain another dimension.

Chapter Eight

THE HILLTOP

by Richard Hodges

The top of Colle della Torre (or Colle dell'Isola, as Pantoni (1980a: 18) called it) is today overgrown and difficult to penetrate in the summer. Photographs taken in the '60s, however, indicate that an olive grove was properly tended on the summit of the hill. Moreover, in his picture-book about Castel San Vincenzo, Di Cicco illustrates a gold *solidus* of Prince Sico of Benevento (817-32) which was discovered on this part of the hill (Di Cicco 1974: 16).

In 1981, following many discussions with local farmers, a preliminary survey was made of the hilltop. This involved cutting paths through the vegetation from Terrace 6 up onto Terrace 7. Following this, a series of test-pits was excavated across the area in order to shed light on the archaeology. In addition, a trial trench (TT) was

cut in 1983 to examine the stratigraphy more fully (Fig. 8:1).

The survey of this area revealed that the crown of the hill is contained within a particularly high terrace wall. This terracing is especially impressive on the south side, where the walls stand nearly 15.0 m high, rising virtually straight up from the rock-cut cemetery zone now in the thick woodland below (for example Trench U) (Fig. 0:1). The date of these walls remains something of a mystery. Trench TT suggested that the east terrace wall may have been recent (see below), but good grounds exist for supposing that the south and west stretches of walling may have dated originally from the monastic period.

The survey located remains of two structures,

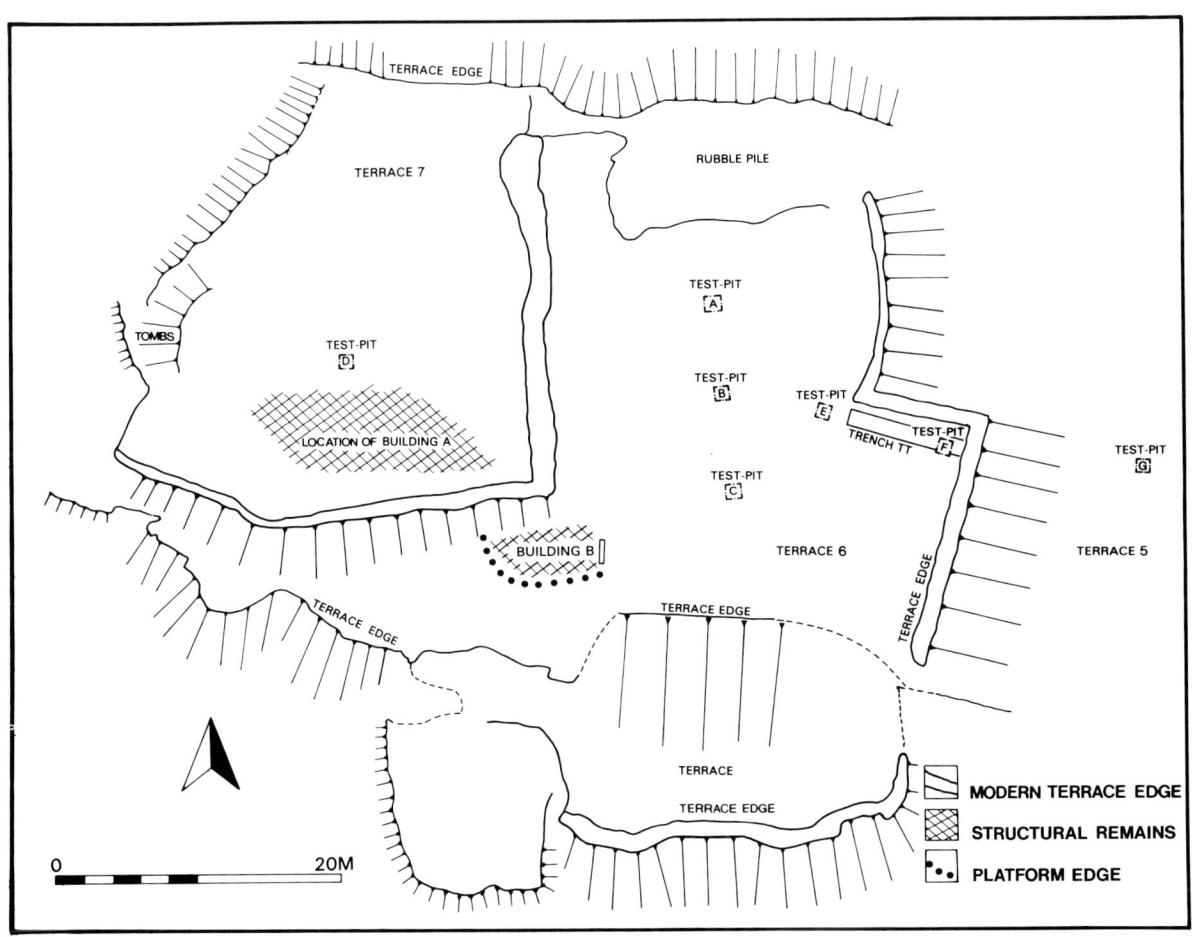

Fig. 8:1 Plan of the hilltop showing the test-pits and Trench TT *(KF)*

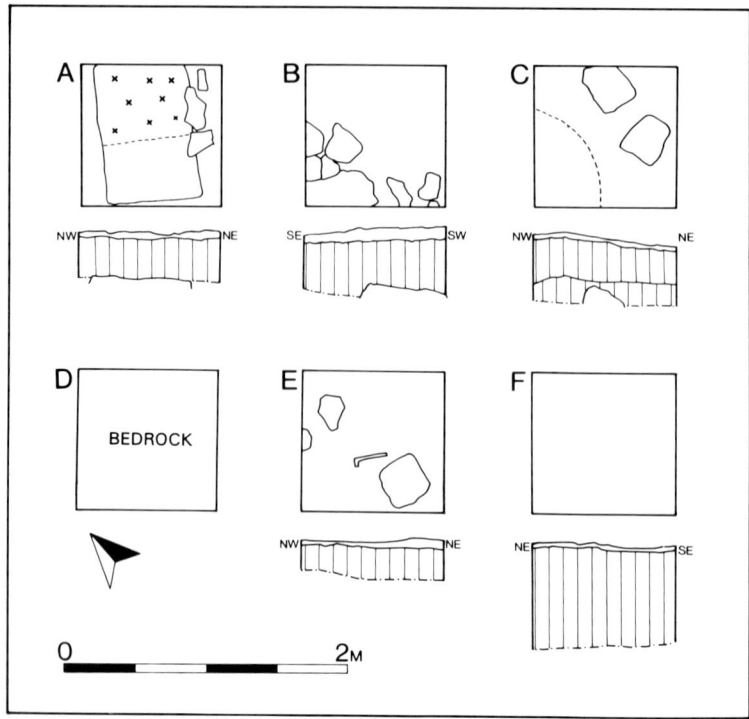

Fig. 8:2 Sections of the test-pits on the hilltop *(KF)*

despite the deep leaf litter. The largest structure (A) commanded the western half of the terrace, and almost certainly had been built out over the terrace wall itself. The exact form of this building was not clear. Two tombs, possibly within a sunken chamber, directly in front of the reinforced terrace wall, *might* imply that building A was a church. Don Angelo Pantoni was emphatic that many years ago these remains clearly showed it to be a church. We shall return to discuss its possible form below. Building B (Fig. 8:1) appears to have stood outside the zone in which A was located, immediately above the high south terracing. All that could be seen were remains of a small platform, about 5.0 m long and 3.0 m wide, with a reused threshold taken from a classical building at its east end.

No traces of buildings were visible on the north side of the terrace, though the leaf litter was especially deep here. In modern times the farmers had removed an enormous quantity of stone from the hilltop, creating a massive pile of rubble over the north terrace edge.

The test-pitting shed a little light on the stratigraphy of the hilltop. Two 1.0 m² pits (G and H) on Terrace 5 showed that there had never been any occupational activity in their vicinity. Terrace 6 appears to have separated the cemetery from the hilltop. A line of pits from the eastern perimeter to the shelving area in front of the tombs showed that the hill had been landscaped (Fig. 8:2). Pit F, just west of the east terrace wall, reached 0.75 m in depth without reaching bedrock, and was filled

with earth which had been brought to this area rather than with material which had accumulated naturally. In contrast, pit D, within the area in front of the tombs in building A, contained no soil cover over the bedrock. The line of pits A-B-C, running north-south across the centre of the terrace, showed that the soil cover amounted to about 0.4 m and contained many fragments of tile. In pit A traces of a mortar surface or a wall were found. A further series of test-pits was excavated on the slope below, beyond the west end of the terrace, but these revealed nothing significant.

The trial Trench TT (10.0 m long and 1.0 m wide) was cut from test-pit F towards test-pit E to examine the subsoil (Fig. 8:1). The result was clear enough: absolutely no traces of human activity were found in the upper 0.4 m or in the metre-deep exposure nearest the eastern terrace wall. (Trench TT was abandoned at this depth as it was quite sterile and appeared to be unhelpful.) It suggests that the earthmoving on the hilltop was executed on a considerable scale, but to precisely what end is not yet clear.

This preliminary survey suggests that the western sector of the hill was levelled and that in some places the limestone platform was exposed. The excess earth was used to create the pronounced terraced enclosure around the crown of the hill, especially on its eastern side.

The principal structure (A) was almost certainly a church, with its apse positioned on the western edge of the hill. Don Angelo Pantoni believed the tombs were especially important ones, held within a crypt. We did not clean these in any way, but they resembled the large slab tombs from the atrium of the Crypt Church, as well as those within the Entrance Hall. The superstructure of the building, however, seems to have been removed, leaving only the platform on which it was created. Associated with this church was at least one substantial structure (B) and possibly others which have not been detected. In parenthesis, we should note that the modern cultivation, as far as could be judged within the test-pits, had been fairly intensive and may therefore have removed more modestly-built structures.

The only other light so far shed on this part of the settlement came from the finds which tumbled down the hillslope from it. A large granite column had rolled down the slope to the north and lay about half a kilometre from the hilltop. Local farmers told us that others had been smashed up or taken away. Of no less interest are the sherds found in Trench U which had clearly come down from the hilltop. These sherds seem to have belonged to a Republican phase of activity on the hilltop. The evidence, as it stands, reaffirms Pantoni's belief that this was an important part of the monastery in so far as there is evidence at least of a large monumental building as well as pre-monastic activities. None the less, it has yet to be established when this area was in use, for what purpose and whether or not it was fortified. Moreover, it is not at all clear if a tower, as referred to in the name of the hill, Colle della Torre, did once occupy the hilltop.

Chapter Nine

THE LATE ROMAN SETTLEMENT AT SAN VINCENZO AL VOLTURNO

by Richard Hodges

The author of the *Chronicon Vulturnense* described the earliest Christian presence at San Vincenzo as an oratory founded by Emperor Constantine as a result of a dream he had whilst he was travelling in this region. The oratory, according to the chronicler, was later transformed into the monastery's earliest abbey-church. The story, of course, is a common one, frequently used by eleventh- and twelfth-century monastic authors to account for the antiquity of their house. The story also relates to the Carolingian fascination with the Constantinian age (Bullough 1975). In effect, it is what Eric Hobsbawm has called an invented tradition (Hobsbawm 1983; cf. Bradley 1987), in which a ritual continuity was being used to establish a genealogy. Examples of villa reoccupation by monks in the early Middle Ages are well-known (cf. Barnish, Chapter 10). In the case of San Vincenzo, therefore, it is not at all unusual to discover that the early medieval monastery was built over, and in part reused, a late Roman settlement. The discovery of this settlement, however, adds a further, critical phase to the long unfolding sequence of occupation at San Vincenzo. In particular, this fifth- to mid-sixth-century settlement is an important addition to a rarely discovered class of monument.

* * *

It seems likely that a major part of the settlement has been uncovered in the excavations. The complex, accordingly, merits detailed description and discussion.

We must begin with the bridge, the Ponte della Zingara, currently giving access to the site. Pantoni (1980a: 91) speculated that the bridge might have its origins in either the early monastic or the classical periods. Samuel Gruber (in Volume 1: 35-6) has shown that Pantoni's view is probably close to the mark. The construction, it can now be said after the excavations, argues against it being early medieval and in favour of its classical date. Whether it belongs to the early or late Roman periods cannot be established without large-scale excavations (which at present would hinder those who use it). The prominent reuse of large ashlar blocks in the bridge abutments on either bank on its south side lend a little support to a late Roman date. Gruber compares it to the supposedly late Antique bridge

at Carpino (Molise) (Monaco 1989: 103). The position of the Ponte della Zingara, though, directly in front of the 'South Church' as opposed to the courtyard/entrance atrium, seems a little unusual. More speculation, however, will not clarify the issue. We might conclude by asserting confidently that the bridge existed in late Roman times, though it might have been an old one by then.

The late Roman settlement appears to have consisted of several clearly separated parts, focused around an atrium garden (Fig. 9:1). To the north of the atrium garden lay a funerary church and, beyond that, a substantial basilican building resembling a church. On the terrace west of the atrium garden there was a tower of Norman proportions. On the south side of the atrium garden there may have been at least one more range of buildings, but the ninth-century Refectory has prevented us from accurately locating it.

The atrium garden itself remains something of an enigma as we were unable to expose fully the late Roman levels. It appears that there was an open area here, to the south of a monumental building beneath the 'South Church', since early Roman times. The exact nature of the early Roman use of this space was not discovered (Volume 1: 191-2). However, in the fifth century the area was clearly covered by a fine soil consistent with it being a garden (Volume 1: 191-2). The late Roman atrium garden was evidently larger than its early medieval successor. In phase 4 the monks constructed the Distinguished Guests' Refectory, as well as a tiled portico, over the eastern extent of the late Roman atrium garden. In other words, it appears that the atrium garden extended towards the river, and that one entered the settlement complex directly from the bridge, along one side of the atrium garden. No traces of a path existed around the south side of the atrium garden, so it seems most likely that the ninth-century north portico overlaid an earlier, late classical version. As the stratigraphy pertaining to this phase remains largely intact there may be an opportunity in the future to clarify the details of this atrium garden. The atrium garden, so it would seem, signalled some continuity with classical Antiquity – a long curated space surrounded by the new buildings of the early Christian age (cf. Littlewood 1992: 128-9).

The complex was clearly dominated by the

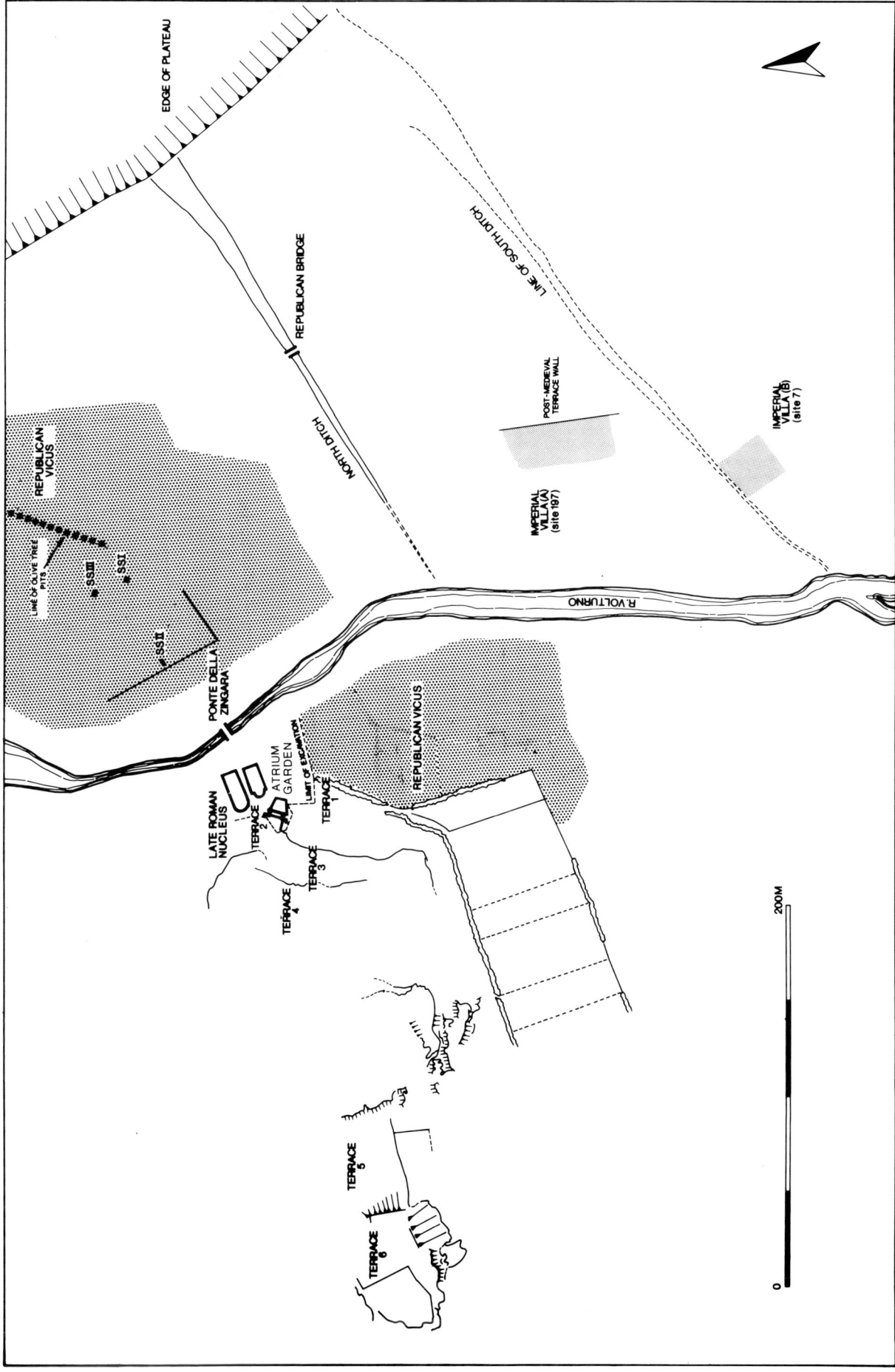

Fig. 9:1 A schematic map of the late Roman and earlier classical settlements at San Vincenzo al Volturno (SC)

Tower on Terrace 2. This was positioned at a slightly different angle to the atrium garden and the two buildings north of it. Less than a quarter of the Tower was excavated, but this was sufficient to indicate its general form and the sequence of building here. Sadly, the architectural aspects of this once imposing building are lost to us as it was finally levelled in the ninth century.

The original Tower was probably set into the hillside, making use of an early Roman structure. However, like the Crypt Church in this period, the early Roman remains do not seem to have been used as footings for the fifth-century structure. The Tower itself (in phase 1a) had a massive east-facing front wall over 1.0 m wide and c. 14.7 m long. Bonded into it were two inner walls of similar massive dimensions which ran upslope, while the outer walls of the building were smaller, c. 0.7 m thick. The plan suggests a rectangular central part, on an east-west axis, with flanking rooms on the north and south sides. Sheila Gibson has reconstructed this as a three-storey building, with flanking rooms, that gave access to the main part, and a deep ground floor in which the vaults rested upon a central pier (Fig. 5:6).

It is not known how the Tower was approached in phase 1a. The midden covering the east-facing slope below the Tower suggests that entry was made from the south along the face of the slope, due west of the later Refectory. Traces of a stairway, ascribed to phase 1b, were found tacked onto the south side of the Tower. However, the south-flanking area and the central area of the Tower were not completely excavated, so we cannot be sure what form these took. Nevertheless, the remains of the building imply a considerable number of people inhabited it, disposing of their refuse outwards in an arc which stretched from the back of the Crypt Church to a point below the pathway up to the south side of the Tower.

In phase 1b the Tower was remodelled and a small trapezoidal enclosed area was created on the slope immediately below it (Terrace 1).

The remodelling of the Tower included the addition of an eastward extension resembling a portico. This enlargement involved some skilful building works. A new wall at the front of the terrace had to be constructed: this was braced by two wide walls to the massive central part. There is some suggestion that the north and south ends remained open. The exact purpose of this addition is not clear. Was it merely to enhance the façade? Was it to create more living room? Had the function of the building altered? Whichever, the construction was technically well executed with good, strong mortar. The enclosure also effectively separated the Tower from the atrium garden, and the access-route to the Tower from the funerary church. The layout of the settlement, and with it attitudes to space, was clearly being reconsidered.

The clean clayey fill (9110) associated with the small trapezoidal enclosed area hints that it was in fact a garden. It certainly brought an end to the disposal of refuse along the eastern side of the building. Attitudes to refuse evidently altered: new means of disposing of rubbish, presumably some distance away from the Tower, were now instituted.

It was at this time, or possibly a little afterwards, that a cistern was constructed alongside the south wall of the Tower. The cistern was 4.5 m wide (internally), but its exact length along the slope is a matter of speculation. The cistern was competently constructed, partially excavated out of the natural rock. It is likely that it resembled the long narrow cisterns from Campanian villas like Posto and San Rocco (Francolise) (Cotton 1979: 27; Cotton and Métraux 1985: 57). Does it suggest increased water needs, improved water facilities, or declining rainfall? These questions cannot be answered without at least uncovering the entire Tower.

We have discussed the architectural features of the Tower in Chapter 5. Suffice it to reiterate here that it appears to belong to the trend of the fortification of villa complexes noted over a wide geographical area in the later Roman period. The mosaics from Tabarka illustrate this form most clearly (Fig. 9:2; Dunbabin 1978: pls XLIV.111, 112 and XLV.113), but the remains of similar towers at Anguillara (Van der Noort and Whitehouse 1992), San Giovanni Di Ruoti (Small 1983: fig. 8) and Torba, near Castelseprio (Mazza 1978-79), as well as the description of Nicetius's villa, near Trier (Percival 1976: 175), all add weight to the notion that this example from San Vincenzo may have belonged to a more general phenomenon, and need not be considered unusual.

Indeed, there is a suspicion that tower houses, like nucleation, were a feature of socio-economic change in the late Roman period, commencing in provinces like Britain (for example at the provincial centre of March (Cambridgeshire): Potter and Whitehouse 1982) some decades before being adopted in Italy. Certainly by the sixth century fortified villas were a common feature in North Africa and the eastern Empire (Mattingly and Hayes 1992; Pentz 1992: 24-7).

The two buildings to the north of the atrium garden appear to have been churches. It seems likely that they occupied the area which had formerly been the site of an early Roman monumental building. The 'South Church' was the better preserved. This was a funerary church – a rustic version of the great metropolitan martyria (Krautheimer 1971). The church was approximately 17.0 m long and about 7.0 m wide internally, with a simple, axially-aligned, apse (Volume 1: 179-86). Between the western apse and the rock-face was a simple ambulatory, a little less than 2.0 m wide. A rough open area existed beyond the east front of the church (that is, directly in front of the bridge). The

Fig. 9:2 Mosaic from Tabarka *(From Dunbabin 1978: pl. 45, no. 113; courtesy of Deutsches Archäologisches Institut, Rome)*

graveyard extended some 2.0 m to the south of the south nave wall, and was probably delimited by a wall: however, the phase 4 south wall of the 'South Church' (the north perimeter wall of the phase 4 Garden Court) almost certainly overlaid this churchyard wall and thus we were not able to investigate it.

The funerary church ('South Church' phase 1) itself was a simple building. The walls were inferior in their constructional details to the Samnite/early Roman walls that had existed on the site several hundred years before. The church walls were about 0.5 m wide and made of rubble bonded with a distinctive soft, buff yellow sandy mortar (unlike the robust mortar employed in the Tower). However, as only footings survived, it is possible that the upper fabric was rather more carefully finished. The one outstanding stretch of walling (869) occurred in the east front (cf. Volume 1: 150-1). The northern half of this wall consisted of the eastern face of a monumental Samnite/Republican wall with excellent jointing. In other words, the late Roman builders prised away the western face of this old wall, leaving the eastern face. The old wall, however, did not extend quite far enough to the south, so a conspicuous few metres of carelessly constructed coursing linked the phase 0 wall to the south wall of the nave. As we shall see, this pragmatism is rather out of character with the rest of the late Roman building pattern, for normally pre-existing buildings were not used.

At some time in the late Roman period (tentatively phase 1c: see Volume 1: 160-1), the church was modestly extended by about 2.0 m to the east. A rough-hewn marble slab covered the junction dividing the Samnite wall from its southerly stretch. The extension appears to have created a narrow narthex, accommodating two tombs, one on each side of the slab. The narrowness of the narthex is rather curious, being unlike the spacious entrance hall of the familiar metropolitan churches of this age. It might simply have been a device to enhance the east front, late in the history of the villa, possibly funded by or devised to accommodate those buried in its two prominently positioned tombs.

As far as we could tell there was no altar or raised dais at the west end of the church in late Roman times, although there was an ambulatory beyond the apse. Perhaps, as in the later eighth-century 'South Church', a window was pierced through the west end, through which one might look upon the tomb (40) which was situated in the centre of the ambulatory, directly beyond this window. The tile coffin had been cut into the natural rock. There were also other tombs in the ambulatory. Tombs 57 and 67 were collective burials, typical of those discovered within the church. To these we must add the tile box 55 which contained a few fragments of burnt human bone, a bronze fragment, two cut bone fragments, and an elegant, if broken, ivory handle of an asperge or fan. Tombs 40 and 55, therefore, were unusual and may to some extent shed light on the ambulatory itself.

Ambulatories and the cult of relics were a prominent feature of the late Roman age as Peter Brown, in particular, has shown (1981). Yet ambulatories at this date were normally associated with metropolitan churches (Krautheimer 1980: 86). In the case of San Lorenzo fuori le mura, Rome, according to Richard Krautheimer, visitors peeped through the window of the church into the ambulatory at the special dead contained therein. These tombs would have brought esteem and gifts to the church. At first this metropolitan cult seems rather far removed from a rustic funerary church. Yet it appears that the 'South Church' in late Roman times was not simply an ordinary burial-ground. Tomb 40 would appear to have been a small shrine capable of attracting pilgrims; Tomb 55 may have amounted to much the same. How we interpret this is of some significance for the general appraisal of the complex as a whole. It is a matter to which we must return again, towards the end of this chapter.

The building contained a graveyard of a familiar open-air type (as opposed to the neatly arranged tombs inserted into the floors of municipal funerary basilicas such as San Lorenzo fuori le mura at Rome (cf. Krautheimer 1980: 83-5)). The ground was raised by about 0.4 m during the use of the graveyard. The earliest tombs were all stone-lined (739, 779 and 916) and may have been set out on the old early Roman ground surface. These were then surrounded by clay and earth taken from somewhere close by, leaving only the uppermost edges exposed. The second period of tombs comprised types made with tiles. There is some possibility that the first tile tombs were on an east-west axis and later ones on a north-south axis. Several of these later tombs were positioned directly over earlier ones, possibly indicating some relationship between the deceased in the upper and the lower tomb.

Some 23 tombs were arranged in the (entirely excavated) eastern half of the building during phases 1b and 1c. It is likely that a similar number of tombs occupy the western half, to judge from the exploratory probes made at various places within it. Yet more tombs occurred within the simple ambulatory at the west end, chiefly on its northern side. Burials also occurred on the south side of the funerary church (in the south corridor of the 'South Church'). Most of this area could not be excavated below the level of the fine ninth-century (phase 4) paved floor. However, excavation of a phase 6a tomb (501) in this corridor showed that it was directly above a tile tomb of typical Roman type (Volume 1: 176). Moreover, the tomb had been tucked up against a south wall that by the ninth or tenth centuries, when 501 was placed here, had been made into a stairway leading from the south passage of the 'South Church' to the Lower Thoroughfare. The line of the ninth-century 'South Church' outer (south) wall, therefore, appears to have overlain the

line of the outer wall of the cemetery (see above). We might speculate, accordingly, that up to fourteen tombs may have been located in this area.

In all we estimated, on the basis of about one tomb to every 3 m^2, that about 50-60 tombs were placed in the church and its accompanying cemetery over about 100 to 130 years of use (Volume 1: 180-1). If we estimate that there was an average of three persons per tomb, with an average lifespan of about 35-40 years (Saller 1987), this suggests a population associated with the settlement in the order of 50-60 persons at any one time.

It should be stressed that the graveyard was not packed with tombs, as is sometimes the case in medieval churchyards. A semblance of order remained in the spacing of the dead (see Volume 1: chapter 9, figs 9:3 and 9:32). This order must be contrasted with the visual impact of the graveyard itself. The ground had been churned up time and time again. Human skeletal fragments, smashed glass and pottery vessels from funerary feasting, and a good deal of ash surrounded the tombs. We must also anticipate that the ground was thickly covered with vegetation from time to time, such is the phenomenal speed with which shrubs proliferate here. The tombs themselves may have been distinguished by wooden markers, though we found nothing to indicate this. Clearly the tombs were opened and closed at regular intervals. It is noticeable that no tomb contained a full complement of bones; all had been disturbed. This 'rustic' appearance, therefore, makes a surprising contrast with the ritual nature of the western end of the building.

The building to the north was separated by about 1.5 m from the funerary church. Comparatively little of this building survived, making it difficult to interpret. Its salient features were as follows: it was a basilican building, measuring 14.0 m long (east-west) by 7.0 m wide, with a sunken narthex. The area was to some extent landscaped before the building was raised, in the course of which the early Roman monumental structure was levelled. It is interesting to note that the late Roman builders opted not to found their walls on the levelled footings of the earlier structure. Hence, the south nave wall ran alongside (up against) the preceding early Roman 'nave' wall. Likewise, the east end of the building ran just inside the footings of the early Roman wall (Volume 1: figs 6:12 and 6:13).

The walls of this building were all about 0.5 m wide and constructed of rubble bonded with a bright yellow firm clayey cement. In some places, for example at its west, apsidal end, the building survived to a height of 0.3-0.4 m. The rounded apse originally rested upon the slope of the hill, extending further westward (towards the hillside) than the funerary church to the south. The building also had a narrow narthex at its east end. The floor level within this had been raised up several times with rubbish from elsewhere within the complex. (It is possible that it trapped rainwater, a problem which reoccurred during the ninth century (phase 5).)

The ground floor of the building must have been on two levels with the lower nave floor being situated just above the level of the outcrop of bedrock (once possibly part of the early Roman monumental structure), and the floor within the apse being at a height nearly 1.5 m above this, roughly at the level of the late eighth-century floor.

There is a possibility that the building was re-employed as a church in the early eighth century (Volume 1: 70), and therefore we must speculate whether it served this purpose in the later Roman periods as well. Sadly, the available evidence sheds no light on this. An absence of tombs and church furniture means that we have only the shell of the building from which to draw conclusions. A basilica of these dimensions was found in the contemporary villa at San Giovanni di Ruoti (Basilicata) (Small 1983: 25-8). In this latter case the excavator believes it had a secular use, as a triclinium. However, at San Vincenzo it would seem unlikely that a range used for secular occasions was separated from the main complex by a cemetery. A more feasible alternative would be to envisage this building and the funerary church as forming a religious module within the complex.

The other buildings around the atrium garden are difficult to interpret, as later structures have concealed or obliterated them. It is not at all clear now whether there was a range of buildings due west of the atrium garden. Excavations within the (ninth-century) Entrance Hall only reached sufficient depth to discover whether or not there was a previous building here in room 1 (Volume 1: 216). The evidence was not conclusive. It remains a possibility that a narrow corridor or range lay at the base of the hillslope. Similarly, were there building(s) lying along the southern side of the atrium garden? The excavation of the modern pipe-trench that sliced through part of the early medieval Refectory confirms that it was preceded by a substantial pre-ninth-century building: however, there is some evidence to indicate that this was in fact an eighth-century (phase 3c) building. Likewise the deep footings of the north wall of the Refectory (354), in contrast to the shallow footings of the south wall (502/561/1072), suggest that the phase 4 structure was built in part on a pre-existing structure, possibly of Roman date.

Despite the highly distinctive nature of the late Roman material very little evidence of this period was found beyond the excavations just described. Occasional sherds of late Roman pottery occurred on Terrace 3 and within the hilltop cemetery, as well as in the trenches on the Rocchetta plain (FF, GG and HH). Late Roman *nummi* have been found in the excavations of the workshops (Trench FF), but these may have been coins reused or redeposited in later times.

On the other side of the river remains of a late Roman building were unexpectedly discovered in Trench SSIII (on the edge of a modern terrace) (Volume 4, chapter 1). There was not the opportunity to excavate it, so we can only note its presence and the fact that its roof had collapsed but showed no signs of having been burnt.

* * *

The late Roman settlement, therefore, seems to have covered an area of about half a hectare. The community probably numbered as many as 50-60 persons at any one time. To judge from its material culture it was modestly affluent. There was a great deal of glassware being used in the complex, mostly for lighting and possibly also in connection with the funerary rites (Stevenson 1988). As is shown by Stevenson in Volume 3, the glass assemblage includes numerous examples of a distinctive lamp form which was probably made in Campania. Alpine soapstone jars and early fifth-century African Red Slip tablewares also occurred, though only in small quantities. A range of other south Italian pottery, including one example of a Lucanian red-painted jug, has also been identified (Patterson 1989). The pottery is notable for its highly regional appearance, being very different, for example, to those wares found in the excavations of a villa at Matrice in the Biferno valley (see Cann and Lloyd 1984). Amphorae were virtually absent, as they were at San Giovanni di Ruoti (Freed 1983). Small bronze *nummi* occurred in large numbers, perhaps indicating their limited value, but at the same time revealing the existence of small denominations of coin. These coins were found in most parts of the settlement, though they seem to have been concentrated in the 'South Church'. As a result, it is tempting to interpret the pattern of coins as partly related to funerary activities. Prolific coin-loss is a characteristic of the mediterranean world in late Antiquity. Hendy offers a reason for this (Hendy 1991: 656). Taxes were paid to the state in gold; 'when a tax-payer owed the fisc two-thirds or above a *solidus/nomisma* (the standard gold coin), he was obliged to pay the next whole gold coin above and was then refunded the difference in copper, resulting in an enhanced supply of gold for the state, and in probably an unwanted enhanced supply of copper for the taxpayer' (Hendy 1991: 656). A similar number of coins was found, for example, in the excavations at Alahan, the early Byzantine monastery in the Taurus Mountains of Turkey, an exact contemporary of this settlement (Coulston and Gough 1985: 62-8).

As at San Giovanni di Ruoti (Basilicata), the inhabitants of San Vincenzo appear to have consumed a large amount of pork in the late Roman period (Higgins in Volume 3; Steele 1983; cf. Barnish 1987). The quantity of pork eaten in late

Roman towns has recently attracted much attention, and may be some reflection of the need of the growing numbers of urban poor for cheap 'fast foods' (cf. Whitehouse *et al.* 1985). Places like San Giovanni di Ruoti and San Vincenzo may have been responsible for producing the increased numbers of pigs required by urban populations, though it is a hypothesis that is difficult to test (cf. Clark 1992; Baker and Clark 1993: 60-1). None the less, this argument fails to explain why comparatively small populations with access to a variety of agrarian resources also adopted this diet. It is not as if the community at San Vincenzo, controlling an ecological niche at the boundary between a polycultural economy and a pastoral one, could have been experiencing hardship even with a population of some 50-60 people (cf. Hodges 1993a). In fact, the reverse seems to have been the case, to judge from the material culture revealed by the excavations. The consumption of pork, in other words, might have been a cultural trait, perhaps reflecting later Roman culinary trends, as opposed to an indication of a short-term agrarian regime. Clearly, we need to know what sort of settlement it was, and to what extent it was responding to circumstances in its region.

To pursue this question, let us consider the evidence for the chronology of the settlement. Over a hundred late Roman coins were found, of which about ten per cent could be identified accurately. The worn nature of these coins implies that they were in circulation for some time. Most, it might be deduced, were lost or thrown away either in the later fifth or earlier sixth century. A corroded *nummus* of Marcian (457-74) from the top of the early Roman ground surface in the funerary church suggests – but no more – that burial here did not begin before this date. Only one late sixth-century coin – a *nummus* of Justin II (565-78) from a phase 3 context (923) in the 'South Church' – hints that the zenith of the place was over before this. The other datable finds serve to confuse this chronology. The African Red Slip seems to belong to the early fifth century, though of course fine-wares of this kind might have been in circulation for several generations. This group would appear to belong to the increased production of D wares at the end of the fourth century, noted by Fentress and Perkins (1988: 208-9). The glass vessels, by contrast, predominantly belonged to the sixth or even the seventh centuries.

The phase 1b settlement clearly involved some development and possible aggrandizement of the initial complex. The Tower was enlarged and the churches were constructed at this time. A walled enclosure, probably a garden, separated off the slope in front of the Tower from the atrium garden as well as the churches, in this period, and it seems that the residents built a cistern. In short, the settlement reached its architectural apogee a generation or two

after its foundation, possibly around AD 475-500. Does this sketchy history shed any light on its function?

There seem to be two possible alternatives for this site: was it a typical estate centre of the late Antique age, or, bearing in mind its later history, was it an ecclesiastical complex of some kind? Let us consider both of these alternatives (and see also below, Chapter 10).

Most of the evidence relates to secular use. The Tower, surrounded by domestic refuse, seems to have been a residential building (though, of course, it should be recalled that Saint Benedict occupied a tower at Monte Cassino (Pantoni 1980b: 103-22; Scaccia Scarafoni 1944)). The creation of an atrium garden in front of it in phase 1b suggests that some minor aristocratic family and its domestic staff lived here, conspicuously separated from its agrarian workforce, in the manner of the later Roman villas illustrated on the Tabarka moasaics (Dunbabin 1978: 122-3). The funerary church, however, contained the tombs of many families. Many of the skeletons in these tombs showed the results of hard manual labour, as might be expected of a peasant community. The material culture of the settlement might not be inconsistent with the idea of a centre engaged in regional exchange systems. Indeed, the large number of coins raises the possibility that it was located beside some minor trading place, midway between the high mountain pastures of the Abruzzo and the polycultural economies in the areas to the south (cf. Barnish, Chapter 10; Gabba 1988; and Cavallo and Giardina 1993: 324-5 on *nundinae*, periodic fairs). Another possibility, slight though the evidence is, is that glassware was produced at the settlement (cf. Stevenson 1988), lending the place some esteem as an artisanal centre. San Vincenzo at this date seems to have been the appropriate successor of the imperial Roman community which once occupied the riverside meadows opposite.

Other late Roman centres in Molise are known to lie near deserted middle Roman sites. Countless reports by local informants at Rocchetta al Volturno indicate that tile tombs (of Roman date) lie strung along the edge of the Rocchetta plain, west of Rocchetta Nuova and close to the 'villa' (San Vincenzo survey site no. 42) discovered below Vacchereccia (cf. Hodges *et al.* 1984). Similar descriptions of scattered later Roman burials were obtained from villagers at Colli a Volturno and Montaquila as well as, more specifically, at Filignano (presumably connected to a possible villa some 3 km to the west (San Vincenzo survey no. 196)).

At this point it should be noted that at San Giovanni di Ruoti (Basilicata) no remains of a graveyard have been reported. Evidently there was some diversity between later Roman villa types. San Vincenzo, on the one hand, seems to be close to the type of later Roman villa which, according to Pietri

(1986), was owned by an aristocratic family (see Barnish, Chapter 10). At such places, Pietri contends that it was commonplace to establish an oratory. This was normally dedicated to the ancestors of the family or to a local saint. A typical example of this occurred in the fifth-century villa of A. Pompeiacus near Agen, where an oratory was dedicated in honour of his ancestors and the martyred Saint Vincent (Pietri 1986: 770, n. 50). Similarly, at San Vincenzo the enlarged tower, the construction of the churches, and, notably, the ambulatory and reliquary features adjoining the 'South Church', all point to the growing aspirations of a minor aristocratic family seeking to promote its status at a time of increasing political turbulence.

Nevertheless, how might a villa-estate be distinguished, for example, from an early Benedictine-type monastery? What would a late Roman monastery have looked like? The best-preserved monasteries of this age are to be found in the Eastern Roman Empire. Monasteries such as those in Coptic Egypt or early Byzantine Turkey appear to have contained several churches in a fashion rather reminiscent of the Carolingian age (cf. Gough 1985). These monasteries appear to reflect the pronounced asceticism of early monasticism – being generally remote places –, yet each possessed a high cultural profile which was most apparent in their spectacular architecture. However, in Italy, Saint Benedict's monastery, like Cassiodorus's *Vivarium*, is described in altogether different terms. (Note that the eighth-century Codex of the *Institutiones divinarum et saecularium litterarum* in the Staatsbibliothek, Bamberg, depicts *Vivarium* as a mighty tower house: Cavallo and Giardina 1993: 333.) These were working farms – villa-estates – closer, in many respects, to the papal *domuscultae* of the early Carolingian age in South Etruria. The remains found at Monte Cassino (Leccisotti 1987; Pantoni 1973) and at Copanello, the site regarded as *Vivarium* (Bougard and Noyé 1986; 1989: 217; Noyé 1991), reveal that the principal churches in these monasteries were of the same proportions as, for example, the 'South Church' and Crypt Church (see Fig. 9:3, A and B). San Martino di Copanello, the sixth-century triconch which probably served as the main church at *Vivarium*, was 15.0 m long and 5.0 m wide, while the late Roman church at Monte Cassino was about 19.0 m long and 12.0 m wide (Fig. 9:3, C and D). In sum, as well as their being working farms, there is evidence that the monasteries of Monte Cassino and *Vivarium* were first and foremost cult centres. San Vincenzo is in some respects similar, although the pre-eminence of the Tower might indicate a lesser significance in terms of a cult centre, as would its less impressive material culture and the 'rustic' nature of the religious structures. On the basis of the archaeological evidence, however, the possibility that San Vincenzo was a monastery at this time could not be ruled out (cf. below, pp. 134-7).

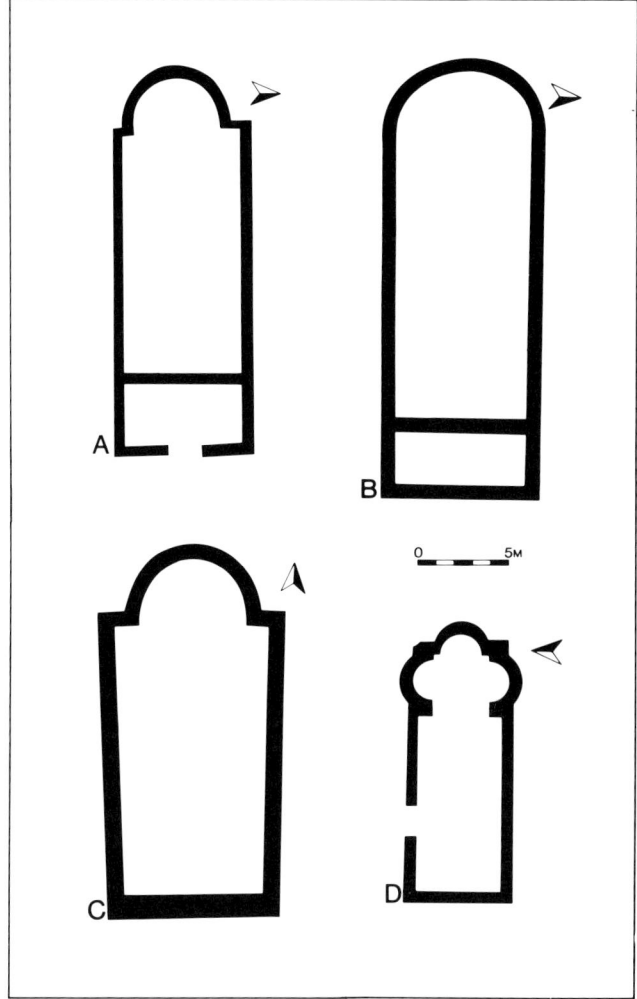

Fig. 9:3 Comparative plans of late Roman churches: A. 'South Church'; B. Crypt Church; C. Monte Cassino (after Pantoni 1973: fold-out between pages 98 and 99); D. San Martino di Copanello (after Bougard and Noyé 1986: fig. 10) *(KF)*

One further consideration is that this might have been a minor bishop's seat. The absence of a baptistery seems compelling evidence against this hypothesis (cf. Barnish, Chapter 10); but had such a building existed it would most probably have been in the area due north of the Crypt Church, which has not been excavated. The evidence for this idea is contentious (Petroccia 1980; 1981; J. Patterson 1985; La Regina 1990). At the Council of Pope Symmachus on 6 November 502, a list of bishops mentions one *Marcus Samninus*. He is listed between the bishops of *Vulturnum (Paschesius Vulturnensis)* and *Nuceria (Aprilis Nucerinus)*, indicating that his diocese lay in central Italy. This is one of the eight references to a place called *Samnium*. Paul the Deacon also refers to this place, listing it after Chieti, Alfedena and Isernia, as an ancient place. At about the same time, in a charter granting land at Benevento to San Vincenzo, Charlemagne refers to it as occupying the *partibus Samnie* (J. Patterson 1985: 191). The evidence is too scanty to be certain whether San Vincenzo is really *Samnium* or if the upper Volturno valley was a locality traditionally known as *Samnium*. However, it must remain a hypothesis that Bishop Marcus Samninus had his seat at San Vincenzo, that he lived in the Tower, that the Crypt Church was his cathedral, and that the upper Volturno valley was his diocese. This might account for the later usage of *Samnium* in the *Chronicon* and by Charlemagne. It is a hypothesis which cannot be tested fully.

* * *

All in all, the evidence from San Vincenzo suggests that it was a minor cult centre in the late Roman period. Although in terms of material culture it was modestly affluent, its architecture was evidently plain and unembellished. No inscriptions of this period and only the poorest of objects associated with funerary ritual were found. In every sense the funerary church was rustic in character, designed principally, so it seems, for local families and individuals of modest status. The brief history of this settlement is not at all inconsistent with the rhythms of the empire at large. Is it not an illustration of the Church colonizing the countryside, carving out a congregation here as it had already done in the great municipalities? The late Charles Pietri wrote that 'with the parish, the countryside ceased to be a desert' (Pietri 1986: 761). The local élite used cult features around which to build a new community. On this basis, like San Giovanni di Ruoti, it seems to have shared in the modest readjustments and short-term affluence which occurred during the fifth century. It may be contrasted with the makeshift continuity of unfortified sites like, for example, the Roman settlements at

Mola di Monte Gelato (Lazio) (Potter 1993) and Canneto sul Trigno (Ferrara 1988). San Vincenzo's apogee towards the end of the fifth century mirrored the expectation that the integration of the mediterranean mountain economies with those of the seaboards would continue and grow. This expectation was not realized (Hodges and Whitehouse 1983: chapters 2 and 3; Panella 1986; Randsborg 1991; Panella 1993). By the second quarter of the sixth century the mediterranean economy was contracting dramatically. Such a recession was bound to hit hardest those communities further from the coastal plains. Indeed, such was the scale of the economic reversal that, while Naples continued to flourish (Arthur 1991), it appears that inland places like San Giovanni di Ruoti and San Vincenzo no longer served any commercial rationale. Thereafter, San Vincenzo's existence was governed by its traditional place in the late Roman society of the upper Volturno valley: as a place of worship and burial. Even so, the scale of depopulation during this period accelerated so much that the community at the end, possibly in the mid to later sixth century, almost certainly numbered only a few persons. (For a pertinent discussion of depopulation on late Roman estates see Alcock (1989).) In sum, the late Roman settlement at San Vincenzo, like the preceding early and middle Roman sites, belongs to a greater mediterranean story. Its ecological niche, however, like the fabric of its buildings, did not disappear entirely. The countryside may have been abandoned to become overgrown, and the buildings may have fallen into disrepair, but both remained to shape substantially the history of the early medieval monastery.

Chapter Ten

CHRISTIANS AND COUNTRYMEN AT SAN VINCENZO,
c. AD 400-550

by Samuel Barnish

Among the most interesting features of the late Roman phase (phase 1) at San Vincenzo is the close resemblance of its chronology to that of the great Lucanian villa excavated recently at San Giovanni di Ruoti near Potenza (Gualtieri, Salvatore and Small 1983; Small and Freed 1986). Both were founded, or thoroughly rebuilt, early in the fifth century and and further expanded *c.* 475; and both, as settlements, were in a state of decay or collapse by *c.* 550. Furthermore, both are situated in remote, but far from inaccessible, uplands of south-central Italy; and pigs seem to have played an important part in the farming practices of both (see Higgins in Volume 3; Steele 1983). It is possible to see the two sites as sharing similar fortunes in the political economy of southern Italy, and, indeed, of the mediterranean world (Barnish 1987).

There, however, the resemblance ends. At San Giovanni, the basilican hall which dominated the site shows no sign of religious use; this may be contrasted to the situation at San Vincenzo, where it seems that the 'South Church' had a religious function in its late Roman phases (and the Crypt Church building may have had a similar purpose). Whilst San Vincenzo had a sizeable funerary church, San Giovanni did not, although funerary inscriptions suggest that there may have been a cemetery a few hundred metres away, at least into the fourth century (Buck and Small 1985). Whilst from the finds it appears that San Vincenzo was modestly affluent, it has yielded no bath suite, none of the mosaics, and little of the fine pottery which distinguish San Giovanni. Yet San Vincenzo has produced more than a hundred fifth- to sixth-century bronze coins, occurring in all types of contexts, not only funerary-related ones. San Giovanni has yielded only six coins, scattered in its latest occupation layer, none later in date than Valentinian I (364-75) (A. Small pers. comm.). All of this suggests that the social and even, to some extent, the economic, functions of these two large rural sites should be interpreted very differently.

The secular ownership of San Giovanni has been established (Small 1983: 34-5). Could San Vincenzo also have been a lay-owned property, if of a rather different type? The foundation of funerary chapels by the pious Italian laity for their dependents, and of non-funerary estate churches, often equipped with relics, as San Vincenzo may have been, is well attested from the fifth century onwards (Violante 1980: 983-1013). In the tomb-obsessed Roman world, the important role played by burial may have done much to root Christianity and its buildings in rural life. In the diocese of Sora, under Pope Gelasius (492-6), the high ranking lady Magetia set up chapels '*in possessionibus propriis*' for '*suorum corpuscula*'; Trigetius, bearer of a senatorial name, founded an estate church in the diocese of Potenza; and two officials of the Ravenna court established another near Larinum. From Gelasius onwards, the popes showed a two-fold concern to license and control such work in their suburbicarian territories.

Firstly, they tried to ensure that no ordinary church was used for burials, or was founded on a burial site; that no funerary church should be used for public services; and that relics should be provided or approved by the popes themselves. Here, they seem to have been afraid of the growth of irregular cults around tombs or relics ascribed to spurious, even non-Christian saints.[1] Their cause for concern is demonstrated by instances such as the case of a fourth-century tomb, built by a minor official for himself, on his own land, near Ronciglione, which had developed into a place of cult and pilgrimage by the late sixth century, and which eventually became the core of a parish church (Nestori 1979; 1981).

Secondly, the popes also tried to limit the founders' rights to attendance at services and no more (cf. Gelasius, *Ep.* 33-5; *LD* X-XI). The diversion of fees and offerings, and of the funds for upkeep, lighting, and support of clergy, is attested in both Italy and Spain. For an unscrupulous founder, an estate church might well be a source of some profit.[2] Moreover, the founder's gift also threatened to weaken the control of the church hierarchy over religion. The establishment of permanent priests by

---

[1] Gelasius, *Ep.* 33, 35; *RPR* I, no. 630; *LD* XI-XIV, XVI. On the efforts made by the Merovingian Church hierarchy to control holy men and relics, see Brown (1982: 162ff., 222-50), perhaps taking its successes too much on trust. For private churches, heresy and their control in the East, note also *Novella Iustiniani* 131, 7-8, 14.1. Also important are Settia 1980: 453-9; Pietri 1981: 428-9; 1986: 770-2, 775-8, 781; and Bullough 1983: 197-200.

[2] Gelasius, *Ep.* fr. 21; second Council of Braga (a. 572), v-vii; third Toledo (a. 589), xix; note also Lérida (a. 524/46), iii (Vives 1963).

the founder was forbidden; if the founder wanted a mass said, he had to request a celebrant for the occasion from his bishop. Only in the seventh century did the addition of baptisteries to estate churches become lawful (Violante 1980: 997ff., 1011).

San Vincenzo fits this pattern of licensed and unlicensed activity rather well. No baptistery has been found. The funerary church and the Crypt Church basilica are quite distinct, and the former seems to have at least one tomb of special note and sanctity ('South Church' ambulatory, Tomb 40) associated with it. The Crypt Church (whose function is less certain) appears to have been deserted much earlier, perhaps when a troubled diocese could no longer spare the services of a priest. The coin finds, which are exceptional in the context of Roman rural sites in general,[3] seem to begin at about that point in the mid-fifth century at which these structures were built. These may be evidence for burial fees, or simply for offerings, and the flow of pilgrims and visitors through a minor religious centre. We might envisage San Vincenzo as a backwoods version of Cimitile (near Nola) in Saint Paulinus's day, when the cult of Saint Felix attracted pilgrims from far and wide, and pigs and calves vowed by the peasantry were slaughtered and distributed to the poor.[4]

Such scenes recall pagan religious festivals; and here it is worth citing Bishop Zeno of Verona's attack on late fourth-century Christian landowners. Not only did these landowners turn a blind eye to the shrines and temples on their estates, but 'every day you go to law lest anyone should deprive you of legal rights over the temples'.[5] Like churches, temples could evidently be a source of profit to the landowner. There is evidence to suggest that San Vincenzo, near the source of an important river, was a site of ancient sanctity (see Chapter 12, and Pantoni 1980a). Pious offerings may not have been the only benefits; in the ancient world, religion and trade went hand in hand. Pagan shrines and festivals were common locations and dates for rural fairs, often encouraged by the landowner; and this continued in the Christian environment (Gabba 1975; Shaw 1981; Vryonis 1981: 200-14; Lane Fox 1986: 41-6). The most notable Italian example is the great fair of *Marcellianum* near *Consilinum* in early sixth-century Lucania, held on Saint Cyprian's day, at a sacred spring, now Christianized by a baptistery (Cassiodorus, *Variae* viii. 33). San Salvatore at Fonti del Clitunno may be a second spring that was transformed into a Christian cult centre in this period. San Vincenzo may have been another and minor case, serving the

Upper Volturno, focused on the river god Volturnus, and perhaps, as was the case with the nineteenth-century fair at that place, acting as a point of exchange between the communities of the river valley and of the mountains. If so, the vicissitudes of the site would have their implications for the changing patterns of regional commerce. Imported pottery occurs in moderate quantities, but is not an outstanding feature of the site (cf. Patterson 1989). Glassware, however, is relatively common, and may have been brought to San Vincenzo if it was not made at the villa (see Stevenson in Volume 3). Objects such as the ivory handle of an asperge or fan from a tile-lined box (context 55 in the ambulatory around the apse of the 'South Church') and a fine bone spatula certainly suggest a place of minor affluence.

However, the general prosperity of a site is only partly reflected in the standard of living of its occupants. As noted, the San Vincenzo villa lacks luxurious elements of material culture when compared with San Giovanni, and contrasts dramatically with the high luxury of the great Sicilian estate-centres. Skeletons from the funerary church show signs of a strenuous physical life (Higgins 1985; see also Higgins in Volume 3). The skeletal evidence suggests that the population was similar to a typical peasant community; although we should note that late Roman gentry were often keen huntsmen, and sometimes took a very active part in the farming of their estates (cf. Sidonius Apollinaris, *Epistulae* i. 6; vii. 15; viii. 8; Paulinus of Pella, *Eucharisticon* 187-219).

The evidence from the cemetery population suggests a complex inhabited by a number of families. *Villae rusticae* of this kind, perhaps the products of partible inheritance, are not unknown in widely separated parts of the Roman world (Tchalenko 1953: 321; Wightman 1975: 598ff., 651-2). The possibility of a community comprising several families also corresponds with those many late Roman sites where a villa-site may have expanded, over time, to form the core of a medieval village (cf. Percival 1976: 176-7). Gregory of Tours tells of a fifth-century villa, a *domus magna* in the Gironde, with a baptismal church nearby; the place seems to have housed a number of Gothic and Roman families (*LGC* 47). The *Charta Cornutiana* of 472 records the foundation of a church by the barbarian general Valila on his *massa* near Tivoli. The church itself included a *confessio*, and therefore relics. Its precinct, and the area set aside for the houses and gardens of its clergy, were legally distinguished from the adjoining *praetorium* (large rural villa) and the enclosed *horti* of the *inquilini*

---

[3]Crawford 1970: 43. The Buccino farms and perhaps the late Roman phase at San Rocco conform to this pattern: cf. Dyson 1983: 67ff., 121, 138, 168, 174; Crawford 1985: 129ff.

[4]Paulinus, *Carm.* xx. 67-209, 312-436; xxvii, 449-79. For a similar festival at an Anatolian monastery, *c.* 600, see *The Life of Theodore of Sykeon* in Dawes and Baynes 1948.

[5]*Tractatus* i. 25.10. A relation between crop offerings and landlord's rent is suggested by the Council of Elvira, canon 40 and by Maximus of Turin's *Sermones* 91.2, 107.2 (Mutzenbecher 1962). Pliny, *Epistulae* ix. 39 links rural temple, popular festival, and landlord's benefaction.

(note plurals) who inhabited it.[6] So too, at San Vincenzo, the building of the church(es) seems to have been accompanied by a reorganization of space, where a garden, possibly walled, helped to separate the residential tower from the ecclesiastical area.

There are a number of possible explanations for the building of churches within late Roman villa complexes. We might imagine a landlord of the mid-fifth century who wished to distance himself from the rest of his community, and who at the same time wished to strengthen his social standing and enhance his political power by building churches (cf. Chrysostom, *Homiliae in Acta Apostolorum* xviii. 4-5, *PG* 60, 148-9; Cassiodorus, *Institutiones* I. xxx. 2). Perhaps Tomb 40 in the 'South Church' belonged to some respected person of the manor, whose prestigious burial would reinforce the authority of an heir. Another possible scenario would be a partnership in church-founding by new tenants at a time of rising agricultural prosperity (Jones 1964: 809-10; Violante 1980: 1040-1).

All this would be consistent with the coin and pottery evidence. Broadly speaking the coins began to appear in significant numbers in archaeological contexts when African Red Slip ware drastically declined. The incidence of fine tablewares of African Red Slip must be related to the fluctuations in the marketing of these pots (we should, perhaps, contrast the pottery finds from *Venafrum* and *Saepinum* (H. Patterson 1985: 86-8), and the material from Canosa in Apulia (Volpe 1985), as well as the trading of other serving dishes in metal, for instance, which have perished (Whittaker 1983; Vera 1986)). The reasons for the growth in coin use are complex and problematic. The tenants needed to buy goods, and to pay travelling merchants or pedlars for them in cash. They may have paid their taxes directly (in coin), and marketed their own goods to raise the money, instead of paying in kind to a landlord who enjoyed the privilege of *autopragium*. They may also have formed a labour pool, earning cash for seasonal services, perhaps in the *Venafrum* olive-harvest (cf. Chrysostom, *Homiliae in Matthaeum* lxi. 3, *PG* 58, 592 – though his labourers are drawn from a very oppressed and lowly stratum). No less possible, however, would be a landlord forced into residence by the loss of other estates through war or partible inheritance, with a concomitant increased interest in his property. Rural coin use may also have been stimulated by the creation of a sales and purchase tax in 445 (the *siliquaticum*, still surviving under the Ostrogoths), to be collected at official *nundinae*, both

in towns and *in regionibus*. Unlicensed markets in villages and estates were also used for tax evasion at this time (Valentinian III, *Novellae* 15 (a. 445), 24 (a. 447)).

San Vincenzo could, however, be interpreted differently. Its ecclesiastical character has been emphasized, and one suggestion is that it was either an episcopal estate-centre (a phenomenon well attested in late sixth-century Gaul (cf. Venantius Fortunatus, *Carmina* i. 18-20; iii. 12; x. 11)) or an early monastery. The first alternative compares well with two north Italian sites. At Spina, near Comacchio, Bishop Aurelian of Ravenna (519-21) built a complex consisting of church and baptistery, associated with an older cemetery, which may have had a role in Adriatic trade.[7] Palazzo Pignano (Cremasco) is still more relevant. There, a martyrium-type basilica, probably of the mid-fifth century, and underlying an eleventh-century church, adjoins an extensive complex with a portico and a mosaic-decorated apsidal hall, of similar date and design. Mirabella Roberti has suggested that this was a country residence of the bishop of Lodi Vecchio, who is known to have had jurisdiction in the area at a later date; the name may even indicate a gift by the senator Pinianus (Mirabella Roberti 1970: 115-16; Roffia 1978: 34; Massari *et al.* 1985). This explanation of the site is, however, highly speculative; and, at both Palazzo Pignano and at San Vincenzo, the absence of a baptistery seems to tell against episcopal involvement. (We should contrast this with Spina, Cimitile, *Marcellianum*, and, for the eighth-century, *Capracorum* (Santa Cornelia), though not Santa Rufina (Remondini 1747-57: 428-33; Goldschmidt 1940: 70; Potter 1979: 150-4; Christie 1991).) The absence of a baptistery would also indicate that Palazzo Pignano and San Vincenzo were not the seats of estate bishoprics (an institution hardly known in Italy) (Massa Nicoterana near Vibo Valentia being the only example I know (*GMRE* vi. 40)), or even parish churches (Castagnetti 1979: 9, 19-20). The architectural simplicity of the San Vincenzo church(es), when compared with the residential tower, enlarged about the time that these structures were built, also tends to count against the episcopal theory. Moreover, as with Bobbio, another church that was in ruins when the eighth-century monks took over the site, the land was given to them by the Lombard ruler, not by a local bishop.[8] Of course, a bishopric weakened or destroyed in the sixth and/or seventh centuries

---

[6] Bruzza 1880: 15-17; *LP* vol. i, cxlvi-vii. Despite one obvious blunder, the twelfth-century manuscript seems to reproduce a genuine late Roman original. The church was probably rather grander than those at San Vincenzo.

[7] Cf. Alfieri 1965; Gentili 1971: 207-8. The trade centre interpretation seems to me far from obvious. Alfieri (1965: 15-16) argues that Agnellus's term *monasterium* for the site (*Liber Pontificalis Ecclesiae Ravennatis* 53) need mean no more than a non-parochial church.

[8] Wickham 1985b: 229-30; see below, Chapter Twelve; Ionas, *Vita Columbani* i. 30. We might compare the eleventh-century refoundation of long-ruined Jarrow by episcopal gifts (Stenton 1971: 451-2, 678).

might well have lost jurisdiction over its property; but the emperor seems the likeliest owner for the site in the mid-fifth century, perhaps leasing it on emphyteutic tenure to a private local *dominus*.[9]

Seventh-century Spanish bishops, however, are known to have founded private chantry-type monasteries (cf. ninth council of Toledo (655), Caballero Zoreda 1984: 581). As for monasteries in general, their formation, with or without continuity, from a *villa rustica*, is a well attested phenomenon (cf. Percival 1976: chapter 9): late Roman San Vincenzo is not the only Italian site to have been so interpreted. At Villaro di Ticineto, in the diocese of Vercelli, a sixth- to seventh-century cemetery was attached to an earlier basilican complex, probably of secular origin. There is no evidence for a parochial or funerary church there in local records, and the excavator has hypothesized a monastic church, formed from a secular estate centre, and acting as a religious focus for its *coloni* (Negro Ponzi Mancini 1980; 1982). We might compare Cassiodorus's *Vivarium* and his remark that monks settled on the properties of Christian *potentes* like birds nesting in the trees (*Institutiones* I. xxx. 2, *Expositio Psalmorum* ciii, 17). At Ribaria, near Cividale, an early Imperial villa and shrine were replaced by a fifth- to sixth-century cemetery and reliquary chapel, with traces of a monastery nearby. This site, however, may have ended up as a lay-owned Lombard *curtis*, with a parish church attached (Brozzi 1972-73). Despite these examples, a late Roman monastery does not initially seem very plausible for the settlement of San Vincenzo: not only the poor quality of these buildings, and their separation from the residential area, but the family tombs in the funerary church would seem to tell strongly against it. However, it is a possibility that we cannot rule out; and it may be illuminating to explore it, and to examine further archaeological and documentary parallels.

Late Roman double monasteries, housing men, women and children, were not uncommon; there is a possibility that San Vincenzo was such a monastery, and this would account for the mixed family burials in the funerary church. In the mainstream tradition, asserted for instance by Martin of Tours, the founder of western monasticism (Sulpicius Severus, *Dialogi* I (II) 11-12), monks were celibate and strictly separated from women even where their establishments had links (Bateson 1899). Thus, the commu-

nities of Basil of Caesarea and his mother and sister, like those of Pachomius and his sister, were divided by a river. The fifth-century Jura nunnery of Lauconum was perched on a precipitous crag above the neighbouring monastery (Basil, *Epistula* 223; *Vita Pachomii* 28, *PL* 73. 248-9 – a translation made in early sixth-century Italy; *Vita Patrum Iurensium* i. 8-9). In the sixth-century East however, *monasteria duplicia*, in which monks and nuns shared the same buildings, had to be suppressed by Justinian (*Codex Iustinianus* i. 3.43; *Novella Iustiniani* 123.36). In the West, about the same period, monks and nuns shared a triple church at Arles, in which both the nuns and their male founder were buried (cf. Bateson 1889: 139ff.). Indeed shared cemeteries for linked houses were known, though sometimes disapproved of.[10] In sixth- to seventh-century Spain, linked male and female foundations are also known, and shared buildings had to be prohibited: however, in Italy, evidence for such double foundations is slight (Bateson 1889: 188-9, 190ff.). In seventh-century Spain, as in eighth-century Northumbria, family pseudo-monasteries, founded by landowners on their property, and encompassing their wives, children, slaves and neighbours, are attested; these may have helped their owners to evade duties to Church and State, and to oppress their neighbours.[11] Even respectable Spanish monasteries might take in whole families in cases of emergency (cf. Fructuosus, *Regula* ii. vi; note *GMRE* i. 48); while, in times of war and disturbance, women might find a less reputable place in male foundations (cf. Pope Siricius, *PL* 13, 1137, to a bishop of Tarragona, a. 385; *GMRE* i. 40; iv. 40; xiv. 16-17). Women and children might also be admitted to a monastery for healing (cf. *Life of Theodore of Sykeon*, translated in Dawes and Baynes 1948: 60, 65, 68, 110), and the reception of child novices was common (cf. Caesarius of Arles, *Regula* i. 7; *RM* 1, 224; Benedict, *Regula* xxx, xxxvii, xxxix, xlv, lix, lxx).

In the fifth century, western Roman nobles sometimes started serious semi-monastic institutions on their estates, in which wives or female relatives might be included.[12] In this context, the mixed burials of San Vincenzo would not seem too anomalous. A founder, or member of special sanctity, could well have achieved the honour of a prestigious tomb (for example that in the 'South Church' ambulatory, context 40, see Volume 1: 125), and such a person's tomb and reputation

---

[9]For the state of *Venafrum*, cf. *GMRE* i. 66; vi. 11. Note *CV* i: 146ff.: Constantine's church at San Vincenzo.

[10]Prohibited by Justinian, *Novella Iustiniani* 133.3; conflicting opinions in Gaul are indicated by differing accounts of Abbot Romanus's burial – *Vita Patrum Iurensium* i. 9.19, Gregory of Tours, *Vita Patrum* i. 6.

[11]Cf. Fructuosus of Braga, *Regula Monastica Communis* II (*PL* 87, 1111ff.), i-ii; Bede, *Epistula ad Ecberctum* – *PL* 94. 662-4. Family control may have been hoped for by the founder of the single-sex Valerian monastery in *GMRE* x. 1. On the tendency in Merovingian Gaul of founders' kin to retain control of monasteries and to strengthen local dominance, cf. Wallace-Hadrill 1983. Note also instances from the third Council of Lérida of churches being disguised as monastic foundations by laymen who wished to retain control of the endowments. On monasteries and the law, cf. *Codex Theodosianus* xiii. 1.63; *Novella Iustiniani* 131.5; *Vita Hilari* 7 I (*Acta Sanctorum*, Mai III, 475); *GMRE* iii.61; Stein 1959: 148-9; Patlagean 1977: 330-3, 339.

[12]On Primuliacum and Nola, cf. Stancliffe 1983: 31, 34-5. At Cimitile (Nola) men and women may have had separate quarters in the same building: cf. Lienhard 1977: 72.

among the pious would then have aided the prosperity of her house.[13]

Such establishments might play important roles in the community. In the early fifth century, the ex-praetorian prefect Claudius Postumus Dardanus, with his wife and brother, founded a *Theopolis* on their estate in the Alpes Maritimes, fortifying the ravine which led to it as a protection for the whole neighbourhood. Behind that guard lay a considerable tract of land which may have included more than one church (*CIL* XII, 1524 (= *ILS*, 1279); Marrou 1954). We cannot be sure that this was a monastic settlement; but the inscription recalls Basil on his monastery – 'there is only one pass, and we control it' (*Epistula* xiv).

A well organized and conscientious monastery could exercise great religious influence, spreading Christianity both on its own estates and further afield (Cassiodorus, *Institutiones* I. xxx.2; *GMD* i. 4; ii. 8-10, 19). Monte Cassino, perhaps like San Vincenzo, was founded on an active pagan cult centre (*GMD* ii. 8-10; Pantoni 1980b: ch. 3). Lay-founded oratories could play a similar part in the community, although both oratories and monasteries may have been hampered by the suspicions and controls of the ecclesiastical hierarchy, at least until the late sixth century.[14]

Monasteries and their monks might also be active in the rural economy. In the East, the great Pachomian houses of Egypt, and those studied by Tchalenko in northern Syria (as too the ordinary churches), were the centres of big estates. We should note the partial socio-economic dependence of the latter area on its olive-oil exports (Tchalenko 1953: 396ff.; Patlagean 1977: 328-33, 338; Jones 1964: 931 (who in my opinion seriously underestimates monastic productivity); Sheehan 1985: 203-4). Augustine and John Cassian gave manual labour a firm place in the western monastic tradition. Ideally, though, the monks would be supported, at least in part, by the rents of their *coloni*, and would busy themselves at work that kept them inside the monastery enclosure (Cassiodorus, *Institutiones* I. xxx.2; *Regula Benedicti* xlviii, lxvi; *RM* lxxxvi, 350 ff.). However, many fifth- to sixth-century rules and anecdotes envisage poor foundations where the brethren tilled their fields in person.[15]

The effect on local farming might be profound. Monasteries and water-mills are associated from an early date (cf. *Vita Patrum Iurensium* i. 17-18; Gregory of Tours, *Vita Patrum* xviii. 2; Cassiodorus, *Institu-*

tiones I. xxix.1); the fifth-century Jura monks cleared primary forest to feed their growing numbers (*Vita Patrum Iurensium* i. 7-8). In the early sixth century the converted ex-courtier Olybrius gave a tract of *agri deserti* to the monastery of Galeata in the northern Apennines, and transferred his 90-strong *familia* there to work it. In ten years, the land was back in cultivation (*Vita Hilari* 6, 473; cf. John of Ephesus, *Life of Addai, Patrologia Orientalis* 17).

Sale of produce from monastic farming and craft work would create an income that could be used to supply the needs of the monks, to raise money-taxes, or for charity. Abbots of rural foundations might be expected to have large sums of money in treasure (cf. *GMD* i. 2; ii. 27). The early fifth-century abbot, Theodosius of Rhosus, near Alexandretta equipped his establishment with a barge for importing and exporting goods (Theoderet, *Historia Religiosa* x. 3). A sixth-century Syrian monastery found money for itself and its charities by attracting Cappadocian buyers for its wine (John of Ephesus, *Life of Addai, Patrologia Orientalis* 17). Saint Benedict and the near-contemporary author of the *Regula Magistri* tell of the sale of low-priced craft-goods. This mercantile activity should have been done by lay-agents, well away from the monastery, to keep the monks untouched by the world (*Regula Benedicti* lvii; *RM* lxxxv, 346-7). In many cases though this must have been impossible, or was simply not enforced. Basil of Caesarea advocated low prices to attract custom to the site, and so save the brethren from journeys to market, while deploring fairs and markets held at monastic martyria (*Long Rules* 39-40; *PG* 31, 1018-21).

Alahan, a late fifth- to early seventh-century Isaurian monastery has yielded 106 late Imperial bronze coins. Unlike those of San Vincenzo, about a quarter of the Alahan coins are of the large reformed types, more common and useful in towns than in the country, and suggesting visits by urban merchants or pilgrims to the site.[16] Alahan appears to have fared better than San Vincenzo in terms of the amount of sixth- and seventh-century fine-wares imported from long distance (Williams 1985:37-8). Monastic marketing on site could be another explanation for the latter's coins. A further possible explanation would be charitable donations: while monastic rules insist on communism of property, and Gregory the Great savagely rejected the private hoarding of money by his monks, the life of

---

[13]For a female founder of a male monastery at Syracuse, see *GMRE* x.1; for a monastery which may have grown around its founder's tomb, see Sheehan 1985: 207-8.

[14]Cf. the attack on Equitius in *GMD* i. 4; *LD* XI-XIV, XVI, XXIX-XXX. *LD* XXIX, which licenses a baptistery for an estate church and hints at its role in conversion, may be developed from Gregory the Great's practices: cf. Violante 1980: 1011, though at 1112-3 he argues that bishops and lay landlords, unlike monks, were not keen on missionary activity.

[15]Rules: *Regula Benedicti* vii, xxii, xlviii; *RM* xvii, 1; 1v, 85-6, 236, 258-9; *Vita Hilari* 6, 474; *Regula Ferreoli* 26, 28, 34-5; *PL* 66, 968-72; *Regula Tarnatensis* 8-9, 12, 981-2; Basil, *Long Rules* 38; *PG* 31, 1016-17. Anecdotes: *Vita Patrum Iurensium* i. 8, 11.5; Gregory of Tours, *Vita Patrum* xviii. 1-2; *Liber in Gloria Confessorum* 97; *GMD* i. 4; ii. 6, 32; Marcus; Cassinensis, *Carmina de S. Benedicto, PL* 80, 185-6; John of Ephesus, *Life of Addai, Patrologia Orientalis* 17, 129. Discussion: de Vogüé 1964b.

[16]Cf. Harrison 1985: 27 on the urban role of large bronzes, and Patlagean 1977: 410, 314ff. Note their importance in the excavation at Villa Clelia, a suburban cemetery and church complex near Imola; cf. Ercolani Cocchi 1978.

Theodore of Sykeon (c. 600) tells of a share-out of donated coins to individual brethren in a monastery (Dawes and Baynes 1948: 142; *GMD* iv. 55; cf. Sulpicius Severus, *Vita Martini X*, 5-8).

In layout, the phase 1 San Vincenzo site seems at least compatible with what is known of late Roman monasteries, East and West. If there were two churches, this recalls those of Sulpicius Severus at *Primuliacum*, and of Cassiodorus at *Vivarium*, the latter pair well separated, but one perhaps a funerary church.[17] The site of Cimitile, not far from San Vincenzo, was an extensive pagan and Christian cemetery. There the two main churches were set at right angles across an atrium with a fountain supplied by cisterns and an unreliable aqueduct. The older of the two churches was a *martyrium* of Felix, with other burials adjoining his tomb. The other probably had a baptistery, and was so planned that the tomb of Saint Felix, in the old church, could be seen from it. At San Vincenzo there may also have been means of direct sight and communication between the Crypt Church and the 'South Church'. The second Saint Felix basilica was built for liturgical use, but, unlike San Vincenzo's Crypt Church, was also funerary, with a collection of relics, and aisle chapels provided as *memoriae* of religious persons and members of the household. (Compare the narthex added to San Vincenzo's 'South Church'.) From a third side of the Cimitile atrium projected another basilica, a large dwelling-house, compared by Paulinus to a *castellum*, with porticoes and rooms on two floors, flanking either a central hall or an open cloister. It lay so close to the new church that nocturnal services disturbed the pilgrims sleeping there, and there was some danger that their rowdy songs might interrupt the ritual. It also lay so close to the martyrium that the shrines of the saints were visible from the upper rooms, as they probably would have been from the Tower at San Vincenzo, despite its awkward angle to the 'South Church' and Crypt Church. West and south of this complex, most of which was built by Paulinus, there perhaps lay four lesser churches (Paulinus, *Epistula* xxix. 13; xxxii. 10-16; *Carmina* xxi. 379-94; xxvii-xxviii; also Goldschmidt 1940; Chierici 1957; Weis 1957; Lienhard 1977; Testini 1985).

The model plan which emerges from Tchalenko's study of the larger monasteries in the Antiochene hinterland shows a central court with the monastery church on one side, and, adjoining it on the inside an important tomb or martyrium. Facing this complex is a range of communal buildings, and, linking them, a range of living quarters on the one side, on the other a porticoed building, perhaps a combined hostel and refectory. This, again, is not dissimilar

from San Vincenzo; though we should contrast a possible seventh-century Spanish monastery, founded on an earlier villa, where the cruciform church, with a sarcophagus niche in one transept, formed the centre of the complex (Caballero Zoreda 1984). Like the local villas and San Vincenzo, many of these Syrian foundations had towers, in at least two cases used for living quarters. One fine specimen with a loggia on top may even have been the abbot's lodging. (Monte Cassino, too, had a tower-lodging for the abbot, standing above a large dormitory building; *GMD* ii. 35.) The churches of the fifth to early sixth centuries were the principal buildings of their monasteries and were very large, a point of difference with San Vincenzo. Like those of San Vincenzo, however, they were placed prominently and were easily accessible from the outside (Tchalenko 1953: 162-9, 173).

Alahan, Cimitile or the Jura houses, and other such foundations, were often shrines of important saints. Such monasteries were the homes of charismatics and centres of pilgrimage, where access took high priority.[18] There was, however, another strain in the monastic tradition which stressed conventual privacy and isolation. According to one biography, the Jura abbot Romanus was buried ten miles from his monastery so that women could reach his tomb for healing without disturbing the living monks (Gregory of Tours, *Vita Patrum* i. 6). In the sixth to seventh century, the *Liber Diurnus* formula licensed the addition of an oratory to a monastery only if the laity, at least those who were not local, were excluded from its service and the monks allowed to worship God in peace (*LD* XXIII; cf. *GMRE* v. 49). Even in sixth-century Syria, churches tended to become smaller and more closely linked to the other monastic buildings (Tchalenko 1953: 162-3). Both East and West, moreover, even in pilgrimage monasteries, usually symbolized isolation by the circuit of hedges, fences, walls and ditches that enclosed the buildings and grounds (Tchalenko 1953: 174, 215-16; James 1981: 40-1). This feature has not yet emerged at San Vincenzo, although the walled enclosure adjoining the Tower tends to separate it from the church area, like the *sepis* of the *praetorium* garden on the *Massa Cornutiana*. The river may have acted as an effective natural means of limiting access to the monastery, isolating it from the rest of the Rocchetta plain.

In general, when considering these monastic plans we should note a high degree of regional variation. The foundations of the Monophysite Antiochene hinterland differ considerably from those of the Chalcedonian territory of Apamea, not far away. Further south in the Hauran,

[17] Cf. Paulinus, *Epistula* xxxii. 1 (note a baptistery between the churches); O'Donnell 1979: 194-8. On the liturgical function of multiple churches, cf. James 1981: 41ff.; but, as noted, normal services were discouraged in funerary churches. Such a complex might be useful in a double monastery.

[18] For the East, cf. *Life of Theodore* 71 (village church), 112-13 (monastery church); for the West, *Vita Patrum Iurensium* i. 4; ii. 3; Sidonius Apollinaris, *Epistulae* iv. 25.5; Paulinus, *Carmina* xxi. 383. This may have been generally true of Italian churches – note how the term '*processio*' is used by Gelasius and the *Liber Diurnus* to refer to their services.

monasteries show a closely integrated design of church and cloister which looks back to local Antonine villas, and forward to western foundations of the high Middle Ages. Mauretania has yielded a similar specimen, without parallel in the secular architecture of the region, and perhaps influenced by Syrian layouts.[19] The aspects discussed above suggest that resemblances to San Vincenzo may be wholly or partly coincidental, possibly the result of common religious functions, but perhaps just of the courtyard-centred plan which was used by so many Roman villas.

Such doubts demonstrate the problem of distinguishing lay and ecclesiastical structures at this period. In the same way that pious *potens*, dedicated *conversus* and monk blend into one another, so do the buildings which they inhabited. Hostile neighbours denounced Abbot Hilarius of Galeata to Theoderic for withdrawing his followers from the state corvée system; they may even have represented him almost as a brigand noble or a *Bacauda*, seducing the king's men from his service, and meditating rebellion against the peace of the realm.[20] Which aspect would have been dominant at such a monastery: church, villa or *castrum*? On balance, I would see San Vincenzo, after 450, as still a secular complex, for the most part like the *Massa Cornutiana*, but with potential for further religious development. By the tenth century, the latter foundation had turned into the parish church of Saint Stephen; the fate of its *praetorium* we do not know.[21] Another parallel might be Monte Canino in the *Ager Capenas*. In late Antiquity, the cemetery of this early Imperial *villa rustica* was centred on a rectangular building with an ambulatory, and was used at least into the eighth century. By 794, it may have become associated with the parish church of Santa Cristina. The villa itself remained in occupation for some time, overlapping with the cemetery building (Jones 1962; Wickham 1978; 1979; Potter (1979: 127ff.), however, seems to doubt the overlap between settlement and cemetery). Other sites in that area may show a comparable pattern of development, as may certain parish churches in the region of Lake Garda.[22]

Evolution from villa to village church or monastery is a familiar phenomenon in early medieval archaeology. Continuity is often surmised, but inevitably hard to demonstrate. At San Vincenzo, where continuity was broken, stages of change are plain to see, but the minutiae of the archaeological stratigraphy cannot assist us in clarifying these broad changes. We can only put the site in the general context of the Church's growing rivalry, to State and élite, as the major Italian landlord; but, whoever controlled it, late Roman San Vincenzo eventually failed. Burials continued for a while after the settlement was abandoned, perhaps illustrating the religious priorities of the neighbourhood; but by 703 even the funerary church was apparently disused, and ownership was in the hands of the dukes of Benevento. However, it seems that, as with Bobbio 100 years before, memories of former sanctity remained in the area, and drew back devout Christians to the site, to start the medieval monastery on its long and glorious career.[23] San Giovanni di Ruoti, with its purely secular structures, suffered a quicker death, and was not reborn.

---

[19]Cf. Tchalenko 1953: 178ff.; Seston 1934. Apamea has much more compact plans resembling the North Syrian villas, with oratories included in the main building, rather than as separate churches. Liebeschuetz 1979: 21 suggests, but does not account for, this relation of doctrine to architecture – it is hardly applicable in Italy.

[20]*Life of Hilarus* 7, 475. The version compiled by the Bollandist editors gives the charge of refusal of *angariae* and *opera publica*; that presented by Rubeus 1589: 136, note e summarized in the *Acta Sanctorum* the charge of rebellion. I would prefer the former. To the latter, John of Ephesus, *Life of Thomas the Armenian, Patrologia Orientalis* 17. 290, 294-5, may give an eastern parallel.

[21]Cf. *Regesto* V, a. 978, p. 35, *fundum qui appellatur cornuti. cum plebe sancti stephani*; Bruzza 1880: 179. It seems to have changed its dedication and been ruined by the eighteenth century: cf. Castritius 1972: 235.

[22]Cf. Jones 1963: 105-6, 134; Brogiolo 1980: 284-5, 292-5. Note the Council of Vaison, a. 528, i, on the ecclesiastical schools often attached to Italian parish churches: would they sometimes have needed villa-type accommodation?

[23]*CV* i: 129 tells us of annual masses held there. For Bobbio, cf. Ionas, *Vita Columbani* i. 30. Do the virtues of the site as reported to Agilulf denote natural or supernatural qualities? I suspect the former. For a possible parallel, in the tenth- to eleventh-century refoundation of seemingly disused churches, cf. Toubert 1973: 865-6.

Chapter Eleven

MONASTIC LANDS AND MONASTIC PATRONS

by Chris Wickham

The eighth-century devotional account by Ambrosius Autpert is the earliest description of the foundation of San Vincenzo al Volturno in the duchy of Benevento. He ascribed it to three noble kinsmen from Benevento, Paldo, Taso and Tato, who were acting with the advice of the abbot of Farfa in the duchy of Spoleto (*CV* i: 104-23).[1] The traditional date of the foundation is 702-3, which cannot be far out: Duke Gisulf I of Benevento was the donor of most of the large block of land inside which the monastery was built, some 300 km^2 of mountain land at the northwestern corner of his duchy, and he ruled from 689 to 706 (Wickham 1985a: 13-14). (Bertolini (1985), however, regards 702 as the date of Paldo's consecration as abbot, and the monastery as having already existed for some years.) Farfa and Spoleto had little or no influence on the monastery after its foundation. San Vincenzo was henceforth, for most of the time, politically as well as territorially part of Benevento: it was closest in its monastic relationships to its immediate neighbour, Monte Cassino, also a border monastery based, from its refoundation in the early eighth century, on large gifts from the Beneventan dukes. Indeed, as we shall see, the two neighbouring monasteries had strikingly similar histories until the end of the tenth century.

San Vincenzo developed slowly. It had a reputation as a place of learning in the eighth century, and was already becoming a centre of monastic life for more than its immediate neighbourhood: Ambrosius Autpert was a noted theologian as well as the monastery's historian, and was, like many of his fellow monks by the last quarter of the century, from the Frankish lands beyond the Alps (Mancone 1960; Leonardi 1968). San Vincenzo was not yet particularly rich, as we shall see, but was certainly influential; Pope Stephen II thought it worthwhile to seek the mediation of the abbots of San Vincenzo and Monte Cassino when attacked by the Lombard king Aistulf in 752 (*LP* i. 441 – the mediation was unsuccessful, and the pope had to call in the Frankish king Pipin instead). Not surprisingly, the monastery was caught up in the whirl of events that accompanied the conquest of the Lombard kingdom by Pipin's son, Charlemagne, in 773-4. Autpert, a supporter of Charlemagne, was himself briefly abbot in 777-8, but then resigned, his place soon taken by the anti-Frankish Poto (782-3/5), whom Charlemagne deposed (see below p. 146). The Frankish king was building up to a full-scale attack on Benevento, whose duke, Arichis II (758-87), had declared himself an independent prince in 774. Shortly before Arichis's death, Charlemagne moved in, and for a few years achieved recognition from the new prince, Grimoald III (Bertolini 1965). But the Franks never did manage to subdue the South; by 791 Grimoald was already independent, and he survived the resultant series of wars with little difficulty. San Vincenzo remained on the frontier between the Frankish kingdom of Italy and the principality of Benevento.

From this time onwards, under abbots Joshua (792-817), Talaricus (817-23) and Epyphanius (824-42), the monastery became rich, above all through a series of substantial gifts from the Beneventan aristocracy. The height of the monastic building programme dates from these years. The gifts stopped when the Beneventan civil war (839-49) ended, but San Vincenzo remained wealthy and powerful. Along with its sister monastery above Cassino, it gained a sort of religious extraterritoriality under the protection (*defensio*) of the Frankish emperor Louis II (845-75) when the South was split between the princes of Benevento and Salerno in 849 (*MGH LL* iv. 222). Trouble only came with the Arab mercenaries, hired by the princes, and their marauding relatives from North Africa; San Vincenzo had to pay off an invading force in 860-2, and, in 881, the Arabs sacked the monastery and dispersed its inhabitants. In 883 the same fate befell Monte Cassino; and by the start of the tenth century the miserable remnants of both houses had found refuge in the most powerful local political centre, Capua.

The Arab sack is a crucial event in the history and the archaeology of the monastery; it is amply discussed in this and the previous volume. San Vincenzo never fully recovered from it. The material remains from the site show as much; so

---

[1] I am grateful to Michael Hendy and Richard Hodges for reading a first draft of this text, and for their useful suggestions. The following convention has been used in this chapter for references to the *Chronicon Vulturnense*: where the reference is to a page number, the volume number has been given, as a small Roman number (e.g. *CV* i: 185 – would be page 185 in volume i); where the reference is to a document, an arabic number only is given (e.g. *CV* 185 – would be document number 185).

do the monastic documents, which reveal the monks, after their return from Capua in 914-16, principally interested in the agrarian reorganization of their central territory, the *terra sancti Vincentii*, by means of the process of *incastellamento*. The international importance of the monastery in the previous 150 years had disappeared, and was not henceforth reclaimed. I have discussed San Vincenzo's *incastellamento* in detail elsewhere (Wickham 1985a); it is enough to say here that it was, although economically successful, perhaps insufficiently militarily oriented – certainly less than was the same process at Monte Cassino. At any rate, when in the eleventh century local nobles and, later, Normans began to threaten the monasteries, it was Monte Cassino which managed to adapt better to the new political and military situation. San Vincenzo was not yet poor, but it was on the defensive; by contrast, its sister monastery became ever richer, and began to re-establish its position as the spiritual centre for the whole of central and southern Italy (Dormeier 1979; Toubert 1979; Cowdrey 1983: 1-45; Wickham 1985a: 42-5; Bloch 1986). San Vincenzo's relative weakness was such that it could not even prevent its central territory from being occupied by the aristocracy; the new Norman rulers of the mid to late eleventh century instead lavished their patronage on Monte Cassino, which was at that point reaching its height. From now on, indeed, our knowledge of the monastery on the river Volturno virtually ceases.

The outlines of this account are well-known, and have been studied by many authors (including Del Treppo 1953-54; Cilento 1966b; Wickham 1985a; the various contributors in Avagliano 1985). I set them out here simply to give context to two historical problems of considerable importance for the understanding of the excavations at San Vincenzo: the issue of the landed wealth at the disposal of the monastery at each moment of its history, and the issue of its changing relations to its patrons. These will allow us to pose the problem of how the monks could pay for everything they built, and, maybe, of why the various building programmes took the form they did. We can get closer to an understanding of what was going on in the monastery, above all between, say, Autpert and Epyphanius (777-842), in this way. It must be admitted at the outset, however, that these analyses will not help to make the extensive and obscure rebuildings of the late eleventh and twelfth centuries much less mysterious.

Almost all the evidence we have for the resources of the monastery comes from one source, the early twelfth-century history of San Vincenzo, the *Chronicon Vulturnense* (*CV*) by the monk John. (See Wickham 1985a: 13 and Avagliano 1985 for bibliography.) The *Chronicon Vulturnense* includes over 200 documents, mostly (at least after *c*. 800) genuine, which must be the basis for all our research. John was writing at a bad time for the monastery, and sought to glorify the past; the sparse narrative of monastic history that accompanies the documents he includes is very seldom historically reliable, and is anyway, where not based on surviving sources, mostly very much later than the events it describes. Other narratives and charter collections do not mention San Vincenzo much after 881, and even before that date are not often illuminating about its resources. However, as we are forced to rely on nothing except the charters in the *Chronicon Vulturnense* for our reconstruction of monastic wealth, we must recognize two serious problems. The first is that there are rather few documents at our disposal, by contrast with other monasteries (Farfa's historian Gregorio di Catino, working in the decades before and after 1100, transcribed over 3,000), and not all of John the monk's texts are reliable. Vincenzo Federici, editor of the *Chronicon Vulturnense*, could usually identify forgeries and interpolations fairly well (even taking into account the criticisms of Brühl (1971: 77-8), and the general criticisms of his edition by Hoffmann (1966)); I have in general used him as an initial guide (Federici 1925). But the small number of the documents surviving cannot be got around. Many texts must have been lost in 881, and John did not by any means include all he had for the tenth century (Wickham 1985a: 31, 34). Much of my analysis will necessarily involve some fairly intricate hypotheses as to what sorts of documents might or might not have been lost or excluded; and the overall history of the monastery's properties and their exploitation will largely remain guesswork.

The second problem to be faced is methodological. Our charters tell us about the boundaries of properties, not about their resources, potential or actual: not about wealth, but simply about land. Only detailed estate rentals, such as the ninth-century polyptychs of the Rhine-Seine region or the Po plain, could tell us directly about resources, and there are none for our area; the leases that survive in the *Chronicon Vulturnense* are too few to allow us to build up a picture of exactly how much money or kind San Vincenzo ever took from the estates under its control. In addition, there are many variables involved when we try to guess it, ranging from the natural fertility of the soil (low, in much of the monastery's Apennine land) to the reliability of aristocratic lessees of outlying estates or the tractability of their inhabitants; in many cases, these were equally low. We have to be very cautious about moving from the scale of monastic lands to the level of monastic economic liquidity: not only can no figures be provided, but even the relationship between the two is suspect. Land was not particularly liquid in the Middle Ages, even less than it is now, and there were under normal circumstances few other resources for a church – or an aristocrat, or a king – to draw on. (Churches often had treasure, and San Vincenzo certainly did, as we shall see; but it was far outweighed in importance by landed wealth.) It is by no means clear, indeed, whether most people even distinguished between land as an economic resource and land as power, for power was what most landowners wanted in the Middle Ages, and wealth was only a means to that end. But we, at least, have to pose the question; San Vincenzo's congregation did need, at certain times, readily available funds, for it was on the latter that they relied to finance the remarkable – and expensive – series of buildings excavated around the sides of Colle della Torre. (The monks, and doubtless their dependents, participated in building – see *CV* i: 221; but the cost of materials and the wages of imported specialist craftsmen must have been immense.) Our texts do sometimes speak in terms of ready cash; at other times I will guess my way towards an idea of the scale of usable monastic income. Landowners were, after all, not fools, even if they were not accountants; they may have managed their finances from a box under the bed, but they did know if they had any gold and silver in it.

The high number of forgeries in the *Chronicon Vulturnense* for the first century of the history of San Vincenzo is significant; John wished there to be as many documents as possible to testify to the early wealth and status of the monastery, but in the twelfth century they were entirely lacking. Nor do I think they had ever existed. The Arab sack of 881 did destroy documents (as *CV* 79, a. 899, explicitly states), but the dozens of lay gifts from the early ninth century certainly survive in large part, and I think that eighth-century texts, had there been many, would therefore have done so as well; in my view the documents destroyed without trace in 881 may have largely been relatively recent (below, p. 148). If we restrict ourselves to genuine or partly genuine texts, however, we only have three for the period before 774 (*CV* 9, 12, 69), and another six from 774-800 (*CV* 22-7); only half a dozen others can be deduced to have existed from references in other texts in the *Chronicon Vulturnense* (22, 26, 28, 29, 55, 69, 77), together with two from other sources (*CDL* v. 29, a. 761; Erchempert, *Historia Langobardorum Beneventanorum* c. 3, in *MGH SRL* 236). We should spend some time looking at what these texts mean.

* * *

San Vincenzo seems throughout the eighth century to have been relatively modestly off in terms of its usable landed resources (Fig. 11:1). Gisulf I and then, in 758/60, Arichis II, gave it the northern and southern parts of the *terra sancti Vincentii*, the great block of mountain land at the top of the Volturno valley (*CV* 9, 12; Wickham 1985a: 14-23). This was not entirely abandoned or unexploited land, but it was not exactly the economic centre of southern

Italy either; it is remote even today, and was doubtless even more so in the eighth century. Document 9 in the *Chronicon Vulturnense* says that Gisulf also gave churches, two monasteries and a great tract of land in the plain of Capua, but much of the list is demonstrably false; the two monasteries (San Pietro di Benevento and Santa Maria in Loco Sano, the latter probably Luogosano southeast of Benevento, in the province of Avellino) are not mentioned in genuine monastic documents until 892 (*CV* 80), the church of Santa Maria in Cinquemiglia not until 981 (*CV* 148), and the Capua lands are copied from a diploma of Louis the Pious, itself probably forged (*CV* 29). We are left with two abandoned churches, both called Santa Maria, in the mountains at the top of the rivers Trigno and Sangro. To this may be added a third, the nearby Santa Maria *ad Castanietum* outside Castropignano (province of Campobasso), referred to plausibly enough as Gisulf's gift in a court case of 897 (*CV* 77); it is probable that the charter of gift, which still existed in 897 (after 881, note), was not kept because the court record was itself sufficient for monastic purposes. But that is all – three mountain properties, in addition to the monastic core, itself in the mountains, as the basis for monastic life at San Vincenzo at its foundation.

In the decades to follow, things did not greatly change. Duke Godescalc (739-42) gave the monastery of Santa Maria in Isernia, but Gisulf II (742-51) confiscated it. A resultant settlement in 766 (*CV* 69) allowed San Vincenzo to keep some of its properties, but the total amount was small – Santa Maria can never have had more than a handful of tenant houses. In the duchy of Benevento, it is hard to say if the monks got much else. John claims (*CV* i: 148) that Beneventan nobles from as early as Gisulf I's time (many of them taking the monastic habit) gave properties, which the duke subsequently confirmed. We do have one later document in which Arichis II confirms a lay gift of a few tenant houses in the territory of Capua (*CV* 22, a. 778), though not by a postulant; but it was certainly common for postulants to give land, and as the monastery increased in size many of them presumably did so. We have one text, copied into the Farfa register (*CDL* v. 29, a. 761), which shows San Vincenzo monks from the Sabina in the duchy of Spoleto selling to Farfa some of their family land there, with the permission of their abbot: San Vincenzo clearly regarded itself as having some authority over its monks' family land, although, equally evidently, it did not prevent them from doing what they chose with it. None the less, if such gifts were substantial, we would expect to find more record of them, either the texts themselves (as with those after 800), or ducal confirmations; we find neither. Only for Spoleto do we have some more information. Duke Lupus (745-51) gave the monastery some tenant houses in Amiterno, beyond

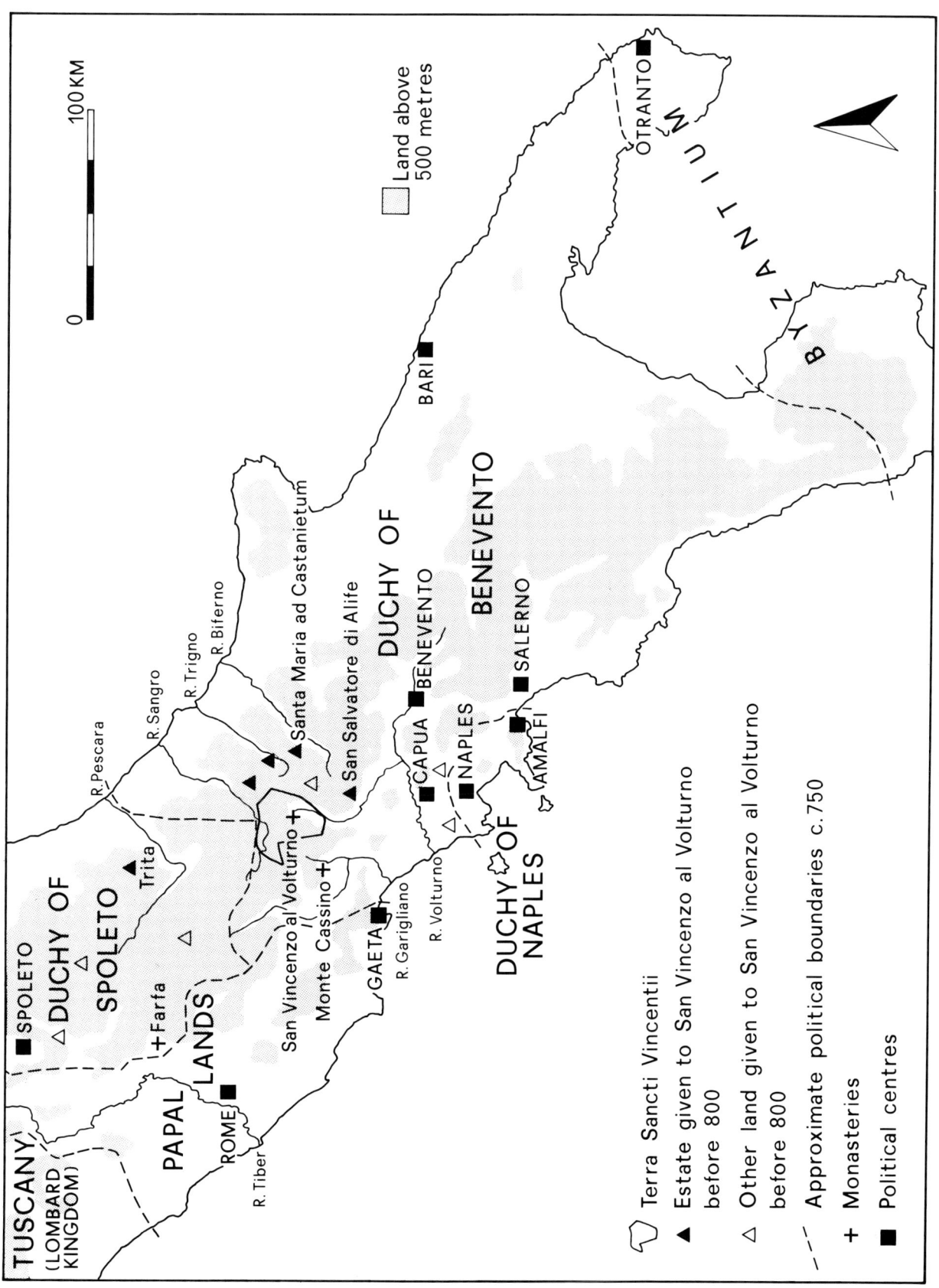

Fig.11:1 San Vincenzo and its *terra* in the eighth century *(SC)*

L'Aquila, and an annual render in animals (gifts referred to in *CV* 28, 55, aa. 816, 831); and King Desiderius gave the estate of the Valle Trita and part of the hills above it, just below the Gran Sasso, presumably in the period he directly controlled the duchy of Spoleto (758-62: referred to in *CV* 26, *c.* 787). Lupus's gifts were minor, of course. The Valle Trita, by contrast, was a substantial block of land with some economic potential, but San Vincenzo had great difficulty in controlling its inhabitants, and arguably never succeeded in doing so (Wickham 1982: 18-28). The importance of the gift lies more in the interest thus shown by the rulers of the North than in its economic use for the monastery.

This completes the gifts recorded for San Vincenzo before 774. The monastery was expanding, none the less, with monks not only from Benevento but, as we have seen, from Spoleto; and, of course, from the Frankish lands as well. These latter, at least, are unlikely to have brought land with them, though they might well have given movable gifts, in treasure or kind (compare the documented gift for treasure by Arnipert of Conza (or Canosa) to Monte Cassino in 823, edited by Gattola (1734: 27-8) and by Citarella and Willard (1983: 126-8)). The possibility of such gifts might in part help to explain the small number of gifts of land that survive, though we cannot do more than speculate on such a matter.

Between 774 and 800 there are a few more texts, but most of them are either confirmations of properties, grants of immunity, or records for San Vincenzo's long run of attempts to subdue the Valle Trita (*CV* 22-7). There is some evidence, however, of an increase in princely and ducal interest in the monastery on the part both of Arichis II (d. 787) and Hildeprand of Spoleto (773-88), as its position became more central in the political strategy of Charlemagne. Hildeprand gave more food renders, some tenant houses in Marsica on the southern border of Spoleto, and, suspiciously, a substantial area of marsh in the plain of Capua, land he had no right to control (*CV* 28). Maybe he got the latter in Charlemagne's Beneventan campaigns of 787-8; if so, however, he must have ceded it straight away. Arichis, for his part, gave his newly-founded monastery of San Salvatore di Alife, in a lost document (Erchempert, *Historia Langobardorum Beneventanorum* c. 3, in *MGH SRL* 236; cf. *CV* i: 354).

These texts are put in perspective by the fact that both rulers made similar gifts to Monte Cassino, but on a far larger scale: Arichis gave his major prestige foundation Santa Sofia di Benevento (Erchempert, *Historia Langobardorum Beneventanorum* c. 3; cf. *CC* i. 9) and lands in the plain of Capua (*CC* i. 14), and Hildeprand gave substantial estates all over the Abruzzo (Gattola 1734: 18; *CC* i. 14, 39). Monte Cassino had been as slow as San Vincenzo to pick up land in the eighth century after its initial cessions from Gisulf II (*CC* i. 5, 6 and Gattola 1733: 27-8 for

Gisulf; Gattola 1733: 27; 1734: 11; cf. *CC* i. 6, 10; these are the only lay gifts before the late 790s). Princely and ducal interest in the decade after 774 were thus as clear a novelty for Monte Cassino as for San Vincenzo, and in both cases point up the relative absence of gifts recorded for anyone in the previous decades. However, it must be stressed that this renewed interest, whether for religious or strategic reasons, benefited Monte Cassino very much more than the monastery on the Volturno. The contrast in Hildeprand's gifts is obvious. Arichis gave monasteries to each, but San Salvatore di Alife seems from tenth-century texts to have been relatively small (*CV* 96, 97, 133); Santa Sofia di Benevento, by comparison, was already extremely rich, and before 800 certainly had more land than either San Vincenzo or Monte Cassino on their own (Poupardin 1907: 66-9; Delogu 1977: 3-36). San Vincenzo was said by Paul the Deacon in the 790s to have a large monastic congregation, and Paul, himself living in Monte Cassino, clearly thought of the two monasteries as a pair, for he wrote of them in the same chapter of his history (*Historia Langobardorum* vi. 40, in *MGH SRL* 179). But Paul's own monastery was already the better off of the two in the years before both really began to expand their direct landowning.

To sum up so far: by the year 800 San Vincenzo al Volturno was becoming quite a substantial landowner, with land that could be estimated as reaching some 650 km^2, of which two-thirds was in its central territory (Fig. 11:1); but this land was very largely in the high mountains of the Abruzzo and Molise, and consisted of unproductive limestone country. The number of tenant houses under monastic control outside these blocks of marginal land may not have numbered more than two or three dozen. San Vincenzo's usable landed resources, actual or potential, were not yet particularly large, above all not by comparison with those it would have 50 years later (Fig. 11:2). Any wealth in the form of treasure would presumably have been less than that held in the future by much the same proportion. This picture is important, for it is the material background to the earliest levels of the excavated monastery (phases 3a and 3b), as well as its first major rebuilding, perhaps after 774, on a larger scale (phase 3c). I will return to the possible patrons of these buildings further on; but the local economic basis for their construction must be recognized as being as yet relatively slight.

In 800 and the years following things began to change rapidly, above all because San Vincenzo began to be the recipient of large-scale lay patronage (Fig. 11:2). Between 800 and 819, under abbots Joshua and Talaricus, nineteen private charters of gift are recorded (plus three public cessions, two of them from princes of Benevento and one from Louis the Pious); three or four lay gifts, plus an increasing number from the princes, are attested from the 830s

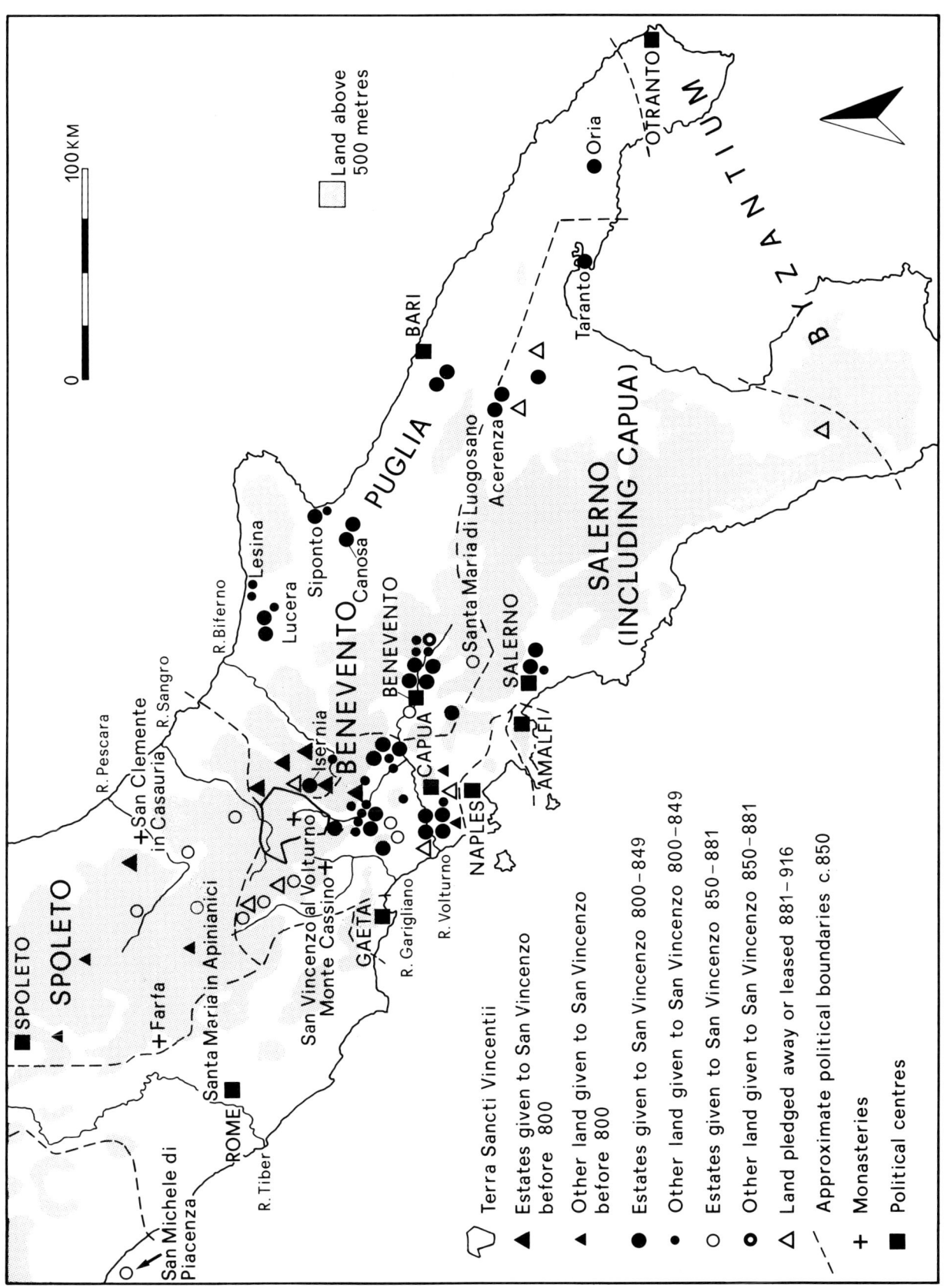

100KM

Land above
500 metres

San Michele di
Piacenza

ROME

R. Tiber

SPOLETO
■ SPOLETO
▲ SPOLETO

+ Farfa

Santa Maria in Apinianici

+ San Clemente
in Casauria

R. Pescara

R. Sangro

R. Biferno

Lesina

Lucera

Siponto

Canosa

R. Garigliano

GAETA

San Vincenzo al Volturno +
Monte Cassino +
Isernia

R. Volturno

NAPLES

CAPUA

AMALFI

BENEVENTO
BENEVENTO

Santa Maria di Luogosano

SALERNO

SALERNO
(INCLUDING CAPUA)

Acerenza

BARI

PUGLIA

Taranto

Oria

OTRANTO

B Y Z A N T I U M

Terra Sancti Vincentii

Estates given to San Vincenzo
before 800

Other land given to San Vincenzo
before 800

Estates given to San Vincenzo 800–849

Other land given to San Vincenzo 800–849

Estates given to San Vincenzo 850–881

Other land given to San Vincenzo 850–881

Land pledged away or leased 881–916

Approximate political boundaries c.850

Monasteries

Political centres

Fig. 11:2 San Vincenzo and its *terra* in the ninth century (*SC*)

and 840s, under abbots Epyphanius and James. Significantly, in these years forgeries and reworked documents become very much rarer, with the exception of a set associated with Louis; the monastic chronicler could by now mostly be satisfied with the records he had. We can therefore proceed much faster with their discussion.

The gifts to the monastery under Joshua and Talaricus are overwhelmingly from private donors, Beneventans, frequently from the princely court. The princes themselves gave relatively little – only two small gifts are recorded for the period (*CV* 31, 67, both probably from Grimoald IV, 806-17; the latter is a problematic text, however, and is certainly reworked). Louis the Pious is associated with some substantial gifts in the marshes of the Capua plain in 817, as well as, in John's narrative, the cession of a *templum antiquissimum in territorio Capuano* (*CV* 29; i: 220). The former text is, however, almost certainly wholly forged, and the latter is best seen as one of the numerous fabulous stories inserted by John the monk; Louis cannot plausibly be imagined as ever having had political power in the plain of Capua at all, and is indeed not known as a donor to the monastery in any authentic text.[2] However, the private gifts were substantial, and also, for the first time, very widely spread across Benevento: they numbered nearly 60 estates and a dozen lesser properties or areas of marginal land, making the monastery, in the space of two decades, one of the largest owners in southern Italy. Fourteen of these properties were in the immediate vicinity of the monastery, near Venafro above all (Wickham 1985a: 19-22), but also Vairano and Isernia (*CV* 31, 34, 35, 37, 44, 50; i: 275); those around Venafro

were certainly often quite small, a few tenant houses each, but one at Isernia had more than two dozen.[3] Another ten properties came from the valley between Alife and Benevento (*CV* 34, 36, 38, 39, 47, 49); four or five from the plain of Capua (*CV* 34, 36, 40, 44, 47); one from the Salernitano (*CV* 36). No less than thirteen properties, furthermore, came from the plains of Apulia at the opposite end of the principality, from Lesina, Siponto, Lucera, Canosa, Acerenza, Taranto and Oria (*CV* 34, 41-3, 45, 47, 51). Only a few are entirely unidentifiable: the only texts that mention substantial unlocated properties are *CV* 38, 43, 46, 48, half a dozen estates at the most; the geographical balance I have outlined would not be upset if we could locate them.

San Vincenzo therefore came to own property most widely in the valleys closest to the monastery, as one would expect, but it also held land in and around all the political centres of the Lombard South (Benevento, Capua, Salerno), and right across to Apulia. Its lands in the (by now Carolingian) duchy of Spoleto, by contrast, did not increase; indeed, no private owner from north of the border is known to have given land to the monastery before the year 1000. Almost all this land, it must be emphasized, was lowland property, largely a natural result of it being predominately private in origin – so much of the mountains being public land. The effect on San Vincenzo's economic prosperity must have been immediate. In 800 the monastery had relatively little usable revenue from its lands; by 820 such revenues must have been immense. Treasure may well have come as well (compare the parallels given by Citarella and Willard (1983)). It was in these years that the

---

[2]The stress laid on Louis the Pious in the *Chronicon Vulturnense* as a donor of land is considerable, but corresponds to little that can be demonstrated to be true, or even likely. He appears as the author of four documents, *CV* 28, 29, 55, 63. The last is obviously forged. Document 28 (a. 816) and document 55 (a. 831) are simply confirmations of properties given by dukes Lupus and Hildeprand of Spoleto, and of court cases dealing with the Valle Trita. The gifts from Hildeprand confirmed by *CV* 28 are tenant houses in Marsica and the *waldo Liburiano* (for *waldo* see Wickham 1982: 26-8, 36-44; Liburia was the plain of Capua, essentially the later Terra di Lavoro). That Hildeprand had rights in the plain of Capua is just possible; but Louis's other involvements in the area are not. In *CV* 29 (a. 817) it is claimed that Louis gave several properties in the plain of Capua and the Salernitano, and that he confirmed others in the Capuano, including two more *waldi* and marshlands; these latter are described as having been given respectively by Duke Gisulf and Prince Sicard (who only began to rule in 833). *CV* 56 (a. 833), from Sicard himself, confirms both gifts, but ascribes both of them to Gisulf. Even 56 is not free of doubt, however; although it has a genuine base, its references to Gisulf seem to relate to interpolated passages in *CV* 9 that themselves depend on *CV* 29. (Federici muddies the waters by confusing 28 and 29, and arbitrarily substituting Hildeprand's name in 56 for Gisulf's.) I would read all this as a confused attempt to give an early date to San Vincenzo's marshland properties in the plain of Capua, which were all in reality probably given by Sicard; and to give a major material role to Louis the Pious, who is also described in the *Chronicon Vulturnense* (i: 219) as Abbot Joshua's brother-in-law, without any contemporary documentation, and, as mentioned in the text, as donor to Joshua of a temple in the plain of Capua (*CV* i: 220). Louis never came south of Rome, and indeed for all of Joshua's rule (792-817) the king of Italy was not Louis, but his brother and his nephew, Pipin and Bernard (781-817); Louis did not succeed his father as emperor until 814. There is no reason why he should ever have had rights in the plain of Capua; after 791 no prince of Benevento would have consented to such a thing, and nor would the Franks have been able to enforce it in that period against the prince's will. (Louis was, it is true, later requested to intervene by the Neapolitans to save them from Beneventan attack (cf. Erchempert, *Historia Langobardorum Beneventanorum* c. 10, and the *Gesta episcoporum Neapolitanorum* c. 57, in *MGH SRL* 239, 431), but without much effect. That the Neapolitans also held substantial portions of the plain of Capua, often in common with the Beneventans (for example, *CV* 105, 126, 140; Cassandro 1969: 129-56), does not increase the likelihood that Louis got his hands on any of them.) What we are left with for Louis is merely two confirmations, of gifts of the dukes of Spoleto and of *placita* in Spoleto, quite normal and neutral acts for any Frankish emperor. *CV* 29 in its present form must be regarded as forged. Compare, for a similar conclusion, Brühl 1971: 78, though his criteria for forgery can be excessively rigorous – he also considers *CV* 22 for Arichis II to be forged, only because its formulae have been altered; but why ever would one forge a confirmation of a gift of three slave families? By contrast, however, his demolition of *CV* 30, a supposed gift by Hildeprand (Brühl 1971: 77-81), is a model of diplomatic analysis.

[3]*CV* i: 275 is the Isernia gift. It is an account of a gift rather than the text itself, but it fits with *CV* 51, which it immediately succeeds (the gift-giver is the same, Graffolus), and is for the Isernia estate described in *CV* i: 372 (after 881); someone must have given this latter to San Vincenzo, and there seems no reason to doubt that it could have been Graffolus. The word 'estate' that I use in the text represents for the most part the word *curtis*; for its varying meanings in southern Italy see Del Treppo 1955; Wickham 1982: 44-8; 1985a: 21. A *curtis* in the South did not always have to be either particularly large or run particularly coherently.

luxurious monastic rebuildings of phase 4 are most probably to be placed; and indeed the wealth of such properties could easily have paid for the Epyphanian aggrandizement of phase 5a in the second quarter of the ninth century as well.

After 819 the intensity of gift-giving slackened; we have in fact no documents at all for the 820s. In 833-6, however, Prince Sicard issued several diplomas for the monastery (*CV* 56-9), some confirming property already given by laymen in texts that have not survived, others adding new gifts: two or three more properties in Venafro, two marshes in the plain of Capua, an estate in Acerenza in Basilicata. In the 840s, during the civil war, there was another bout of lay gifts (*CV* 62, 64, 65), still involving land stretching from Capua to Apulia. After 849 they stopped, but San Vincenzo can hardly have worried much; it was one of the few forces in the South to have gained from the civil war, which concluded, as I have already said, with a declaration of its neutrality under Frankish protection. This neutrality was shared by Monte Cassino, and in this period, as before, the whole pattern of development of the latter monastery was strikingly similar to that of San Vincenzo. Lay gifts to Monte Cassino also began around 800 and tailed off in the mid-century (in the 850s, a little later than those for the Volturno house). They, too, included lands stretching all the way across the Beneventan principality down to Acerenza and Taranto, and almost none in Spoleto, apart from one gift by the emperor, Lothar I, in 835 (Gattola 1734: 18-21, 27-8, 30-2, 34; *CC* i. 14, 18-19, 22-4; *MGH D. Loth I.* 24). Indeed three texts (*CV* 38, 41, 43) show Beneventan aristocrats giving gifts to both monasteries at once, '*qui forciores sunt*' as one said; the two were still evidently seen as a pair.

By 850, the monastery of San Vincenzo was at its height, with all its great Carolingian-period buildings completed and a vast patrimony spread all the way across the South. Before we follow the history of its lands across the next two centuries, however, we should look at the political context of the arc of time 750-850. It is in this context that the issue of the relationships between the monastery and its patrons can be seen most clearly, and in the light of these relationships we may be able to understand better the type of socio-political environment in which the various buildings excavated at San Vincenzo were put up. This is not an unstudied theme, in particular for the reign of Charlemagne; many articles have discussed the role of San Vincenzo in the stand-off between the Frankish conquerors of the north of Italy and the princes of Benevento, the only people in Italy capable of resisting Frankish power, despite their relative military weakness (although the Franks were bad at conquering peninsulas, for some reason: Brittany and Denmark had similar improbable survivals). In this context, Del Treppo (1953-54), Bertolini (1965), Felten (1982), and

Houben (1985) are the major recent contributors to the debate. San Vincenzo, like Monte Cassino, was a border monastery, as has been noted often enough; its core lands were bounded to the north by the Lombard-Carolingian duchy of Spoleto. It was then on no significant road, it is true (less than Monte Cassino, for sure), but the *terra sancti Vincentii* was not entirely cut off; it was certainly crossed by drove-roads, and indeed, in the later Middle Ages, by the major inland road route of the Italian peninsula. The patronage of the monastery could easily have had strategic purposes, understanding the word 'strategy' in its widest sense. We must look at this patronage more closely, accepting some repetition as inevitable, to understand what effect the border did have on San Vincenzo's wealth and (of course) its buildings.

* * *

Although the foundation of San Vincenzo fits quite well into the period of Beneventan northern expansion of the years around 700, its subsequent history does not (cf. Del Treppo (1953-54: 45), although he argues against any links at all between the monastery and the dukes – oddly, since it was in Benevento and endowed by the dukes with their own land; see Bertolini (1985) as a corrective). San Vincenzo was not generously treated by any Beneventan duke or prince between Gisulf I and the end of the eighth century; if Gisulf thought of it as a 'ducal' monastery, along the lines that San Salvatore di Brescia was thought of by King Desiderius, or any of the Carolingian *Reichsklöster*, his successors certainly did not. We do not, it is true, have many Beneventan comparisons – documents have survived from too few places – but one of these, Santa Sofia di Benevento, is clear enough. Founded by Arichis II, by his death it had gifts of 22 separate properties from him, many of them vast (Poupardin 1907: 66-8; Bertolini 1926: 29). Arichis did give to San Vincenzo, as we have seen, part of its core territory and also San Salvatore in Alife; but this is nothing by comparison. The monastery was in effect left alone by the Beneventans for the whole of the eighth century; it did not form part of what one could call their geopolitical strategy.

San Vincenzo was thus left free to be taken up by other political environments, and so it was. Del Treppo (1953-54: 37-50) and Picasso (1985: 238-44) insist on its closeness to Rome, in my view excessively; but papal links did play a role in the history of the Volturno monastery, as with its sister monastery above Cassino, and both had the position of religious establishments on an international level. The second of the two always had more status, as the preferred retirement home of kings of both the Lombards and the Franks in the 740s, and with Anglo-Saxon links as well; but San Vincenzo was already attracting monks from Francia well before Charlemagne came into

Italy, and not, as far as we know, for particularly political reasons. Not that politics remained entirely absent, however. The people who seem to have responded to this first were Duke Lupus of Spoleto (745-51) and King Desiderius around 760. Lupus was a protégé of the kings of the North (Gasparri 1978: 80-1), and may well have wished to establish political links with an increasingly important religious centre just beyond his southern border, perhaps already as a southward extension of royal politics. It was Desiderius, however, whose donation of the Valle Trita in c. 760 most smells of strategic thinking. Desiderius wanted to control both Spoleto and Benevento; Arichis II himself, duke from 758, was his son-in-law. Desiderius certainly recognized the strategic use of monasteries (Schmid 1972); what better than to link a Beneventan border house both to Spoletan land and to himself?

It is in this context of a greater politicization of an existing international role that San Vincenzo confronted the problems of Charlemagne's conquest of the Lombard kingdom. Tension rose between its Frankish and Lombard monks; Autpert, for the pro-Frankish party, denounced his second successor Poto in 783 for (allegedly) refusing to take part in prayers for the Frankish king and for insulting Franks in general and Charlemagne in particular, and Poto was deposed on Charlemagne's orders. There is no need to go over the incident; the above-mentioned articles on Charlemagne do so very fully, only disagreeing in detail (Bertolini (1965: 625-31) presents the most straightforward and convincing analysis). It is enough to note that politics did matter in the abbey; and also that Charlemagne was prayed for (and capable, we do not know how, of deposing abbots) beyond his borders well before he descended militarily into Benevento in 787. It is also worth noting that Autpert's most immediate protector was Duke Hildeprand of Spoleto (773-88), a Frankish ally even if not totally a Frankish dependent (Ruggiero 1966-67: 77-8, 87-91). Hildeprand, indeed, seems to have had his own designs in Benevento; he followed Desiderius's example in giving land to San Vincenzo and, in his case, Monte Cassino too. His role in the crisis of 783 was not, in other words, only as Charlemagne's military representative. Arichis, by contrast, was on the defensive, unable to extract the border monasteries from the Frankish/Spoletan orbit. He did give gifts to them, however, in particular to Monte Cassino; it is reasonable to see these gifts as a preliminary attempt, for the first time since before 750, to associate the two houses more closely with the Beneventan court, by using the same politics of gift-giving as did the Lombards of the North.

Charlemagne did not give land. This was not because San Vincenzo was unimportant to him, but because gifts of land to the church were not the currency in which he dealt. There are few gifts of any kind in the 33 diplomas to Italian churches and monasteries that survive from his reign; all but six are simply confirmations of property and grants of immunities from secular legal interference. In Spoleto and Benevento, none are gifts at all; the eight diplomas for Farfa are all confirmations and immunities, and so also are the near-carbon-copy diplomas for San Vincenzo, Monte Cassino and the cathedral of Benevento granted by the king when he was in Capua and Rome with his army in March 787.[4] Charlemagne evidently regarded immunity as the most important privilege he had to give, and indeed it was one fully exploited by the border monasteries later on when they wanted to remain clear of the division of the Beneventan principality in 849, as we have seen. It was through this, and of course through direct control over the choice of abbot, that Charlemagne sought to influence monastic politics, and not through the more delicate gift-exchange that underlay landed patronage. It is not to be excluded, however, that he gave treasure; he was certainly not short of it, and he certainly did give it to the church in Rome. If he did, then the years between 783 and 788, when he was on the offensive in the South and directly involved in monastic politics, would seem the most likely time. It is indeed quite likely that he could have financed the early enlargements of the monastery (in phase 3c), although his gifts cannot have matched the monastic wealth of the following century: the phase 3c monastery, in comparison with its successors, was still small.

The situation changed in the 790s. Between 791 and 812 the Franks and the Beneventans fought a series of inconclusive wars (Bertolini 1965: 657-71), and thereafter the former recognized the de facto independence of the latter; only in the 840s, with the Beneventan civil war and the Arab threat, did Frankish and Spoletan political influence begin to weigh on the South again (Cilento 1966b; Ruggiero 1966-67). It was in these years that San Vincenzo really began to prosper. The first of the builder-abbots, Joshua (792-817), is claimed by the *Chronicon Vulturnense* to have been a Frank, and linked closely to Louis the Pious (i: 219-22). Frank he may have been – there were plenty to choose from at San Vincenzo; but, as I have already argued (n. 2), Louis probably had little involvement in giving land to San Vincenzo, and little political influence in southern Italy at all. On the other hand Gisulf, Monte Cassino's builder-abbot (796-817), an exact contemporary of Joshua, was a noble from Benevento (*CC* i. 17-18). The economic underpinning for

---

[4]*MGH D. Kar* 80, 113, 155, 201, 207, 214 are gifts to north Italian institutions; 125, 131, 133-5, 150, 164, 174-5, 177, 183, 196-7, 200, 202 are confirmations, judgements and immunities. *MGH D. Kar* 98-9, 111, 146, 160, 171-2, 199 are for Farfa; 156 for Benevento; 158 for Cassino; 157 and 159 (*CV* 27, 26) for San Vincenzo.

the ninth-century rebuilding of both monasteries is entirely Beneventan, the sudden explosion of gifts from the aristocracy of the principality. Indeed, the best way of understanding these gifts is to see them as the Beneventan reaction to the passing of the Frankish danger, and as the recognition of (and desire to preserve) San Vincenzo and Monte Cassino as henceforth securely in the Beneventan political orbit. The princes themselves gave very little land; but many of the donors to the monastery were their courtiers, and they must have been granting land in an atmosphere of princely benevolence and even encouragement. Until the arrival of Louis II in 848-9 to help end the war and divide the principality, and, still more, until his campaigns in the South after 866, San Vincenzo was essentially a great Beneventan monastery, with few links to the North that can be identified through the documentary sources. For that matter, despite Louis II's own gifts, it remained so; it was to Capua that the monks fled in 881, not to Spoleto or Rome.

But if San Vincenzo's political and economic links in the early ninth century, the context for the great rebuildings of phase 4, were totally Beneventan, why does phase 4 seem (in part at least) so influenced by Carolingian monastic models? One reason must be the Carolingian dominance of the issue of monastic reform. In 816 and 817 leading churchmen from all over Europe came to Aachen to draw up a reformed Benedictine Rule (McKitterick 1983: 112-24). The abbot of Monte Cassino, original home of the Rule, must have been there (cf., but not explicitly, *CC* i. 16). Equally naturally, the *Chronicon Vulturnense* claims that Joshua was there too (*CV* i: 122). There is no independent evidence of his presence, but it is likely enough (at least in the 816 council – he was dead by the second). This gives us a context for Louis the Pious's claimed involvement with the monastery, and may even explain the *Chronicon Vulturnense*'s insistence on his patronage. Louis was not particularly interested in Benevento; but he was interested in monastic reform and monastic expansion. Monte Cassino and, by extension, San Vincenzo were major spiritual sources for Louis's reform programme.

If Louis was a material supporter of San Vincenzo's rebuildings, then, he was so as a religious patron, not a political one: San Vincenzo could not by now be removed from the Beneventan political network as easily as that. But the Carolingians may have gained, all the same; San Vincenzo was, after all, primarily a religious rather than a secular building. The fact is that by the first decades of the ninth century the Carolingians had a cultural hegemony in Latin Europe that was almost total, stretching well outside even the widest interpretation of the boundaries of their political power. Anglo-Saxon England was certainly part of this cultural network; its political and ecclesiastical institutions were permanently affected by it, as was its architecture. The Beneventans were less safe from the Franks, and therefore perhaps more suspicious; but they could not entirely avoid such influences.[5] Any great Benedictine monastery built or rebuilt in the early ninth century would, of necessity, be affected by the cultural presuppositions emanating from Aachen, Reichenau and St Gall. Even a building programme explicitly put into action against Carolingian political claims (and this we cannot prove for San Vincenzo in the early ninth century, when Frankish-Beneventan relations were at least intermittently polite) would, in this period, have almost inevitably been expressed in a common Carolingian religious and architectural language, made all the more telling by imperial patronage of the 816-17 Aachen decrees. The only alternative model would have been Constantinople, as with Arichis II's Santa Sofia di Benevento; but this at least is probably to be excluded for San Vincenzo, judging by what survives – Byzantine influence in Italy was anyway not great in these decades. Beneventan though San Vincenzo was, and Beneventan though many of its builders and artists were (both in phase 4 and, even more, in phase 5a under Epyphanius), it looked Carolingian. So too, probably, did Monte Cassino. After the 780s, San Vincenzo would never again be a real political fulcrum – unlike, for example, Farfa on the trickier boundary between Spoleto and Rome, where religious and secular politics more obviously fitted together. But in its Beneventan period it paradoxically fitted Carolingian cultural-imperialist aspirations almost as well as it would have done if explicitly built and controlled by the Frankish rulers themselves; as a great rural Benedictine monastery, with an immunity from secular jurisdiction, it would remain a symbol of a world view that owed far more to Frankish (and north Italian) preconceptions than those of the Lombard South. (By contrast, Santa Sofia, the princely foundation *par excellence*, was urban, and had no immunity until it got one from Otto I; see Martin (1980: 556-8) for the absence of immunities in the Lombard principalities.) San Vincenzo stood as a Carolingian cultural symbol, right on the border of the independent lands of the South; but it was only after it had ceased to be a key to international power politics that it really began to prosper in economic terms, as a centre of a Beneventan 'national' political-religious identity.

* * *

After 850, the patterns of political patronage of San Vincenzo al Volturno can be more directly linked to the gifts of land that we have in the *Chronicon*

---

[5] The best-developed parallel to the Beneventan situation is probably by now Brittany, a quasi-independent protectorate also heavily influenced by Carolingian culture: see now the model survey in Smith 1992.

Vulturnense, or that we can deduce from it. How they changed is not, however, wholly straightforward: in the years before 881, in particular, we will still have to proceed quite carefully, in order to tease out the real changes in monastic landowning; and in the tenth century, even though we are not short of documents, it is important, as I shall argue, not to read them too naïvely.

There are few documents in the *Chronicon Vulturnense* for the period between 850 and 881: nine, to be precise, of which two are court cases for the Valle Trita (*CV* 71, 72), two are lists of servile dependents on Abruzzese estates (*CV* 176; i: 333-7 (Wickham 1982: 44-6)), and one is a general confirmation from the emperor, Louis II, dating from 866, on his entry into the South to fight the Arabs (*CV* 70). Two more are exchanges of land with princes of Benevento and Salerno, from which San Vincenzo did not gain significantly (*CV* 66, 68, to which should be added the lost charter referred to in i: 315). Only two gifts are recorded, one by a layman, of an estate on the plain of Capua (*CV* 73, a. 874), and one by Prince Adelchis of Benevento, a lost text of 861 confirmed by the prince himself in 878 (*CV* 78), for properties unknown. This is scarcely a large haul of documents. The period may not, however, have been as unpropitious for San Vincenzo as the group might make appear. In the decades after the Arab sack of 881, which were very bleak indeed for the monastery and certainly not a period of generous gift-giving, we begin to find references to very substantial monastic properties, often monasteries themselves, whose donors are entirely unknown. They include the rich monastery of Santa Maria in Apinianici[6] in Marsica, first cited in 885 (*CV* 70); the substantial Beneventan houses of San Pietro on the Sabato (outside Benevento itself) and Santa Maria di Luogosano, first recorded as San Vincenzo's in 892 (*CV* 80; cf. also 79, 81) and San Michele di Piacenza in the Po plain, referred to in 899 in an original from Piacenza itself (*CV* iii: 146-8). Other estates that fall into the same category include one in Teano (*CV* 88, a. 936); two in Valva (the territory of Sulmona (Wickham 1982)), San Rufino di Rota near Sulmona and Baratta above the Valle Trita (*CV* 89, 90, aa. 926, 936); and perhaps the set in Marsica and Valva that Otto II declared in a diploma of 981 to have been lost after the Arab sack (*CV* 148). Other tenth-century Abruzzese properties, of which there were many in the hands of San Vincenzo, probably came with Santa Maria in Apinianici (see, for example, *CV* 120, 176). John the monk was well aware of the gaps in his record of gifts; not surprisingly, most of these properties turn

up in the eighth-century forged cessions to the monastery (*CV* 9, 10, 15, 17, 19). But early Luogosano documents, some of which eventually came into San Vincenzo's own archive and were transcribed into the *Chronicon Vulturnense* (32, 33, 53, 60, 61, aa. 754-839) show no signs that the former was under the latter's control. For Luogosano, the situation changed between 839 and 881, the period when we have relatively little documentation in the *Chronicon Vulturnense*. I would propose that the same is true of the others, and that they came, to be more precise, into monastic hands in the period after 850 when the record of gifts and of all documents in the *Chronicon Vulturnense* sharply drops back.

The obvious reason for this gap in information is the sack of 881; but why did it only destroy records of the last 30 years? There may be entirely contingent reasons for such a pattern of survival. An alternative, however, if a risky one, is the existence of a cartulary of the mid-ninth century that collected the preceding texts, which John could use and (on occasion) abuse; and, of course, add to, with the few other surviving texts from before 881 and the rather larger number after. No explicit reference to such a cartulary exists in the *Chronicon Vulturnense*, and no such text survives in Italy from before the *Codex Bavarus* of the late tenth century (Rabotti 1985; cf. Pratesi (1976) and Feller (1988) for a probable Abruzzese example from *c*. 1025); but they did exist in ninth-century Francia (see Goffart (1966) for one example, the rather disreputable collection from Le Mans), and in their insistence on effective written record they had something in common with the polyptychs, which are ninth-century texts *par excellence*. This would solve the problem of the balance of the texts most neatly, although it raises other, most notably diplomatic, problems; I leave the issue open, but it is in my view one that is worth exploring further.

More important for this discussion is, however, the question of who actually gave these properties. In the case of Santa Maria di Luogosano, the answer is almost certainly the prince of Benevento (most likely Adelchis, ruling in 853-78), for that monastery looks pretty clearly to be under direct princely control in a court case of Sicard in 839 (*CV* 61). The same may be true of San Pietro di Benevento. Almost all the other properties, however, come from Marsica and Valva in the duchy of Spoleto, and one actually from northern Italy; the pattern of these gifts points most directly at the period 866-73, when Louis II was in the South, and, even though fighting the Arabs, had an eye firmly fixed on the possibility of taking over the Lombard

---

[6]Apinianici is the least easy of San Vincenzo's major properties to locate, in the main because Marsica so far lacks any serious study. The fourteenth-century *Rationes Decimarum* mention a monastery of Santa Maria de Apamia near Pescina east of the lago Fucino (Sella 1936: 518, 717, 723); the linguistic link is weak enough, but the area is probably about right (it is near to the dependencies Santa Maria is known to have had in Valva and Penne: *CV* 120), and I have so placed it on the maps. (Bloch, in a book which only appeared when the basic text of this article was already submitted, confirms this location, with extra supporting arguments (1986: 831). Bloch's large book, it may be added, is mostly focused on tenth- to twelfth-century Monte Cassino, and its long-awaited appearance does not affect the discussions in this chapter.)

states as well (Delogu 1968: 178-85). Louis, unlike some of his ancestors, did give gifts to monasteries, at least in part for political reasons. He founded his own monastery of San Clemente in Casauria in the eastern Abruzzo, largely to counterbalance the dukes of Spoleto, and endowed it massively. He gave Abruzzese lands to Monte Cassino in 867, too (*CC* i. 36; cf. i. 39), and was one of the major contributors to the remarkable set of Cassinese lands along the Adriatic recorded by Abbot Berthar in the years before the sack of that monastery in 883 (Gattola 1733: 78-9; *CC* i. 45). It would not have been at all surprising, given the traditional parallelisms between the two houses, if he had given Apinianici, Rota, and Baratta to San Vincenzo at the same time, just as it is extremely likely that it was his wife Angilberga, owner of many properties in Piacenza, who gave San Michele there (Del Treppo 1955: 41).[7] Louis may have been attempting with these substantial gifts not only to tempt the monasteries away from Beneventan dependence, but also to undermine Spoletan power, since it was probably ducal land he was ceding. Adelchis's gift of Luogosano may even have been in response.

I have insisted at some length on these undocumented gifts for two reasons. Firstly, they show as clearly as anything some of the problems of the *Chronicon Vulturnense*; I would not wish anyone to think that what is contained in it, even when genuine, always has the certainty of a well-dated sealed archaeological deposit, even supposing these were common in early medieval excavations. Secondly, they show that, despite the troubles of the period after 850, when the Arabs were at large throughout the South,[8] the monastery was still expanding its resources, thanks now to public rather than private generosity. Luogosano and Apinianici, in particular, must have been very substantial acquisitions. But San Vincenzo did not have time to exploit them: in 881 the Arabs burnt the monastery and took its treasure. Indeed, they sacked Apinianici and San Salvatore di Alife too (*CV* 74; ii: 40), and, in 883, following the usual logic, Monte Cassino. San Vincenzo remained abandoned, or at least devoid of monks, for 33 years (Wickham 1985a: 25-6).

After 881, the Carolingian monastery of San Vincenzo ceased to exist; we can thus afford to look at its subsequent documents (over two-thirds of the total in the *Chronicon Vulturnense*) in less detail, and I will draw the lines of its development rather more broadly. The first point to note is that there is a small group of texts, from the years between 881 and the reoccupation of the monastic area in 914-16, that for

once make the relationships between the monks' financial needs and the extent of their landholdings very explicit. They show Abbot Maio (872-901) leasing and pledging away monastic lands for low rents, in return for lump sums of money for the restoration of monastic fortunes (*CV* 74-6; ii: 14, 30). These lands were all over the South: in or around Capua, north of Cassino, in Basilicata. They were not necessarily inaccessible or devastated lands; they would not have been much use if so to their lessees. The texts show, however, that for all the extent of San Vincenzo's lands, they were not capable of producing revenue for sudden immediate expenditures. This is an important point to bear in mind when considering the expense of the monastic foundation at the beginning of the century. The analogy may not be exact, none the less: times were changing. San Vincenzo's direct economic control over its own lands, the essential prerequisite for its ability to turn landowning into usable resources, was weakening. In the tenth century, as we shall see, the monastery often leased to aristocrats who in reality already totally controlled the lands they were 'leasing'. This pattern was already beginning to appear before 900 too. Soon after 881, and possibly even before, a Beneventan prince gave away monastic property (Santa Maria *ad Castanietum*) to a lay follower in benefice, as *CV* 77 (a. 897) tells us; and many other lands that San Vincenzo had before 881 must have been lost in the confusion of these decades, for they are never mentioned again. We have a list of lost lands in the territory of Isernia (*CV* i: 372-3), and there were beyond doubt many others, which were certainly not balanced by the occasional gift recorded for these years (*CV* 85; and perhaps ii: 40). The low point for the monastery may well have been around 900, when the monks were even poorer than in the immediate aftermath of the Arab sack.

In the tenth century, and above all in the 100 years after 950, there was a certain reconstitution of the lands of San Vincenzo, both old and new (Fig. 11:3). The impression of an increase in Volturno property is most graphically expressed by the steady rise in lands confirmed by popes, princes, and Italian kings and emperors: nine estates and monasteries were confirmed in 930 (*CV* 91), 23 in 944 (*CV* 106), 30 in 983 (*CV* 144), 38 in 1038 (*CV* 187), and 54, or perhaps 68, in 1059 (*CV* 204). It is certain that this corresponds to some real increase in monastic lands, for we have some of the charters of gift, such as *CV* 140 (a. 964), a substantial cession by Prince Pandulf I of Capua-Benevento of land in the plain of Capua. Private gifts also exist for Isernia and the Capua plain for the period 963-86

---

[7] John the monk made a similar link, in his entirely fabulous legend of the Magdalen-like Ymilla, sister of Louis II, and her donation of masses of property in Valva, including Rota, to San Vincenzo (*CV* i: 226-30). Maybe this reflects some monastic tradition, maybe (and more likely) not; still, it would be unfair to doubt that Louis II could be responsible for the Rota gift just because John came to a similar conclusion.

[8] The Arabs had already in 860-2 removed 3,000 *aurei* from San Vincenzo's treasury in return for not sacking it: Erchempert, *Historia Langobardorum Beneventanorum* c. 29, *MGH SRL* 245. They apparently did not do the same to Monte Cassino, this time, but the latter's treasure had been largely expropriated earlier, in 843-4, by Siconolf of Salerno (Citarella and Willard 1983).

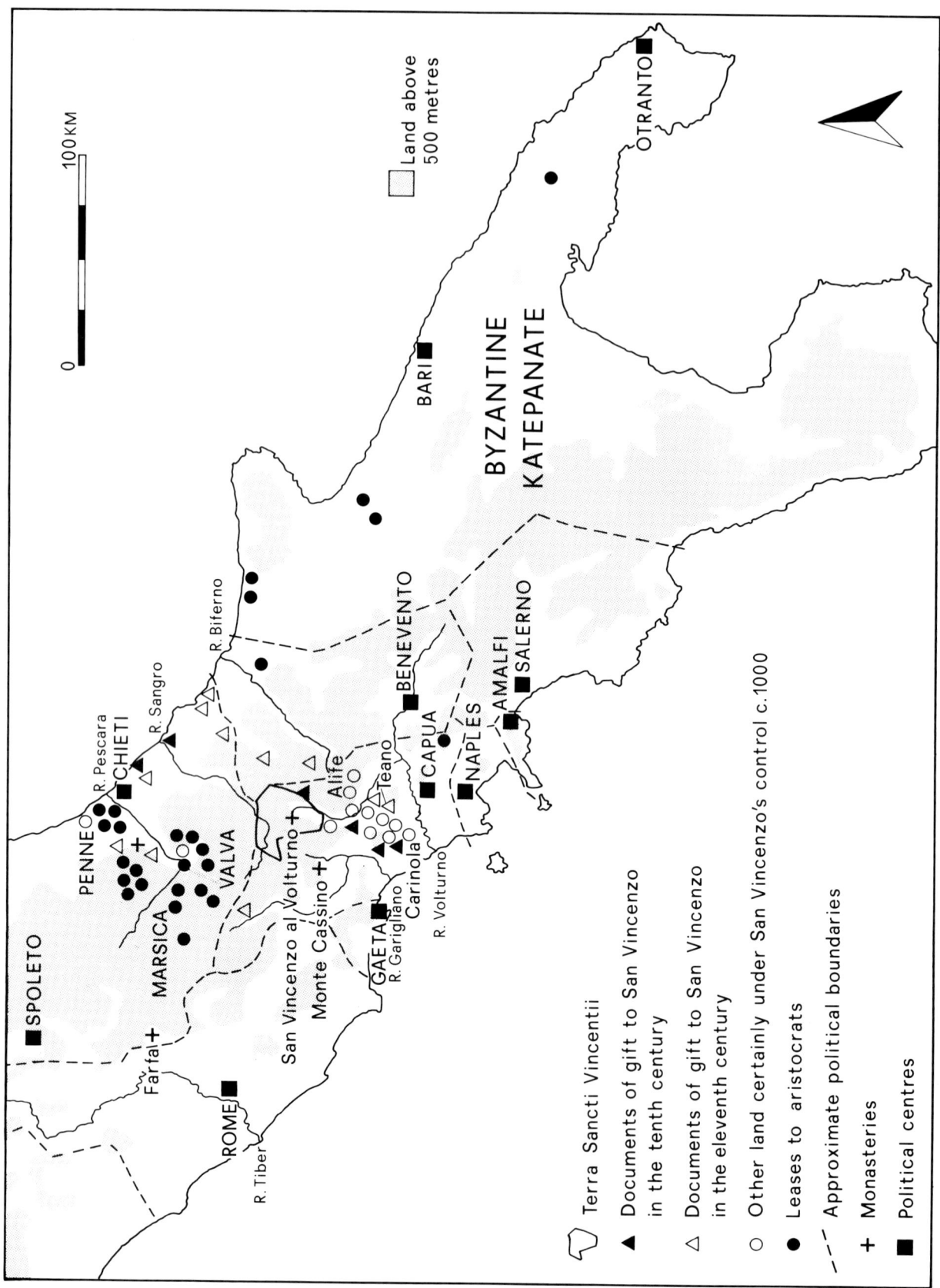

Fig.11:3 San Vincenzo and its *terra* in the tenth and eleventh centuries *(SC)*

(*CV* 138-9, 168-9); and there was a certain number from after 1000, as we will see in a moment. However, this does not mean that we can trust these lists of properties to any significant extent. The other documents we have for the period point in quite a different direction; they show San Vincenzo with far from full control over its territories. Take Apulia, for instance: even in 1059 the monastery still claimed two churches there, at Lesina and Lucera (*CV* 204); but in reality five of the six documents we have for the region after 900 are leases to aristocrats, usually for nominal rents, and none come from the period after 980 (*CV* 101-2, 128-9, 131-2) – monastic power in Apulia had, in effect, ceased.

The best example of the lack of relationship between monastic claims and monastic control is, however, the case of San Vincenzo's lands in the Abruzzo, in the duchy of Spoleto. The monastery claimed over twenty estates there in 1059: indeed, we have 37 documents for the region in the tenth and eleventh centuries, by far the largest group of texts for the period that survive. It seems that San Vincenzo was returning to being a high mountain power, its centre of gravity moving closer to the Spoletan border, thanks above all to the patronage of Louis II. This view would probably exaggerate the importance of Louis's gifts, in fact; but, even if it did not, it would certainly misrepresent the realities of the tenth and eleventh centuries. Most of the documents for Santa Maria in Apinianici are court cases which complain that the monastery is in the hands of laymen; the defendants often do not even bother to turn up in court (*CV* 120-2, 146, 149). All the other texts for Marsica, most of those for Valva, and many for Penne, are leases to local aristocrats for nominal rents, but also for enormous 'gifts' of movables and money for the restoration of the monastery (*CV* 89, 90, aa. 926-36; 155-7, 161-2, 173-5, 177-9, 181-2; ii. 330-1, aa. 982-98). These show that the monastery could no longer hope to control its lands directly, or indeed at all; these leases were in effect sales, which legitimated aristocratic possession without formally alienating monastic property, and also released some much-needed resources to be spent, as has been argued more than once, on San Vincenzo's *incastellamento* and agrarian reorganization in its immediate *terra*, and then, after 998, on the rebuilding of the monastic mother church (Toubert 1973: 521-7; Wickham 1985a: 45-6).

If we leave these texts and instead restrict ourselves to those where San Vincenzo leased lands to cultivators, thus demonstrating direct control of the properties concerned, the situation changes sharply. No such texts survive from Apulia, and only two from the Abruzzo (*CV* 134, 153, one from the plain of Sulmona and one from Penne). There are seven from the Alife-Teano-Carinola area, between San Vincenzo and the sea (*CV* 133, 135-7, 158, 163, 198). All the others, twenty-odd in

number, come from the *terra sancti Vincentii* itself and the lands bordering on it, and most relate directly to the *incastellamento* process (Wickham 1985a: 24-52). Around 1000, say, San Vincenzo still controlled the *terra* and a group of estates just to its south, extending as far as the plain of Capua; but beyond this its real control was probably restricted to a few fragments of land. By the late tenth century, in effect, the monastery had returned to the sort of scale of landowning it had had in the late eighth century, with only two advantages: the exploitation of the monastic *terra* was, for the first time, systematic; and the opportunity presented itself of gaining once-for-all windfall gifts, as San Vincenzo in effect sold off its Marsican and Sulmonese lands to their real controllers one by one. It must have been with these resources that abbots John IV (998-1007) and Ilarius (1011-45) finally rebuilt the main church of San Vincenzo (*CV* ii: 342; iii: 78); conversely, the financial straits of the monastery are clearly shown by the fact that it took the monks over 80 years from their return to do so.

The eleventh century was a time of paradoxes for the monastery. We have references to almost twenty gifts from the period 994-1045, almost all under the rule of Ilarius: ten in surviving documents are for the Adriatic coast, a set of gifts spearheaded by the counts of Chieti, though the others are spread all across Spoleto and the southern Lombard lands. It is very likely that these cessions, some of them substantial, further aided Ilarius's building programmes. Did they continue, though, as they would for Monte Cassino? The *Chronicon Vulturnense* is unfinished, and in effect breaks off with Ilarius's abbacy; its continuations are fragmentary. It is certainly conceivable that more leasing for lump sums and more gifts made San Vincenzo rich enough for the last builder-abbots, John V, Gerard, Benedict and Amicus (1053-1139) to be able twice to rebuild and decorate in the way so enthusiastically described in our surviving narrative fragments (*CV* i: 37; iii: 89-90, 106-7, 169-70). Three late texts, two gifts and a lease, for 1064-70 (*CV* 180, 193, 1), would fit into such a hypothesis. But I doubt it, all the same. While the counts of Chieti were being generous on the coast, less pious Lombard nobles were beginning to occupy the monastic *terra* itself, and in the 1040s and 1050s took almost half of it; the Normans after the 1060s took much of the rest (Wickham 1985a: 34-5, 42). The *terra* was, by now, the core of San Vincenzo's prosperity; if it lost that, estates on the Adriatic would not help it much, even supposing it could keep control of them as the Normans moved steadily up from Apulia (Gatto 1974). It is thus far from clear how the rich rebuildings of the late eleventh and early twelfth centuries could have been financed from the revenues from monastic lands.

The twelfth century, the age in which the *Chronicon Vulturnense* was actually written, is by far the obscurest period for San Vincenzo since its foundation. Its monastic building was evidently impressive; it had relations with popes and with the Norman princes of Capua; and it still had the self-confidence to commission a chronicle, which, however defensive and inadequate, was clearly in the tradition of the great monastic histories by Gregorio di Catino for Farfa and Leo Marsicanus for Monte Cassino, and expensively illustrated as well (cf. Loud 1985: 233-5 and *passim*). On the other hand, its lands were no longer extensive. Exactly how substantial they were we have, it must be admitted, no clear idea. The *Catalogus Baronum* of 1150 (Jamison 1972) does not mention San Vincenzo, which indicates that it was exempt from military service to King Roger II (cf. Wickham 1982: 35, 44). We can hardly rely on absences in a text like the *Catalogus*, which in no sense has the comprehensiveness of a Domesday Book, but it is none the less worth noting that absences from the military fiefs of 1150 also include Luogosano, Apinianici and Trita; these may have remained monastic properties in some sense at least. On the other hand, over two-thirds of the *terra* was now out of monastic control; San Vincenzo's land was restricted here to the four or five villages closest to the abbey. As late as the fourteenth century it was still the second richest monastery in the former principality of Capua (Loud 1985: 235), but its wealth was by now barely fifteen per cent of that of Monte Cassino; San Vincenzo would never again be anything more than an ordinary provincial house.

In this context, it is worth stressing that from the 1070s onwards many of the abbots of San Vincenzo, starting with the builders Gerard and Amicus, came from Monte Cassino (*CC* iv. 42, 55). If San Vincenzo was becoming in the late eleventh century more and more provincial, its old sister monastery was, as I have said, reaching its height. It may well have been with Cassinese money, in effect already as a Cassinese daughter house, that the monastery on the Volturno was rebuilt for the last time. There is nothing of this in John the monk, but that may not be surprising; though a protégé of Amicus and heavily influenced by Leo Marsicanus (Hoffmann 1966), John at least was not Cassinese, and, whether or not he became Abbot John VI in 1139 (as Federici thought (1941: 84-6); but cf. Hoffmann (1966: 183-4)), he may well have been part of that wing of the monastery that had certainly come to be hostile to Monte Cassino's claims by 1137 (*CC* iv. 118). The last patron of San Vincenzo was probably, then, its own sister monastery, which indeed wholly took over after John VI's death in *c.* 1150 (Federici 1941: 74 ff.). The

lavish building of the years around 1100 was, perhaps, not so much the curiously late flowering of a declining independent house, as the first (and only) reward of a patronage relationship that was to continue to the present day.

* * *

I have focused this account on monastic resources: a plain enough subject, but vital as a background to our understanding of the shape and pace of monastic building and rebuilding across the centuries. It must be recognized, however, that the history of San Vincenzo's lands is in no way unusual. I have emphasized at all points the peculiarly close parallels between the Volturno house and its neighbour overlooking Cassino; until the early eleventh century their histories were nearly identical. Moreover, both reflect more or less precisely the cycles of ecclesiastical property-owning everywhere in Italy, and, with greater variability, elsewhere in western Europe too (Herlihy 1961; Wickham 1988). For every church or monastery, the very early ninth century (or, alternatively, the late eighth) was a high point in the accumulation of land; for every one the early tenth century was similarly a low. It was not necessary to be sacked by the Arabs to find oneself losing one's lands; such losses were the product of more general social developments, in which local military families struggled to find or expropriate the land that would establish themselves as personally noble, in a world where the public structures of power and hierarchy were breaking up (Tabacco 1979: 189-206, for example). It is not surprising that this land usually came to them at the expense of the church, less a part of the military hierarchy that produced aristocratic status and less able to defend its own (by now extensive) land. Similarly in most of Italy the destinies of churches and monasteries could change substantially after 1000; the new aristocratic stratum was still taking land from the church, but, once families established themselves, they also handed it back, often generously, to their own chosen foundations. It was at this point that San Vincenzo struck unlucky, with its second cycle of land accumulation cut short or rendered useless by external forces invading its own heartland; the Cassinese experience was not only more fortunate (indeed, fortunate on an international level), but in this respect actually more typical. The changing patterns of San Vincenzo's resources, if carefully studied, thus contribute not just to an understanding of its buildings, but also to a model for social developments on a wide scale, far beyond the history of a poor mountain valley in the most unconsidered region of Italy.

Chapter Twelve

SAN VINCENZO AL VOLTURNO AND THE PLAN OF ST GALL

by Richard Hodges

The discovery of the ruins of San Vincenzo al Volturno was quite unexpected. The immense body of data associated with these remains, much of it described in this report, brings a new dimension to the archaeology of the early Middle Ages (cf. Plate 12:1). In some ways it is as though a new chronicle had been discovered – not in a well-known archive or familiar place, but in a territory which until that point had figured modestly in the history of the first millennium AD. The original intention of the project, to indicate the size and extent of the monastery and at the same time to examine the archaeology of its villages, has proved difficult to achieve simply because of the magnitude of the archaeological remains. Nevertheless, in this closing chapter it is appropriate to recall the aims of the project and to consider what light these discoveries shed on the Plan of St Gall and the concept of a Carolingian monastic design. This question is bound up inherently with the other principal aim of the project: the determination of the extent to which San Vincenzo depended upon its territory in its rise to become one of the great places of Charlemagne's Europe. First, however, it is necessary to examine the chronology of the medieval settlement. The phasing of the sequence of monasteries at San Vincenzo al Volturno constitutes one of the most important discoveries made during the project.

THE PHASING

The essence of modern archaeology is not what has been termed the 'Pompeii premise' – the prospect of finding a place fossilized from one moment in time (cf. Binford 1981) – but the reverse, the opportunity to record how a place has evolved through time. Time-depth, in the form of a stratigraphic sequence spanning a millennium, can be traced on one spot. The archaeological sequence at San Vincenzo embodies not only the form of the settlement, but also information about production, distribution and consumption, and about the ideological attitudes of the people who lived there. Together, this information, normally so elusive for this period, permits some scale to be placed upon the many levels of history embodied in the monastery. At one level it enables us to assess the details of the *Chronicon Vulturnense*, a source compiled long after the principal events described in its pages. At another

level the excavated data allow us to evaluate the impact of European influences belonging to mainstream political, economic and cultural history. The phasing, of course, throws light on all aspects of the place: its artistic history, its architectural history, its religious history, its technological history and so on.

Yet we should be clear about the nature of the phasing. None of the medieval phases discussed in Volumes 1 and 2 were dated by coins or radiocarbon dating; medieval coins were intriguingly absent, while funds were insufficient to consider radiocarbon dates. Instead, a relative sequence has been devised, framed largely by the chronology of San Vincenzo as described in the *Chronicon Vulturnense*, and dated more closely by the material culture. The paintings in the Crypt Church, for instance, were considered to be a fixed dating point when the project began, and have remained a benchmark when assessing the chronology of the stratigraphy in the Crypt Church and 'South Church' areas. Many of the excavated remains, as it happens, belong to the age of these paintings. Indeed, one is tempted to think of San Vincenzo as a Pompeii of the Carolingian Renaissance – a place trapped, archaeologically-speaking, in a moment in time. It is an illusion, of course, because the ninth-century monastery was formed over several generations, during stratigraphic phases 4 and 5. (Given the ambitiousness of the phase 4 building project, it is prudent to recall that some buildings probably took the entire span of a phase to construct. Churches like Cologne, Reims and Saint Denis, for example, were the work of several generations of masons (cf. Riché 1978: 157-8).) Then, no sooner was the building programme finished, there is evidence that the place was beginning to fall into decline, even before it was sacked by the Arabs in October 881. Nevertheless, this cataclysmic end, marked by a spread of burning across the site, within which tell-tale Saracenic arrowheads occurred, is reminiscent of the infamous volcanic eruption that overwhelmed Pompeii.

The sequence of settlement areas seems to be as follows (Figs 12:1 and 12:2).

Phase 3a

The first monks arrived at San Vincenzo to discover the dilapidated, but far from completely ruined,

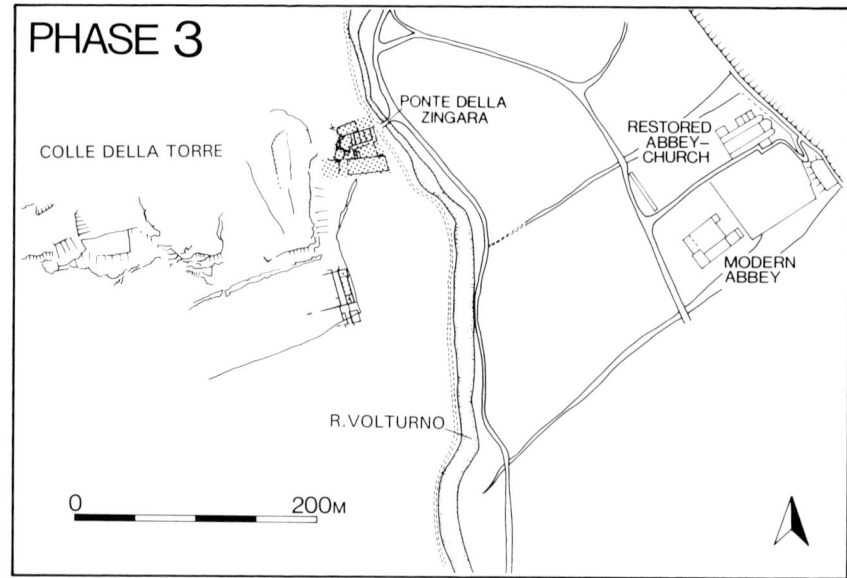

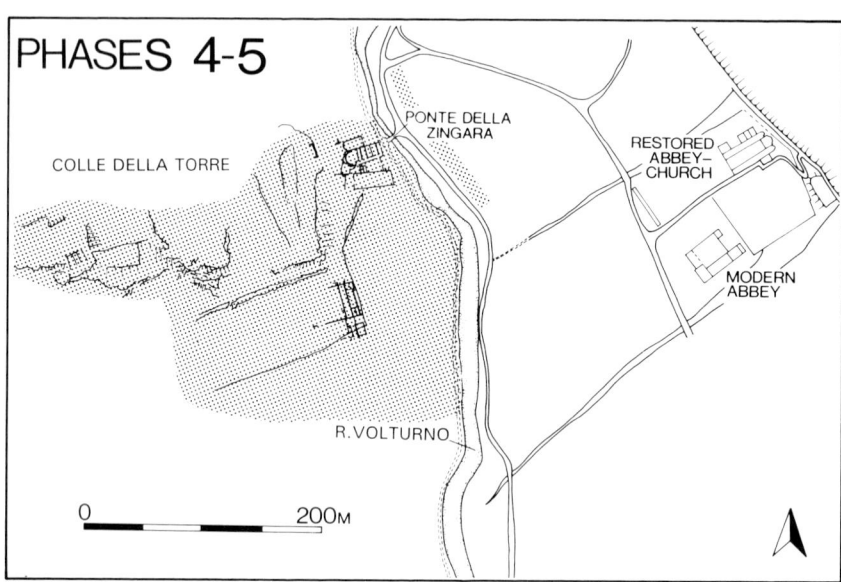

Fig. 12:1 Settlement plans for phases 3 to 5 at San Vincenzo *(KF)*

buildings of the late Roman settlement. This settlement covered an area of about half a hectare, and in all likelihood the fifth-century residential Tower (on Terrace 2) made it a prominent landmark at the north end of the Rocchetta plain. Like the better-known tower at Torba, Castelseprio, it was a conspicuous place in which to found a monastic community (cf. Mazza 1978-79; Bertelli 1988a; 1988b). The archaeology of phase 3 at San Vincenzo is difficult to interpret. The late Roman funerary church was rebuilt and appears to have been transformed into the first abbey-church, while the adjacent Crypt Church, to the north, was either used briefly or not at all. The *Chronicon Vulturnense* leads its readers to assume that the abbey-church founded by Paldo, Tato and Taso was situated in the same place as the large church built by Abbot Joshua in AD 808, called San Vincenzo Maggiore by the chronicler. In practice, the excavations have

indicated the likelihood that San Vincenzo Maggiore occupied a new site (see below). Hence, we have termed the first abbey-church as San Vincenzo Minore, to distinguish it from the later, ninth-century building. San Vincenzo Minore made use of the pre-existing funerary church. The residential Tower on the terrace above almost certainly became the focus of the monastic cemetery, while it must be assumed (at the moment) that late Roman buildings to the south of the 'South Church' provided the community with accommodation.

Little else found in the excavations can be assigned to this phase. The material culture of the monastery in the early eighth century was almost certainly impoverished.

Phase 3b

The first major change to the form of the settlement

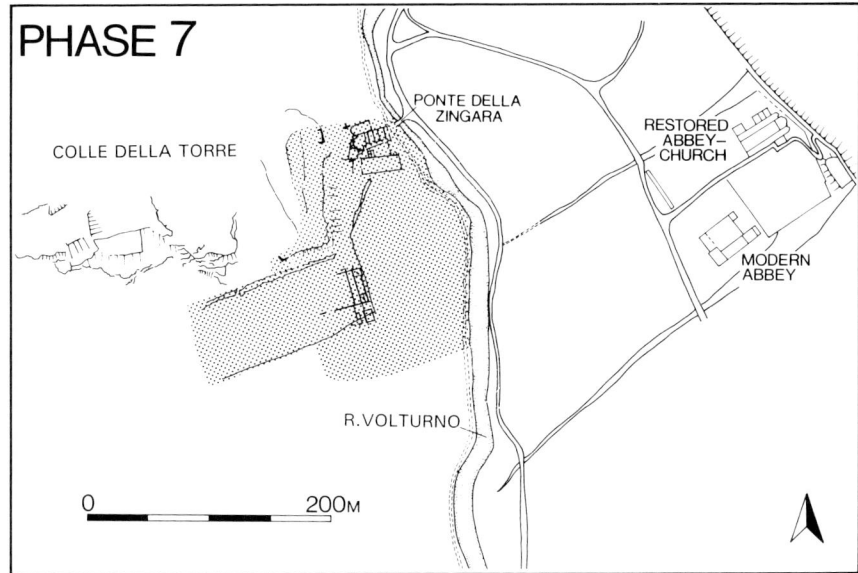

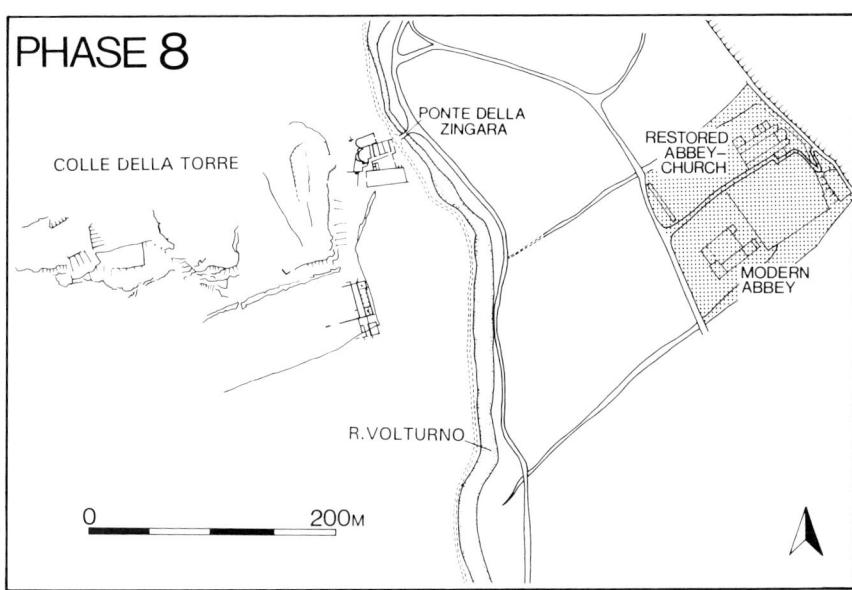

Fig. 12:2 Settlement plans for phases 7 and 8 at San Vincenzo *(KF)*

was the demolition of most of the late Roman Crypt Church, and the construction of the new Crypt Church. This latter building had a short, poorly built nave, which was bonded onto the late Roman apse. The nave was built upon the remains of an earlier Republican structure, and had a façade embellished by the reuse of cornices to support its corners (reminiscent of the use of *spolia* in the façade of the more or less contemporary Spoletan funerary chapel, known as the Tempietto di Clitunno (Benazzi 1985)).

The idea of a small chapel flanking the mother church on a parallel axis was not uncommon in this period. Such a feature has been noted at Saint Martin, Angers from the early eighth century and at Saint John at Müstair and at Farfa from the later eighth century (McClendon 1987: 56). A second change of some significance was the creation of a

primitive ambulatory for San Vincenzo Minore by constructing a rudimentary wall to close off the south end of the passage which existed between the apse of this church and the rock-face beyond. The effect resembles the primitive later eighth-century church of Santa Maria Annunziata at Prata di Principato Ultra, near Avellino, where an ambulatory lay between the painted apse and the natural rock-face (Belting 1968; Pavan 1990: 291-5). In the case of San Vincenzo Minore, the construction of this short stretch of wall, comprising rubble and a clayey mortar, resembled the poorly made remains of the nave wall of the Crypt Church. However, this addition cannot be more precisely dated. There had been an ambulatory of sorts between the late Roman 'South Church' and the rock-face below Terrace 2 during the fifth century. The presence of the ambulatory perhaps reflects the assimilation of a late Antique scheme by the monks. The ultimate model may have been the ring-crypt built into the apse of Old Saint Peter's in the time of Pope Gregory the Great (590-604), which became the model for many similar crypts, not only in ninth-century Rome, but also in the Frankish kingdoms from the later eighth century onwards (Krautheimer 1980: 86; cf. McClendon 1987: 58). However, the primitive nature of their achievement must be emphasized; no architect as such designed this new structure.

Phase 3c

The first elements of a monastic plan can be attributed to this phase. As Figure 12:3 shows, it comprised San Vincenzo Minore (the 'South Church'), with a church (the Crypt Church) on its north side, a possible passage (the south corridor of the 'South Church', leading from the Ponte della Zingara along the north side of the Garden Court to the ambulatory of San Vincenzo Minore, and a comparable north-south passage leading from the

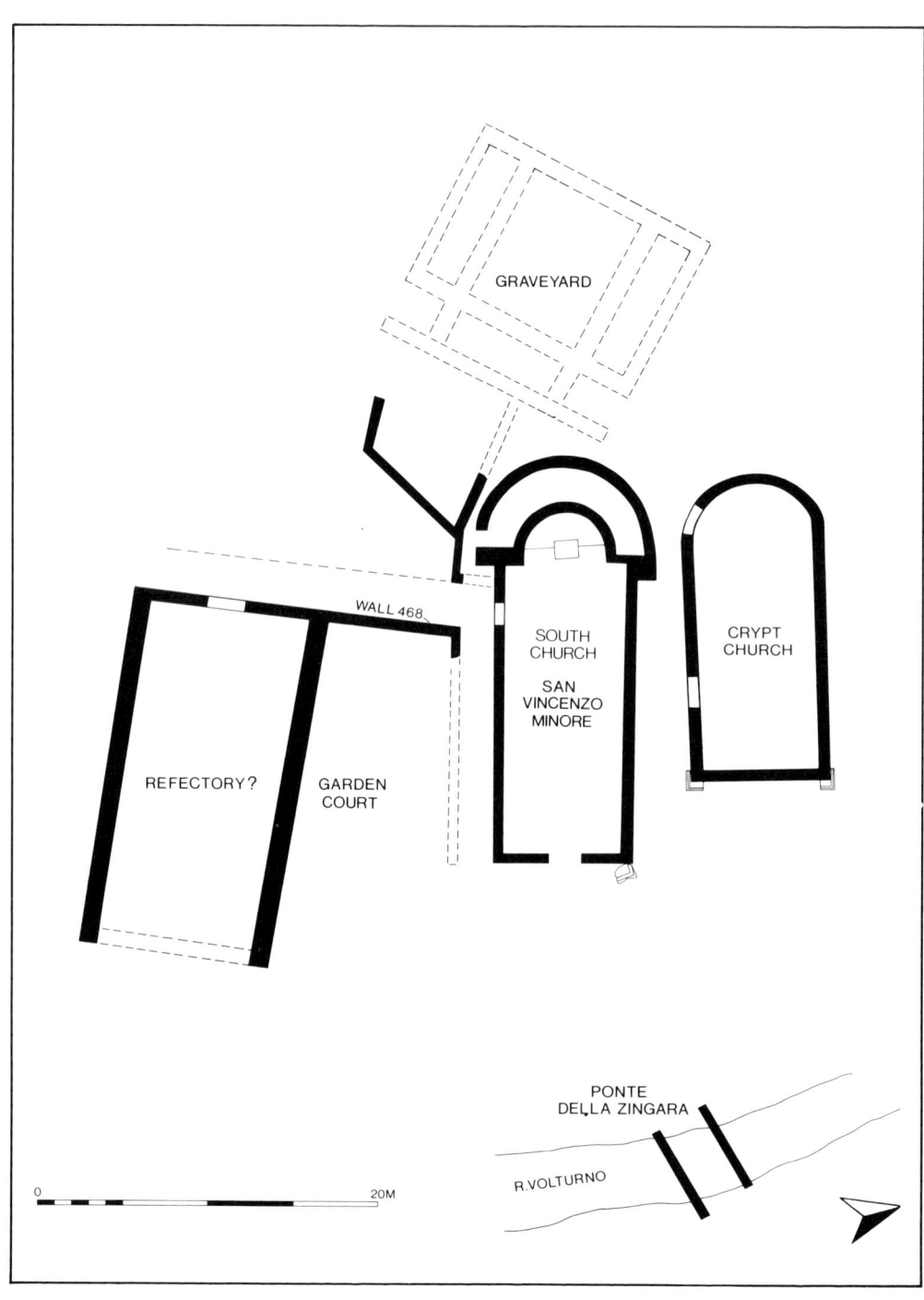

Fig.12:3 Schematic plan of San Vincenzo in phase 3c *(SC)*

south doorway of San Vincenzo Minore along the west side of the Garden Court to a large rectangular building tentatively identified as a refectory.

San Vincenzo Minore was significantly altered. A finely built new ambulatory replaced the simple affair constructed in phase 3b. The near-perfect symmetry of the new addition to the church, its level coursing and hard lime mortar rendering, distinguished this from the earlier buildings in the monastery. The painted altar found in the apse of this church also probably belonged to this phase.

North of the 'South Church', the (late Roman) apsidal end of the Crypt Church was rebuilt at this time. Its scheme of decoration may date from this period; it was more or less contemporary with the painted apse of the phase 3 'South Church', incorporating bands of blue-grey, dull red, pale orange-red, cream and yellow, with thin white lines along the divides. Traces of figurative painting were also found.

An arrangement of corridors around the pre-existing Garden Court appears to date from this phase. The south corridor beside the 'South Church', defined on its south side in phase 4 by wall 506, probably followed the line of a late Roman enclosure wall which had bounded the south side of a cemetery at that time (see Volume 1: 172). This corridor provided a means of access from the Ponte della Zingara to the new ambulatory. The corridor turned south at the western end of the Garden Court. Here, exiting through the south doorway of San Vincenzo Minore, the passage, defined on the east (Garden Court) side by wall 468, led to a building sealed beneath the later Refectory. The outline of the earlier building, possibly an earlier refectory, could be made out from the undulations in the tiled floor of the phase 4 Refectory and was confirmed in the re-excavation of the modern pipe-trench that bisected this building. This building was approximately 11.6 m wide by 21 m long, sufficiently spacious to accommodate about a hundred monks dining at tables.

Several points can be made about these alterations. Firstly, a new plan was being grafted onto the existing one. Secondly, this plan embodied rather more clearly, and much more competently, the features introduced to San Vincenzo in phase 3b. Thirdly, the new ambulatory was possibly the most proficient construction discovered in the excavations from any phase. The exactitude of the symmetry (despite the fact that the ambulatory was constructed against the rock-face), the level coursing, and above all the distinctive hard mortar rendering stand out in contrast to the rustic efforts of phase 3b. San Vincenzo's masons could not have changed so suddenly; the services of a *sapiens architectus* – an architect-builder – must have been responsible for these works (cf. Hodges, Gibson and Hanasz 1990). Lastly, the context for this redevelopment, if the building beneath the phase 4 Refectory was a phase

3c refectory, must have been the rapidly increasing size of the monastery's community. It is tempting to identify this remodelling as a response to the changing needs of the great community at San Vincenzo which Pope Hadrian I and Paul the Deacon described in the late eighth century (*Codex Carolinus: MGH, Epistolae Merowingici et Karolini aevi I (= MGH Epp. III.* 66, 594); *HL:* 283).

Phase 4a

Great changes, far exceeding those envisaged in phase 3c, were made in this period. Unlike the phase 3c programme, when new parts were grafted onto old ones, most of the phase 4 building programme was conceived as a new venture in which the pre-existing structures were modestly accommodated.

The major change was to shift the ritual axis of the monastery from its position beside the Ponte della Zingara (that is within the late Roman settlement) to a new site on the southern edge of the old remains, overlooking the Rocchetta plain (Fig. 12:4). It is proposed that San Vincenzo Maggiore was constructed upon a high terrace at the base of Colle della Torre, dominating the plain, and visible from the mountain road from Isernia to Sulmona, above and to the northeast of Cerro al Volturno. As a result, the 'South Church' no longer served as the principal church of the monastery; instead, it is proposed, it was radically transformed into a grand guest-hall.

The exact plan of the monastery at this date is very far from known, but its bare outlines can be tentatively pieced together. The new abbey-church (see Volume 1: 19-20; and Volume 5) was almost certainly the pivot around which the monastery was spread out. Immediately to its southeast lay collective workshops, where glass and fine metalwork for liturgical and secular use were made (see Volume 5). In this same area, on the edge of the Rocchetta plain, were possibly situated the farms and industries needed to support this large settlement. Judging from the plough-scatter debris, the settlement spread 75-100 m south of San Vincenzo Maggiore.

On the north side of the abbey, beside the river, lay the claustrum. The architect was expedient in devising this complex. The phase 3c(?) refectory/range (described in Chapter 4) was enlarged into a great thatched barn of a refectory in phase 4. The kitchen and stores must have been situated close by, and it is probable that together they formed an east wing, with convenient access to the river. In this general area, too, it is likely that there was a dormitory for the monks. This might have formed a south wing of a cloister, if the complex took a standard medieval form. While the exact layout of the claustrum remains a matter of speculation, it is clear that unlike the Plan of St Gall (see Fig. 12:5), as well as many later Romanesque monasteries, the claustrum was not situated immediately alongside

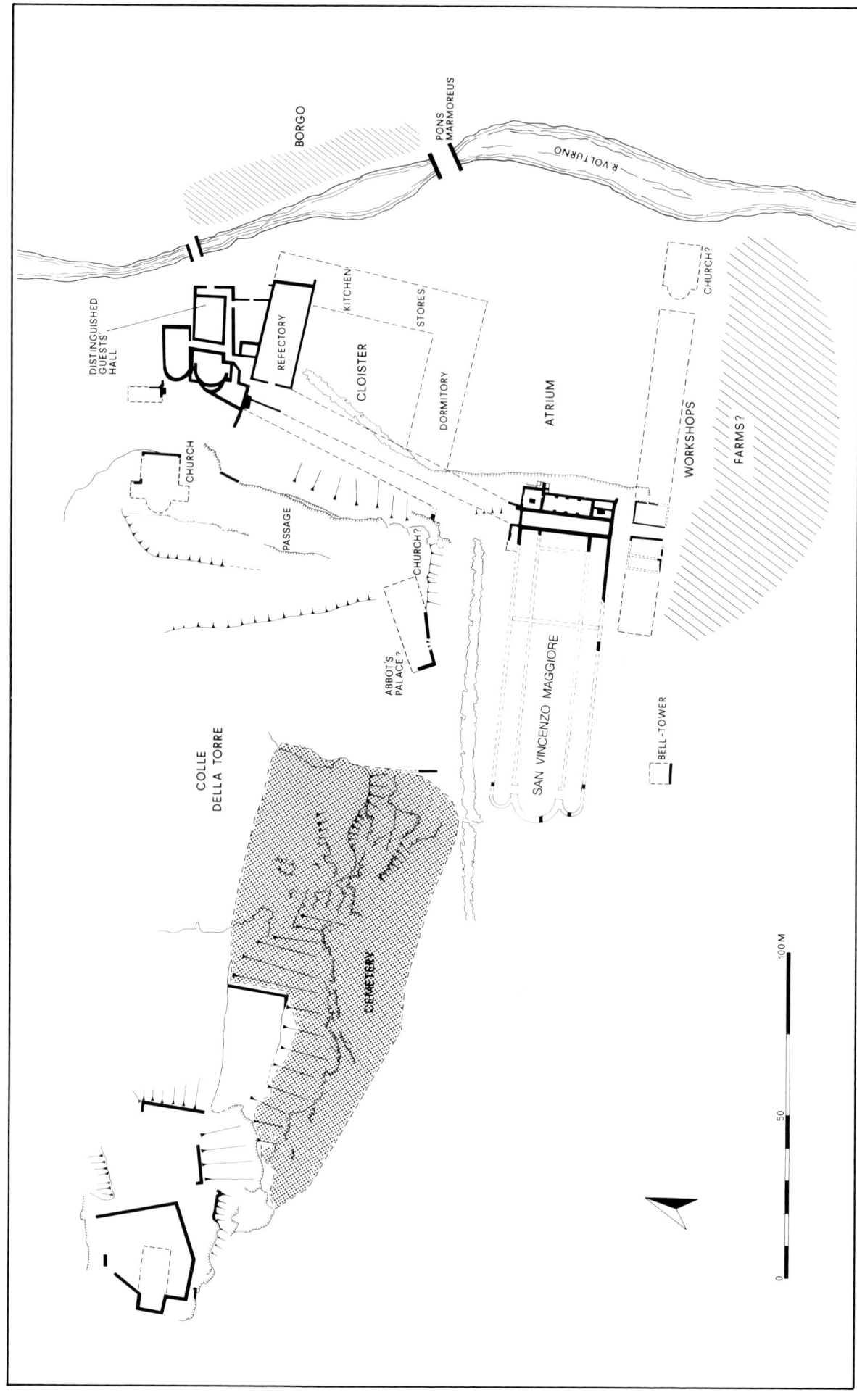

Fig. 12:4 Schematic reconstruction plan of San Vincenzo in the ninth century (SC)

the new church. Instead, it seems to have been placed at a little distance, much as seems to have been the case, for example, at Saint John, Müstair (Switzerland) (Davis-Weyer 1987). The size of the Refectory may offer a clue on this score. Several hundred monks needed to be accommodated in this complex. Evidently the architect, while calculating the space necessary for such large buildings, decided to retain a significant part of the old (phase 3) nucleus. Otherwise, it might be deduced, he would have constructed the claustrum in the fields due south of the new abbey-church (where the collective workshops were in fact built). The integration of the new complex with the original monastery is a feature of the phase 4 plan. Two long passages linked the new abbey to the old northern sector. The Lower Thoroughfare, which included the Assembly Room, connected the monks' quarters to the abbey-church. This passage, furthermore, continued through a small covered courtyard (the Vestibule) to the distinguished guests' quarters situated in the old phase 3 nucleus. The Upper Thoroughfare followed virtually the same route, but outside the claustrum and at a higher level (on Terrace 1). This passage almost certainly provided access to buildings on the terraces above, as well as linking the abbey-church (San Vincenzo Maggiore) to the distinguished guests' quarters. A wall at the back of Terrace 2, on which remains of painted decoration were found, follows the same line as these two passages, emphasizing the existence of a coherent plan in the arrangement of the new monastery (Volume 1: 21, figs 3:10 and 3:11).

The Assembly Room, at the north end of the Lower Thoroughfare, immediately outside the monks' Refectory, may conceivably have served as a place for meetings. Its principle purpose, however, was as a space where the monks might gather before proceeding to the Refectory. The paintings in this room were certainly outstanding. The line of prophets along the west wall was by artists working in a fashionable Lombard idiom, while the scheme of (painted) marbled panelling around the room, as in other rooms, reveals the aspiration to recreate the elegant grandeur of the Roman past.

The old 'South Church' (San Vincenzo Minore) was entirely rebuilt. It incorporated a chapel at its west end (half the phase 3c church, including the altar). This was separated by a cross-passage(s) from a two-storey hall: on the ground floor there were three rooms whilst on the first floor there were apartments. The quality of the paintings, as well as the marble *opus sectile* floors associated with these first-floor rooms, indicates that this was a grand building. Like the Assembly Room, the first-floor hall of this building had a scheme of overlapping particoloured scales reminiscent of late Antique practice, perhaps decorating wall-benches, as well as dados painted in imitation of painted marble panels. There were also traces of fine figurative decoration

similar in style to the Prophets in the Assembly Room. One section of the room, however, contained a painted dado in red porphyry and red speckled grey granite, arranged in such a way as to suggest cut marbled panels. This was a decorative scheme of the highest quality. Below the hall, the ground-floor rooms included stabling for horses and simple accommodation. A south corridor, painted with a dado in imitation of panelled *opus sectile* revetment, led visitors from a narthex in front of the Ponte della Zingara to a grand marble staircase (in the Entrance Hall), situated on the south side of the hall. In its new function, therefore, the 'South Church' incorporated grand apartments in its upper storey, a chapel, a small stable and possibly primitive ground-floor accommodation. This range of features points to the building being the Hall for Distinguished Guests. Its model was perhaps the duke's palatial complex at Salerno (Peduto 1990: 320-6), or the much-admired palatial complex at Benevento, in the vicinity of Santa Sofia (Peduto 1990: 319). Such building complexes are well-known from Carolingian Europe (see Volume 1: 188-9). For example, the ninth-century reformer, Abbot Haito of Reichenau, informs us that '(the) auditorium of the abbot lies between the claustrum and the gate ..., so that he can receive in conference the brethren without inconvenience to the guests, and the guests without inconvenience to the brethren' (*SM*, chapter 4).

Next to the Entrance Hall lay a small porticoed Garden Court. The east portico was particularly fine. Here, reused fluted columns supported the roof, while, in classical Campanian fashion, the arrangement was skilfully evoked in the paintings on the back wall of the portico. Following Roman fashion still further, it is likely that a large late second-century marble vase stood either in the centre of the Garden Court, or between two of the columns around it. To the immediate east of the Garden Court, and entered from the colonnaded east portico, was a long narrow 'building' which contained fine paintings. The scheme of decoration was badly burnt in 881, but traces of Egyptian blue were found, suggesting that this was no ordinary room. The presence of smashed vessel-glass of fine quality in this room, destroyed in 881, lends weight to the hypothesis that this was the refectory for the distinguished guests, which was entered from the Garden Court.

The Crypt Church was probably not altered at this time. It could only be entered from the south, by a cross-passage, at ground-floor level leading from the Lower Thoroughfare through the 'South Church' complex. Whether the late Roman residential Tower remained in use in this phase is not known, but on Terrace 3 above it is likely that another church stood at the north end of the terrace. The remains of an eleventh-century church identified in Trench R almost certainly were associated with an earlier, eighth- or ninth-century church founded on this prominent point on Colle della Torre. Remains of another large building directly overlooked the new abbey-church on the south-facing slope of Colle della Torre. This building seems a likely candidate for the abbot's palace. Further up the hill was situated a large cemetery. Only a small sample of the cemetery was investigated. Nevertheless, it seems probable that at least several hundred people were buried here over a comparatively short period of time. A few were buried in fine tombs, including two rock-cut arcosolia, while others were placed in simpler rock-cut tombs (see Chapter 7). Further up the hill, occupying the summit of Colle della Torre, was yet another complex of buildings (see Chapter 8).

It appears that the phase 4 monastery spread well beyond Colle della Torre. During the ploughing of the fields on the east bank of the river Volturno, traces of a further stretch of buildings came to light. The spread of debris here covers almost a hectare. It suggests that there was some kind of 'extra-mural' *borgo*, possibly containing the dwellings of craftsmen, traders and lay dependents, as at *Eulogimenopolis*, the *borgo* later known as San Germano on the Via Casilina below Monte Cassino (see below, Fig. 12:6) (Leccisotti 1987: 38; cf. Delogu 1992: 307).

During phase 4, San Vincenzo became one of the largest monasteries in Europe. With an estimated population of at least 300 monks in the early to mid ninth century, judging from the dining space in the Refectory, and, as was normal (Horn and Born 1979: vol. 1, 268), possibly as many lay dependents, San Vincenzo would have ranked amongst the largest monasteries in Latin Christendom. Contemporary texts offer population numbers of monastic communities of comparable size. Centula boasted 400 monks under Abbot Angilbert, Fontanella (Saint Wandrille) may have briefly had as many as 300 monks, whilst Fulda, with an estimated 270, and St Gall, with about 120, were smaller than San Vincenzo (Horn and Born 1979: vol. 1, 343). In terms of settlement area, the ninth-century monastery at San Vincenzo far exceeded the better-known ones at Farfa (McClendon 1987), Monte Cassino (Pantoni 1973), Müstair (Davis-Weyer 1987: Müstair, it should be noted, had consistently less than 50 monks at its zenith during the ninth century), and Novalesa (Cantino Wataghin 1985; Wataghin 1989).

Three features of the phase 4 monastery stand out. Firstly, there is its sprawling size; secondly, the fact that virtually every room and passage was painted; and thirdly, the conscious use of classical *spolia* and classical ideas in every part of the complex. The paintings associated with this phase suggest that it dates to either the last years of the eighth or the first years of the ninth century. The *Chronicon* offers a clear context for this colossal enterprise when it describes how Abbot Joshua (792-817) rebuilt the abbey-church in 808 with the assistance of Louis the Pious. As Wickham shows in Chapter 11, Louis the Pious's contribution may be a legend of little substance. None the less, if Joshua extended his building works to include not just the abbey, but the entire monastic plan, there is little doubt that his later reputation as an abbot with royal connections was in certain respects justified. The distinctive, if expedient, construction technique common to all these buildings suggests the work was executed rapidly over a short period. In many cases it became necessary to repair the buildings at a later date. The two thoroughfares and the back wall of Terrace 2 are the best index of the common purpose behind this project. These formed the spine of the new monastery, connecting the new abbey-church to the distinguished guests' sector. Around this spine, we may suspect, the other buildings were constructed. There can be little doubt that a plan of sorts was put into effect, executed under the direction of a *sapiens architectus*, involving the creation of an enormous monastic city similar in concept to the new Italian towns of the age (Marazzi 1994). Much of this work was probably undertaken by the monks and lay people using locally available materials. A good deal of the stone, for example, was probably found on Colle della Torre. But at the same time the scale of the enterprise, the inclusion of distinctive architectural concepts then in fashion, such as the hall for distinguished guests, the extensive use of glass windows, tiled pavements and classical *spolia*, as well as the presence of a northern Lombardic idiom in much of the decoration, all indicate that this settlement was the product of many connections and influences, masterminded by an abbot as ambitious as any in Europe in this period of intense ecclesiastical development (contra Devroey 1993: 239).

Phase 4b

Minor alterations were made to the rooms on the ground floor of the 'South Church'.

Phase 5a

It is our contention that the alterations to the Crypt Church occurred as another phase of major works was undertaken throughout the monastery. The portrait of Abbot Epyphanius in the crypt of the Crypt Church dates the paintings here to his period in office (824-42). The crypt itself, it now seems clear, was made in this period; a good case has been put forward for it being designed as an elaborate funerary chapel of a kind that was in fashion in the Carolingian age. Above it, the sanctuary of the Crypt Church was remodelled as well. In addition, an atrium was now created at its east end and the building might be entered directly from the Ponte della Zingara. A number of fine tombs were inserted into the atrium. These changes, as those in earlier stages of the monastery's history, accompanied a programme of rebuilding of the 'South Church' guest hall. The alterations necessitated the closure of the north-facing doorways of the 'South Church' undercrofts. These could no longer be used as stables; instead, the building(s) north of the Crypt Church (found in Trench EE) might have provided these facilities. In the west end of the 'South Church', the chapel was filled in, and a high third apse was constructed. The high third apse of the 'South Church' would have necessitated the demolition of part of the late Roman residential Tower on Terrace 2 (although it should be noted that the Tower may have been demolished before this). The aggrandizement of this building was probably accompanied by the addition of a monumental loggia-like extension to the Entrance Hall (with its arcading reminiscent of the façade of the church of Santa Maria delle Cinque Torri at Monte Cassino (Scaccia Scarafoni 1946)), on the south side of the building, and by the addition of a finely painted bench in the east portico of the Garden Court. In sum, the entire complex appears to have been refurbished, with, in functional terms, the old chapel within the 'South Church' being replaced by the Crypt Church. The alterations to the Entrance Hall may have been the occasion for the construction of a bridging passage, westward from the first floor of this building, over the hitherto open yard in the Vestibule to Terrace 1. This caused the Vestibule below to be covered, at which stage its walls were decorated and a tiled pavement was laid. Here, within a generation or so, a fine tomb was inserted. In time, it may be surmised, the conspicuous break between the monks' quarters and the distinguished guests' sector was made increasingly less apparent. Above the ubiquitous marbled dado in this room were several images of young, gaily painted saints. The artist responsible for these figures was working in the tradition of those who in phase 4 had painted the Prophets in the adjacent Assembly Room, but a generation later. At about the same time, the Refectory was extended eastward with the addition of an annexe.

The monastic community had reached its zenith.

Phase 5b

The patched cracks in the lower walls of the 'South Church', as well as the bowed form of its south wall, could relate to the earthquake of 848 (Guidoboni 1989: 614-15). Generally, however, few other building works and virtually no decoration could be attributed to the central and later decades of the ninth century. The monastery's heyday was plainly over.

Phase 5c

The widespread burning throughout the monastery, in some cases associated with heavy arrowheads, as fired from a composite bow, must have been the result of the Arab sack in October 881. The most dramatic evidence came from the workshops on the edge of the Rocchetta plain (see Volume 5). Here the door had been burnt down, probably by fire-arrows, and had crashed inwards onto shelves or cupboards inside the east room (cf. Moreland 1985). The entire building then ignited. Scrap bronze, similar to that excavated in this building, was found in a pit (D 320) in the Upper Thoroughfare, perhaps hastily concealed, or abandoned, during the attack. Arrowheads were also found in the distinguished guests' Garden Court. These were probably shot from the Ponte della Zingara, and may have been intended to fire the thatched Refectory. Both refectories burnt to the ground, leaving little but ash. A timber beam, however, crashed into the east portico beside the Garden Court, and remained where it fell for over a hundred years. The fire swept along the south ground-floor corridor of the 'South Church' (the distinguished guests' quarters), and through it, to the edge of the Crypt Church. Parts of the Entrance Hall were badly burnt, while the tiled roof of the Vestibule collapsed. The roof at the north end of the Assembly Room also collapsed, blocking the doorway leading to the Vestibule. Traces of the fire were also found in the building(s) behind the Crypt Church. Without any doubt the sack was devastating.

Phase 6a

The vestiges of the monastery occupied in the tenth and early eleventh centuries tell a sorry tale. The Crypt Church possibly fared the best; only its atrium fell into dilapidation. The 'South Church' ground-floor rooms may have been used intermittently, but the state of the apartments above is not known. Tombs, however, were cut into the apsidal end. These were probably part of the cemetery focused upon the Entrance Hall. In the Entrance Hall itself tombs were inserted into many of its rooms, and there is a strong impression that it had become a matryrium housing, initially, those who perished in 881. In the 'South Church' corridor, alongside, as well as beside the Upper Thoroughfare and on Terrace 2, there were still more tombs. In addition, a tomb was cut into the north bench of the Refectory immediately beside the Entrance Hall.

The Refectory itself was devastated, but a small room of some makeshift kind was made within the northwest corner of the old building. A rough doorway was chopped through the Refectory wall here, providing access to the Entrance Hall and to the 'South Church'. Further south, we must presume the abbey-church stood in ruins, while the workshops were burnt out. It is tempting to interpret the ruins as an index of San Vincenzo's dismal fate in the tenth century. The community, according to the chronicler, had shrunk to a handful of monks who used some buildings and were unable to repair others. The integrated plan no longer functioned, but the Entrance Hall cemetery may have been intended to inform visitors of the dreadful calamity suffered by the community. Was the Crypt Church the Santa Maria beside the gate (re)built, as related by the twelfth-century chronicler, by Abbot Rambald soon after the monks returned from exile? Is San Salvatore, the church which was, the chronicler informs us, used while the abbey stood in ruins, to be identified with the building situated on the summit of Colle della Torre or was it a shrine at the entrance to the abbey-church? Between these surviving buildings – islands in a sea of ruins – there were doubtless thickets of brambles concealing the devastation of October 881.

Phase 6b

The demolition of the monastery was a systematic affair. All but the apse of the 'South Church' was levelled to below first-floor height. This level then became the height of the demolished Entrance Hall, and the filling-in level of the Vestibule, the Assembly Room, the peristyle Garden Court as well as the refectories. The buildings behind the Crypt Church were also pulled down at this time. The tips in some cases were nearly 2.0 m deep and contained a great deal of ninth-century material which presumably had been lying about for 150 years. The Crypt Church, however, survived. New building works were also underway as the demolition progressed. A large mortar-mixer bedded on the initial tips overlying the east portico of the distinguished guests' Garden Court is some indication of this. Elsewhere we have associated this mortar-mixer with Abbot John V's major redevelopment of the monastery in about 1055 (Volume 1: 206-8; Table 0:1). It should be noted, though, that the scale of the demolition and the ruthless disposal of ecclesiastical objects provides a modest glimpse of the new energy behind San Vincenzo's eleventh-century revival as a community.

Phase 7

The abbey-church (San Vincenzo Maggiore) was almost certainly rebuilt in the late tenth century by Abbot John IV, but no evidence of this phase was discovered during the 1980-86 excavations. Later, under Abbot John V, a new claustrum was constructed on its south side. Traces of the claustrum were found overlying the workshops in Trench FF, as well as in Trench GG and Trench PP nearby (Hodges 1985; Volume 5). The dimensions can be estimated as 52 m east-west by 45 m north-south. An enclosure wall probably belonging to this period, still surviving to a height of almost 1.0 m, appeared to define the new south side of the Romanesque complex (Volume 1: 21). To the north, however, little of the original ensemble of buildings survived. With the exception of the Crypt Church, which appears to have remained in use throughout the eleventh century, the other ninth-century buildings in front of the Ponte della Zingara were levelled and were mostly sealed beneath a yard reminiscent of that around the great eleventh-century monastery of Cluny (Conant 1968). The Crypt Church itself was altered at some time in the eleventh century when its sunken atrium was filled in. All that survived of the 'South Church' was an enigmatic gate in front of the Ponte della Zingara, a low wall on top of the old south wall of the hall, and the apse (see Volume 1: 177-8, 190). This presumably separated the area where the 'South Church' had once stood, and perhaps also the Crypt Church, from the yard immediately to the south. The wall might also have drawn visitors crossing the Ponte della Zingara either towards the apse of the 'South Church' or along the corridor once beneath the 'South Church' to the south doorway of the nave of the Crypt Church. The survival of the 'South Church' apse and the Crypt Church is difficult to explain: perhaps there was a tradition associated with these buildings, relating to the foundation of the monastery, which led to their exemption from the otherwise thorough demolition at this time.

In the yard itself traces of a small brick-built kiln were found, set up against the largely demolished back wall of the Lower Thoroughfare. The kiln was probably used for making pottery, though no wasters were discovered in the excavation. Close by were traces of post-built structures as well as pits. These may have related to short-lived and small-scale industrial activities concentrated in this area.

Phase 8

Late in the eleventh century Abbot Gerard decided to abandon the old settlement and to shift the community to a more readily defensible site on the edge of the Rocchetta plain. Gerard, formerly a monk at Monte Cassino when Desiderius was abbot there, may have been seeking to emulate the achievements of the Cassinese. It is as likely, though, that he was conscious of the vulnerable location of the abbey at a time when the Borrelli family was becoming increasingly powerful in the upper Volturno valley (Wickham 1985a; 1985b).

Parts of the grand Romanesque abbey were excavated by Pantoni when the building was restored in the 1960s (Pantoni 1980a), and some evidence of the plan of the monastic ranges survives. It was here, during the twelfth century, that the monk John compiled the *Chronicon Vulturnense*, recalling the great history of his forebears at San Vincenzo. As he was writing, the old site was being turned into terraces which were cultivated more or less continuously until 1980.

Discussion

Before considering the implications of the phasing, one point needs to be emphasized. The phasing represents a sequence of archaeological time-slices: these may be equated to historical time in certain instances with some precision; in others only broad indications are possible. For example, the chronology of the ninth-century (phases 4-5) building works at San Vincenzo appears to be fairly exact. However, the sub-divisions of phase 3 are relative to one another and must be treated as time-slices of as yet unknown numbers of years in the eighth century. Likewise the chronology of phases 6 and 7 must be treated as time-slices of which only the limits are exact in historical terms.

THE MORPHOLOGY OF THE MONASTERY: AD 703 - *c.* 1100

The overall form as well as the individual components of the monastery altered greatly between the eighth and twelfth centuries (Figs 12:1 and 12:2). The phase 3 monastery covered about half a hectare in area; the ninth-century monastery covered at least five hectares; the size of the phase 6 monastery is impossible to estimate, given the present state of our knowledge; the phase 7 monastery may have covered two to three hectares at most; and the phase 8 monastery covered just over two hectares. These rough estimates are as much as we hoped to achieve at the start of the San Vincenzo project. We need to note that the earliest (phase 3) monastery was essentially a modified Roman villa. In common with many monasteries throughout western Europe at this date, the founders made use of existing classical buildings. In phase 3b, however, there was a conscious attempt to alter the existing 'South Church' and the Crypt Church, perhaps to meet new liturgical needs. However, the first great changes occurred in phase 3c. The new buildings display an architectural capability that was never again equalled at San Vincenzo. The contrast to the phase 3b additions could not be greater. The Refectory, believed to belong to this new complex, was capable of accommodating about a hundred monks at a sitting. Evidently much had changed in the monastery. Not least, to judge from the phase 3b building works, the quality of the construction implies that an architect must have been employed to manage the work. A good parallel for this exists from precisely this time. The Frank, Walcharius, archbishop of Sens and apparently an engineer long in the confidence of both the papal and Frankish courts, was summoned to Rome to act as a consultant to Pope Hadrian on the project to refurbish Saint Peter's (Krautheimer 1980: 112). In the case of San Vincenzo it is tempting to regard the outcome as an image of the large community to which both Paul the Deacon and Pope Hadrian referred (cf. Del Treppo

1955). Wickham (see Chapter 11) argues that it was Carolingian patronage granted to Abbot Paul that made this new layout possible. Here in the late 780s and early 790s, just as at the abbey of Farfa (McClendon 1987: 6), we might surmise that the mixed rule in practice at the abbey since its foundation was replaced by the exclusive use of the Rule of Saint Benedict, a move in keeping with Charlemagne's precepts for monastic reform. However, the phase 3c monastery was a small undertaking by comparison with what happened under Abbot Joshua's direction. San Vincenzo's buildings expanded to cover an area approximately ten times larger than Paul's monastery. Moreover, the community of monks (and probably their lay dependents also) almost certainly tripled or quadrupled in number. Pre-eminent amongst the new buildings was a grand abbey-church, San Vincenzo Maggiore. Paradoxically, although references were made to classical Antiquity in almost every part of the new complex, Abbot Joshua's monastery marks a break with the classical villa form and the beginnings of a medieval layout.

The decoration and material culture of the monastery, however, embody the spirit of the Lombard cultural revival of the mid-eighth century (cf. Belting 1968; Mitchell 1990; 1994; and in Volume 3; Peduto 1990), although the new Frankish political and cultural presence in northern and central Italy may be evident in the scale and design of the monastic buildings and in certain aspects of their ornamentation. Classical *spolia* were prominently positioned throughout the monastery. Cartloads of Antique capitals, columns, bases, inscriptions, and furniture were incorporated into the phase 4 buildings. The ninth-century paintings, as in other parts of Italy during this period, employed certain ideas and motifs commonly found in Antiquity. The decision of the abbot and monks to build ambitiously and to embellish their buildings with rich painted schemes was largely determined by the practice of the Italian Lombard courts in the preceding generations. The Lombard king and his dukes, in an open spirit of mutual rivalry and emulation, had devised traditions of spectacular cultural display in which classical reference and resonance were always present. The Carolingian invaders of Italy were to adopt these strategies and to deploy them widely and effectively in the next century. The *Chronicon* also leads us to suppose that much emphasis was placed upon the traditional importance of the place as *Samnium* (cf. J. Patterson 1985; La Regina 1989). It remains contentious whether this was an invented tradition, in so far as the eighth- to ninth-century community could have known almost nothing of what *Samnium* looked like. Finally, there was a pronounced Beneventan dimension to the monastery's outward appearance. Abbot Joshua must have found a body of skilled (and, in all probability, prized) craftsmen to serve him in this great enterprise. Even though the monks may have assisted in the work, as the chronicler asserts, a glass-maker would have been needed to make the windows and the lamps vital for the lighting; tile-makers would have been required to instruct in the production of the thousands of tiles used in the floors and roofs; smiths would have been needed to make the huge number of nails employed in the roofs; and masons would have been needed to mix the mortar and design the buildings. The archaeological evidence confirms Lynn White's contention (1962) that the diffusion of technology in medieval Europe was the achievement of a Carolingian-period monastic movement, such as has been discovered at San Vincenzo.

The phase 5 additions to Joshua's monastery took two forms. Firstly, the guest-house facilities were aggrandized, and secondly, to judge from the changes to the Vestibule, the integration of the monastic plan was improved when the complicated phase 4 steps, linking the Upper Thoroughfare to the northern sector, were replaced by a first-floor passageway which bridged the Vestibule, arriving at the first floor of the Entrance Hall. The painted decoration in the monastery took a new form in this period too. The northern Lombard idiom apparent in the phase 4 decorations was further assimilated and its implications developed by a second generation of painters (Mitchell 1994).

However, after the fury of changes and building spanning the period c. 790-830/40, the momentum slowed. Little evidence existed for mid to later ninth-century renovations or buildings of any substance. The phase 6 monastery was seemingly a sad, decrepit place, where the levels of artistic and of artisanal practice matched those exhibited in the eighth century. But ninth-century skills were not entirely forgotten and lost. In the eleventh century the monastery was refurbished and then entirely rebuilt on two further occasions. These Romanesque monasteries were more compact, less ambitious versions of the ninth-century model, and rooted in a central Italian tradition almost certainly springing from Monte Cassino (Carbonara 1979).

The arrangement of the settlement also betrays interesting attitudes to space and form through time. The compact eighth-century monastery, with its small abbey-church (the phase 3 'South Church'), was markedly different from the succession of plans which followed it. The phase 3c additions, notably the ambulatory, suggest increased emphasis upon ritual connected with the dead and that sufficient visitors were either anticipated or present to warrant the building of special areas to promote the abbey's relics.

The phase 4 monastery was very different. Apart from the overt scale of the new buildings, the settlement was seemingly separated into zones or modules linked by a network of passages and corridors. A large increase in the population at San Vincenzo inevitably caused it to be divided and probably stratified in some way. Monks and lay people would have occupied different quarters and possibly have taken different routes through the monastery. Similarly, distinguished visitors appear to have been allocated palatial quarters, while ordinary pilgrims were probably accommodated in more modest parts of the monastery (possibly close to the main bridge in front of the abbey-church). The cemeteries of this new monastery revealed the same stratification. Some individuals were buried in front of the Crypt Church (perhaps members of the secular élite); ninth-century funerary inscriptions from Trenches FF and HH suggest that the monks' cemetery probably lay within the vicinity of the abbey-church, as it is shown on the Plan of St Gall (cf. the Reichenau cemetery: Zettler 1988: TA 35); and the secular cemetery may have been the one situated on the hill overlooking the principle church and, significantly, the fields where the monastic dependents had once worked.

The tenth-century monastery provides a marked contrast to its predecessor. Collective burials, individual burials in large and small, undecorated and decorated, tombs seem to illustrate the inchoate ideology of this transitory age. The sequence of eleventh-century monasteries begins to emulate the extensive scale of the ninth-century settlement. There was a new cloister, a refurbished abbey-church, probably new workshops and farms; several churches were refurbished by Abbot Ilarius, including one identified in Trench R on Terrace 3; the old cemeteries were still in use; and new quarters were probably built for the abbot and distinguished guests.

The changing attitudes to space manifested in the plan of the monastery can be found also in the history of individual buildings.

All the earliest buildings in the monastery (in phase 3a) owed their origins to antecedent late Roman structures. The environment was primitive, with beaten earth floors not unlike a house from the period. Likewise the clay-based mortar and the rough-hewn rubble walls belong to an age of primitive technology. Clearly, the eighth-century community had little knowledge of construction techniques. By contrast, the buildings of phases 3c and 4 showed considerable competence. The ambulatory and south wall of the 'South Church', in particular, were skilfully built with hewn and reused stone (there being no evidence that stone was quarried until phase 7, that is the mid-eleventh century). Unlike the poor clay-based mortars of phases 3a-b, those used in phases 3c and 4 are lime-based and rather harder.

The form of some phase 4 buildings, such as the hall and the porticoes around the Garden Court, owed a good deal to the construction techniques of classical architecture, but some at least mark the beginnings of a medieval tradition witnessed elsewhere in the principality of Benevento (Belting 1968; Peduto 1990). The Crypt Church was a modest building, quite consistent with eighth- to ninth-century churches found throughout western Europe. The 'South Church' guest hall, by comparison, was a 'triclinium' of a type adopted by the secular and ecclesiastical élites. Its origins were Roman, but in many respects the particular type was medieval. Such palatial complexes appear to have existed at Benevento and Salerno, as a result of the revival of fortunes in the region under Arichis II (cf. Delogu 1977: 26-32; Peduto 1990: 319-26; Delogu 1992; Mitchell 1994). Certainly, the passages, the Entrance Hall, the refectories and the workshops – some with tiled roofs, some thatched – belong to an incipient medieval architectural tradition. A notable feature of this early medieval building tradition at San Vincenzo was its perilous expediency. Buttresses had to be incorporated into the Refectory, the Entrance Hall and the Assembly Room of the Lower Thoroughfare to reinforce the unstable phase 4a-b walls. The roofs too betray the same expediency. A multitude of long nails discovered in the excavations reveals the surprising inability of local carpenters to make neatly jointed roof timbers. Instead, it appears that the beams, trusses and supports were nailed together. This is a feature which would be most unusual north of the Alps at this date. However, Pierre Toubert, in his monograph on the estates of the abbey of Farfa, commented on the rarity of wooden dwellings mentioned in the early medieval sources (1973: 334ff., 660-3). Likewise David Andrews drew attention to the absence of timber buildings in modern times in Italy, and suggests that stone buildings with tiled roofs may have been preferred since classical times (1982: 2-3). However, numerous excavations in recent times have shown that after *c.* AD 500 the majority of domestic buildings in Italian towns and villages was constructed in timber (for examples, see Brogiolo (1989; 1992) for Brescia and neighbouring villages, and Ward-Perkins (1981) for Luni). Construction of buildings in timber and the use of thatch for roofing appear to mark a genuine break with Antiquity. Even the small classical farms in the upper Volturno valley had been roofed with tiles. Either the monastic tile-maker(s) found the task of covering these many roofs too great, or (more probably) the builders considered the poorly-built walls too weak to support a tiled roof on so large a building. Straw and reeds for thatching were readily available on the Rocchetta plain, and while thatch was perhaps considered a covering of inferior status it was nevertheless cheap, easily repaired and retained the heat in winter. Less rubble and *spolia* were included in the Romanesque buildings. The use of more ashlar appears to distinguish this phase.

This archaeological evidence about the sequence of monastic plans, including the layout and architecture of the settlements and their individual buildings, makes it possible to study afresh the Plan of St Gall, one of the original aims of the San Vincenzo Project. Obviously, the excavations do not reveal an entire plan with which to make comparisons with the ninth-century drawing. Nevertheless, we are in a position to test empirically the theory of a standardized plan spread throughout the Carolingian territories. San Vincenzo, contra the view recently expressed by Laurence Nees (1986: 4), is not peripheral to this problem.

SAN VINCENZO AND THE PLAN OF ST GALL (FIG.12:5)

The Plan of St Gall (Stiftsbibliothek, Ms. 1092) has been analysed and lavishly published by Walter Horn and Ernest Born (1979). The drawing is composed of five separate pieces amounting to 0.77 x 1.12 m in size. Just on the grounds of its size it is an extraordinary document for its age. The plan of the monastery was drawn in red ink and had been annotated by the architect. A dedication discloses, so Horn and Born argue, that it was made in the scriptorium at Reichenau (now in south Germany), having been drawn up at the request of Abbot Gozbert who presided over the nearby monastery of St Gall from 816-36. Horn believes the author was Haito, bishop of Basle, 803-23, and simultaneously abbot of Reichenau. Haito, according to Horn, was a leading participant in the reform synods held at Aachen in 816 and 817. The synods debated Benedict of Aniane's proposals for a universal rule (*una consuetudo*) for the spiritual and temporal conduct of monastic life, to replace the mixed rule (*regula mixta*) that had prevailed in the preceding period. The outcome of the synods was a compromise between the liberals and the ascetic reformers like Benedict. These views, Horn argues, were embodied in the Plan of St Gall, which he contends is a paradigmatic blueprint drawn up by Abbot Haito as a model for future monastic building (Horn and Born 1979: vol. 1, 21-2). Horn argues that it demonstrates the defeat of Benedict's attempt to recreate the simpler, egalitarian monastery of an earlier age. Some stratification was retained within the rules of the monastery, notably permitting the abbot separate facilities (*ibid.*: vol. 1, 22). Horn asserts that the Plan of St Gall reveals a 'consummate conceptual and technical homogeneity ... a mosaic of perfect order and rationality. This order is tight and consistent. It does not show, at any place, the kind of break or formal incompatibility that one associates with an architectural composition pieced together from heterogeneous parts' (*ibid.*: vol. 1, 53). This homogeneity, in Horn's view, stems from the blueprint for unity (*forma unitatis*) encompassed by the directives for canons and canonesses framed at the synods of 816 and 817. Yet, as he acknowledges, the unity of empire of which the unity of the church was a precondition had been a prevailing aspect of the Carolingian world since the late eighth century: 'the drive for

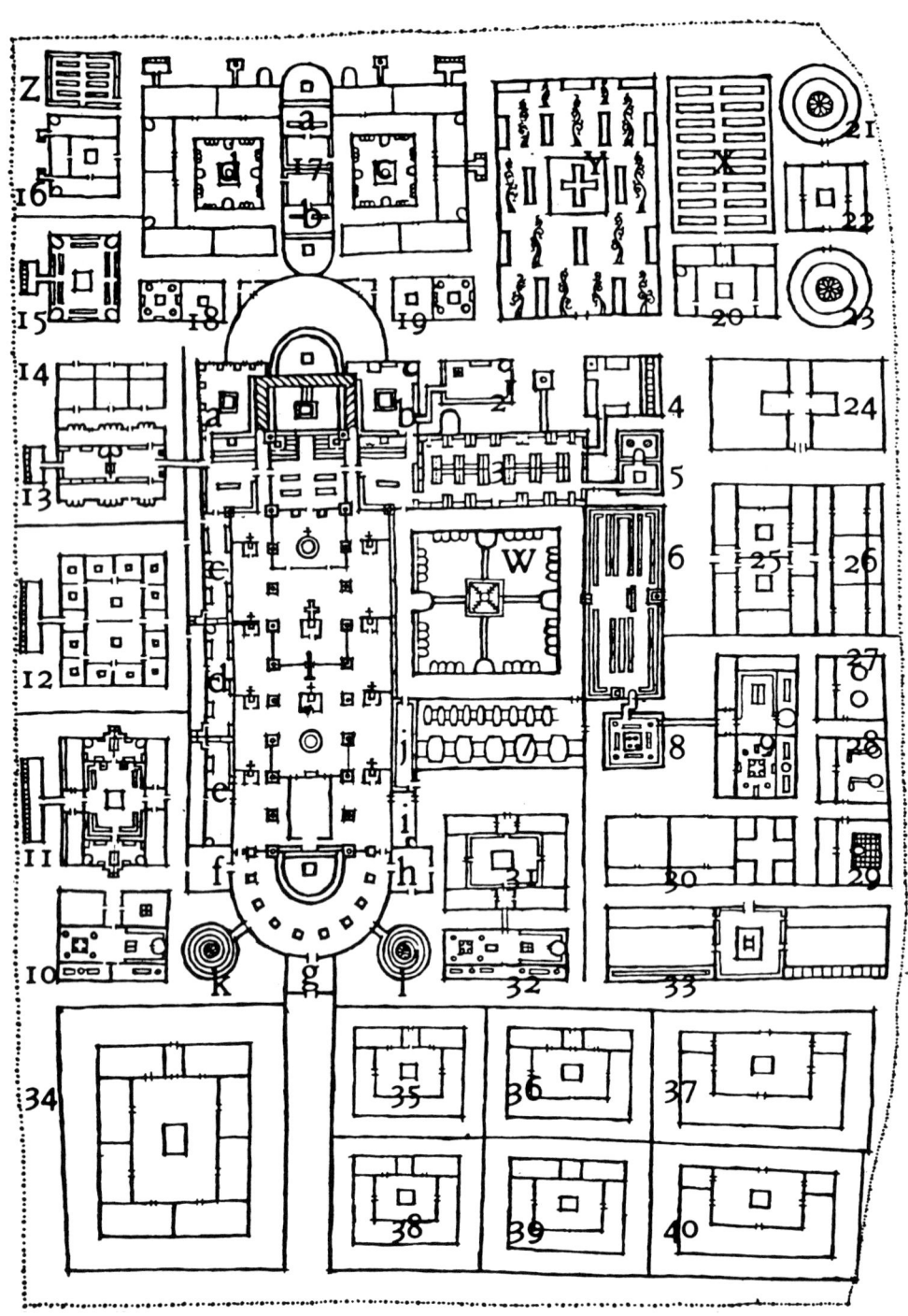

Fig. 12:5 A schematic drawing of the Plan of St Gall *(After Horn and Born 1979: vol. 1, xxiv)*

Key: 1: (a) Scriptorium below, library above; (b) Sacristy below, vestry above; (c) Lodging for visiting monks; (d) Lodging of master of the outer school; (e) Porter's lodging; (f) Porch giving access to house for distinguished guests and to outer school; (g) Porch for reception of all visitors; (h) Porch giving access to hospice for pilgrims and paupers and to servants' and workmens' quarters; (i) Lodging of master of the hospice for pilgrims and paupers; (j) Monks' parlor; (k) Tower of St Michael; (l) Tower of St Gabriel; (2) Annex for preparation of holy bread and holy oil; (3) Monks' dormitory above, warming room below; (4) Monks' privy; (5) Monks' laundry and bathhouse; (6) Monks' refectory below, vestiary above; (7) Monks' cellar below, larder above; (8) Monks' kitchen; (9) Monks' bake and brew house; (10) Kitchen, bake, and brew house for distinguished guests; (11) House for distinguished guests; (12) Outer school; (13) Abbot's house; (14) Abbot's kitchen, cellar, and bathhouse; (15) House for bloodletting; (16) House of the physicians; (17) Novitiate and infirmary; (18) Kitchen and bath for the sick; (19) Kitchen and bath for the novices; (20) House of the gardener; (21) Goosehouse; (22) House of the fowlkeepers; (23) Henhouse; (24) Granary; (25) Great collective workshop; (26) Annex of the great collective workshop; (27) Mill; (28) Mortar; (29) Drying kiln; (30) House of coopers and wheelwrights, and brewers' granary; (31) Hospice for pilgrims and paupers; (32) Kitchen, bake, and brew house for pilgrims and paupers; (33) House for horses and oxen and for their keepers; (34) House for the vassals and knights who travel in the emperor's following ?; (35) House for sheep and shepherds; (36) House for goats and goatherds; (37) House for cows and cowherds; (38) House for servants of outlying estates and for servants traveling with the emperor's court ? - cf. 34; (39) House for swine and swineherds; (40) House for brood mares and foals and their keepers; (W) Monks' cloister yard; (X) Monks' vegetable garden; (Y) Monks' cemetery and orchard; (Z) Medicinal herb garden.

uniformity was programmatic and universal' (*ibid.*: vol. 1, 22). Consequently, Horn seeks the union of schematism and reality in the Plan of St Gall not only in Roman military plans, but also in the planning inherent in existing churches such as Cologne cathedral (*ibid.*: vol. 1, 27-31). Indeed, he concludes that the Plan of St Gall displays 'a *largesse d'esprit* that appears more akin to the educational and administrative policies promoted by Charlemagne and his advisers than to the constrictive atmosphere prevalent in monastic life at the time of Louis the Pious' (*ibid.*: vol. 1, 27).

Horn's thesis owes much to the tradition of art and architectural history which emerged in the late nineteenth century, and was widely admired in the 1930s. Erwin Panofsky (to whom Horn and Born dedicated their book), in his classic book, *Renaissance and Renascences in Western Art* (1960), offers a clear statement of this tradition: 'when Charlemagne set out to reform political and ecclesiastical administration, communications and the calendar, art and literature, and – as a basis for all this – script and language ... his guiding idea was the *renovatio imperii romani*' (Panofsky 1960: 44).

Hardly surprisingly, the publication of Horn and Born's book has generated much controversy. The most substantive charges have been made by Paul Meyvaert (1980), Dom Adalbert de Vogüé (1984), Warren Sanderson (1985) and Alfons Zettler (1990), all of whom contend that the dedicatory inscription on the plan, which (as was noted above) Horn and Born took to be axiomatic evidence that the plan is (i) a copy, and (ii) officially prescribed, indicates quite the contrary! The critics, who accept Bernhardt Bischoff's translation of the dedication (1962), believe that the plan concerned a specific building project at St Gall, and thus cannot be interpreted as paradigmatic. The critics appear to have a solid and convincing argument (cf. Jacobsen 1992; Zettler 1988). Jacobsen, in particular, has demonstrated that the plan was not a copy, as Horn and Born suggested (1979: vol. 1, 15-19), but a palimpsest of complex drafting (Jacobsen 1992: 35-106). But does this entirely undermine the central tenet of Horn and Born's study? In some ways it appears to. For example, Lawrence Nees in a review of the volumes, describes this as a 'severely antiquated' approach which has distorted and produced 'a rather one-sided view of Carolingian art' (1986: 5). Yet he, like all the critics, offers no alternative approach, except to emphasize the importance of understanding the detail of the Plan of St Gall as part of the Carolingian movement. It seems that he (and most of the other reviewers) would prefer to consider the Carolingian renaissance as an assemblage of loosely connected traditions rather than a single, clearly directed movement of the kind proposed by Panofsky. But there are just as many dangers in particularism as in the generalizations that underpin Panofsky's sweeping perspective of the Carolingian age. The Plan of

St Gall surely offers us a remarkable model for a ninth-century monastery, even if it is not a blueprint? The pendulum of opinion on this matter has swung between generalization and particularism, much as it has on many other historical issues during the twentieth century. To a large extent this is a consequence of the restricted nature of the database. Jacobsen, in his recent study of the Plan of St Gall, has been able to examine the church thanks to countless excavations over the past century, but the other buildings, and thus the plan as such, remain beyond the scope of all but the bold because the archaeological data still do not exist (cf. Jacobsen 1992). The San Vincenzo excavations, however, shed some new light on the issue, not simply because they provide new information on monastic plans, but also because the monastic complex as a whole has been sampled using modern archaeological methods as opposed to being investigated using antiquarian techniques. As a result a number of significant observations can be made about the Plan of St Gall.

Three different plans can be identified at San Vincenzo during the Carolingian age:

(1) the phase 3c plan of the 780s/790s (Abbot Paul's plan);

(2) the phase 4a plan of the period 792-817 (Abbot Joshua's plan);

(3) the phase 5a revisions to the phase 4a plan in the period 824-42 (Abbot Epyphanius's plan).

Abbot Paul's plan

The phase 3c plan, although little of it survived, appears to have had the aim of enhancing the primitive phase 3b monastery. Two features stand out about this phase: firstly, the high calibre workmanship involved, and, secondly, the imposing ambulatory added to the small eighth-century abbey-church (San Vincenzo Minore) (cf. Volume 1: fig. 9:57). These features point to a programme of works designed to replace the disparate parts of the earlier eighth-century monastery with an integrated plan. In addition, there was an emphasis upon the promotion of San Vincenzo's relics. However, there was no evidence to show that the new plan included the variety of additional settlement units, such as a farm and workshops, which figure on the Plan of St Gall. The principal evidence for this is the virtual absence of materials such as glass and tiles in this phase, notably in the phase 3c levels sealed beneath the phase 4 floors in the ground-floor rooms excavated in Trench G, the 'South Church'. Workshops and other facilities may have existed, but these were not situated in those areas in which there have been excavations.

Abbot Joshua's plan

The phase 4a plan was conceived on an urban scale. It included a great many different sectors, in addition to an enhanced emphasis upon the ritual focus of the monastery. Workshops for glass-working, fine metalwork, ironworking, the carving of bone and horn, carpentry, tile-production, and many other crafts, occupied at least one sector. Other sectors, it might be surmised, included Terrace 3, with a church, in all probability, at the northern end, and the hilltop of Colle della Torre, separated from the main body of the monastery by the cemetery. But was it a planned settlement in the sense that its architect was working from a blueprint?

Several features suggest that parts of it were planned, in so far as someone designed a new, much larger monastic layout than had existed in the phase 3c monastery. The principal evidence to indicate the presence of an architect working with a blueprint of some kind consists of the two long corridors (the Upper and Lower Thoroughfares), as well as the back wall of Terrace 2, which appear to have been built first, as the axis, linking the old abbey-church to San Vincenzo Maggiore: the rest of Abbot Joshua's monastery was developed around this axis. These corridors simultaneously divided and connected the component parts of the settlement. The means to undertake this work, of course, was a critical factor. The architect must have had available a pool of artisans, who were familiar with mixing lime mortar, with monumental construction techniques, with making tiles for pavements and roofing, with making window panes and glass lamps for lighting, and many other allied crafts. Abbot Joshua's achievement was not a piecemeal enterprise, but the ambitious creation of a settlement which exceeded the ambitions of Christendom's new town-builders (see, for example, Haslam (1987) on ninth-century Mercian towns and Marazzi (1994) on ninth-century new towns in central Italy). Phase 4 was a 'monastic city' in the sense described by McKitterick (1994). Its closest parallel, it may be supposed, was Monte Cassino, where Abbot Gisulf at this time built a new town, called *Eulogimenopolis*, immediately east of Roman *Casinum*, astride the ancient Via Casilina (Fig. 12:6) (Leccisotti 1987: 38). Other parallels are to be found at Fontanella (Saint Wandrille), Saint Riquier (where in 831 2,500 houses were grouped into specialized quarters around the monastery (Riché 1978: 38-9)), and Saint Denis (Fig. 12:7), where parts of the *borgo* have been excavated recently (Héron and Meyer 1991; Meyer 1993).

But Abbot Joshua's monastery, while it embodies a unity of purpose and spirit, is not readily comparable to the Plan of St Gall (cf. Fig. 12:5). The modular character of the Plan of St Gall bears

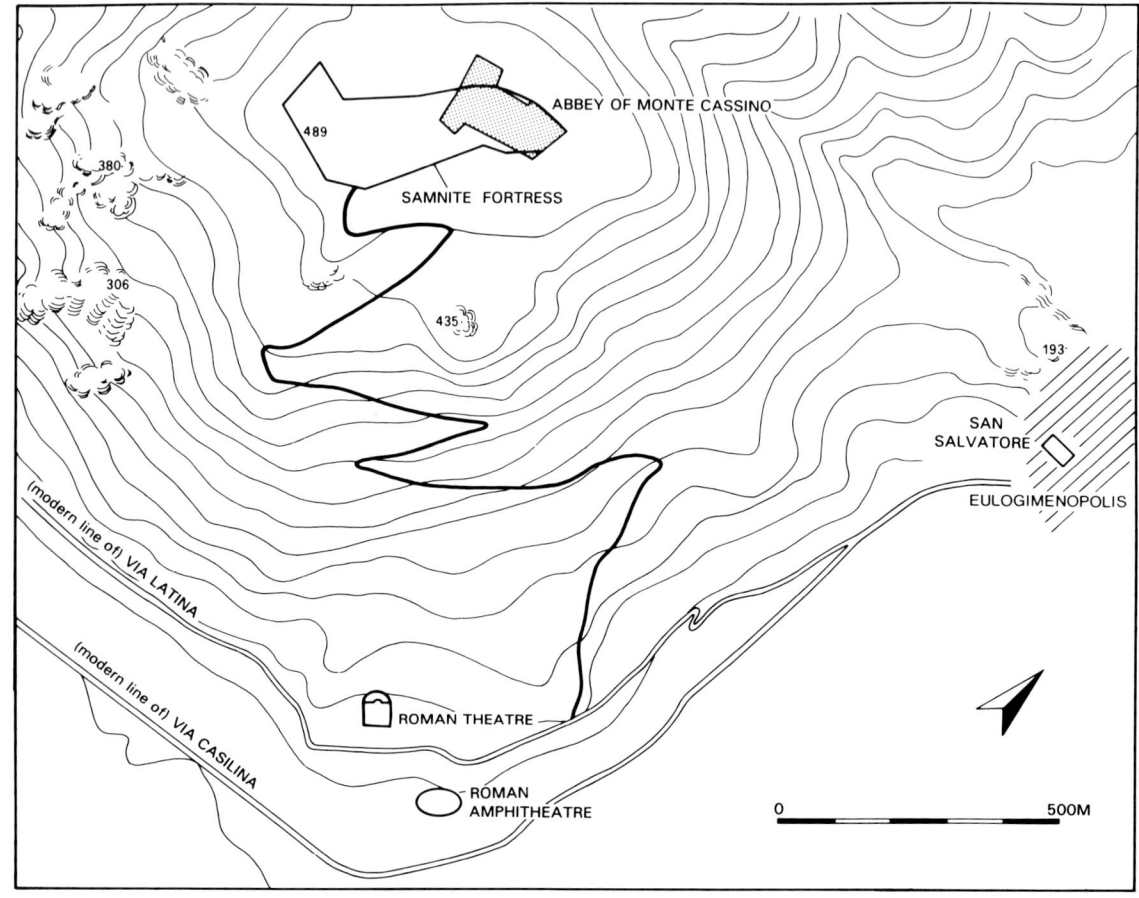

Fig. 12:6 Map showing the location of the abbey of Monte Cassino and ninth-century *Eulogimenopolis (SC)*

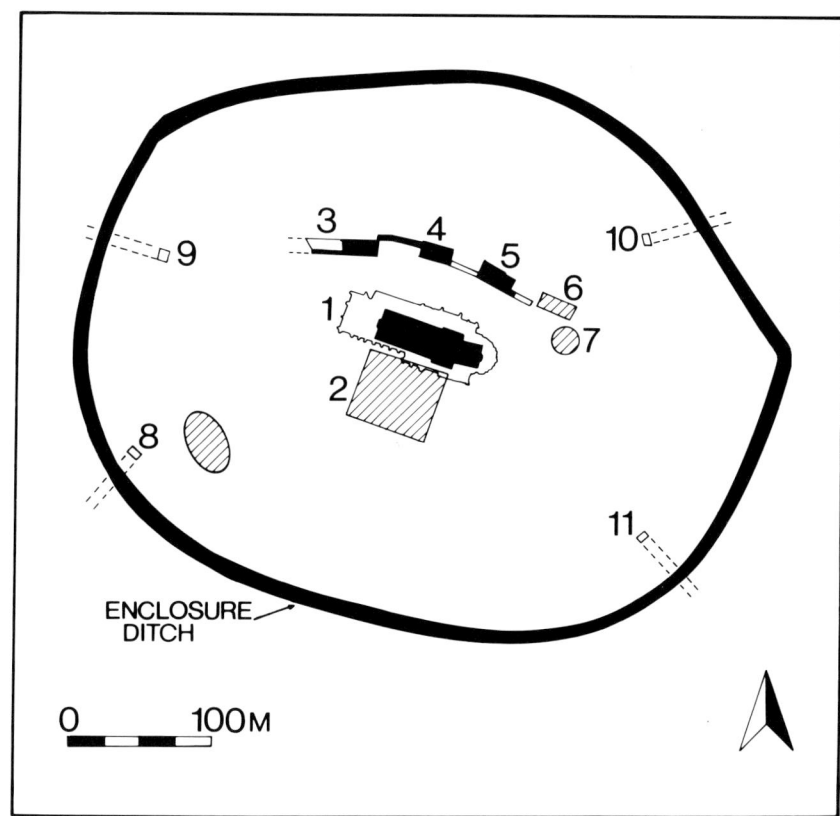

Fig. 12:7 The monastic city of Saint Denis *c.* 869: 1. Carolingian abbey; 2. Monastery; 3. Guest house; 4. Church of Saint Bartholemew; 5. Church of Saint Peter; 6. Church of Saint Paul; 7. Church of Saint John the Baptist; 8. Paris gate; 9. Compoise gate; 10. Bazoin gate; 11. Saint James gate *(After Meyer 1993: 92)*

witness to a hierarchy within the place, yet, in the absence of passages or corridors, paradoxically it appears that there existed a fluid access between all parts of the settlement. The layout, on the other hand, offers no hint of the history of St Gall – of pre-existing buildings, modified, for example, to the needs of a new liturgy (see, however, Zettler 1990). At San Vincenzo, by contrast, it is important to note that the architect decided to retain the old monastery, albeit in a remodelled form, within the loosely ordered structure of his new plan. Reason and history were grafted together in an intriguing form. Thus the architect resisted the opportunity of creating a new settlement on the Rocchetta plain, as Abbot John V, Desiderius of Monte Cassino's ambitious contemporary, was to do in the mid-eleventh century. The configurations of the landscape, as a result, also prevented the architect from creating an ideal symmetrical scheme. In addition, the bridges, long corridors, yards and gardens, intersections of a sort, served to break up the plan and to accentuate the differences between the sectors.

San Vincenzo in phase 3c had been dominated by its abbey-church, San Vincenzo Minore, with its pronounced west end including the enlarged ambulatory. By contrast, the monastery in phase 4 was dominated by two buildings roughly at either end of the settlement: at the south end, the new abbey-church of San Vincenzo Maggiore (measuring 36 *passus* (paces) by 16 *passus* and raised on a platform built to command the southern aspect of the place), and, towards the north end, the 'South Church' (measuring 31 m long and 14.0 m wide), completely remodelled as the abbot's guest-house for distinguished visitors. Long corridors connected these two nodal points in the monastery, much as we are led to believe that Charlemagne's audience-hall at Aachen was connected by a long passageway to his palace-chapel (cf. Heitz 1980). Essentially, the plan and profile of the place lay emphasis not upon unity, but upon the twin pillars of society, the Church and the secular élite. In short, it is tempting to interpret the phase 4 monastic plan as an expression of the transition from the early Carolingian concept of unity to a monastic zeal where for a while, at least, abbots recognized and sought to influence the aristocracy.

Abbot Epyphanius's plan

The phase 5 revisions to the phase 4a plan almost certainly belonged to the age of Abbot Epyphanius. The essential layout of the monastery was not altered, but significant parts of it were aggrandized. Visitors would have found it to be an even more impressive place. The distinguished guests' complex was enlarged with a new, high west apse. Associated with this was a fine arcosolium tomb in the corridor leading beneath the 'South Church' to the refurbished Crypt Church with its exquisitely made crypt. The emphasis upon refurbishments can also be found in the Vestibule, where the yard separating the claustrum and distinguished guests' sector was roofed and the area was decorated. The Entrance Hall was also decorated, using an imposing pilastered façade with an arcaded loggia in the upper storey. Concomitant alterations were also made to the abbey-church at this time (Hodges 1994).

Individuals were certainly being given greater emphasis in the refurbishments. There was a new cemetery in the atrium of the Crypt Church. It is argued in Volume 1 that the crypt itself was constructed for the child of a donor. However, this point is most explicitly illustrated by the portraits of Abbot Epyphanius himself, two deacons and the occupant of the tomb in the cycle of paintings in the crypt.

Discussion

How are we to interpret this sequence of plans at San Vincenzo in the light of the discussion about the Plan of St Gall? The Plan of St Gall was drawn up in the wake of Charlemagne's death, at a time when the relationship between the nobility and the Church was beginning to come under strain. Whether it was a paradigmatic blueprint or simply a design for a major monastery, as a unique artefact it is of paramount importance for any interpretation of the Carolingian age. How are we to judge its significance?

The Carolingian empire had become the largest political entity in western Europe between the end of the Roman empire and Napoleon's short-lived polity a millennium later. Unlike the Romans and, indeed, Napoleon, Charlemagne had few administrators at his disposal – only learned churchmen like Alcuin and Einhard – and no legions. To unify this polity, as most historians agree, he sought to make use of the Church rather than armies. Christian ideology was explicitly fashioned to bind the disparate regions together by restraining the political aspirations of potentially hostile aristocrats. The Church, in short, provided a constitution for the empire, a *Klosterpolitik*. Monasteries were no longer retreats, but outward-looking centres of civilization promoting the new ethos (see, for example, McKitterick 1994). Senior churchmen were well aware of their growing power in the empire, especially after the loss of Charlemagne's charismatic leadership. As a result, the synods of 816 and 817 were designed not only to build upon the spirit of reform, then already two generations old, but also to develop the role of the Church in the formation of the State.

Central to these meetings was the part played by Benedict of Aniane, sometimes described as Louis the Pious's vice-regent. According to Ardo, Benedict's biographer, it was the reformer's intention to promote 'such a state of unity that it seemed as though they had been instructed by one master and in one place' (Noble 1976: 249). But was this spirit of unity already jeopardized by a generation of discussion, dispute and, above all, the passing of Charlemagne? By *c.* 820 the stability of the empire rested upon the twin pillars of society, the nobles and the senior churchmen, and the use that they made of an incipient third order, (skilled) workmen (cf. Duby 1980; Le Goff 1980; Andreolli and Montanari 1983: 129-45, esp. 144). Benedict of Aniane's monastic concept had necessarily been superceded by a more pragmatic entity (cf. Heitz 1980; Jacobsen 1992: 321-32). Monasteries modelled upon Aachen, in which long passages played an important axial role, connecting, yet separating, secular and ecclesiastical poles, already existed at Centula (Saint Riquier (Taylor 1975)) and, in all likelihood, at Farfa (McClendon 1987: 64ff.) and Monte Cassino (cf. Pantoni 1973, where he illustrates the sequence of abbey-churches). This was the inevitable consequence of Charlemagne's strategic use of the Church in the later eighth century. He had directly and indirectly invested power in the ecclesiastical élite in order to control the secular aristocracy (cf. Schmid 1972).

Such a policy meant that monasteries needed rooms for public receptions and for accommodating guests, to bring spiritual influence to bear on their aristocratic visitors – to involve them in the new Benedictine ideology. The Plan of St Gall – this unique artefact betraying a contemporary perspective of a centre of civilization – illustrates the comparative importance of visitors. Four separate houses are allocated for the reception of royal visitors, according to Horn: '1, a house for the emperor and his immediate entourage; 2, an ancillary building containing the kitchen, bake and brewing facilities pertaining to this house; 3, a house for visiting servants; and if my interpretation is correct, 4, a house for the emperor's vassals and others of knightly rank travelling in the emperor's train' (Horn and Born 1979: vol. 2, 155). Horn and Born calculated that the total surface area taken up by these houses and their surrounding courts amounted to a little over one-fifth of the surface area of the entire monastic complex. Nevertheless, unlike the distinguished guests' complex at San Vincenzo, with its own access over the Ponte della Zingara, and which was then connected by a corridor to the abbey-church, the great abbey-church on the Plan of St Gall dominates the guests' quarters in its shadow. St Gall's guest-houses were evidently lesser buildings. The Plan of St Gall, of course, may reflect the circumstances where the authority of Carolingian government was strong and abbots were not called upon to manipulate local élites (that is in the Rhineland and the transalpine region). On the other hand, beyond the core region of the empire the reverse may have been more likely to have occurred. In the principality of Benevento, for example, which was intermittently (although not after *c.* 790) compelled to pay tribute to the Carolingian Empire, it seems likely that the authority and skill of individual churchmen (and their craftsmen) to manipulate the aristocracy would have been an issue of enormous, indeed critical, significance. Accordingly greater importance was attached to the independence and grandiosity of the guests' accommodation.

In sum, San Vincenzo took part in a cultural renaissance, much as St Gall did. In San Vincenzo's case, the need to cultivate the local élite was more necessary than at St Gall, and this purpose is more explicit in the layout of the phase 4 monastery than it is on the St Gall plan. On the other hand it would be misguided to interpret everything from San Vincenzo as explicitly Carolingian in origin when it is clear that the monastery was Beneventan, and conspicuously displays strong cultural affinities with the southern and northern Lombards. On reaching this conclusion, it is appropriate to consider the other aim of the San Vincenzo project, the context of the monastery.

THE CONTEXT OF THE MONASTERY

Chris Wickham (in Chapter 11; see also Wickham 1985a; 1985b) has outlined the historical context of San Vincenzo as a great monastic landlord. As he describes it, the monastery's history fits satisfactorily within the broader sweep of Beneventan history (cf. Del Treppo 1968; Peduto 1990). Its eighth-century phases mirror the circumstances of the duchy of Benevento in the age before Arichis II, whereas its great expansion appears to have followed hard upon the changes wrought by him; and the monastery suffered from the political ramifications of the Beneventan civil war, after the second quarter of the ninth century; only late in the tenth century and during the first half of the eleventh century did circumstances revive once more (Wickham 1981: 159; cf. Chapter 11, p. 149). In fact, it seems that the *Chronicon Vulturnense* was the last great achievement of the abbey. Thereafter, the place passed into obscurity. The achievements of San Vincenzo's great builders, abbots Paul, Joshua and Epyphanius seem all the greater because of the apparent remoteness (in modern terms) of the monastery.

Far from the heartlands of the principality of Benevento, the monastery lies in a mountain valley, almost equidistant from the coastal littorals of the peninsula. Significantly, as Hayes shows in Volume 1, chapter 2, the settlement is located at the intersection between two climatic zones: that is, the mediterranean climatic zone and the mountain continental climatic zone. In the continental zone winters are hard and long with a good deal of snow, while summers vary between temperate and humid high temperatures, with many thunderstorms. By contrast, mild wet winters and long hot summers typify mediterranean climates. Apart from the obvious differences in living conditions, climate has major implications for agrarian regimes. The mediterranean climate supports polyculture with olives, vines and cereals, but the upper limit of this cultivation is at the 800 m contour. A continental climate, by contrast, chiefly gives rise to stock-raising and the cultivation of hardy cereals. The nineteenth-century sheep-fair held beside the abbey (witnessed by the Hon. Keppel Craven) clearly illustrates this point, for it was the place where shepherds and peasants working two entirely different landscapes met.

It appears that this strategic location was first occupied in later Samnite times when a *vicus* was founded at San Vincenzo. This settlement was located a little over half way between Venafro or Isernia (both situated in classic mediterranean territory) and Alfedena (located in classic continental upland territory). The half way point, as the crow flies, occurs at about Colli a Volturno. But the half way point on foot, bearing in mind the steep climb from San Vincenzo up the mountainous face of the Mainarde to Alfedena, is roughly on the Rocchetta plain.

However, the potential of such a location could only be realised fully once intra- and interterritorial exchange became possible and important, at that point in time when the bulk production and distribution of regionally-specific agrarian goods could be coordinated by society. The archaeology of the upper Volturno valley demonstrates that this momentous change occurred in the last centuries BC. At this time the hilltop settlements were finally abandoned in favour of sites where the agrarian resources could be efficiently exploited. A local family or a provincial government may have established a sanctuary site at San Vincenzo, which, over the course of several generations, became the hub of a small, loosely aggregated, urban settlement. This settlement, while perhaps inheriting some traditions from local hilltop sites, was explicitly situated at the northern end of the Rocchetta plain on poor but readily defensible ground, where full advantage might be made of communications up the valley, on the one hand, and, on the other, of the potential of the plain for grazing stock and growing cereals. It remains a matter of speculation whether this was the site of *Samnium* (J. Patterson 1985; La Regina 1989; 1990).

The complex history of San Vincenzo's classical Antiquity led the form of the settlement to alter from a *vicus* to a villa. But nevertheless, over 600 or 700 years the locational advantages of the place must have changed little until classical society and its economy collapsed. The late Roman settlement was the final relic of the integrated economies that connected the mountains and the Mediterranean (Hodges 1993a). Perhaps as much for a tradition spanning many centuries as for its immediate late Antique past, after its desertion in the sixth century, it continued to be used intermittently as a burial ground by local peoples who upheld the tradition of burial at this place. But these peoples were few in number; they were occupying hilltop locations, such as the hills around Colli a Volturno and Vacchereccia, for a variety of reasons, and their impoverished material culture expresses the drastic downswing in the economy of this region (Hodges 1990). In effect, this inland valley had returned to its prehistoric condition, where the mountain resources might satisfactorily maintain only a small population.

This economic potential may have been recognized, in a sketchy sense at least, by the Beneventan founders, Paldo, Tato and Taso, in the early eighth century, but its full potential was certainly not realized by them. Of course, it is unlikely that the monks chose the site for its economic qualities; instead, they were guided, we may suppose, by such matters as the historic associations of the place, close to the source of the river Volturno, which had enjoyed 700 years of virtually uninterrupted settlement, as well as by its position close to the Beneventan frontier.

According to the *Chronicon Vulturnense*, the monks were given a largely defunct landscape. The chronicler describes it as a wild, abandoned zone, evoking the image of a pioneering age (cf. Wickham 1985a: 13-23; 1994: 157). (In this instance, Le Goff's analysis of the desert-forest image in texts of this period, wherein later chroniclers attempted falsely to conjure up origins that resembled biblical primitivism, is now all the more interesting as the archaeological evidence for settlement continuity is very limited (Le Goff 1988; cf. Wickham 1994: 157; for a review of the archaeological evidence see Hodges 1990; 1992).) In one sense, however, the founders of San Vincenzo may have been seeking a mystical isolation that had parallels with the history of the people of Israel (Le Goff 1988). The duke of Benevento's generosity needs to be measured in these terms. At Benevento, as in many southern Italian towns, it is very likely that the classical community had dwindled to little more than an élite settlement (Peduto 1990: 312-19; contra La Rocca Hudson 1986; cf. Brogiolo 1987; 1989). The nearby colony of ancient *Venafrum*, for example, appears to have lost its bishopric by the seventh century, after which only its northwest corner was occupied by the fortified residence of a count (Morra and Valente 1993: 29-30, 89). Nevertheless, some elements of classical life outlasted the regional devolution of the Roman state. Notions of Roman property ownership survived the eclipse of the empire (cf. Wickham 1981: 92-114; 1994: 99-118). Was the duke's largesse towards Paldo, Tato and Taso designed, therefore,

not only to secure his vulnerable northern frontier, but also to encourage the development of what was a marginal zone? Were the monks part of a modest plan to revive the integration of mountain and mediterranean resources within the duchy? If an early medieval fair had been located at San Vincenzo, it would have eluded the archaeological investigations for two reasons. First, it would have been located, in all probability, outside the monastic perimeter, possibly on the Rocchetta plain or on the east side of the river Volturno (cf. Volume 1: 24-5). Secondly, bearing in mind that we have failed to pinpoint the locus of the ninteenth-century fair witnessed by the Hon. Keppel Craven (1838: 62-5), identifying the remains of such a temporary (seasonal) activity would prove very difficult.

According to the chronicle, pre-eminent in the minds of San Vincenzo's founders was the development of a religious retreat dedicated to Saint Vincent. Within a century, though, the tiny sanctuary had been developed beyond the imagination of any early eighth-century monk. Similarly, one wonders if the Samnite founders of the sanctuary at San Vincenzo would have recognized the *vicus* at its apogee in the early first century AD, covering as much as ten hectares and including the numerous monumental buildings which grew up around it. This difference, though, cannot be ascribed to San Vincenzo's relics, or the creation of a cult, as this was never a celebrated attribute of the monastery (Geary 1978: 166-7). The real difference is revealed in the comparison of the patterns of settlements in the region in Republican and early medieval times.

The field survey of the upper Volturno valley shows that the Republican settlement formed part of an extensive system to which many small farms or cottages belonged. Small farms were dotted at regular intervals around this territory. This is an index of the integrated competitive market system of which each settlement was one part. By contrast, the monastic settlement system before AD 1000 was altogether different. Very few medieval farms were found in the field survey. Excavations at Vacchereccia, however, suggest that the farms of the seventh century onwards were small, unprepossessing settlements already situated on hilltops (Hodges *et al.* 1984). These excavations, as well as those at Colle Castellano (tenth-century *Olivella*) (see Volume 4), show that these farms had an impoverished material culture up until the age of *incastellamento*, at about the turn of the millennium, making them archaeologically difficult to identify (Hodges 1990). In short, the survey as well as the excavations of villages within the two differing ecological and climatic zones constituting the *terra* indicate that San Vincenzo was slow to develop its own domain. Only small churches, possibly *plebes* (Settia 1991: 3-4), such as that excavated at Colle Sant'Angelo (above Colli a Volturno), offer any illustration of San Vincenzo's extraordinary wealth (Hodges 1992; to be published in Volume 4). Modest churches like Colle Sant'Angelo, it appears, rather like the sanctuaries surrounding the great Samnite hilltop settlement of Monte San Paolo, were the monastery's limited investment in diffusing its spirit as a centre of civilization to the dispersed families in *condumae* in its immediate environs (Hodges 1990). San Vincenzo evidently looked further afield for its resources.

Wickham (Chapter 11) shows that San Vincenzo acquired numerous estates in the heartland of the principality of Benevento, places illustrated by Peduto in his recent appraisal of the duchy (Peduto 1990: 362ff.). The scale of Abbot Joshua's achievement, as Wickham argues, cannot simply be measured in terms of the phase 4 monastery, for in his period as abbot San Vincenzo became one of the great landowners in Italy. Clearly, the monastery managed to influence many of the lower-ranking Beneventan nobility at a time when the old Lombard duchy assumed a new political shape as a coalition of princely households, and as the territory began to sense its precarious position between the two superpowers, the Carolingian and Byzantine empires (Cilento 1966a: 209; Delogu 1977; 1990; Peduto 1990).

The significance of the estates donated to San Vincenzo lies in their location. Almost all were close to the major centres within the principality, on the mediterranean littoral as opposed to in the mountains. A fortified centre of this kind (possibly princely) (Hodges and Wickham, forthcoming) was investigated at Santa Maria in Civita in the Biferno valley, 30 km from the Adriatic coast, again close to the northern frontier of the principality (Fig. 12:8) (Hodges, Barker and Wade 1980).

At Santa Maria all the features (for example, the enclosure wall, a church serving the community, associated cemeteries, a non-nucleated habitation pattern) of a late tenth-century *castello* in the upper Volturno valley were found to exist in the early to mid-ninth century (Fig. 12:8) (Hodges and Wickham forthcoming). The settlement was processing and storing cereals in some quantity (Van der Veen 1985), and in receipt of mass-produced pottery as well as some glassware. It exhibits some of the traits of the Carolingian agricultural developments documented on other estates in the early ninth century

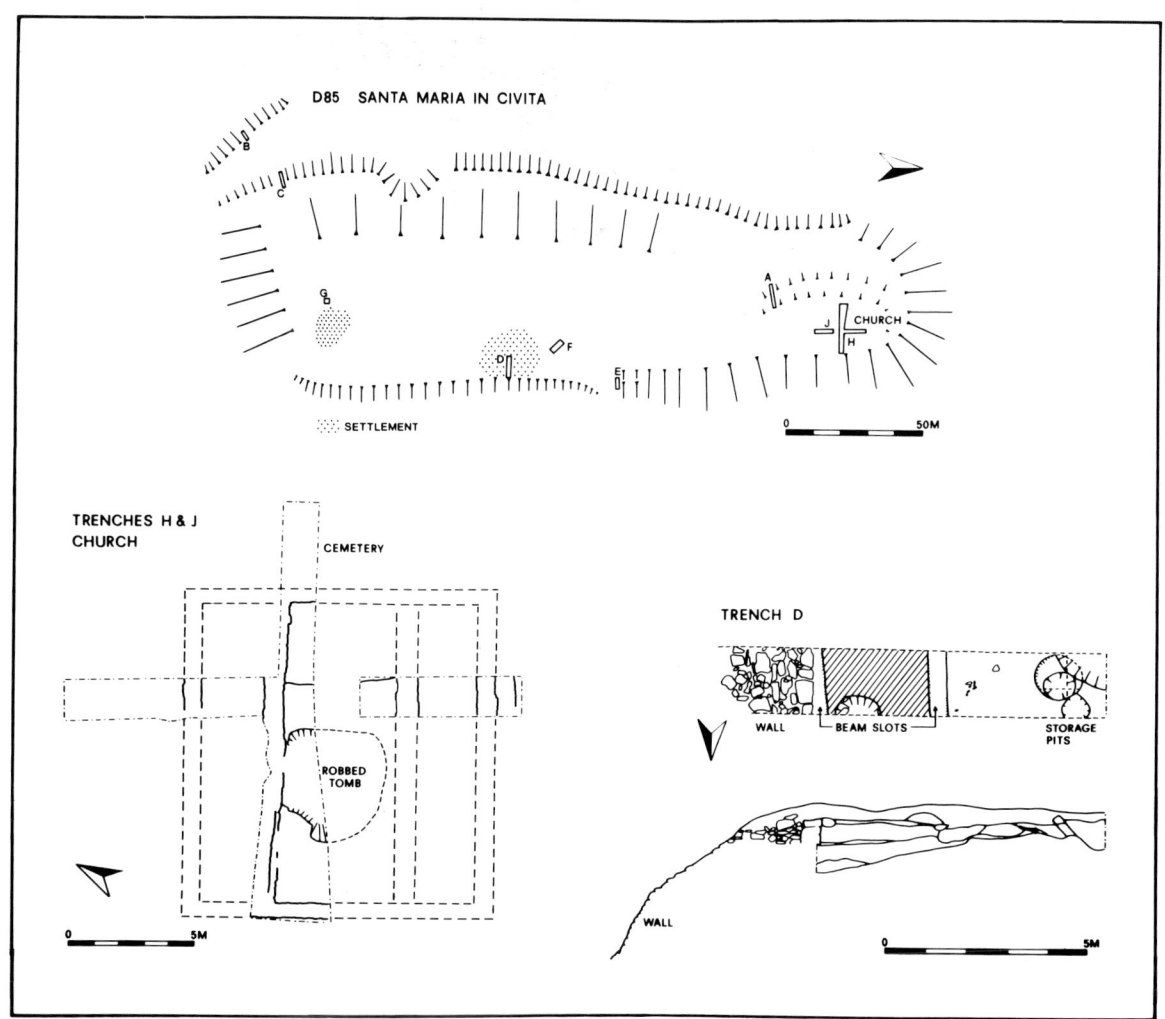

Fig. 12:8 D85: Santa Maria in Civita. Top: plan of the early medieval settlement. Bottom left: plan of Trenches H and J – the church. Bottom right: plan of and section through the fortification wall and associated dwelling in Trench D *(SC)*

Fig. 12:9 The excavations at San Vincenzo: recording skeletons in Trench G
(the 'South Church') *(RH)*

(Andreolli and Montanari 1983). In this respect it constitutes a part of the scientific and technical development encouraged by the Carolingians, illustrated in many other forms in Abbot Joshua's monastery, but notably absent in rural settlements such as Vaccchereccia in the upper Volturno at this time. Put another way, the archaeology of Santa Maria in Civita strongly suggests that the expansion of agricultural production was taking place within parts of the Beneventan heartland, but not within the upper Volturno.

But why did San Vincenzo seek to acquire estates around Benevento, Capua, and Salerno, where similar agrarian developments were perhaps underway, when it failed to invest in its own *terra*? In part, of course, land, especially in these areas, was a measure of status and power. Benevento and Salerno had experienced a significant urban revival under

Arichis II (Delogu 1977; 1990; 1992; Peduto 1990), not so very dissimilar from the revival of Rome itself (Delogu 1988; Hodges 1993b). Not surprisingly, San Vincenzo's neighbour, Monte Cassino, had built up a similar reputation as a landowner in Benevento (Toubert 1976), and, under Abbot Gisulf (797-817), was able to rebuild the abbey-church on a large scale, as well as found the new town beside the ruins of ancient *Casinum* (Leccisotti 1987; Pantoni 1973). Neither San Vincenzo nor Monte Cassino could have consumed the produce of their estates, and much of it must have been redistributed to their many dependent houses. Some of it doubtless was also traded to the monasteries' mountain communities in the Abruzzo. However, it is tempting to speculate that some small part of it was traded via middlemen beyond central Italy.

The excavations at San Vincenzo (Figs 12:9-10)

Fig. 12:10 The excavations at San Vincenzo: work in the Refectory in 1984 *(RH)*

permit us to show how there was a programme embracing not simply the revival of classical imagery, but, more lastingly, the reintroduction to élite centres, at least, of classical technology (cf. Plate 12:1). Yet to enlarge this picture we need to examine the monastery's farms, probably located on the Rocchetta plain, and the putative extramural settlement (see Volume 1: 24-5), situated on the east bank of the river Volturno. Beyond this, the archaeological data remain frustratingly slight. It still remains imperative that we examine the material culture of the peasantry to establish the extent of the reverberations of this programme. Santa Maria in Civita provides a clue, as, in a rather different, ideological measure, does the church at Colle Sant'Angelo, that local communities were being 'cultivated' to support the new spirit. In rural German contexts, for example, Heiko Steuer has illustrated the development of more effective, fixed management of rural resources in this period, associated with the construction of local stone-built churches (Steuer 1989); Theuws has demonstrated the same in the Kempen region of eastern Flanders (Theuws 1991). Even in Anglo-Saxon England there is evidence to show that the adoption of new estate practices accompanied the ideological reorientation of this age (cf. Hodges 1989: 116-49). At the other end of Europe were abbots like Joshua attempting to introduce similar, more intensive forms of resource control? In so far as this remains a matter of speculation, the San Vincenzo project failed to achieve all its objectives.

In conclusion, the archaeology of San Vincenzo sheds light on the significance of the Plan of St Gall, illuminating both what it is and what it is not. The large-scale investigations at San Vincenzo lend some qualified support to Horn's sweeping contention that: 'Superbly executed, and possibly the most accomplished architectural creation of the age of Charlemagne, the Plan of St Gall owes its existence to a striving for cultural unity that pervaded the whole of Carolingian life: unity embodied in a common language, Latin; a common belief, Christianity; a common legal and spiritual authority vested in the offices of Emperor and Pope; and unity of monastic custom and observance. It was the search for unity in the conduct of monastic practice – *unitas regulae* – that by inner necessity also required creation of an ideal scheme to standardise and guide monastic architecture for the future' (Horn and Born 1979: vol. 1, 356). Yet, as is now clear from excavations at Reichenau and St Gall, Horn plainly overstated the significance of the ideal scheme to standardize. Nevertheless, the archaeology of San Vincenzo at its apogee splendidly illustrates a striving desire to evoke a spirit of unity and renaissance far from the source of its conception. The paintings, the prolific display of script, the explicitly positioned pieces of classical *spolia*, and the revival of technology, show that San Vincenzo's abbots sought to be part of a programme that drew upon Lombard and even Frankish connections, as well as to exploit fully the renaissance of Beneventan political life that followed the reign of Arichis II. This led to great monastic riches, lifting the monastery out of its natural and social context, and, paradoxically, in this manner contributing to its inevitable demise.

REFERENCES

Alcock, S. (1989) Roman imperialism in the Greek landscape. *Journal of Roman Archaeology* 2: 5-34.

Alfieri, N. (1965) La chiesa di S. Maria in Padovetere nella zona archeologica di Spina. *Atti del II congresso nazionale di archeologia di studi bizantini*: 1-33. Ravenna, Edizioni A. Longo.

Andreolli, B. and Montanari, M. (1983) *L'azienda curtense in Italia. Proprietà della terra e lavoro contadino nei secoli VIII-XI*. Bologna, Editrice CLUEB.

Andrews, D. (1982) Architecture and archaeology. Medieval domestic architecture in northern Lazio. In D. Andrews, J. Osborne and D. Whitehouse (eds), *Medieval Lazio. Studies in Architecture, Painting and Ceramics (Papers in Italian Archaeology III)* (BAR International Series 125): 1-122. Oxford, British Archaeological Reports.

Ariès, P. (1976) *Western Attitudes toward Death from the Middle Ages to the Present*. London, Marion Boyars.

Artese, G. (1993) *La guerra in Abruzzo e Molise 1943-44 Vol. 1*. Lanciano, Casa editrice Rocca Carabba.

Arthur, P. (1991) Naples: a case of urban survival in the early Middle Ages? *Mélanges de l'École Française de Rome. Moyen Age* 103 (2): 759-84.

Avagliano, F. (ed.) (1985) *Una grande abbazia altomedievale nel Molise. San Vincenzo al Volturno (Atti del I convegno di studi sul medioevo meridionale) (Miscellanea Cassinese 51)*. Montecassino.

Baker, P. and Clark, G. (1993) Archaeozoological evidence for medieval Italy: a critical review of the present state of research. *Archeologia medievale* 20: 45-77.

Barello, F. and Cardosa, M. (1991) Casignana Palazzi. *Mélanges de l'École Française de Rome. Moyen Age* 103 (2): 669-87.

Barnish, S.J.B. (1987) Pigs, plebeians and *potentes*: Rome's economic hinterland c. 350-600 AD. *Papers of the British School at Rome* 55: 157-85.

Basile, G. (1988) Abbazia di San Vincenzo al Volturno: restauri in corso. *Arte medievale* 2 (1): 153-61.

Bateson, M. (1899) Origin and early history of double monasteries. *Transactions of the Royal Historical Society* n.s. 13: 137-98.

Behn, F. (1934) *Die Karolingische Klosterkirche von Lorsch an der Bergstrasse nach den Ausgrabungen von 1927-1928 und 1932-1933*, 2 vols. Berlin/Leipzig, Walter de Gruyter.

Belting, H. (1968) *Studien zur Beneventanischen Malerei (Forschungen zur Kunstgeschichte und Christlichen Archäologie 7)*. Wiesbaden, Franz Steiner Verlag.

Benazzi, G. (1985) *I dipinti murali e l'edicola marmorea del Tempietto sul Clitunno (Restauri a Spoleto 3)*. Todi, Ediart.

Bertelli, C. (1988a) *Gli affreschi nella torre di Torba (I quaderni del fondo per l'ambiente italiano 1)*. Milan, Electa.

Bertelli, C. (1988b) Castelseprio e Milano. In *Bisanzio, Roma e l'Italia nell'alto medioevo (Settimane di studio del centro italiano di studi sull'alto medioevo 34)*, vol. 2: 869-917. Spoleto, Centro italiano di studi sull'alto medioevo.

Bertolini, O. (1926) I documenti trascritti nel '*Liber Preceptorum Beneventani Monasterii S. Sophiae*' (Chronicon S. Sophiae). In *Studi di storia napoletana in onore di Michelangelo Schipa*: 11-47. Naples, ITEA editrice.

Bertolini, O. (1965) Carlomagno e Benevento. In H. Beumann (ed.), *Karl der Grosse*: 609-71. Düsseldorf.

Bertolini, P. (1985) I duchi di Benevento e San Vincenzo al Volturno. Le origini. In F. Avagliano (ed.), *Una grande abbazia altomedievale nel Molise. San Vincenzo al Volturno (Atti del I convegno di studi sul medioevo meridionale) (Miscellanea Cassinese 51)*: 85-177. Montecassino.

Bethmann, L. and Waite, G. (eds) (1878) *Monumenta Germaniae Historica, Scriptores rerum Langobardicarum et Italicarum saec. VI-IX*. Hanover, Hahniani.

Binford, L.R. (1971) Mortuary practices: their study and potential. In J.A. Brown (ed.), *Approaches to the Social Dimensions of Mortuary Practice (Memoirs of the Society for American Archaeology 25 = American Antiquity 36 (no. 3, pt 2))*: 6-29.

Binford, L.R. (1981) Behavioral archaeology and the 'Pompeii Premise'. *Journal of Anthropological Research* 37 (3): 195-208.

Bischoff, B. (1962) Die Entstehung des Sankt Galler Klosterplanes in paläographischer Sicht. In J. Duff (ed.), Studien zum St Galler Klosterplan. *Mitteilungen zur Vaterländischen Geschichte* 42: 67-78.

Bloch, H. (1986) *Monte Cassino in the Middle Ages*, 3 vols. Rome, Edizioni di storia e letteratura.

Bloch, M. and Parry, J. (1982) Introduction: death and the regeneration of life. In M. Bloch and J. Parry (eds), *Death and the Regeneration of Life*: 1-44. Cambridge, Cambridge University Press.

Bluhme, F. (ed.) (1868) *Monumenta Germaniae Historica, Leges*. Hanover, Hahniani.

Bougard, F. and Noyé, G. (1986) Squillace (Prov. de Catanzaro). *Mélanges de l'École Française de Rome. Moyen Ages – Temps Modernes* 98 (2): 1195-1212.

Bougard, F. and Noyé, G. (1989) Squillace au moyen âge. In R. Spadea (ed.), *Da Skylletion a Scolacium. Il parco archeologico della Roccalletta*: 215-30. Rome, Gangemi editore.

Bradley, R. (1987) Time regained: the creation of continuity. *Journal of the British Archaeological Association* 140: 1-17.

Bradley, R. (1990) *The Passage of Arms*. Cambridge, Cambridge University Press.

Breul, A. (1876) *Receuil des chartes de l'abbaye de Cluny*. Paris.

Brogiolo, G.P. (1980) Lettura archeologica di un territorio Pievano: l'esempio Gardesano. In *Cristianizzazione ed organizzazione ecclesiastica delle campagne nell'alto medioevo: espansione e resistenze (Settimane di studio del centro italiano di studi sull'alto medioevo 28)*, vol. 1: 281-300. Spoleto, Centro italiano di studi sull'alto medioevo.

Brogiolo, G.P. (1987) A proposito dell'organizzazione urbana nell'altomedioevo. *Archeologia medievale* 14: 27-46.

Brogiolo, G.P. (1989) Brescia: building transformations in a Lombard city. In K. Randsborg (ed.), *The Birth of Europe. Archaeology and Social Development in the First Millennium AD (Analecta Romana Institutum Danici Supplementum 16)*: 156-65. Rome, L'Erma di Bretschneider.

Brogiolo, G.P. (1992) Trasformazioni urbanistiche nella Brescia longobarda: delle capanne in legno al monastero regio di S. Salvatore. In C. Stella and G. Brentegani (eds), *S. Giulia di Brescia. Archeologia, arte, storia di un monastero regio dai Longobardi al Barbarossa*: 179-210. Brescia, Comune di Brescia.

Brown, P. (1981) *The Cult of Saints. Its Rise and Function in Latin Christianity*. Chicago, University of Chicago Press.

Brown, P. (1982) *Society and the Holy in Late Antiquity*. London, Faber and Faber.

Brozzi, M. (1972-73) Ribaria: un *fundus* trasformatosi in *curtis*. *Rivista della Società Friulana* 48-9: 1-9.

Brühl, C.R. (1971) Chronologie und Urkunden der Herzöge von Spoleto im 8. Jahrhundert. *Quellen und Forschungen* 51: 1-92.

Bruzza, P. (ed.) (1880) *Regesto della chiesa di Tivoli*. Rome.

Buck, R.J. and Small, A.M. (1985) Inscriptions from near San Giovanni di Ruoti (Potenza). *Epigraphica* 47: 98-109.

Bullough, D. (1975) *Imagines regum* and their significance in the early medieval west. In G. Robertson and G. Henderson (eds), *Studies in Memory of David Talbot Rice*: 223-76. Edinburgh, Edinburgh University Press.

Bullough, D. (1983) Burial, community and belief in the early medieval west. In P. Wormald, with D. Bullough and R. Collins (eds), *Ideal and Reality in Frankish and Anglo-Saxon Society. Studies Presented to J.M. Wallace-Hadrill*: 177-201. Oxford, Basil Blackwell.

Caballero Zoreda, L. (1984) Un típo cruciforme de iglesia visigoda: Melque, La Mata y Bande. In T.F.C. Blagg, R.F.J. Jones and S.J. Keay (eds), *Papers in Iberian Archaeology* part ii (BAR International Series 193): 570-86. Oxford, British Archaeological Reports.

Cann, S. and Lloyd, J. (1984) Late Roman and early medieval pottery from the Molise. *Archeologia medievale* 11: 425-36.

Cantino Wataghin, G. (1985) L'abbazia di Novalesa alla luce delle indagini archeologiche: verifiche e problemi. In *Dal Piemonte all'Europa: Esperienze monastiche nella società medievale (XXXIV congresso storico subalpino 1985)*: 569-85. Turin, Deputazione subalpine di storia patria – regione Piemonte.

Carbonara, G. (1979) *Iussu Desiderii. Monte Cassino e l'architettura Campano-Abruzzese nell'undicesimo secolo*. Rome, Istituti di fondamenti dell'architettura (Università degli studi di Roma).

Cassandro, G. (1969) Il ducato bizantino. In *Storia di Napoli* ii (1): 1-408. Naples, Società editrice storia di Napoli.

Cassels, J. (1955) The cemeteries of Cyrene. *Papers of the British School at Rome* 23: 1-43.

Castagnetti, A. (1979) *L'organizzazione del territorio rurale nel medioevo. Circoscrizioni ecclesiastiche e civili nella 'Langobardia' e nella 'Romania'*. Turin, Giappichelli editore.

Castritius, H. (1972) Zur Sozialgeschichte der Heermeister des Westreichs nach der Mitte des 5. JH.: Flavius Valila qui et Theodovius. *Ancient Society* 3: 233-43.

Cavallo, G. and Giardina, A. (1993) L'iconografia delle campagne nel libro antico. In A. Carandini, L. Cracco Ruggini and A. Giardina (eds), *Storia di Roma III. L'età tardoantica. I. Crisi e trasformazioni*: 323-48. Turin, Einaudi.

Chierici, G. (1957) Cimitile. *Palladio* n.s. 7 (1): 69-73.

Christie, N. (ed.) (1991) *Three South Etrurian Churches: Santa Cornelia, Santa Rufina and San Liberato (Archaeological Monograph of the British School at Rome* 4). London, The British School at Rome.

Cilento, N. (1966a) *Italia meridionale longobarda.* Milan/Naples, Riccardo Ricciardi editore.

Cilento, N. (1966b) *Le origini della signoria capuana nella Longobardia minore (Studi storici* 69-70). Rome, Istituto storico italiano per il medio evo.

Citarella, A.O. and Willard, H.M. (1983) *The Ninth-Century Treasure of Monte Cassino in the Context of Political and Economic Developments in South Italy (Miscellanea Cassinese* 50). Montecassino.

Clark, G. (1992) Town and countryside in medieval Italy: a critical evaluation of the sources for understanding the mechanisms of supply and demand. *Anthropozoologica* 16: 75-82.

Colvin, H. (1991) *Architecture and the After-Life.* New Haven/London, Yale University Press.

Conant, K. (1968) *Cluny. Les églises et la maison du Chef d'Ordre (Medieval Academy of America Publication no. 77).* Mâcon, Imprimerie Protat frères.

Cotton, M.A. (1979) *The Late Republican Villa at Posto, Francolise.* London, British School at Rome.

Cotton, M.A. and Métraux, G. (1985) *The San Rocco Villa at Francolise.* London, British School at Rome.

Coulston, J. and Gough, M. (1985) The coins and small finds at Alahan. In M. Gough (ed.), *Alahan. An Early Christian Monastery in Southern Turkey. Based on the Work of Michael Gough (Studies and Texts* 73): 62-74. Toronto, Pontifical Institute of Mediaeval Studies.

Coutts, C.M. and Mithen, S. (1985) The late Roman and early medieval cemeteries at San Vincenzo al Volturno: an evaluation of the mortuary data. In R. Hodges and J. Mitchell (eds), *San Vincenzo al Volturno: The Archaeology, Art and Territory of an Early Medieval Monastery (BAR International Series* 252): 61-81. Oxford, British Archaeological Reports.

Cowdrey, H.E.J. (1983) *The Age of Abbot Desiderius: Montecassino, the Papacy, and the Normans in the Eleventh and Early Twelfth Centuries.* Oxford, Clarendon Press.

Cramp, R. (1976) Monastic sites. In D.M. Wilson (ed.), *The Archaeology of Anglo-Saxon England:* 201-52. London, Methuen.

Craven, K. (1838) *Excursions in the Abruzzi and Northern Provinces of Naples.* London, Bentley.

Crawford, M.H. (1970) Money and exchange in the Roman world. *Journal of Roman Studies* 60: 40-8.

Crawford, M.H. (1985) Coins. In M.A. Cotton and G. Métraux, *The San Rocco Villa at Francolise*: 129-31. London, British School at Rome.

Davies, G. (1977) Burial in Italy up to Augustus. In R. Reece (ed.), *Burial in the Roman World (Research Report* 22): 13-19. London, Council for British Archaeology.

Davis-Weyer, C. (1986) *Early Medieval Art.* Toronto, University of Toronto Press.

Davis-Weyer, C. (1987) Müstair, Milano e l'Italia carolingia. In C. Bertelli (ed.), *Il millennio ambrosiano. Milano, una capitale da Ambrogio ai carolingi*: 202-37. Milan, Electa.

Dawes, E. and Baynes, N.H. (trans.) (1948) Theodore of Sykeon. In E. Dawes and N.H. Baynes (trans.), *Three Byzantine Saints*: 85-192. Oxford, Basil Blackwell.

De Hartel, G. (ed.) (1894) *Sancti Pontii Meropii Paulini Nolani Opera I, Epistulae; II, Carmina (Corpus Scriptorum Ecclesiasticorum Latinorum* 29-30).

Delogu, P. (1968) Strutture politiche e ideologia nel regno di Lodovico (Ricerche sull'aristocrazia carolingia in Italia, II). *Bullettino dell'istituto storico italiano per il medio evo e archivio muratoriano* 80: 137-89.

Delogu, P. (1977) *Mito di una città meridionale (Salerno, secoli VIII-XI) (Nuovo Medioevo* 2). Naples, Liguori editore.

Delogu, P. (1988) The rebirth of Rome in the eighth and ninth centuries. In R. Hodges and B. Hobley (eds), *The Rebirth of Towns in the West, 700-1050 (Research Report* 68): 32-42. London, Council for British Archaeology.

Delogu, P. (1990) Longobardi e Romani: altre congetture. In S. Gasparri and P. Cammarosano (eds), *Langobardia*: 111-67. Udine, Casamassima.

Delogu, P. (1992) Patroni, donatori, committenti nell'Italia meridionale longobarda. In *Committenti e produzione artistico-letteraria nell'alto medioevo occidentale (Settimane di studio del centro italiano di studi sull'alto medioevo* 39), vol. 1: 303-39. Spoleto, Centro italiano di studi sull'alto medioevo.

Del Treppo, M. (1953-54) Longobardi, Franchi e papato in due secoli di storia vulturnese. *Archivio storico per le province napoletane* 73 (n.s. 34): 37-59.

Del Treppo, M. (1955) La vita economica e sociale in una grande abbazia del Mezzogiorno; San Vincenzo al Volturno nell'alto medioevo. *Archivio storico per le province napoletane* 74 (n.s. 35): 31-110.

Del Treppo, M. (1968) *'Terra Sancti Cincenci'. L'abbazia di S. Vincenzo al Volturno nell'alto medioevo.* Naples, Libreria scientifica.

Dessau, H. (1892-) *Inscriptiones Latinae Selectae.* Berlin, Weidemann.

De Vogüé, A. (ed.) (1964a) *Caesarius of Arles, Regula I. 7; Regula Magistri 1.*

De Vogüé, A. (1964b) Travail et alimentation dans les régles de Saint Benôit et de Maître. *Revue Bénédictine* 74: 242-51.

De Vogüé, A. (1984) Le Plan de Saint-Gall, copie d'un document officiel? Une lecture de la lettre à Gozbert. *Revue Bénédictine* 94: 295-314.

Devroey, J.-P. (1993) '*Ad Utilitatem Monasterii*'. Mobiles et préoccupations de gestion dans l'économie monastique du monde franc. *Revue Bénédictine* 103: 224-40.

Di Cicco, A. (1974) *Castel San Vincenzo*. Castel San Vincenzo/Bugatti, Biblioteca comunale.

Dormeier, H. (1979) Montecassino und die Laien im 11. und 12. Jahrhundert (*Schriften der Monumenta Germaniae Historica* 27). Stuttgart, Hiersemann.

Douglass, W.A. (1969) *Death in Murelaga: Funerary Ritual in a Spanish Basque Village* (*American Ethnological Society Monograph* 49). Seattle/London, University of Washington Press.

Duby, G. (1974) *The Early Growth of the European Economy. Warriors and Peasants from the Seventh to the Twelfth Century*. London, Weidenfeld and Nicolson.

Duby, G. (1980) *The Three Orders. Feudal Society Imagined*. Chicago/London, University of Chicago Press.

Duchesne, L. (1886-92) *Le Liber Pontificalis. Texte, introduction et commentaire*, 2 vols (*Bibliothèque des Écoles Françaises d'Athènes et de Rome, 2ᵉ série*). Paris, Ernest Thorin.

Dunbabin, K.M.D. (1978) *The Mosaics of Roman North Africa. Studies in Iconography and Patronage*. Oxford, Clarendon Press.

Dyson, S.L. (1983) *The Roman Villas of Buccino* (BAR International Series 187). Oxford, British Archaeological Reports.

Eco, U. (1983) *The Name of the Rose*. London, Secker and Warburg.

Ercolani Cocchi, E. (1978) La circolazione monetale fra tardo antico e alto medioevo: dagli scavi di Villa Clelia. *Studi romagnoli* 29: 367-99.

Federici, V. (ed.) (1925) *Chronicon Vulturnense del monaco Giovanni*, 3 vols (*Fonti per la storia d'Italia* 58-60). Rome, Istituto storico italiano.

Federici, V. (1941) Ricerche per l'edizione del Chronicon Vulturnense del monaco Giovanni. *Bullettino dell'istituto storico italiano per il medio evo e archivio muratoriano* 57: 71-114.

Feller, L. (1988) Pouvoir et société dans les Abruzzes autour de l'an mil: aristocratie, *incastellamento*, appropriation des justices (960-1035). *Bullettino dell'istituto storico italiano per il medio evo e archivio muratoriano* 94: 1-72.

Felten, F.J. (1982) Zur Geschichte der Klöster Farfa und S. Vincenzo al Volturno im achten Jahrhundert. *Quellen und Forschungen* 62: 1-58.

Fentress, E. and Perkins, P. (1988) Counting African Red Slip Ware. In A. Mastino (ed.), *L'Africa romana (Atti del V convegno di studio, Sassari, 11-13 dicember 1987)* 5: 205-14. Sassari, Dipartimento di storia, Università degli studi.

Fentress, J. and Wickham, C. (1992) *Social Memory*. Oxford, Basil Blackwell.

Fernie, E. (1983) *The Architecture of the Anglo-Saxons*. London, Batsford.

Ferrara, V. (1988) *Canneto sul Trigno*. Vasto, Arte della stampa Cannarsa.

Février, P. (1978) Problèmes de l'habitat du Midi méditerranéen à la fin de l'antiquité et dans le haut moyen âge. *Jahrbuch des Römisch-Germanischen Zentralmuseums Mainz* 25: 208-47.

Foulke, W.D. (trans.) (1974) *Paul the Deacon, History of the Lombards*. Philadelphia.

Freed, J. (1983) Pottery from the late middens at San Giovanni. In M. Gualtieri, M. Salvatore and A. Small (eds), *Lo scavo di San Giovanni di Ruoti ed il periodo tardoantico in Basilicata*: 91-106. Bari, Adriatica editrice (for the Centro accademico canadese in Italia and the Soprintendenza archeologica della Basilicata).

Gabba, E. (1975) Mercati e fiere nell'Italia Romana. *Studi classici e orientali* 24: 140-63.

Gabba, E. (1988) *Del buon uso della ricchezza. Saggi di storia economica e sociale del mondo antico*. Milan, Guerini e associati.

Garwood, P., Jennings, D., Skeates, R. and Toms, J. (eds) (1991) *Sacred and Profane* (*Monograph* 32). Oxford, Oxford University Committee for Archaeology.

Gasparri, S. (1978) *I duchi longobardi* (*Studi storici* 109). Rome, Istituto storico italiano per il medio evo.

Gatto, L. (1974) Ugo Maumouzet, conte di Manoppello, normanno d'Abruzzo. In *Studi sul medioevo cristiano offerti a Raffaello Morghen per il 90° anniversario dell'istituto storico italiano (1883-1973)* i (*Studi storici* 83-7): 355-73. Rome, Istituto storico italiano per il medio evo.

Gattola, E. (1733) *Historia abbatiae cassinensis per saeculorum seriem distribuita*, 2 vols. Venice.

Gattola, E. (1734) *Accessiones ad historiam abbatiae cassinensis*, 2 vols. Venice.

Geary, P.J. (1978) *Furta Sacra. Thefts of Relics in the Central Middle Ages*. Princeton, Princeton University Press.

Gentili, G.V. (1971) Scavi e scoperte negli ultimi dieci anni nell'Emilia e nella Romagna. *Atti del II congresso nazionale di archeologia cristiana*: 205-32. Rome, L'Erma di Bretschneider.

Goffart, W. (1966) *The Le Mans Forgeries. A Chapter from the History of Church Property in the Ninth Century* (*Harvard Historical Studies* 76). Cambridge (Mass.), Harvard University Press.

Goldschmidt, R.C. (1940) *Paulinus' Churches at Nola*. Amsterdam, N.V. Noord-Hollandsche Vitgevers Maatschappij.

Goldstein. L. (1981) One-dimensional archaeology and multi-dimensional people: spatial organisation and mortuary analysis. In R. Chapman, I. Kinnes and K. Randsborg (eds), *The Archaeology of Death*: 53-69. Cambridge, Cambridge University Press.

Gough, M. (ed.) (1985) *Alahan. An Early Christian Monastery in Southern Turkey. Based on the Work of Michael Gough* (*Studies and Texts* 73). Toronto, Pontifical Institute of Mediaeval Studies.

Gualtieri, M., Salvatore, M. and Small, A. (eds) (1983) *Lo scavo di S. Giovanni di Ruoti ed il periodo tardoantico in Basilicata*. Bari, Adriatica editrice (for the Centro accademico canadese in Italia and the Soprintendenza archeologica della Basilicata).

Guidoboni, E. (ed.) (1989) *I terremoti prima del mille in Italia e nell'area mediterranea*. Bologna, Istituto nazionale di geofisica (SGA Storia-geofisica-ambiente).

Gundlach, W., Dümmler, E. and Arndt, W. (1892/1957) *Monumenta Germaniae Historica, Epistolae III*. Berlin, Weidmann.

Gutmann, D. (1977) Dying to power: death and the search for self-esteem. In H. Feifel (ed.), *New Meanings of Death* (new edition): 336-47. New York/London, McGraw Hill.

Harrison, M. (1985) The inscriptions and chronology of Alahan. In M. Gough (ed.), *Alahan. An Early Christian Monastery in Southern Turkey. Based on the Work of Michael Gough* (*Studies and Texts* 73): 21-34. Toronto, Pontifical Institute of Mediaeval Studies.

Haslam, J. (1987) Market and fortress in England in the reign of Offa. *World Archaeology* 19 (1): 76-93.

Heitz, C. (1980) *L'architecture religieuse carolingienne. Les formes et leurs fonctions*. Paris, Picard.

Hendy, M. (1991) East and West: divergent models of coinage and its use. In *Il secolo di ferro: mito e realtà del secolo X* (*Settimane di studio del centro italiano di studi sull'alto medioevo* 38), vol. 2: 637-79. Spoleto, Centro italiano di studi sull'alto medioevo.

Herlihy, D. (1961) Church property on the European continent, 701-1200. *Speculum* 36: 81-105.

Herlihy, D. (1985) *Medieval Households*. Cambridge (Mass.)/London, Harvard University Press.

Héron, C. and Meyer, O. (1991) L'environnement urbain du monastère de Saint-Denis. *Les dossiers d'archéologie* 158: 76-89.

Higgins, V. (1985) A preliminary analysis of some of the early medieval human skeletons from San Vincenzo al Volturno. In R. Hodges and J. Mitchell (eds), *San Vincenzo al Volturno: the Archaeology, Art and Territory of an Early Medieval Monastery* (BAR International Series 252): 111-24. Oxford, British Archaeological Reports.

Higgins, V. (1990) *Health patterns in rural agricultural communities of the late Roman and early medieval periods: a study of two skeletal groups from San Vincenzo*. Unpublished Ph.D. thesis, Department of Archaeology and Prehistory, University of Sheffield.

Higham, N.J. (1993) *The Kingdom of Northumbria, AD 350-1100*. Stroud, Alan Sutton.

Hobsbawm, E. (1983) Introduction: inventing traditions. In E. Hobsbawm and T. Ranger (eds), *The Invention of Tradition*: 1-14. Cambridge, Cambridge University Press.

Hodges, R. (1981) Excavations and survey at San Vincenzo al Volturno, Molise: 1980. *Archeologia medievale* 8: 483-92.

Hodges, R. (1985) Excavations at San Vincenzo al Volturno: a regional and international centre from AD 400-1100. In R. Hodges and J. Mitchell (eds), *San Vincenzo al Volturno. The Archaeology, Art and Territory of an Early Medieval Monastery* (BAR International Series 252): 1-36. Oxford, British Archaeological Reports.

Hodges, R. (1989) *The Anglo-Saxon Achievement*. London, Duckworth.

Hodges, R. (1990) Rewriting the rural history of early medieval Italy: twenty-five years of medieval archaeology reviewed. *Rural History* 1 (1): 17-36.

Hodges, R. (1992) Villaggi altomedioevali nell'alta valle del Volturno. *Almanacco del Molise* (2): 71-96.

Hodges, R. (1993a) Il declino e la caduta: San Vincenzo al Volturno. In A. Carandini, L.C. Ruggini and A. Giardina (eds), *La storia di Roma III (ii)*: 255-78. Turin, Einaudi.

Hodges, R. (1993b) The riddle of St Peter's republic. In L. Paroli and P. Delogu (eds), *La storia economica di Roma nell'alto medioevo alla luce dei recenti scavi archeologici*: 353-66. Florence, All'Insegna del Giglio.

Hodges, R. (1994) In the shadow of Pirenne: San Vincenzo al Volturno and the revival of mediterranean commerce. In R. Francovich and G. Noyé (eds), *La storia dell'alto medioevo italiano (VI-X secolo) alla luce dell'archeologia*: 109-28. Florence, All'Insegna del Giglio.

Hodges, R. and Patterson, H. (1986) San Vincenzo al Volturno and the origins of the medieval pottery industry in Italy. In *La ceramica medievale nel mediterraneo occidentale*: 13-26. Florence, All'Insegna del Giglio.

Hodges, R. and Whitehouse, D. (1983) *Mohammed, Charlemagne and the Origins of Europe. Archaeology and the Pirenne Thesis*. London, Duckworth.

Hodges, R. and Wickham, C.J. (forthcoming) The evolution of hilltop villages in Molise. In G. Barker (ed.), *The Archaeology and History of a Mediterranean Valley*. Leicester, Leicester University Press.

Hodges, R., Barker, G. and Wade, K. (1980) Excavations at D85 (Santa Maria in Città): an early medieval hilltop settlement in Molise. *Papers of the British School at Rome* 48: 70-124.

Hodges, R., Gibson, S. and Hanasz, A. (1990) Campo La Fontana: a late eighth-century triconch and the Ponte Latrone at the entrance to the territory of San Vincenzo al Volturno. *Papers of the British School at Rome* 45: 273-97 + plates.

Hodges, R., Grierson, P., Herring, P., Higgins, V., Nowakowski, J., Patterson, H. and Wickham, C. (1984) Excavations at Vacchereccia (Rocchetta Nuova): a later Roman and early medieval settlement in the Volturno valley, Molise. *Papers of the British School at Rome* 52: 148-94 + plates.

Hoffmann, H. (1966) Das *Chronicon Vulturnense* und die Chronik von Montecassino. *Deutches Archiv für Erforschung des Mittelalters* 22: 179-96.

Hoffmann, H. (ed.) (1980) *Chronica monasterii Casinensis, Monumenta Germaniae Historica, Scriptores* 34. Hanover, Hansche Buchhandlung.

Hope-Taylor, B. (1977) *Yeavering: an Anglo-British Centre of Early Northumbria*. London, HMSO.

Horn, W. and Born, E. (1979) *The Plan of Saint Gall. A Study of the Architecture and Economy of, and Life in, a Paradigmatic Carolingian Monastery*, 3 vols. Berkeley, University of California Press.

Houben, H. (1985) Karl der Große und die Absetzung des Abtes Potho von San Vincenzo am Volturno. *Quellen und Forschungen aus Italienischen Archiven und Bibliotheken* 65: 405-17.

Hubert, J., Porcher, J. and Volbach, W.F. (1969) *Europe of the Invasions*. New York, George Braziller.

Hugot, G. (1965) Die Pfalz Karls des Grossen in Aachen. In W. Braunfels and H. Schnitzler (eds), *Karolingische Kunst − Karl der Grosse, Lebenswerk und Nachleben* III: 534-72. Düsseldorf, L. Schwann Verlag.

Huntington, W.R. and Metcalf, P.A. (1979) *Celebrations of Death: the Anthropology of Mortuary Ritual*. Cambridge, Cambridge University Press.

Jacobsen, W. (1992) *Der Klosterplan von St. Gallen und die Karolingische Architektur*. Berlin, Deutscher Verlag für Kunstwissenschaft Berlin.

Jaffé, P. (ed.) (1885) *Regesta Pontificum Romanorum ab condita Ecclesia ad annum post Christum Natum, MCXCVIII*, 2 vols. Leipzig, Veit et Comp.

James, E. (1977) *The Merovingian Archaeology of South-West Gaul*, 2 vols (BAR International Series 25). Oxford, British Archaeological Reports.

James, E. (1978) Cemeteries and the problem of Frankish settlement in Gaul. In P.H. Sawyer (ed.), *Words, Names, and Graves: Early Medieval Settlement*: 55-89. Leeds, The School of History, University of Leeds.

James, E. (1981) Archaeology and the Merovingian monastery. In H.B. Clarke and M. Brennan (eds), *Columbanus and Merovingian Monasticism* (BAR International Series 113): 33-55. Oxford, British Archaeological Reports.

Jamison, E. (ed.) (1972) *Catalogus Baronum (Fonti per la storia d'Italia pubblicate dall'istituto storico italiano per il medio evo* 101). Rome, Istituto storico italiano per il medio evo.

Jones, A.H.M. (1964) *The Later Roman Empire 284-602*, 3 vols + maps. Oxford, Basil Blackwell.

Jones, G.D.B. (1962) Capena and the Ager Capenas. *Papers of the British School at Rome* 30: 116-210.

Jones, G.D.B. (1963) Capena and the Ager Capenas. Part II. *Papers of the British School at Rome* 31: 100-58.

Krautheimer, R. (1971) *Studies in Early Christian, Medieval and Renaissance Art*. London, University of London Press Limited.

Krautheimer, R. (1980) *Rome: Profile of a City, 312-1308*. New Jersey, Princeton University Press.

Kreusch, F. (1965) Kirche, Atrium und Portikus der Aachener Pfalz. In W. Braunfels and H. Schnitzler (eds), *Karolingische Kunst − Karl der Grosse, Lebenswerk und Nachleben* III: 463-533. Düsseldorf, L. Schwann Verlag.

Krier, J. and Wagner, R. (1985) Zur frühgeschichte des Willibrordus-Klosters in Echternach. *Revue d'histoire Luxembourgeoise* 1: 15-51.

Lane Fox, R. (1986) *Pagans and Christians*. London, Viking.

La Regina, A. (1989) I Sanniti. In G. Pugliese Carratelli (ed.), *Italia omnium terrarum parens*: 299-432. Milan, Scheiwiller/Credito italiano.

La Regina, A. (1990) Safinum dal conflitto con Roma alla 'Tota Italia'. In N. Paone (ed.), *Il Molise. Arte, cultura, paesaggi*: 31-5. Rome, Palombi.

La Rocca Hudson, C. (1986) 'Dark Ages' a Verona: edilizia privata, aree aperte e strutture pubbliche in una città dell'Italia settentrionale. *Archeologia medievale* 13: 31-78.

La Rosa, A. (1971) Siracusa – lavori nella latomia di S. Venera. *Notizie degli scavi di antichità; Atti della accademia nazionale dei lincei*, Ser. 8, 25: 575-80.

Lauer, P. (1911) *Le palais de Latran*. Paris, E. Leroux.

Leccisotti, T. (1987) *Monte Cassino (Abbazia di Montecassino scritti vari 1)*. Montecassino, Abbey of Monte Cassino.

Le Goff, J. (1980) *Time, Work, and Culture in the Middle Ages*. Chicago/London, University of Chicago Press.

Le Goff, J. (1988) The wilderness in the medieval west. In J. Le Goff, *The Medieval Imagination*: 47-59. Chicago/London, Chicago University Press.

Le Maho, J. (1993) Le groupe épiscopal de Rouen du IVᵉ au Xᵉ siècle. In J. Stratford (ed.), *Medieval Art, Architecture and Archaeology at Rouen*: 20-30. London, British Archaeological Association.

Leonardi, C. (1968) Spriritualità di Ambrogio Autperto. *Studi medievali* 9 (1): 1-131.

Leveau, P. (1983) La ville antique et l'organisation de l'espace rural: villa, ville, villages. *Annales. Économies – Sociétés – Civilisations* 38 (4): 920-42.

Liebeschuetz, W. (1979) Problems arising from the conversion of Syria. *Studies in Church History* 16: 17-24.

Lienhard, J.T. (1977) *Paulinus of Nola and Early Western Monasticism*. Cologne/Bonn.

Linklater, E. (1951) *The Campaign in Italy*. London, HMSO.

Littlewood, A.R. (1992) Gardens of Byzantium. *Journal of Garden History* 12 (2): 126-53.

Löfstedt, B. (ed.) (1971) *Zenonis Veronensis tractatus (Corpus Christianorum, Series Latina 22)*. Turnholt, Brepols.

Loud, G.A. (1985) *Church and Society in the Norman Principality of Capua, 1058-1197*. Oxford, Clarendon Press.

Mancone, A. (1960) Ambrogio Autperto. In *Dizionario biografico degli italiani* 2: 711-13. Rome, Istituto della enciclopedia italiana.

Marazzi, F. (1994) Le 'città nouve' pontificie e l'insediamento laziale nel IX secolo. In R. Francovich and G. Noyé (eds), *La storia dell'alto medioevo italiano (VI-X secolo) alla luce dell'archeologia*: 251-78. Florence, All'Insegna del Giglio.

Marrou, H.I. (1954) Un lieu dit Cité de Dieu. *Augustinus Magister Congres International Augustinien* I: 101-10. Paris.

Martin, J.-M. (1980) Eléments préféodaux dans les pricipautés de Bénévent et de Capoue (fin du VIIIᵉ siècle-début du XIᵉ siècle): modalités de privatisation du pouvoir. In *Structures féodales et féodalisme dans l'occident méditerranéen (Xᵉ-XIIIᵉ siècles) (Collection de l'École Française de Rome 44)*: 553-86. Rome, École Française de Rome.

Massari, G., Roffia, E., Bolla, M. and Caporusso, D. (1985) La villa tardoromana di Palazzo Pignano (Cremona). In G. Pontiroli (ed.), *Cremona romana. Atti del congresso storico archeologico per il 2200 anno di fondazione di Cremona (Cremona, 30-31 maggio 1982) (Annali della biblioteca statale e libreria civica di Cremona 35 (1984))*: 185-227. Cremona, Biblioteca statale e libreria civica di Cremona.

Matthiae, G. (1967) *Mosaici medioevali delle chiese di Roma*. Rome, Istituto poligrafico dello stato.

Mattingly, D. and Hayes, J.W. (1992) Nador and fortified farms in North Africa. *Journal of Roman Archaeology* 5: 408-18.

Mazza, S. (1978-79) Il complesso fortificato di Torba. *Sibrium* 14: 187-215.

McClendon, C.B. (1987) *The Imperial Abbey of Farfa. Architectural Currents of the Early Middle Ages (Yale Publications in the History of Art 36)*. New Haven/London, Yale University Press.

McKitterick, R. (1983) *The Frankish Kingdoms under the Carolingians, 751-987*. London, Longman.

McKitterick, R. (ed.) (1994) *Carolingian Culture: Emulation and Innovation*. Cambridge, Cambridge University Press.

Meyer, O. (1993) Le bourg monastique de Saint-Denis. In M. Petit and M. Depratère-Dargery, *L'Ile-de-France de Clovis a Hugues Capet du Vᵉ siècle au Xᵉ siècle*: 91-6. Condè-sur-Noireau, Editions du Valhermeil.

Meyvaert, P. (1980) Review of 'The Plan of St Gall'. *University Publishing* 9: 18-19.

Migne, P.G. (1844-63) *Patrologiae cursus completus, series latina*.

Migne, P.G. (1857-76) *Patrologiae cursus completus, series graeca.*

Mirabella Roberti, M. (1970) Una basilica e una villa a palazzo Pignano. *Arte lombarda* 15: 115-16.

Mitchell, J. (1985) The painted decoration of the early medieval monastery. In R. Hodges and J. Mitchell (eds), *San Vincenzo al Volturno. The Archaeology, Art and Territory of an Early Medieval Monastery* (BAR International Series 252): 125-76. Oxford, British Archaeological Reports.

Mitchell, J. (1990) Literacy displayed: the use of inscriptions at the monastery of San Vincenzo al Volturno in the early ninth century. In R. McKitterick (ed.), *The Uses of Literacy in Early Medieval Europe:* 186-225. Cambridge, Cambridge University Press.

Mitchell, J. (1994) The display of script and the uses of paintings in Longobard Italy. *Testo e immagine nell'alto medioevo* (*Settimane di studio del centro italiano di studi sull'alto medioevo* 41): 887-951. Spoleto, Centro italiano di studi sull'alto medioevo.

Monaco, D. (1989) La via latina nel territorio dell'alto Volturno. In E. Nocera (ed.), *Almanacco del Molise* (2): 83-103.

Moreland, J. (1985) A monastic workshop and glass production at San Vincenzo al Volturno, Molise, Italy. In R. Hodges and J. Mitchell (eds), *San Vincenzo al Volturno. The Archaeology, Art and Territory of an Early Medieval Monastery* (BAR International Series 252): 37-60. Oxford, British Archaeological Reports.

Morra, G. and Valente, F. (1993) *Il Castello di Venafro. Storia-arte-architettura.* Campobasso, Edizione enne.

Mühlbacher, E. *et al.* (eds) (1906) *Monumenta Germaniae Historica, Diplomata Karolinorum.* Hanover.

Mutzenbecher, A. (ed.) (1962) *Maximi episcopi Taurinensis Collectionem Sermonum antiquam, nonnullis sermonibus extravagantibus adiectis* (*Corpus Christianorum, Series Latina* 23). Turnholt, Brepols.

Narroll, R. (1962) Floor area and settlement population. *American Antiquity* 27: 187-9.

Neal, D. (1982) Romano-British villas: one or two storied. In P.J. Drury (ed.), *Structural Reconstruction. Approaches to the Interpretation of the Excavated Remains of Buildings* (BAR British Series 110): 153-71. Oxford, British Archaeological Reports.

Nees, L. (1986) The Plan of St Gall and the theory of the program of Carolingian art. *Gesta* 25 (1): 1-8.

Negro Ponzi Mancini, M.M. (1980) Villaro di Ticineto (AL). Note per lo studio del popolamento rurale e della dinamica del territorio. In *Studi di archeologia dedicati a Pietro Barocelli*: 151-89. Turin, Soprintendenza archeologica del Piemonte.

Negro Ponzi Mancini, M.M. (1982) Villaro di Ticineto (Alessandria). La chiesa paleocristiana e altomedievale. Notizie preliminari sulle campagne 1975-1976. In *Atti del V congresso nazionale di archeologia cristiana*: 211-25. Rome, Viella.

Nestori, A. (1979) Monumentum Fl. Eusebi fatto *Ecclesia S. Eusebi* presso Roncaglione (*Studi di antichità cristiana* 34). Vatican City, Pontificio istituto di archeologia cristiana.

Nestori, A. (1981) In *Atti del convegno paleocristiano nella Tuscia*: 69-75. Viterbo.

Noble, T.P.X. (1976) The monastic ideal as a model for Empire: the case of Louis the Pious. *Revue Bénédictine* 86: 235-50.

Nordberg, D. (ed.) (1982) *Gregoria Magnus, Registrum Epistularum.* Turnholt, Brepols.

Noyé, G. (1991) Les *Bruttii* au VIe siècle. *Mélanges de l'École Française de Rome. Moyen Age* 103 (2): 505-51.

O'Donnell, J.J. (1979) *Cassiodorus.* Berkeley/London, University of California Press.

Osborne, J. (1983) The tomb of Alfanus in S. Maria in Cosmedin, Rome and its place in the tradition of Roman funerary monuments. *Papers of the British School at Rome* 51: 240-7.

O'Shea, J. (1981) Social configurations and the archaeological study of mortuary practices: a case study. In R. Chapman, I. Kinnes and K. Randsborg (eds), *The Archaeology of Death*: 39-52. Cambridge, Cambridge University Press.

Pallottino, M. (1937) Capena. Resti di costruzioni romane e medioevali in località 'Montecanino'. *Notizie degli scavi di antichità; Atti della accademia nazionale dei lincei,* Ser. 6, 13: 7-28.

Panella, C. (1986) Le merci: produzioni, itinerari e destini. In A. Giardini (ed.), *Società romana e impero tardoantica. Vol. 3. Le merci, gli insediamenti*: 432-59. Rome/Bari, Laterza.

Panella, C. (1993) Merci e scambi nel Mediterraneo tardoantico. In A. Carandini, L.C. Ruggini and A. Giardina (eds), *La storia di Roma III (ii)*: 613-97. Turin, Einaudi.

Panofsky, E. (1960) *Renaissance and Renascences in Western Art.* Stockholm, Almqvist and Wiksell.

Pantoni, A. (1970) *San Vincenzo al Volturno e la cripta dell'abate Epifanio 824/842.* Monte Cassino, Edizioni dell'abbazia di Montecassino.

Pantoni, A. (1973) *Le vicende della basilica di Montecassino attraverso la documentazione archeologica* (*Miscellanea Cassinese* 36). Montecassino.

Pantoni, A. (1980a) *Le chiese e gli edifici del monastero di San Vincenzo al Volturno* (*Miscellanea Cassinese* 40). Montecassino.

Pantoni, A. (1980b) *L'acropoli di Montecassino e il primitivo monastero di San Benedetto* (*Miscellanea Cassinese* 43). Montecassino.

Parker, E.C. and Little, C.T. (1994) *The Cloisters Cross, its Art and Meaning*. London, Harvey Miller.

Parker Pearson, M. (1993) The powerful dead: archaeological relationships between the living and the dead. *Cambridge Archaeological Journal* 3 (2): 203-29.

Patlagean, E. (1977) *Pauvreté économique et pauvreté sociale à Byzance 4e-7e siècles*. Paris-La Haye, Mouton.

Patterson, H. (1985) The late Roman and early medieval pottery from Molise. In R. Hodges and J. Mitchell (eds), *San Vincenzo al Volturno. The Archaeology, Art and Territory of an Early Medieval Monastery* (BAR International Series 252): 83-110. Oxford, British Archaeological Reports.

Patterson, H. (1989) *The Later Roman and Early Medieval to Medieval Pottery from San Vincenzo al Volturno, Molise: Production and Distribution in Central and Southern Italy, AD 400-1100*. Unpublished PhD thesis, Department of Archaeology and Prehistory, University of Sheffield.

Patterson, J. (1985) A city called Samnium. In R. Hodges and J. Mitchell (eds), *San Vincenzo al Volturno. The Archaeology, Art and Territory of an Early Medieval Monastery* (BAR International Series 252): 185-200. Oxford, British Archaeological Reports.

Pavan, G. (1990) Architettura del periodo longobardo. In G.C. Menis (ed.), *I Longobardi*: 236-98. Milan, Electa.

Peduto, P. (1990) Insediamenti longobardi del ducato di Benevento. In S. Gasparri and P. Cammarosano (eds), *Langobardia*: 307-74. Udine, Casamassima.

Peebles, C.S. and Kus, S. (1977) Some archaeological correlates of ranked societies. *American Antiquity* 42: 421-48.

Pentz, P. (1992) *The Invisible Conquest. The Ontogenesis of Sixth and Seventh Century Syria*. Copenhagen, National Museum of Denmark.

Percival, J. (1976) *The Roman Villa. An Historical Introduction*. London, Batsford.

Petroccia, D. (1980) Il problema di Samnia. Città eponima dei Sanniti I. *Samnium* 53: 160-85.

Petroccia, D. (1981) Il problema di Samnia. Città eponima dei Sanniti. *Samnium* 54: 29-61.

Picasso, G. (1985) Il pontificato romano e l'abbazia di San Vincenzo al Volturno. In F. Avagliano (ed.), *Una grande abbazia altomedievale nel Molise. San Vincenzo al Volturno* (*Atti del I convegno di studi sul medioevo meridionale*) (*Miscellanea Cassinese* 51): 233-48. Montecassino.

Pietri, C. (1981) Aristocratie et société clericale dans l'Italie Chrétienne au temps d'Odacre et de Théoderic. *Mélanges de l'École Française de Rome. Antiquité* 93 (1): 417-67.

Pietri, C. (1986) Chiesa e comunità locali nell'occidente cristiano (IV-VI D.C.): L'esempio della Gallia. In A. Giardina (ed.), *Società romana e impero tardoantica. Vol. 3. Le merci, gli insediamenti*: 761-95. Rome/Bari, Laterza.

Potter, T.W. (1979) *The Changing Landscape of South Etruria*. London, Elek.

Potter, T.W. (1993) The Mola di Monte Gelato: a microcosm of the history of Roman and early medieval Rome? In L. Paroli and P. Delogu (eds), *La storia economica di Roma nell'alto medioevo alla luce dei recenti scavi archeologici*: 137-52. Florence, All'Insegna del Giglio.

Potter, T.W. and Whitehouse, D.B. (1982) A Roman building in the Cambridgeshire fens and some parallels near Rome. *World Archaeology* 14 (2): 218-23.

Poupardin, R. (1907) *Les institutions politiques et administratives des principautés Lombardes de l'Italie méridionale (IXᵉ-XIᵉ siècles)*. Paris, Honoré Champion.

Pratesi, A. (1976) Cronache e documenti. In *Fonti medioevali e problematica storiografica* i: 336-50. Rome.

Pringle, D. (1981) *The Defence of Byzantine Africa from Justinian to the Arab Conquest*, 2 vols (BAR Supplementary Series 99). Oxford, British Archaeological Reports.

Rabotti, G. (ed.) (1985) *Breviarium ecclesiae Ravennatis (Codice Bavaro), secoli VII-X* (*Fonti per la storia d'Italia pubblicate dall'istituto storico italiano per il medio evo* 110). Rome, Istituto storico italiano per il medioevo.

Randsborg, K. (1991) *The First Millennium A.D. in Europe and the Mediterranean. An Archaeological Essay*. Cambridge, Cambridge University Press.

Raspi Serra, J. (1976) Una necropoli altomedioevale a Corviano (Bomarzo) ed il problema delle sepolture a 'Logette' lungo le sponde Mediterranee. *Bollettino d'arte* 61: 144-69.

Remondini, G. (1747-57) *Della Nolana eclesisastica storia alla Santitá di N.S. Sommo Regnante Ponteficie Benedetto XIV dedicata*, 3 vols. Naples, G. di Simone.

Rhein, P. (1986) *Altenmünster und die Lorscher Klöster. Führungsblatt zu den drei Mittelalterlichen Klosterstandorten von Lorsch im Landkreis Bergstraße (Archäologische Denkmäler in Hessen* 61). Wiesbaden, Abteilung für Vor- und Frühgeschichte im Landesamt für Denkmalpflege Hessen.

Riché, P. (1978) *Daily Life in the World of Charlemagne.* Liverpool, Liverpool University Press.

Roffia, A. (1978) In *Notiziario di archeologia medievale* Dec: 34.

Rossi, P. (1993) Elementi per l'individuazione di una tipologia di ambone 'romano' in epoca altomedievale. *Arte medievale* 7 (1): 1-13.

Rubeus, H. (1589) *Historiae Ravennates III.* Venice.

Ruggiero, B. (1966-67) Il ducato di Spoleto e i tentativi di penetrazione dei Franchi nell'Italia meridionale. *Archivio storico per le province napoletane* 84-5: 77-116.

Saller, R.P. (1987) Men's age at marriage and its consequences in the Roman family. *Classical Philology* 82: 21-34.

Sanderson, W. (1985) The Plan of St. Gall reconsidered. *Speculum* 60 (3): 615-32.

Saxe, A.A. (1970) *Social Dimensions of Mortuary Practices.* Unpublished Ph.D thesis, University of Michigan.

Scaccia Scarafoni, E. (1944) La 'torre di S. Benedetto' e le fabbriche medioevali di Montecassino (ricerche di topografia). *Bullettino dell'istituto storico italiano per il medio evo e archivio muratoriano* 59: 137-83.

Scaccia Scarafoni, E. (1946) La chiesa cassinese detta 'S. Maria delle Cinque Torri'. *Rivista di archeologia cristiana* 22: 139-89.

Schieffer, T. (ed.) (1966) *Monumenta Germaniae Historica, Diplomata Lotharii I.* Berlin.

Schmid, K. (1972) Zur Ablosung der Langobardenherrschaft durch den Franken. *Quellen und Forschungen aus Italienischen Archiven und Bibliotheken* 52: 1-36.

Sella, P. (ed.) (1936) *Rationes decimarum italiae. Le decime dei secoli XIII-XIV, Aprutium-Molisium (Studi e Testi* 69). Vatican City, Biblioteca Apostolica Vaticana.

Semmler, A. (ed.) (1963) *Statuta Murbacensia. Corp. cons. mon.* 1, 448.

Seston, W. (1934) Le monastére d'Ain Tamda et les origines de l'architecture monastique en Afrique du Nord. *Mélanges d'archéologie et d'histoire* 51: 79-113.

Settia, A.A. (1980) Pievi e cappelle nella dinamica del popolamento rurale. In *Cristianizzazione ed organizzazione ecclesiastica delle campagne nell'alto medioevo: espanzione e resistenze (Settimane di studio del centro italiano di studi sull'alto medioevo* 28), vol. 1: 445-93. Spoleto, Centro italiano di studi sull'alto medioevo.

Settia, A.A. (1991) *Chiese, strade e fortezze nell'Italia medievale (Italia sacra. Studi e documenti di storia ecclesiastica* 46). Rome, Herder Editrice e Libreria.

Shaw, B.D. (1981) Rural markets in North Africa and the political economy of the Roman Empire. *Antiquités africaines* 17: 37-83.

Sheehan, M.M. (1985) Religious life and monastic organization at Alahan. In M. Gough (ed.), *Alahan. An Early Christian Monastery in Southern Turkey. Based on the Work of Michael Gough (Studies and Texts* 73): 197-220. Toronto, Pontifical Institute of Mediaeval Studies.

Shennan, S. (1975) The social organization at Branc̆. *Antiquity* 49: 279-88.

Sickel, Th.E.Ab. (ed.) (1889) *Liber diurnus Romanorum Pontificium ex unico Codice Vaticano.* Vienna, C. Geroldi.

Small, A. (1983) Gli edifici del periodo tardo-antico a San Giovanni. In M. Gualtieri, M. Salvatore and A. Small (eds), *Lo scavo di S. Giovanni di Ruoti ed il periodo tardoantico in Basilicata*: 21-46. Bari, Adriatica editrice (for the Centro accademico canadese in Italia and the Soprintendenza archeologica della Basilicata).

Small, A. and Freed, J. (1986) S. Giovanni di Ruoti (Basilicata). Il contesto della villa tardoromano. In A. Giardina (ed.), *Società romana e impero tardoantico. Vol. 3. Le merci, gli insediamenti*: 97-129. Rome/Bari, Laterza.

Smith, J.M.H. (1992) *Province and Empire: Brittany and the Carolingians.* Cambridge, Cambridge University Press.

Stancliffe, C. (1983) *St Martin and his Hagiographer. History and Miracle in Sulpicius Severus.* Oxford, Clarendon Press.

Steele, G. (1983) The analysis of animal remains from two late Roman middens at San Giovanni di Ruoti. In M. Gualtieri, M. Salvatore and A. Small (eds), *Lo scavo di S. Giovanni di Ruoti ed il periodo tardoantico in Basilicata*: 75-84. Bari, Adriatica editrice (for the Centro accademico canadese in Italia and the Soprintendenza archeologica della Basilicata).

Stein, E. (1959) *Histoire du bas-empire. Tome I, 1-2: De l'état romain à l'état Byzantin (284-476).* Bruges, Desclée de Brouwer.

Stenton, F.M. (1971) *Anglo-Saxon England*, third edition. Oxford, Clarendon Press.

Steuer, H. (1989) Archaeology and history: proposals on the social structure of the Merovingian kingdom. In K. Randsborg (ed.), *The Birth of Europe. Archaeology and Social Development in the First Millennium AD* (*Analecta Romana Institutum Danici Supplementum* 16): 100-22. Rome, L'Erma di Bretschneider.

Stevenson, J. (1978) *The Catacombs: Rediscovered Monuments of Early Christianity*. London, Thames and Hudson.

Stevenson, J. (1988) Glass lamps from San Vincenzo al Volturno, Molise. *Papers of the British School at Rome* 56: 198-209.

Tabacco, G. (1979) *Egemonie sociali e strutture del potere nel medioevo italiano*. Turin, Einaudi.

Tainter, J.A. (1975) Social inference and mortuary practices: an experiment in numerical classification. *World Archaeology* 7 (1): 1-15.

Tainter, J.A. (1977) Modeling change in prehistoric social systems. In L.R. Binford (ed.), *For Theory Building in Archaeology*: 327-51. London, Academic Press.

Tamponi, P. (1897) Noto vecchio (*Netum*) – esplorazioni archeologiche. *Notizie degli scavi di antichità; Atti della accademia nazionale dei lincei*: 69-92.

Taylor, H.M. (1975) Tenth-century church building in England and on the continent. In D. Parsons (ed.), *Tenth-Century Studies. Essays in Commemoration of the Millennium of the Council of Winchester and 'Regularis Concordia'*: 141-68. London, Phillimore.

Tchalenko, G. (1953) *Villages antiques de la Syrie du Nord. Le massif du Bélus à l'epoque romaine I*. Paris, Paul Geuthner.

Testini, P. (1985) Note per servire allo studio del complesso paleocristiano di S. Felice a Cimitile (Nola). *Mélanges de l'École Française de Rome. Antiquité* 97 (1): 329-71.

Theuws, F. (1991) Landed property and manorial organisation in Northern Austrasia: some considerations and a case study. In N. Roymans and F. Theuws (eds), *Images of the Past. Studies on Ancient Societies in Northwestern Europe*: 299-407. Amsterdam, Instituut voor Pre- en Protohistorische Archeologie Albert Egges van Giffen (IPP).

Thiel, A. (ed.) (1868) *Epistulae Romanorum Pontificum Genuinae*. Brunsberg.

Toubert, P. (1973) *Les structures du Latium médiéval. Le Latium méridional et la Sabine du IXe siècle à la fin du XIIe siècle* (*Bibliothèque des Écoles Françaises d'Athènes et de Rome* 221). Rome, École Française de Rome.

Toubert, P. (1976) Pour une histoire de l'environnement économique et social du Mont-Cassin (IXe-XIIe siècles). *Comptes rendus de l'académie des inscriptions et belles-lettres*: 689-702.

Toubert, P. (1979) La terre et les hommes dans l'Italie normande aux temps de Roger II: l'exemple campanien. In *Società, potere e popolo nell'età di Ruggero II* (*Atti del centro di studi normanno-svevi, Università degli studi di Bari* 3): 55-71. Bari, Dedalo libri.

Ullmann, W. (1969) *The Carolingian Renaissance and the Idea of Kingship. The Birkbeck Lectures 1968-9*. London, Methuen & Co.

Van der Noort, R. and Whitehouse, D. (1992) Le mura di Santo Stefano and other medieval churches in South Etruria: the archaeological evidence. *Archeologia medievale* 19: 75-89.

Van der Veen, M. (1985) An early medieval hilltop settlement in Molise: the plant remains from D85. *Papers of the British School at Rome* 53: 211-24.

Vera, D. (1986) Forme e funzioni della rendita fondiaria nella tarda antichità. In A. Giardina (ed.), *Società romana e impero tardoantico. Vol. I. Istituzioni, ceti, economie*: 367-447. Rome/Bari, Laterza.

Violante, C. (1980) Le strutture organizzative della cura d'anime nelle campagne dell'Italia centro-settentrionale (secoli V-X). In *Cristianizzazione ed organizzazione ecclesiastica delle campagne nell'alto medioevo: espansione e resistenze* (*Settimane di studio del centro italiano di studi sull'alto medioevo* 28), vol. 2: 963-1162. Spoleto, Centro italiano di studi sull'alto medioevo.

Vives, J. (ed.) (1963) *Concilias Vizigòticos e Hispano-Romanos*.

Volpe, G. (1985) La documentazione ceramica. In R. Cassano, C.A.M. Lagnara Fabiano and G. Volpe, Area del Tempio di Giove Toro a Canosa, relazione preliminare: 505-10. *Archeologia medievale* 12: 501-15.

Vryonis, S. Jr. (1981) The Panegyreis of the Byzantine Saint. In S. Hackel (ed.), *The Byzantine Saint* (*Sobornost Supplement* 5). London.

Wallace-Hadrill, J.M. (1983) *The Frankish Church*. Oxford, Clarendon Press.

Ward-Perkins, B. (1981) Two Byzantine houses at Luni. *Papers of the British School at Rome* 49: 91-8.

Wataghin, G. (1989) Monasteri di età longobarda: spunti per una ricerca. *XXXVI corso di cultura sull'arte ravennate e bizantina*: 73-100.

Weis, A. (1957) Die Verteilung der Bidzykliken des Paulin von Nola in den Kirchen von Cimitile (Campanien). *Römische Quartalschrift für Christliche Altertumskunde und Kirchengeschichte* 52: 129-50.

White, L. (1962) *Medieval Technology and Social Change*. Oxford, Oxford University Press.

Whitehouse, D. (1980) Anguillara: an introduction. In K. Painter (ed.), *Roman Villas in Italy. Recent Excavations and Research* (*British Museum Occasional Paper* 24): 111-17. London, British Museum.

Whitehouse, D., Costantini, L., Guidobaldi, F., Passi, S., Pensabene, P., Pratt, S., Reece, R. and Reese, D. (1985) The Schola Praeconum II. *Papers of the British School at Rome* 53: 163-210.

Whittaker, C. (1983) Late Roman trade and traders. In P. Garnsey, K. Hopkins and C. Whittaker (eds), *Trade in the Ancient Economy*: 163-80. London, Chatto and Windus.

Wickham C.J. (1978) Historical and topographical notes on early mediaeval South Etruria. *Papers of the British School at Rome* 46: 132-79.

Wickham, C.J. (1979) Historical and topographical notes on early mediaeval South Etruria: Part II. *Papers of the British School at Rome* 47: 66-95.

Wickham, C.J. (1981) *Early Medieval Italy. Central Power and Local Society 400-1000*. London, Macmillan.

Wickham, C.J. (1982) *Studi sulla società degli Appennini nell'alto medioevo: contadini, signori e insediamento nel territorio di Valva (Sulmona)* (*Università degli studi di Bologna. Quaderni del centro studi sorelle Clarke* 2). Bologna, Editrice CLUEB.

Wickham, C.J. (1985a) *Il problema dell'incastellamento nell'Italia centrale: l'esempio di San Vincenzo al Volturno* (*Studi sulla società degli Appennini nell'alto medioevo* II; *Quaderni dell'insegnamento di archeologia medievale della Facoltà di lettere e filosofia dell'Università di Siena* 5). Florence: All'Insegna del Giglio.

Wickham, C.J. (1985b) The *terra* of San Vincenzo al Volturno in the eighth to twelfth centuries: the historical framework. In R. Hodges and J. Mitchell (eds), *San Vincenzo al Volturno. The Archaeology, Art and Territory of an Early Medieval Monastery* (BAR International Series 252): 227-58. Oxford, British Archaeological Reports.

Wickham, C.J. (1988) L'Italia e l'alto medioevo. *Archeologia medievale* 15: 105-24.

Wickham, C.J. (1994) *Land and Power. Studies in Italian and European Social History, 400-1200*. London, British School at Rome.

Wightman, E.M. (1975) The pattern of rural settlement in Roman Gaul. *Aufstieg und Niedergang der Römischen Welt* II.4: 584-657. Berlin/New York, Walter de Gruyter.

Williams, C. (1985) The pottery and glass at Alahan. In M. Gough (ed.), *Alahan. An Early Christian Monastery in Southern Turkey. Based on the Work of Michael Gough* (*Studies and Texts* 73): 35-61. Toronto, Pontifical Institute of Mediaeval Studies.

Young, B.K. (1975) *The Merovingian Funeral Rites and the Evolution of Christianity: a Study in the Historical Interpretation of Archaeological Material*. Unpublished Ph.D. thesis, University of Pennsylvania. Ann Arbor/London, University Microfilms International.

Zettler, A. (1988) *Die Frühen Klosterbauten der Reichenau: Ausgrabungen – Schriftenquellen – St. Galler Klosterplan* (*Archäologie und Geschichte. Freiburger Forschungen zum Ersten Jahrtausend in Südwestdeutschland* 3). Sigmaringen, Jan Thorbecke Verlag.

Zettler, A. (1990) Der St. Galler Klosterplan: Überlegungen zu seiner Herkunft und Entstehung. In P. Godman and R. Collins (eds), *Charlemagne's Heir. New Perspectives on the Reign of Louis the Pious (814-840)*: 655-87. Oxford, Clarendon Press.

Zielinski, H. (ed.) (1986) *Le chartae dei ducati di Spoleto e di Benevento. (Codice diplomatico longobardo* (ed. L. Schiaparelli and C. Brühl)) (*Fonti per la storia d'Italia pubblicate dall'Istituto storico italiano per il medio evo* 66). Rome, Istituto storico italiano per il medio evo.

Appendix One

CONTENTS OF VOLUME 1 AND PROPOSED CONTENTS OF FUTURE VOLUMES

VOLUME 1: 1980-86 EXCAVATIONS PART 1

1. San Vincenzo al Volturno: a general introduction, by Richard Hodges
2. The environmental setting, by Peter Hayes
3. The excavations: an introduction and overview, by Richard Hodges
4. Archaeological strategy and methodology, by Richard Hodges
5. Ponte della Zingara and the river Volturno, by Samuel D. Gruber and Richard Hodges
6. The Crypt Church, by Richard Hodges and John Mitchell, with a contribution by Sheila Gibson
7. The crypt reappraised, by John Mitchell
8. The excavations behind the Crypt Church, by Richard Hodges, with Catherine M. Coutts and John Mitchell
9. The 'South Church': a late Roman funerary church (San Vincenzo Minore) and the Hall for Distinguished Guests, by Richard Hodges and Steven J. Mithen, with contributions by Sheila Gibson and John Mitchell
10. The Garden Court, by Ian Riddler, with contributions by Richard Hodges and John Mitchell
11. The Distinguished Guests' Refectory, by Ian Riddler, with contributions by Sheila Gibson, Richard Hodges and John Mitchell
12. The Entrance Hall or Monumental Staircase, by Richard Hodges, with contributions by Sheila Gibson and John Mitchell

VOLUME 3: THE FINDS FROM THE 1980-86 EXCAVATIONS

1. The Roman inscriptions, by John Patterson
2. The medieval inscriptions, by John Mitchell
3. Personal names from the inscriptions of San Vincenzo al Volturno, by Nicoletta Francovich Onesti
4. The Roman and medieval sculpture, by John Mitchell with Amanda Claridge, with an appendix by Amanda Claridge, Catherine M. Coutts and John Mitchell
5. The window-glass, by Debbie Hodges
6. The tiles and modillions, by John Mitchell with Helen Patterson

7. An analysis of the painted plaster, by Helen Howard
8. The coins, by Philip Grierson and David Barrett
9. The pottery, by Helen Patterson, with an appendix by Paul Arthur
10. The vessel-glass: a catalogue and preliminary assessment, by Judith Stevenson
11. The soapstone, by Helen Patterson
12. The bronze and silver, by Paola Filippucci
13. The enamel, by John Mitchell, with an appendix by Mavis Bimson and Ian Freestone
14. A set of sword-belt mounts and associated bridle furniture of iron inlaid with silver, by John Mitchell
15. The iron and lead objects, by Catherine M. Coutts
16. The sword pommel/scabbard chape of nephrite jade, by John Mitchell
17. Ivory and bone, by Richard Hodges, John Mitchell and Ian Riddler
18. Miscellaneous finds (flint, spindle whorls, hones), by Richard Hodges
19. The livestock economy, by Valerie Higgins
20. The bird bones, by Sheila Sutherland
21. The molluscs, by C.O. Hunt
22. The human populations at San Vincenzo al Volturno: the demographic data, by Valerie Higgins
23. The cultural history of San Vincenzo, by John Mitchell

VOLUME 4: VOLTURNO STUDIES

1. The Republican *vicus* and Imperial villa at San Vincenzo al Volturno, by Amanda Claridge, Samuel D. Gruber, Richard Hodges and John Patterson
2. The early classical settlement sequence at San Vincenzo al Volturno, by Richard Hodges and John Patterson
3. The twelfth-century monastery of San Vincenzo al Volturno, by Samuel D. Gruber with Richard Hodges
4. The San Vincenzo survey, by Peter Hayes, Richard Hodges, John Patterson and Paul Roberts
5. Excavations, survey and the ethnoarchaeology of transhumance in the Mainarde mountains, by Frederick Baker

6. Early medieval villages in the upper Volturno valley, by Richard Hodges
7. Excavations at Colle Castellano, by Stefano Coccia, Gillian Clark, Richard Hodges and Helen Patterson
8. Excavations at Colle Sant'Angelo, by Patrick Foster and Richard Hodges

VOLUME 5: SAN VINCENZO MAGGIORE AND THE COLLECTIVE WORKSHOP

Excavations 1982-94

INDEX

References for *San Vincenzo al Volturno 1* are given first; those for *San Vincenzo al Volturno 2* follow and are in bold.